KU-761-395

A wealth of recipes, old and not so old, drawn from all parts of Scotland, from palace and from cottage, lavish and simple.

First published in 1929, *The Scots Kitchen* is much more than an unusual cook book, for it explores the traditions and lore of Scottish hospitality as well as revealing the secrets of the kitchen.

By the same author

The Scots Cellar

F. Marian McNeill

The Scots Kitchen

Its Traditions and Lore
with Old-Time Recipes

A MAYFLOWER BOOK

GRANADA
London Toronto Sydney New York

Published by Granada Publishing Limited in 1974
Reprinted 1976, 1979, 1981

ISBN 0 583 19748 5

First published in Great Britain by
Blackie & Son Ltd 1929
Copyright © F. Marian McNeill 1929

Granada Publishing Limited
Frogmore, St Albans, Herts AL2 2NF
and
36 Golden Square, London W1R 4AH
866 United Nations Plaza, New York, NY 10017, USA
117 York Street, Sydney, NSW 2000, Australia
100 Skyway Avenue, Rexdale, Ontario, M9W 3A6, Canada
61 Beach Road, Auckland, New Zealand

Made and printed in Great Britain by
Richard Clay (The Chaucer Press) Ltd
Bungay, Suffolk
Set in Monotype Times

PREFACE TO THE FIRST EDITION

The object of this book is not to provide a complete compendium of Scottish Cookery, ancient or modern – for many of the dishes prepared in the Scots kitchen are common to the British Isles; some, indeed, to Europe – but rather to preserve the recipes of our old national dishes, many of which, in this age of standardization, are in danger of falling into an undeserved oblivion. Recipes available in contemporary Scottish cookery books are as a rule omitted, unless hallowed by age or sentiment.

All parts of the country, from the Shetlands to the Borders, have been levied, and all types of kitchen, from Old Holyrood to island sheiling. A few of the simple folk recipes collected in Orkney and the Hebrides have, I believe, never before been published.

In the preliminary sketch, I have tried to show how from the earliest times – through the period of romantic semi-savagery in the Highlands, the period of cosmopolitan elegance (Edinburgh's golden age) in the days of the Auld Alliance, the sober kail-and-brose period that succeeded the Reformation, and on to modern times – the pageant of Scottish history is shadowed in the kitchen.

In Scotland today, as perhaps the world over, there is of good home cooking less and less. The old women say there is neither the variety there used to be, nor the respect for quality. But we may rest confident that out of the domestic travail through which our women folk are now passing there will emerge a new delight in the home, and, not least, in the kitchen.

'Lean gu dlùth ri cliù do shinnsre,' says the Gaelic proverb: Let us follow in the brave path of our ancestors.

Edinburgh, 1929   F. M. MCNEILL

PREFACE TO THE SECOND EDITION

By a happy paradox, the more the peoples of the world draw together in amity, the less do they desire assimilation in a common culture. Standardization is, in fact, the antithesis of culture, which consists in those subtle differences, those nuances, which give colour and character to every aspect of the national life. It is right and desirable that in the arts and sciences, in products and manufactures, the nations should borrow freely from one another and thus share in the general progress of the human race; but it is no less right and desirable that each should cherish its distinctive traditions and customs, as evidence not of antiquarian zeal, but of a healthy national sentiment.

Needless to say, food and drink form an important part of a nation's heritage, and the opportunity to enjoy the national and regional dishes of the country one is visiting gives an added zest to travelling abroad. There is, in fact, nothing more wearisome to the palate than an unrelieved diet based on *la haute cuisine*. The people who have lived for generations in a particular region may be depended upon to deal wisely and interestingly with the products of that region.

The Scot does not take to high sophistication in cookery (or in anything else) but he is wise to follow his instinct in using the simplest methods in dealing with foodstuffs of the first quality, with which his national larder is so well endowed. An unspoiled palate appreciates the essential flavour of the meat, fish or vegetable that is so easily destroyed by any but the most subtle seasoning.

'Up to the middle of the last century,' writes that distinguished dietician, Lord Boyd Orr, 'the people of Scotland were eating natural foodstuffs. With the introduction of machinery . . . natural foodstuffs have been changed into

6

artificial foodstuffs, with the very substances purified away that the Almighty put there to keep us in perfect health.'

In our modern civilization, it is true, such methods of food preservation as canning and refrigeration are undoubtedly a boon, even a necessity – at least to city-dwellers; but it should be borne in mind that canned or frozen foods are always, or nearly always, a second-best to foodstuffs that come straight from the soil or the sea, since they lack the 'subtle elements of freshness' that are the basis of sound nutrition.

Since this book was first published I have garnered a good deal more about the history and traditions of the Scots kitchen, and this material, together with a number of new recipes, I have incorporated in the revised edition.

Edinburgh, 1963   F. M. McNeill

ACKNOWLEDGEMENTS

I am indebted to the following for their courtesy in permitting me to quote from copyright works:

Edward Arnold & Co. for extracts from A HUNDRED YEARS IN THE HIGHLANDS, by Osgood Mackenzie; John Carswell, for extracts from THE SCOTS WEEK-END, edited by Donald and Catherine Carswell; Constable and Sons, for three recipes from THE COOKERY-BOOK OF LADY CLARK OF TILLYPRONIE; Elizabeth Craig and André Deutsch, for a recipe from THE SCOTTISH COOKERY-BOOK; Ian Finlay, for an extract from SCOTLAND; Mrs. Gina MacKinnon for one of her special Drambuie recipes; the Rev. Dr. Kenneth Macleod, for THE RUNE OF HOSPITALITY; Lily Macleod and Faber and Faber, for two recipes from A COOK'S NOTE-BOOK; THE OBAN TIMES, for extracts from MYTH, TRADITION AND LEGEND FROM WESTERN ARGYLL, by Mrs. Katherine W. Grant; Mrs. George Shield and Faber and Faber, for an extract from WHEN I WAS A BOY, by General Sir Ian Hamilton; and Oliver and Boyd and Dr. William Watson, a former Professor of Celtic in the University of Edinburgh, for extracts from CARMINA GADELICA, edited by Alexander Carmichael.

My thanks, too, to friends and correspondents all over the country for their invaluable help.

F. M. McN.

CONTENTS

AN HISTORICAL SKETCH

RECIPES

APPENDICES

ILLUSTRATIONS

Products of Soil and Sea

I. OLD WATER-MILL AT MILNGAVIE
   (*BY PERMISSION OF HUGH ALLISON, ESQ.*)

II. A CATCH OF HERRING,
   from a British Council photograph
   (*BY PERMISSION OF THE CENTRAL OFFICE OF INFORMATION*)

Old Domestic Utensils

GROUP I. *Wooden Luggie; Fro'-stick; Plump-Churn*

GROUP II. *Three-legged Pot; Brander; Spurtle or Porridge-stick; Toasting-stone; Bannock-spathe; Girdle*
   (*BY PERMISSION OF THE NATIONAL MUSEUM OF ANTIQUITIES OF SCOTLAND*)

THE BREAKFAST,
   from the painting by Sir David Wilkie
   (*BY PERMISSION OF THE RT. HON. THE COUNTESS OF SUTHERLAND*)

GRACE BEFORE MEAT,
   from the painting by Sir David Wilkie
   (*BY PERMISSION OF THE CITY MUSEUM AND ART GALLERY OF BIRMINGHAM*)

AN ORKNEY INGLE-NEUK
   from a photograph by Miss Sinclair, Kirkwall
   (*BY PERMISSION OF MRS. METZGER, NEW YORK*)

A FISHING COMMUNITY IN ST. ANDREWS, 1890
   from a photograph by Messrs Yerbury, Edinburgh
   (*WITH THEIR PERMISSION*)

To
The 'Land o' Cakes and sister Scots
Frae Maidenkirk to Johnnie Groat's,'
and over the Firth to
Orkney and Shetland

AN
HISTORICAL SKETCH

I

INTRODUCTORY: INSTITUTION OF THE CLEIKUM CLUB

'Man,' said Mr. Peregrine Touchwood, 'is a cooking animal.'

The occasion was a memorable one – none other than the institution of the celebrated Cleikum Club at the old Border Inn presided over by Meg Dods[1] and immortalized by Sir Walter Scott in *St. Ronan's Well*. This red-letter day in the annals of Scottish gastronomy is commemorated in the introduction to *The Cook and Housewife's Manual*, by Mistress Margaret Dods (Edinburgh, 1826),[2] a work not

---

[1] Lockhart, in his *Life* of Scott, tells us that Scott borrowed the name from Mrs. Margaret Dods, at whose little inn at Howgate, among the Moorfoots, with Will Clark, and John Irving, and George Abercrombie, he often spent a night during a fishing excursion in their student days. When the novel was published, Clark met Scott in the street and observed, 'That's an odd name; surely I've met with it somewhere before.' Scott smilingly replied, 'Don't you remember Howgate?'

The name alone, however, was taken from the Howgate hostess. According to a well-known Peebles tradition, supported by William Chambers, Miss Marian Ritchie was the true original of the termagant landlady of the 'Cleikum Inn', which, as the 'Cross Keys', still exists. Meg appears to have been a caricature of Miss Ritchie, but the characteristics, though exaggerated, are said to agree, in the main. Marian's Bible, punch-bowl, etc., are still preserved in Peebles. – F.M.McN.

[2] 'The individual who has so ingeniously personated Meg Dods is evidently no ordinary writer, and the book is really most excellent miscellaneous reading. Here we have twenty or thirty grave, sober, instructive, business-like pages right on end, without one particle of wit whatever; then comes as many more, sprinkled with *facetiae* – and then half a dozen of broad mirth and merriment. This alternation of grave and gay is exceedingly agreeable – something in the style of *Blackwood's Magazine*.'
– Christopher North, in *Blackwood's Magazine*, June, 1826.

'We have no hesitation in saying that if the humorous introduction is not written by Sir Walter Scott, the author of it possesses a singular talent of mimicking his best comic manner, and has presented us with an imitation of the great novelist, as remarkable for its fidelity, facility, and cleverness as anything in the *Rejected Addresses*.'
– *The Monthly Review.*

Whether or not Scott had a hand in it, the book was actually compiled by Mrs. Isobel Christian Johnston, the wife of an Edinburgh publisher, the author of *The Edinburgh Tales* and other works, and in after years the editor of *Tait's Magazine*.

'Her sense of humour and power of delineating character are shown in her stories and sketches in *Tait*, and a good example of her ready wit has been told by Mr. Alexander Russell, editor of the *Scotsman*. On a visit to Altrive, Mrs. Johnston and her party were kindly received by the Ettrick Shepherd, who did the honours of the district, and among other places took them to a Fairy Well, from which he drew a glass of sparkling water. Handing it to the lady, the bard of Kilmeny said, "Hae, Mrs. Johnston, ony merrit wummin wha drinks a tumbler o' this will hae twuns in a twalmont." "In that case, Mr. Hogg," said the lady, "I shall only take half a tumbler".'
– Sir Walter Scott: *Journal*, Vol. I, Note.

Mrs. Johnston was born in Fife in 1781 and died in 1857.

unworthy to be placed alongside its French contemporary, Brillat-Savarin's *Physiologie du Goût*.

After the catastrophe which befell the ancient and honourable house of St. Ronan's, our friend Mr. Touchwood, more commonly styled the Cleikum Nabob, was, it appears, in some danger of falling into hypochondria – 'vulgarly, *fidgets*, a malady to which bachelor gentlemen in easy circumstances, when turned of fifty, are thought to be peculiarly liable' – but evaded the disaster by the happy thought of founding a club of gastronomes. In addition to the founder, 'who understood and loved good cheer', the club included Mr. Winterblossom, 'an old coxcomb, but deep in the mystery'; Dr. Redgill, an English divine who chanced to be taking the waters at St. Ronan's,[1] and who, 'like a true churchman, had a strong leaning to dishes as they are'; Mr. Jekyl, a young life-guardsman who had served in the Peninsula, had 'French theory' in the affairs of the kitchen, and was 'to the full as flighty and speculative as the Doctor was dogmatic'; and lastly, on Meg's recommendation, Mr. Matthew Stechy, 'St. Ronan's auld butler, that kept the first hottle in Glasgow'. Mrs. Dods herself was elected 'high priestess of the mysteries'.

The Nabob explains his design to Dr. Redgill:

'"To this ancient hostel now – you will scarce believe it – have been confined scores of admirable receipts in cookery, ever since the jolly friars flourished down in the monastery yonder:

> The Monks of Melrose made fat brose
> On Fridays, when they fasted.

You remember the old stave, Doctor?"

'The doctor remembered no such things. His attention was given to more substantial doctrine. "Sir, I should not

---

[1] St. Ronan's is in fact Innerleithen, in the county of Peebles. Innerleithen had a Spa, known as the Doos' Well, from the flocks of pigeons who made it their haunt. 'The publication of Scott's novel ushered in the period of its greatest glory, and visitors were further attracted by an annual festival established by an association known as the St. Ronan's Border Club. Among those who countenanced, or took part in the proceedings, were Scott and Adam Ferguson, Christopher North and the Ettrick Shepherd, Sheriff Glassford Bell and others.' – W. S. Crockett: *The Scott Originals.*

be surprised if they possessed the original receipt – a local one, too, I am told – for dressing the red trout,[1] in this hereditary house of entertainment."

'"Never doubt it, man – claret, butter, and spiceries. Zounds, I have eat of it till – It makes my mouth water yet. As the French adage goes, 'Give your trout a bottle of good wine, a lump of butter, and spice, and tell me how you like him'. Excellent trout in this very house – got in the *Friar's cast*, man – the best reach of the mere. Let them alone for that. These jolly monks knew something of the mystery. Their warm, sunny old orchards still produce the best fruit in the country. You English gentlemen never saw the Greygudewife pear. Look out here, sir. The Abbot's Haugh yonder – the richest carse-land and fattest beeves in the country. Their very names are genial and smack of milk and honey! But there comes a brother of the reformed order, whom I have never yet been able to teach the difference between Béchamel and buttermilk, though he understands ten languages. Dr. Redgill – give me leave to present you to my friend, Mr. Josiah Cargill, the minister of this parish.[2] I have been telling my friend that the Reformation has thrown the science of cookery three centuries back in this corner of the island. Popery and made dishes, eh, Mr. Cargill? – Episcopacy, roast beef, and plum-pudding – and what is left to Presbytery but its lang-kail, its brose, and mashlum bannocks?"

'"So I have heard," replied Mr. Cargill; "very wholesome food indeed."

'"Wholesome food, sir! Why, your wits are woolgathering. There is not a bare-foot monk, sir, of the most beggarly abstemious order but can give you some pretty notions of tossing up a fricassee or an omelet, or of mixing an olio. Scotland has absolutely retrograded in gastronomy. Yet she saw a better day, the memory of which is savoury in our nostrils yet, Doctor. In old Jacobite families, and in

[1] See p. 144.
[2] The original of Josiah Cargill was the Rev. Alexander Duncan, D.D., the minister of Scott's Smailholm boyhood. See *The Scott Originals*, by W. S. Crockett.

17

the neighbourhood of decayed monasteries – in such houses as this, for instance, where long succeeding generations have followed the trade of victuallers – a few relics may still be found. It is for this reason I fix my scene of experiment at the Cleikum,[1] and choose my notable hostess as high priestess of the mysteries."'

The choice was justified.

'The dinner was served punctual to the second; for Meg and the Nabob, though they did not quite agree in harmony, always agreed in time: a true gourmand dinner; no sumptuous feast of twenty dishes in the *dead-thraw*, but a few well-chosen and well-suited – each relieving each – the boils done to a *popple*, the roast to a *turn*, the stews to the *nick of time*.[2] First came the soup – the hare soup; Meg called it rabbit-soup, as this was close-time.

'"Sir, if you please," replied the doctor, bowing to the tureen, and sipping his heated Madeira, as he answered the inquiry of the Nabob, if he would take soup, "as our great moralist, Dr. Johnson, said of your Scotch barley-broth, Sir, I have eat of it, and shall be happy to do so again."'

'Stewed red trout, for which the house was celebrated; a fat, short-legged, thick-rumped pullet, braised and served with rice and mushroom sauce; a Scotch dish of venison-collops; and though last, not least in the doctor's good love, one of the young pigs, killed since his adventure in the sty: these formed the dinner. And all were neatly dished – the whole in *keeping* that would have done honour to the best city-tavern in London. "Sir, I say city-tavern," said Redgill; "for I humbly conceive that, in all save flimsy show,

---

[1] The name Cleikum derives from the legend of St. Ronan, a seventh-century monk, whose method of dealing with the evil and ignorance of his time was symbolically displayed on the sign hung over the doorway of 'Meg Dods's' establishment, where the saint is represented with his crook 'cleeking* the De'il by the hind leg'. A ceremony in celebration of the saint is performed annually by the schoolboys of Innerleithen

– F. M. McN.

* Catching as by a hook.

[2] '*The Nabob*: The Scots may, or did fail in a grand dinner, Doctor – no doubt of it; but as a *nation* they manage better than most of their neighbours.' – Annals of the Cleikum Club (incorporated in the Introduction and Notes to Meg Dods's *Manual of Cookery*).

business is best understood in the city, however finely they may talk the matter at the West End."'

Cranberry-tart and a copious libation of rich plain cream concluded one of the most satisfactory dinners Dr. Redgill had ever made in his life, and the racy flavour of Meg's old claret completed the conquest of his affections.

After 'much smacking of green seals and red seals', much 'cracking of nuts and of jokes', 'to conclude the entertainment, the Nabob produced a single bottle of choice Burgundy, Mont Rachet; and a special bumper was dedicated to the newcomer. Coffee, four years kept, but only one hour roasted, was prepared by the Nabob's own hands – coffee which he himself had brought from Mocha, and now made in a coffee-pot of Parisian invention patronized by Napoleon.

'The meal concluded, the Nabob wiped his mouth with his ample Bandana and proceeded:

'"Gentlemen, Man is a cooking animal; and in whatever situation he is found, it may be assumed as an axiom, that his progress in civilization has kept exact pace with the degree of refinement he may have attained in the science of gastronomy. From the hairy man of the woods, gentlemen, digging his roots with his claws, to the refined banquet of the Greek, or the sumptuous entertainment of the Roman; from the ferocious hunter, gnawing the half-broiled bloody collop, torn from the still-reeking carcass, to the modern *gourmet*, apportioning his ingredients and blending his essences, the chain is complete!

'"First, we have the brutalized *digger* of roots; then the sly *entrapper* of the finny tribes; and next the fierce, foul feeder, devouring his ensnared prey, fat, blood, and muscle!"

'"What a style o' language!" whispered Mistress Dods. "But I maun look after the scouring o' the kettles."

'"The next age of cookery, gentlemen, may be called the pastoral, as the last was that of the hunter. Here we have simple, mild broths, seasoned, perhaps, with the herbs of the field, decoctions of pulse, barley-cake, and the kid seethed in milk. I pass over the ages of Rome and Greece, and confine myself to the Gothic and Celtic tribes, among whom gradually emerged what I shall call the chivalrous or feudal age of cookery – the wild boar roasted whole, the stately crane, the lordly swan, the full-plumaged peacock, borne into the feudal hall by troops of vassals, to the flourish of trumpets, warlike instruments, marrow-bones, and cleavers."[1]

'"Bravo!"' cried Jekyl.

'"Cookery as a domestic art, contributing to the comfort and luxury of private life, had made considerable progress in England before the Reformation; which event threw it back some centuries. . . . Gastronomy, violently expelled

> [1] The spousal rites were ended soon;
> 'T was now the merry hour of noon,
> And in the lofty arched hall
> Was spread the gorgeous festival.
> Steward and squire, with heedful haste,
> Marshalled the rank of every guest;
> Pages, with ready blade, were there,
> The mighty meal to carve and share;
> O'er capon, heron-shew, and crane,
> And princely peacock's gilded train,
> And o'er the boar-head, garnished brave,
> And cygnet from St. Mary's wave; *
> O'er ptarmigan and venison
> The priest had spoke his benison.
>   – Scott: *The Lay of the Last Minstrel.*
>
>   * St. Mary's Loch, at the head of the Yarrow.

'The peacock, it is well known, was considered during the times of chivalry, not merely as an exquisite delicacy, but as a dish of peculiar solemnity. After being roasted, it was again decorated with its plumage, and a sponge, dipped in lighted spirits of wine, was placed in its bill. When it was introduced on days of grand festivals, it was the signal for the adventurous knights to take upon them vows to do some deed of chivalry, "before the peacock and the ladies".

'The boar's head was also a usual dish of feudal splendour. In Scotland it was sometimes surrounded with little banners, displaying the colours and achievements of the baron at whose board it was served.' – Pinkerton's *History of Scotland*, Vol. I.

'At a Feeste Roiall Pecokkes shall be dight on this manere: Take and flee off the skynne with the fedurs, tayle, and the nekke, and the hed theron; then take the skyn with all the fedurs, and lay hit on a table abrode; and strawe theron grounden comyn; then take the pecokke, and roste hym, and endore hym with rawe zolkes of egges; and when he is rosted, take hym of, and let hym coole awhile, and take and sowe hym in his skyn, and gilde his combe, and so serve hym forthe with the last cours.'
     – From an old coverless Anthology.

At a ball given in the 1840s by the 72nd Highlanders, then stationed at Edinburgh Castle, 'At either end of every long supper-table (there were, I think, three) a peacock sat in state upon his own pie – no doubt incited thereto by old Sanderson, the bird-stuffer – with the tail spread. The peacock is the crest of the regiment. The effect was very fine.' – L. B. Walford (née Colquhoun of Luss): *Recollections of a Scottish Novelist.*

20

from monasteries and colleges, found no fitting sanctuary either in the riotous household of the jolly Cavalier, or in the gloomy abode of the lank, pinched-visaged Roundhead, the latter, as the poet has it, eager to

> . . . fall out with mince-meat and disparage
> His best and dearest friend, plum-porridge,

the former broaching his hogshead of October beer, and roasting a whole ox, in the exercise of a hospitality far more liberal than elegant.

'"But, gentlemen, in our seats of learning the genial spark was still secretly cherished. Oxford watched over the culinary flame with zeal proportioned to the importance of the trust! From this altar were rekindled the culinary fires of Episcopal palaces, which had smouldered for a time; and Gastronomy once more raised her parsley-wreathed front in Britain, and daily gained an increase of devoted, if not yet enlightened worshippers."'

An extended correspondence, we learn, was arranged by the Club 'with well-known amateur gourmands, as well as practical cooks, and also with those clubs, provincial and metropolitan, of which the eating, rather than the erudite preparation of dishes, has hitherto been the leading business'.

Not only Scotland, but Ireland, England and Wales were levied, and several continental countries as well. The later editions of the *Manual* contain over twelve hundred recipes. The unique feature of the work, however, is the section on Scottish National Dishes, and the sixty (or thereabouts) recipes it contains form the nucleus of the present collection.

II

THE NATIONAL LARDER

'The fate of nations depends on how they are fed.' – Brillat-Savarin.

The art of a country always has its roots in the soil, and the study of comparative cookery shows that however plentiful and varied the imported foodstuffs, it is the natural conditions and products that determine the general character of the national cuisine.

Despite certain natural disadvantages, Scotland has always been in a special sense a food-producing country. It is true that little more than a fourth of her total area is under cultivation; the soil, too, though of very diverse quality, is on an average poorer than that of England, and the climate wetter and colder, so that neither crops nor fruits reach the same perfection, nor is the harvest so certain.[1]

'We have a limited area,' writes a leading authority,[2] 'but within that area a soil and climate equal to the best in Europe for the growth of grass, forage crops, potatoes, oats and some bush fruits, and a great variety of vegetables. Our climate is not suitable for the best qualities of wheat and barley. With the exception of the Lincolnshire fens, there are no greater areas of good land in Britain than can be found in the Merse, the Lothians, the East of Fife, the Vale of Strathmore and the Howe of the Mearns. There are no kindlier, nor more responsive soils than the early lands of South Ayrshire. There are no better strains of livestock anywhere in Europe, nor greater skill available for their management.'

---

[1] 'No nation has so large a stock of benevolence of heart as the Scotch. Their temper stands anything but an attack on their climate. They would have you even believe they can ripen fruit; and, to be candid, I must own in remarkably warm summers I have tasted peaches that made excellent pickles. . . . Even the enlightened mind of Jeffrey cannot shake off the illusion that myrtles flourish at Craig Crook.' – Sydney Smith.
[2] The late Sir Robert Greig, of the Department of Agriculture for Scotland.

22

Moreover, in certain sheltered districts in Moray, Ross and the Isles, exotic fruits and flowers grow freely in the open air. And nowhere in the world are farming and gardening prosecuted with greater skill and enterprise.[1]

In olden times, when the population was small and sparse – by the beginning of the sixteenth century it did not exceed half a million – the means of sustenance were on the whole plentiful. The moors and forests abounded with game, whilst in Argyll and elsewhere 'herds of kye nocht tame' with flesh 'of a marvellous sweetness, of a wonderful tenderness, and excellent delicateness of taste' ranged the hills. Rivers, lochs, and seas teemed with fish. Sheep were valued mainly for their wool, cows for their milk. Butter and cheese were in use in the earliest times, and the oat and barley crops have always provided the staple bread.[2]

Although barley bread (in the form of bannocks) was popular throughout the country for centuries and is still popular in the north, 'It was not for his benefactions to broth-pot and bake-board,' as Hugh Haliburton points out, 'that John Barleycorn got title to rank as King of Grain. It was for the gift of his own heart's blood. . . . From the Lothians in the south to the scarcely inferior barley-soils of Moray in the north, the great mass of the bear harvest is destined for distillation and brewing, and only an insignificant proportion will find its way to the mill. The flower of it goes to the brewer; the distiller gets the inferior quality; but even when barley-bread was a staple food in the farmhouses and burgh towns of Scotland, it was still the lighter

[1] There have been two remarkable developments within the present century – first, the transformation of the industry by science and technology and the creation of a whole new range of essential farming skills; and, secondly, the astonishing variety of produce which so small a country as Scotland can offer from its soil and waters.
Each year our southern neighbours look to us for cereals and potato seed bred to high and rigorous standards of health and purity. Our farm produce is exported in various forms. From whisky to Aberdeen-Angus beef, from salmon to grouse, the products of our countryside enjoy a high and, in many cases, an international reputation for quality.'
– John Jenkins, President of the National Farmers' Union of Scotland.
[2] '(Oats) were hardly known on the Continent (says a writer of the early seventeenth century), but were raised in Scotland to the highest perfection. One gathers, indeed, that in early times abroad oats were regarded as a weed.'
– Victor Maclure: *Scotland's Inner Man.*

qualities of both bigg and barley that were dressed or ground at the mill for pot or girdle.'[1]

'There is one kind of food,' writes a distinguished physician, 'that is helpful to the brain and to the whole body, throughout childhood and adolescence, and that is oatmeal. Oats are the most nutritious of the cereals, being richer than any other in fats, organic phosphorus and lecithins. . . . At one time it was the mainstay of the Scottish peasant's diet and produced a big-boned, well-developed and mentally energetic race, but it is so no longer, having largely given way to less useful and economic foods.'[2]

Oatmeal has gradually ousted barley from its supremacy, and is in turn threatened by wheaten flour, the victory of which would be regarded by many as a national disaster.[3]

Since the Reformation, which effected a radical change in the national character, the proverbial Scot has been reared on porridge and the Shorter Catechism, a rigorous diet, but highly beneficial to those possessed of sound digestive organs.[4] Many a 'lad o' pairts' who ultimately rose to fame studied his Bain and Aristotle by guttering candlelight in a garret in which one of the most conspicuous articles of furniture was a sack of oatmeal,[5] and regular holidays were

---

[1] *Furth in Field.*

[2] Sir James Crichton-Browne: *Stray Leaves from a Physician's Portfolio.*

'Up to the middle of the last century, the people of Scotland were eating natural foodstuffs. With the introduction of machinery, this has been changed. . . . Natural foods have been changed into artificial foodstuffs, with the very substances purified away that the Almighty put there to keep us in perfect health.' – Lord Boyd Orr.

Lord Boyd Orr, after studying (and being horrified by) the conditions in Glasgow, went to Aberdeen, where the university and the North of Scotland Agricultural College had founded the Rowett Institute for the special study of nutrition.

'There is no more fruitful line of investigation in the world at present,' said Walter Elliot a few years ago, 'than the combination between farmers and scientists in Scotland.'

[3] '*Macdonald*: If beer and beef-steaks have made Englishmen, oatmeal cakes and oatmeal porridge have made Scotchmen.

'*Hilarius*: Specially Scotch brains. There is a notable seasoning of phosphorus in oats which produces the *praefervidum ingenium Scotorum*.'

– John Stuart Blackie: *Altavona.*

When the *Edinburgh Review* was founded in 1800, the motto proposed by Sydney Smith was, 'Tenui musam meditamur avena'. ('We cultivate literature on a little oatmeal.') This was later modified. – F. M. McN.

[4] 'An honest, good sort of fellow, made out of oatmeal,' said Carlyle of Macaulay. The compliment might have been reciprocated. – F. M. McN.

[5] Many a promising lad nevertheless died of over-study and malnutrition, and some who did achieve success were cut off in their prime as the result of a too meagre régime.

formerly granted by the authorities to enable the poor student to tramp back to his native glen and replenish his sack.[1]

'The ancient way of dressing corn,' writes Martin, who visited the Western Isles in 1703, 'which is yet used in several Isles is called Graddan, from the Irish word *Grad*, which signifies quick.... A Woman sitting down, takes a handful of Corn, holding it by the Stalks in her left hand, and then sets fire to the Ears, which are presently in a flame; she has a Stick in her right hand, which she manages very dexterously, beating off the Grain at the very Instant, when the Husk is quite burnt, for if she miss of that, she must use the Kiln, but experience has taught them this Art to perfection. The Corn may be so dressed, winnowed, ground, and baked within an Hour after reaping from the Ground. The Oat-bread dressed as above is Loosening, and that dressed in the Kiln Astringent, and of greater strength for Labourers: but they love the Graddan, as being more agreeable to their taste.'

Another mode was the primitive mortar-mill, which was succeeded by the quern,[2] a hand-mill composed of two circular stones with a hole in the centre of the upper one, through which it is fed with corn, and a wooden handle. The meal falls from all sides on to a wide tray, and by means of a wooden spindle can be ground coarse or fine at will.

> The cronach[3] stills the dowie[4] heart,
> The jurram[5] stills the bairnie,
> The music for a hungry wame[6]
> Is grinding o' the quernie,

says the old song.

---

[1] An annual holiday known as Mealy Monday is still celebrated in the Scottish universities.

Oatmeal has other uses than as an article of food. 'Meat in Scotland is frequently kept a fortnight smothered in oatmeal and carefully wiped every day,' says Mrs. Dalgairns in her *Practice of Cookery* (Edinburgh, 1829), 'and if it should be a little tainted, it is soaked for some hours before it is used in oatmeal and water.'

Oatcakes, mealie puddings, and cheeses are still commonly kept buried in oatmeal in the girnel or meal-chest. Oatmeal was formerly used as soap, and many country lasses still place a small muslin bagful in their ewer overnight for the benefit of their complexions. – F. M. McN.

[2] A.S. *cweorn*.   [3] Gael. *coronach*, lament.   [4] Sorrowful.
[5] Gael. *iorram*, song, lullaby.   [6] Belly.

25

The quern was in common use throughout the Highlands and Islands in the latter part of the nineteenth century, and is still used in the outlying districts, though isolatedly and sparingly.[1] In the burghs, however, and in the more populated areas, it was displaced at an early period by the mill. David I (1123–53) built mills for the Augustinian canons of Holyrood at the village known, appropriately, as Canon-mills, and elsewhere on the Water of Leith there were later established the mills belonging to the Baxters of Edinburgh,[2] who received from the Town Council a monopoly of the making and selling of bread within the burgh, the Council itself fixing the weight and price of the loaves, admitting the burgesses to the Incorporation of Baxters, and regulating the admission of apprentices. Bread had always to be pure, wholesome and sweet.[3]

As in the rural areas, barley-meal and oatmeal were the grains in general use. Wheaten flour was long regarded as a luxury, but was used more extensively as home-grown and imported supplies increased. The many religious establishments throughout the country had their own mills and bake-houses.[4] Not all the town houses had ovens of their own, and much of the food of the people was sent to the public bake-houses.

As oats and barley were the staple grains, so kail (cole-

[1] 'A friend of mine on one occasion . . . visiting an old woman on the heights of Assynt, was pressed to wait and get something to eat; whereupon the old matron went out to the barn, took in a sheaf of corn, and in a minute whipped the oats off with her hand, winnowed it with a fan at the end of the house, then placed it on the fire in a pot to dry; after that it was ready to be ground, and then, being put through a sieve, was ready to bake. The whole thing was done within an hour, from the time she took in the sheaf of corn till the cakes were on the table, and my friend says she never tasted better.' – J. G. Mackay: *Social Life in the Highlands in the Olden Times* (Trans. Gael. Soc. Glasgow).

[2] The Baxters of Edinburgh erected their own altar in the Kirk of St. Giles in honour of St. Cuthbert, their patron saint.

[3] Bread is the staff of life, and as such has always had an almost sacred significance; hence bakers have always been among the most honoured of craftsmen. In ancient Rome, they were the only craftsmen who were freemen of the city, the others being slaves.

[4] The earliest baker whose name is recorded in Scottish history is Genere, a Saxon and a religious brother who worked at his trade in the Iona community in the life-time of St. Columba (A.D. 521–97). He is mentioned in Adamnan's *Life* of the saint.

'The Natives told me that bread baked by the fuel of sea-ware relishes better than that done otherwise.' – Martin Martin: *Description of the Western Islands* (1703).

26

wort) was long the staple vegetable. His kail-yard[1] was, in fact, to the old Scots crofter what his potato-plot was to the Irish peasant. There he planted cabbages for summer and green kail for winter use, in addition, of course, to potatoes.

> Although my father was nae laird,[2]
> 'Tis daffin'[3] to be vaunty,[4]
> He keepit aye a gude kail-yard,
> A ha' hoose[5] and a pantry.[6]

Meg Dods speaks of *The Land o' Kail* as Burns does of *The Land o' Cakes*.[7] The vogue of kail, however, was originally confined to the Lowlands. The Highlander preferred the common nettle in his broth, and appears to have regarded the use of kail as a symptom of effeminacy.[8] In the earlier part of the nineteenth century, however, cabbage and green kail were freely grown in the Hebrides; but after the evictions in South Uist and elsewhere, when the people were deprived of their plots of land, they fell back on certain wild vegetables, most of which were used only in emergency – wild spinach, wild mustard, the goose-foot, and the root of the little silver-weed, trunkfuls of which were stored for winter use. Pennant tells us that the dried roots of the

[1] Kitchen-garden.
The term kail-yard has been applied to a school of fiction including Barrie, Crockett, and Ian Maclaren, who depict Scottish village life. Ian Maclaren took one of his titles, *Beside the Bonnie Brier Bush*, from the song:
> There grows a bonnie brier bush in our kail-yard.
George Douglas's *House with the Green Shutters*, a study of the same theme in colours as sombre as those of the others were roseate, was a protest against the sentimentalism of the 'kail-yairders'. – F. M. McN.
[2] Land-owner. [3] Nonsense. [4] Boastful. [5] A superior type of house with a hall or living-room. [6] *Scornfu' Nansy*, from Ramsay's *Tea-Table Miscellany*, where it is marked as old.
[7] Originally oat-cakes.
[8] 'The Grants, who, living near the Lowland line, had grown fond of it, were condemned as the soft, kail-eating Grants, and a Gaelic poem on the battle of Killiecrankie mocks at Mackay's defeated soldiers as "men of kail and brose".'
– T. F. Henderson: *Old-World Scotland*.
'Kail is still the common name in Scotland for broth, and is even used metonymically for the whole dinner, as constituting, among our temperate ancestors, the principal part. Hence, in giving a friendly invitation to dinner, it is common to say, "Will you come and tak' your kail wi' me? *Black Dwarf*".'
– Jamieson, *Dictionary of the Scottish Language*.
In Edinburgh the bell rung at two o'clock was popularly known as the kail-bell, and that which was rung at eight as tinkle-sweetie, because the sound of it was so sweet to the ears of apprentices and shop-men, who were then at liberty.

cor-meille, or wood pease (*orobus tuberosus*) were the support
of the Highlanders in long journeys where the customary
food could not be obtained. A plant called *shemis* (*ligusticum
scoticum*), possessing aromatic and carminative qualities,
grows on the rocky shores of the Hebrides and western sea-
board, and is used as a green vegetable, boiled or raw. The
wild carrot has always been a favourite 'fruit' of the children
of the Hebrides. The wild garlic, too, is a popular pot-herb.

> Is e mil fo'n talamh
> A th'anns a' churran gheamhraidh,
> E'adar Latha an Naoimh Aindreadh agus An Nollaig.

> Honey underground
> Is the winter carrot
> Between St. Andrew's Day and Christmas.

> Is leighas air gach tinn
> Cheamh 'us im a Mhàigh;
> Ol 'an fhochair sid
> Bainne-ghobhar bàn.

> Garlic with May butter
> Cureth all disease;
> Drink of goat's white milk
> Take along with these.[1]

The potato, like the Gael, travelled to Scotland via
Ireland, and crossed by the self-same route. 'That man has
not been dead many years who first introduced from Ireland
the culture of the potato into the peninsula of Cantyre;
he lived near Campbeltown. From him the city of Glasgow
obtained a regular supply for many years; and from him
also the natives of the West Highlands and Isles obtained
the first plants, from which have been derived those abundant supplies on which the people there now primarily
subsist.'[2] Its first recorded appearance in Scotland is in
1701, when the Duchess of Buccleugh's Household Book
mentions a peck of potatoes as brought from Edinburgh,
and costing half a crown.

[1] Old Gaelic rhymes.
[2] Anderson's *Recreations*, Vol. II (1800).

'About (1733),' Chambers tells us, 'it was beginning to be cultivated in gardens, but still with a hesitation about its moral character, for no reader of Shakespere requires to be told that some of the more uncontrollable passions of human nature were supposed to be favoured by its use. . . . (In 1739) a gentleman styled Robert Graham of Tamrawer, factor on the forfeited estate of Kilsyth, ventured to the heretofore unknown step of planting *a field of potatoes*.[1] His experiment was conducted on a half-acre of ground on the croft of Neilstone, to the north of the town of Kilsyth. It appears that the root was now, and for a good while after, cultivated on *lazy-beds*. Many persons – amongst whom was the Earl of Perth, who joined in the insurrection of 1745 – came from great distances to witness so extraordinary a novelty and inquire into the mode of culture.'[2]

Today, some of the finest varieties of potatoes bear the names of Scottish cultivators, and the growing of seed potatoes for export, principally to England, is an important feature of our agriculture.

Turnips were introduced from Holland about the same period. 'Cockburn of Ormiston . . . sewed turnips in 1725, being the first to raise turnips in drill.'[3]

These innovations were, in fact, part and parcel of the Agrarian Revolution of the early eighteenth century, when various societies for the improvement of agriculture, then deplorably primitive, came into being.[4] The results were improved methods, more varied crops in proper rotation, and the cultivation of waste land. In the Highlands, sheep-

[1] Apparently Robert Graham was not the first in the field.
'According to family tradition, my mother's forbears of the name of Mutter (later changed to Muter), who came over to this country at the time of the Revocation of the Treaty of Nantes and settled in the Lothians, were the first to plant a field of potatoes in Scotland. In a book about the parish of Stenhouse published in 1885, it is stated that in 1719 a William Mutter planted the first field of potatoes in Scotland on the farm of Liberton Mains, near Edinburgh, and got the Earl of Melville's gardener to assist him.'
— Miss E. M. Napier, Cardross, in a letter to the author (1952).
This is twenty years earlier than the Kilsyth experiment.
[2] *Domestic Annals of Scotland.*
[3] *Farmer's Magazine*, 1804.
[4] Of these, the Royal Highland and Agricultural Society of Scotland (popularly known as 'The Highland') which was founded in 1784, still flourishes, and its Annual Show is the most important event of the agricultural year.

farming was introduced into areas where the only money income hitherto had been derived from the rearing of cattle for sale at the Crieff and, later, the Falkirk Tryst. The progress of the Agrarian Revolution was fostered by the Industrial Revolution which soon succeeded it,[1] and by the growth of overseas trade. With the increased fertility of the soil and the importation of foodstuffs from other countries, food became more abundant and much more varied.

There was also a revolution in gardening. By the end of the century Scottish gardens were famed for their beauty and Scottish gardeners for their skill.[2] In the 'best' houses in England a Scottish gardener was now as much *de rigueur* as a French chef, and not a few found their way to the Continent.[3] Nor were they less expert with vegetables than with flowers. Bishop Pococke, who visited Scotland in 1760, writes, 'The most beautiful kitchen-garden, I believe, in the world, was at Blair Castle'.

Long before that date, the kail-wives, or green-wives of Edinburgh were conspicuous in the High Street with their creels of vegetables and garden stuff, the bulk of which came from Musselburgh and its environs.[4] Most of them took up their stances at the Tron. The scene is described by Robert Fergusson:

> If kail sae green, or herbs, delight,
> Edina's street attracts the sight,
> Nor Covent-garden, clad sae braw,
> Mair fouth o' herbs can eithly shaw:
> For mony a yaird is here sair sought
> That kail and cabbage may be bought,

[1] 'The first blast furnaces of the Carron Ironworks, which were lit in 1760, heralded the Industrial Revolution in Scotland.'
  – Stewart Michie: *The Church and Scottish Social Development*, 1780–1870.
[2] 'Scottish gardens are among the most impressive in the world.' – *Sunday Times*, May 27, 1962. Art. *Brief Guide to Some (British) Gardens on Show This Year*.
[3] Among these was Thomas Blaikie, who was in service at the French Court, and was for a time gardener to the Duke of Chartres, who became the Duke of Orleans (Philippe l'Egalité).
[4] A notable member of the kail-wife sisterhood was Jenny Geddes.
  'It happened to be in the Old Kirk (St. Giles) that the celebrated riot of the 23rd of July, 1637, took place, when, on the opening of the new Episcopal service-book, Jenny Geddes, of worthy memory, threw her cutty-stool at the dean who read it – the first weapon, and a formidable one it was, employed in the great civil war.'
  – Robert Chambers: *Traditions of Edinburgh*.

And healthfu' sallad to regale,
When pampered by a heavy meal.[1]

Writing in 1826, Meg Dods tells us that 'much has been done of late years to improve the quality, to hasten the season, and to spread the cultivation of vegetables. Where a turnip, or a cabbage, or a leek was fifty years ago the only vegetable luxury found on a country gentleman's table, we now see a regular succession of not merely broccoli, cauliflower and pease, but of the more recondite asparagus, seakale, endive and artichoke, with an abundance of early small saladings.

'The vegetable markets of most towns have within the same period undergone a wonderful improvement . . . so that a healthful luxury is now within the reach of all classes.'

At the same time, the cultivation of fruit went on apace. Charles McIntosh, one of the ablest horticulturalists Scotland has produced, and head gardener at Dalkeith Palace at a time when these gardens were among the most famous in Europe, writes in 1853:

'Without allowing what may be supposed a spirit of nationality to influence our reason, we must state that many of the districts north of the Forth or the Tay are better adapted for the cultivation of the finer kinds of apples than a great extent of the Border counties on both sides of the Marches. Peaches and apples ripen better at Dunkeld, in Perthshire, and even at Brahan Castle, in Ross-shire, than they do in many gardens in Cumberland and Northumberland, although several degrees farther south.'[2]

As for our own times,[3] the late Mrs. Christine Roebuck[4] wrote to the present writer after a visit to her native Hebrides:

'The quality of the turnips, carrots, leeks and cauliflowers I saw in the islands was unrivalled in my experience.

---

[1] *Edina*, Edinburgh; *fouth*, abundance; *eithly*, easily.
[2] See *The Memoirs of the Caledonian Horticultural Society*.
[3] The mid-twentieth century.
[4] Mrs. Roebuck (née Macpherson) cooked in her day for some of the nobility of Britain and plutocracy of the United States. On her return to Scotland her *céilidhs* became a feature of the social life of Edinburgh. She died in 1943. – F. M. McN.

One turnip, in Uist, weighed twenty pounds. Mushrooms, too, were of admirable quality.

'There are no tomatoes or peaches in America to touch ours for quality. A French chef I met in a Highland house corroborates this view. Of course, except in a few sunny places these have to be grown under glass, but there is something in our soil that accounts for their goodness, and again the fact that we have only one growth in the year means that they have a finer flavour than in countries where they have two or more growths.'

'Piscinata Scotia,' says the proverb. The great salmon-rivers and innumerable lochs and trout streams, together with the wide sea-track that skirts our shores from Stornoway to Eyemouth (proceeding thence to Yarmouth) – the immemorial route of the annual migration of our herring shoals – provide us with a wealth of fish of high quality. The most important of our white fish are haddock, cod, plaice and hake; others are whiting, halibut, turbot, lemon-sole and ling; and in our herring (as in our oats) we possess a foodstuff of the highest nutritional value and of a quality unexcelled in any other part of the world.

During the early Celtic period, when adoration was paid to the waters, fish as food was taboo, and even after the introduction of Christianity it continued for a time to be considered dangerous to the purity of the soul.[1] When, in the eleventh century, the Roman Church superseded the Celtic one, her fast-days and fastings encouraged the development of the fisheries, which at an early period became a source of national wealth. In the twelfth century, David I gave the monks of the Island of May exclusive rights round

---

[1] Aphrodite was born of the sea, and was commonly held to exercise her influence through certain products of the sea, notably (in the Scottish tradition) trout, skate, shell-fish and salt. Skate-bree (the liquor in which skate has been boiled) is a famous old Scottish love-potion. – F. M. McN. See *Caledonian Medical Journal* Ap. 1928, article on Scottish Folk Medicine by Col. D. Rorie, M.D.

'Il y a beaucoup d'amour parmi les paysans écossais.' – Stendhal: *De l'Amour.*

'It is a general Observation on all such as live on the Sea Coast, that they are much more prolific than any other people whatsoever.'
– Martin Martin: *A Description of the Western Islands.*

their own shores, conferred on the community of Holyrood the tithe of his own share of the larger fish caught along the southern shore of the Forth, from the Avon to Cockburnspath, and made over to the monastery of Dunfermline every one of the seals caught at Kinghorn after his own tithes had been set aside;[1] Malcolm IV granted the half of the fat of the royal fishes which might come into the Forth on either shore; and Alexander I gave to the monks of Scone the right to fish in the Tay, near which their house was situated.[2]

By the thirteenth century, Aberdeen was famous for her speldings[3] and other cured fish, and Don Pedro de Ayala, who visited Scotland in 1498, comments on the great quantities of salmon, herring and 'a kind of dried fish which they call stock fish', which were then exported. At an early period the curing of salmon and herrings was an important branch of trade in Glasgow, and by the middle of the seventeenth century had greatly increased. In those days the herring came much farther up the Clyde than they do now, and it is recorded that in some seasons as many as nine hundred boats were employed within the Cloch. The greater part of the catch was taken to Greenock (whose prosperity was largely based on the fishery) to be cured and dispatched to foreign markets.[4]

In 1630, Charles I, alluding in an accompanying letter to Sir William Alexander, Secretary of State, to 'that great blessing offered to us in the abundance of fish on the coasts of our islands', sent instructions to the Privy Council for the erection of a general fishery in Scotland, 'this being a common benefit to all our three kingdoms'.

In the seventeenth century the Dutch fishermen were

[1] Seals were extensively used as food in the Hebrides down to the last century. Adamnan (624–c. 704) speaks in his *Life of St. Columba* of 'the little island (off Iona) where our sea-calves breed' and Martin writes: 'The natives salt the seals with the ashes of burnt sea-ware, and say they are good food' (*Description of the Western Islands*, 1703). – F. M. McN.

[2] See Louis A. Barbé: *Sidelights on Scottish History*.

[3] Called also *speldrins*; small haddock or whiting split, salted and rock-dried – to be distinguished from *finnans*, or smoked haddock. They are mentioned by Boswell.

[4] In 1564, twenty thousand barrels were exported from Greenock to La Rochelle alone, as well as to other French and Baltic ports.

thoroughly at home in Scottish waters.[1] Every season, year in, year out, and almost the whole year round, those patient, plodding, but astute folk came over and fished round our coasts until they had practically established a monopoly, out of which their country made enormous gains. The Firth of Forth was a favourite resort.

> In her the skate and codlin sail,
> The eil, fu' souple, wags her tail,
> Wi' herrin, fleuk,[2] an' mackerel,
>   An' whitens dainty;
> Their spindle-shanks the labsters trail
>   Wi partans[3] plenty.[4]

It was not till the beginning of the eighteenth century that the Scots woke up to the fact that their pockets were being unostentatiously but systematically picked. In 1720, the same year that the South Sea scheme was launched in England, a North Sea scheme was launched in Scotland, its express purpose being to 'ding the Dutch', and to revive and develop the Scottish fisheries, as well as stimulate the boat-building industry. About two million pounds appears to have been subscribed, but soon, 'by a frost the origin and nature of which belongs to the social and political history of those times', the North Sea scheme, like its more celebrated contemporary, was completely blighted.

Of all the varieties of fish we produce, our chief benefactor is the herring.

'Here we have perhaps the most plebeian and common of fish', writes Morton Shand, 'a fish of endless resource and sovereign merit. The love of good red herrings is in our island blood. . . . Loch Fyne herrings are part of the pride of Scotland. Wherever the Briton settles, his homesick appetite for herrings remains unabated. Millions of tins of herrings are exported annually to Australia, New Zealand and South Africa, for herrings are strangers to the Pacific and Indian Oceans. Salted herrings are the staple diet of millions of Scandinavians, Letts, Finns and, above all,

---

[1] There is an old saying that Amsterdam was built on Scottish herring-bones.
[2] Flounder.   [3] The large edible crab.   [4] Fergusson: *Caller Oysters*.

34

Russians, and the majority of those consumed by them are imported from Great Britain.'[1]

Herrings, fresh or salted, have been for centuries a staple article of diet throughout Scotland itself. Until within living memory, the cry 'Caller Herrin'!' (fresh herring) rang or, more correctly, sang through the streets of Edinburgh and other towns. The Newhaven fishwives[2] in their picturesque costumes have now ceased to ply their wares in the residential quarters of the capital, but in many of our fishing-ports the 'luckies' still carry their teeming creels from door to door.

'Wastlin' herrin'!' was another, though less familiar, cry. Loch Fyne herring have always been celebrated for their delicious flavour, and a keg of 'wastlin' (west-coast) herring used to be a popular gift in Edinburgh and the east country. The plump 'Loch Fynes' were jocularly alluded to as 'Glasgow Magistrates'.[3]

[1] *A Book of Food.*
Up to the outbreak of the First World War, the prosperity of the north-east, in particular, had been created largely by our export trade in fish, and one of the greatest tragedies in our social and economic history is the decay and devastation caused by the neglect of the Government to recover the lapsed markets. (Fish, of course, play a much smaller part in the English economy.)
'Scottish herring are the best in the world, but it is a problem now to find out where to market them. At one time vast quantities of salt herring used to be exported to Russia, Germany and the Mediterranean countries, but the future significance of these markets is uncertain. The development of refrigeration of herring and the setting up of plant in the chief ports is a hopeful augury.'
– Peter Anson: Art. *Sea Fisheries in Scotland* (ed. H. W. Meikle, 1947).
[2] 'The Newhaven fish-wives – who has not been in love with "Christie Johnstone"? – have always excited the admiration of visitors, especially the artists. George IV, who was surely a connoisseur, when taken down incog. to the village by Sir Walter, declared that he had never seen a handsomer set of women.'
– James Bertram: *Memories of Men, Books and Events.*
The Peacock Inn was a favourite resort of those who were wont to delight in a fish dinner at Newhaven, 'despite the outside dirt and discomfort of the little town, and its ancient and fish-like smell.' Among the distinguished visitors were Dickens, Thackeray, Macready, Charles Kean, Douglas Jerrold and Henry Irving; and it was here that Charles Reade stayed when collecting material for his novel of fisher-life, *Christie Johnstone*. The verdict pronounced by Dickens was, 'This is immense! The service is not so fine as at Greenwich, but the fish! And the cooking!'
[3] In Glasgow itself, as we learn from entries in the Council's Accounts, barrels of herring were frequently presented by the city to those from whom it had received favours or services. It is to this practice of the Glasgow magistrates that the nickname is attributed. It is now seldom used, but is kept up by the Grand Antiquity Society of Glasgow which, on the occasion of its annual dinner, requests the honour of one's company to 'supper and the meeting of the magistrates' – herring having the place of honour on the bill of fare.
The epic of the growth of the herring industry in the north-east of Scotland has been

The salmon fisheries, too, were of great importance. The Tay, the Spey, the Tweed, the Don, the Dee and lesser rivers produced salmon of superlative quality, and in such quantity that it was long despised by the upper classes;[1] whilst farmhands, when being fee'd, used to stipulate that it should not be served to them more than so many times a week.[2] Eaten fresh in summer and kippered in winter, it played as important a part in the diet of the people who lived in the vicinity of the salmon rivers as did herring and haddock in that of the coast-dwellers. Large quantities, too, were exported.[3]

magnificently told by Neil Gunn in *The Silver Darlings*, and the joys and sorrows of the fisherfolk's life have been immortalized in our folk-songs, notably in Lady Nairne's well-known '*Caller Herrin*':

> Buy my caller herrin'!
> Though ye may ca' them vulgar farin',
> Wives and mithers, maist despairin',
> Ca' them lives o' men.

and in her Cradle-song:

> Baloo-loo lammie, noo baloo, my dear,
> Does wee lammie ken that its daddie's no here?
> Ye're rockin' fu' sweetly on minnie's warm knee,
> But daddie's a-rockin' upon the saut sea.
>
> Noo hush-a-ba, lammie, noo hush-a, my dear,
> Noo hush-a-ba, lammie, ain minnie is here;
> The wild wind is ravin', and minnie's hert's sair,
> The wild wind is ravin', and ye dinna care.

[1] 'I have been told it here as a very good Jest, that a Highland Gentleman who went to London by Sea, soon after his Landing passed by a Tavern where . . . there were among other Things a Rump of Beef and some Salmon: of the Beef he ordered a Steak for himself, "but", he says, "let Duncan have some Salmon". To be short, the Cook who attended him humoured the Jest, and the Master's eating was Eight Pence, and Duncan's came to almost as many Shillings.'
– Burt: *Letters from the North of Scotland* (1730).

[2] Their attitude is understandable, for the salmon, in comparison with the salmon-trout, is a coarse fish, and its richness speedily becomes nauseous.
'Every spring we look forward with a new-found impatience to the first Scotch salmon of the season, and every summer we are surprised anew to find how soon our palates grow indifferent, if not hostile to it.' – P. Morton Shand: *A Book of Food*.
'Salmon fishing on the river Tay and its tributaries opens on January 15 for rod fishing and on February 4 for nets; the fish that is caught during the first fortnight or so is of a delicacy and excellence never to be attained again during the rest of the fishing season.' – André Simon: *An Encyclopaedia of Gastronomy*.
In these degenerate days – our rivers have been greatly over-fished, and much goes to southern markets – the only salmon these same farm-workers taste is the kind that swims the Atlantic in tins. – F. M. McN.

[3] In the reign of James I the popular demand for French wines reached such proportions that in 1431 an Act was passed requiring that half the price of the salmon exported to France should be paid in Gascon wine.

36

Shellfish were always a staple article of diet. So, too, were seaweeds, not only in the isles, where the food problem was often acute, but in all the seaward towns.

The prince of shellfish is, of course, the oyster. A century ago, Edinburgh was a city of oysters, and we have ample testimony as to both the quantity and the quality of the 'natives' bred in the once-renowned oyster-beds of the Firth of Forth.[1]

'What desperate breedy beasts eisters must be,' says the Shepherd in the *Noctes Ambrosianae*, 'for they tell me that Embro devours a hunner thoosand every day.'

'Why, James,' says North, 'that is only about two oysters to every three mouths.'

As to quality, Faujas de St. Fond, the King of France's Commissioner for Wines, who visited Scotland in the 1780s, comments on the plumpness and exquisite flavour of the oysters he consumed at Prestonpans. Such is their reputation, he adds, that they are sent to all the principal towns in England and Wales, and are exported in barrels to all quarters.

Alas, her oyster-beds are one of the many glories that have departed from the capital. Their decay is due to the long course of reckless and improvident fishing to which they were subjected in view of the large gains to be made by selling young oysters and brood to English and Dutch oyster-growers, who relaid and fattened them for the market. In consequence, thousands of pounds have been lost annually to the fishermen of the Forth, to say nothing of the loss to the citizens of Edinburgh (and their overseas and foreign guests) of a delicious regale.[2]

[1] Oysters figure with partans, crabs and other shellfish at the royal banquet at Stirling in 1594, on the occasion of the baptism of Prince Henry (the elder brother of Charles I).

[2] In recent years there has been a revival of oyster fisheries in various parts of England and Wales, and there seems to be no adequate reason why Scotland, and in particular the Firth of Forth, should lag behind. It should be relatively easy to trawl for evidence of any remaining spat (which dies hard if left to itself) of the original stock in the Forth; and, in any case, there is no reason why, if a fresh stock of oysters, home and foreign, were laid down and due precautions taken to protect them from sewage effluents, our Scottish oysters should not once more rival, if not excel, those of England. The market appears to be insatiable. – F. M. McN.

Within the present century the fishing-trade was revolutionized by the introduction of filleting as a commercial process.[1] Fortunes were made by trawler-owners, who could now market fish that had previously been thrown overboard as too small or too unattractive to the eye, though pleasing to the palate.

Meanwhile a scientific staff carries on fishery research from the Marine Laboratory in Aberdeen for the Fisheries Division of the Scottish Home Department.

Relatively speaking, the Scots were always a piscivorous, the English a carnivorous race. Despite the excellence of their beef[2] and mutton, the Scots have never been great meat-eaters. Burt writes: 'The little Highland Mutton, when fat, is delicious, and certainly the greatest of Luxuries. And the small Beef, when fresh, is very sweet and succulent, though it lacks that Substance which should preserve it long when salted. Amongst the poorer Classes in Scotland, Beef is eaten only at Martinmas,[3] when a Mart or Ox is killed; and the only other Butcher-meat they eat throughout the year is an occasional Braxy[4].'

[1] The originator was W. S. Eunson (familiarly known as Old Bill o' Aiberdeen), the son of a Fair Isle fisherman. Although entirely self-educated, he had a strong scientific bent, and after migrating to Aberdeen became an acknowledged expert on fish. Old Bill had no interest in money, and gladly shared his secrets with the fisherfolk, by whom he was held in affectionate esteem.

Old Bill was strongly opposed to trawling limits. 'Give real fishermen adequate boats and gear and say to them, Now, go fish where you like, as you like and when you like. The whole world needs your fish and the coming of your fish will stir up all the shore end of fisheries and they will find a way or make a way to supply the whole world with the best of food.'

[2] The 'roast beef of old England', at its best, is Scots beef, which always fetches a higher price in the London market.

[3] At this season fodder is scarce. The killing of the mart appears to have been originally sacrificial in character, in honour of St. Martin. The name may be derived, as Jamieson suggests, from *Martin*, but more probably it is simply the Gaelic word *mart*, a cow.

[4] *Letters from the North of Scotland* (1730).

Braxy mutton, the salted flesh of sheep which have died of braxy, is commonly eaten by poor herdsmen and shepherds, who may have found its strong flavour palatable. 'In pastoral countries it is used as a food with little scruple,' says Scott in a note to *Redgauntlet*; according to Burns, 'moorland herds like good fat braxies'; and Norman Macleod speaks of 'the occasional dinner luxury of braxy, a species of mutton which need not be too minutely inquired into.'

'The true braxy is an intestinal affection . . . and arises from the habit the sheep have of gorging themselves with food when newly weaned or suddenly placed on

38

Today, with the development of stock-breeding, the scene is vastly changed. The main emphasis is placed on quality beef.[1] Shorthorns of the beef type and the Aberdeen-Angus black cattle attract buyers from all parts of the world to the great Perth sales to bid for bulls.[2]

In the Southern Uplands is to be found another type of black, hornless cattle – the Galloway – a hardy breed much sought after by the butcher. Hardier still are the shaggy Highland cattle, which thrive where other breeds fail. The south-west specializes in dairy herds – healthy, high-yielding cattle. The Ayrshire cow is world-famous.

The ubiquity of sheep has given rise to a large woollen-cloth industry in the valley of the Tweed; but for the table our mountain mutton is on a par with the Welsh, the English Southdown and the *Pré-salé* of France.

As regards pork, Scott, in a note to *The Fortunes of Nigel*, reminds us that 'the Scots, till within the last generation, disliked swine's flesh as an article of food as much as the Highlanders do at present. It was remarked as extraordinary rapacity, when the Border depredators condescended to make prey of the accursed race, whom the fiend made his habitation';[3] and adds, in a note to *Waverley*, 'King Jamie carried this prejudice to England, and is known to have abhorred

---

rich or indigestible pasture. This produces a kind of colic . . . which generally proves fatal.

'. . . A well-known farmer says of the food, "It is wholesome and very digestible. . . . It should, however, be well cooked." ' – *The Scottish National Dictionary*.

Braxy Bree: A soup made with braxy mutton. 'The fine braxy bree o' Kintyr.' – Ibid.

[1] 'I little thought,' a cousin, whose early home was a Banffshire Manse, once commented to the present writer, 'that those rough working-farmers in my father's congregation were producing some of the finest beef in the world, that fetched the highest prices at Smithfield.'

[2] 'It is a triumph for the sagacity and diligence of Aberdonians that today the progeny of Aberdeen and Angus "doddies"* can command five-figure prices in the Americas. The young bulls learn Spanish almost in the byre.'
                    – Douglas Young: Art. *Aberdeen* in *The Scotsman*, April 8, 1961.
* Hornless cattle.

[3] An old Galloway grace before meat runs:

> Bless the sheep for David's sake, he herdit sheep himsel';
> Bless the fish for Peter's sake, he gruppit fish himsel';
> Bless the soo for Satan's sake, he was yince a soo himsel'.

                            – From Dr. Trotter's *Galloway Gossip*.

pork almost as much as he did tobacco'.[1] Nevertheless Burt tells us that Aberdeen, in 1730, was furnishing families with pickled pork, 'for winter provision, as well as for their shipping'; and in the Kingdom of Fife they have an excellent pie, of ancient pedigree, with rabbit and pickled pork as the main ingredients.

To vary the winter diet of salt beef, salt mutton and pickled pork, two articles of diet were cultivated – rabbits and pigeons. Rabbits were particularly popular in the Lowlands – the Highlands had the mountain hare – and as early as the thirteenth century a rabbit warren, with its warrener, was attached to every burgh.[2] The doocot (dove-cote) was a charming feature of our old castles and manor-houses.[3] It dates from the Auld Alliance, and shows marked French influence. Gables are often crow-stepped to provide landing- and perching-places for the birds. A poor man could keep a few pigeons in a 'fuie', which consisted of a small wooden structure on the gable-end of his dwelling, or make entrance holes admitting to nests in the rafters.

In modern times, we have made good our neglect of pork by producing our own method of curing it – the now widely known and highly regarded Ayrshire bacon.

Like the fisheries, poultry-rearing, and indeed husbandry generally, owed much to the fostering care of the monks.

The popular belief that before the Union of the Crowns Scotland was a poor and barbarous country is contrary to fact. Like other countries, she had periods of acute poverty,

[1] Ben Jonson has recorded this peculiarity where the gipsy in a masque, examining the King's hand, says:

> . . . you should by this line
> Love a horse and a hound, but no part of a swine.
> – *The Gipsies Metamorphosed.*

'James's own proposed banquet for the Devil was a loin of pork, a poll of ling, with a pipe of tobacco for digestion.' – Scott: *Waverley*, Note.

'In Scotland we do not manage pork well. In England they kill it at the proper age and size. . . . Servants [in Scotland] will seldom touch it; in London it is the greatest treat they can get.' – Mrs. McEwen: *Elements of Cookery* (1835).

[2] Mak kinnen* and capon ready, then,
And venison in great plentie;
We'll welcome here our royal King.
> – *Ballad of Johnie Armstrang.*

* Rabbits. cf. Gael. *coinnin* and E. *coney.*

[3] There was a pawky old saying that the possessions of a Fife laird were a 'puckle land, a lump o' debt, a doocot and a law plea.'

even of destitution; but at the worst of times she was never much worse off than England, and often she fared much better. Her internal resources were frequently drained by costly wars and by internal feuds which occasionally resulted in social anarchy, and she was further handicapped by a vicious economic system – a survival of the Middle Ages – that set town against town, burgh against burgh. Nevertheless at a very early period she had a considerable foreign trade.[1] Rich dresses were imported by Malcolm III (Canmore) in the eleventh century, oriental luxuries by Alexander I in the twelfth, whilst David I was praised by Fordun for enriching the ports of his kingdom with foreign merchandise. In the thirteenth century, under Alexander III, Scotland had a large and lucrative trade with Flanders, Germany, and the Low Countries, and during the next hundred years, under the wise rule of three successive kings, she attained a remarkable degree of well-being. In the fourteenth century, however, when a truce with England was on the point of conclusion, and Scotland imagined herself safe from attack, she was raided with more than usual ferocity[2] and her richest provinces utterly laid waste.[3]

[1] In the ledger of Andrew Halyburton, an enterprising Scottish commission merchant, we have an authoritative document as to Scottish trade at the end of the fifteenth century. Her foreign trade was based not on any organized industry, but on the primeval callings of fishermen, shepherds, and huntsmen. Her ships took wool, hides, and fish to Flanders, and returned with wine, furniture, and plate. (The Netherlands were long the clearing-houses for European and extra-European trade.) Under James IV, Berwick, the chief Scottish port, was likened to Alexandria, and her customs were reckoned to equal a third of all England. – F. M. McN.

Aberdeen was an early Flemish settlement. 'She served an extensive district – a district which was rich in the staple products of the period. . . . As the bulk of her trade was with the Low Countries, she frequently received accessions to her population from her kinsmen across the water. Down the centuries the true son of Aberdeen has maintained certain characteristics of his own, so much so that even today the typical Aberdonian is different from his fellow-Scots elsewhere.'
– Evan Barron: *The Scottish War of Independence.*

[2] 'The barons of Scotland were not apprised of this invasion, and took the affair much to heart, saying they would revenge it to the utmost of their power.'
– Froissart: *Chronicles.*

[3] 'Between the fertile and civilized part of England and the march of Scotland, lay a hundred miles of barren and thinly peopled country. . . . The Scotch themselves were less fortunate. . . . From the top of the Cheviot ridge the moss-troopers could descry three of the richest shires of Scotland stretched below them, a helpless prey, whilst southward they could see nothing but desolate moors. The fertile Lothians and the Tweed valley could be raided by Percy, but the English midlands could not be touched by Douglas.' – G. M. Trevelyan: *England in the Age of Wyclif.*

Quhen[1] Alysander oure king was dede,
    That Scotland lede in luve and lé,[2]
Away was sons[3] of ale and brede,
    Of wyne and wax, of gamyn[4] and glé;
Oure gold was changed into lede.
    Cryst borne into Virginité,
Succour Scotland and remede[5]
    That stad[6] is in perplexité.[7]

No wonder that, as Froissart tells us, the French troops
were astonished and appalled at the intense poverty of the
country which had produced so much of the flower of
European scholarship and chivalry.

But with normal conditions she invariably recovered.
Taylor, the Water-Poet, primed with travellers' tales of a
bleak, barren, and famine-stricken land, was astonished to
find, on crossing the Border in 1618, that

> There I saw the sky above and earth below,
> And, as in England, there the sun did shine;
> The hills with sheep replete, with corn the dale,
> And many a cottage yielded good Scots ale.

Neither was there any shortage in the Highlands. Of
Lord Lovat (b. 1572) we read: 'The weekly expenditure
of provisions in his house included 7 bolls of malt, 7 bolls of
meal, and 1 of flour. Each year 70 beeves were consumed,
besides venison, fish, poultry, lamb, veal, and all sorts of
feathered game in profusion. His lordship imported wines,
sugars, and spices from France, in return for the salmon
produced by his rivers. He was celebrated for a liberal hospitality, and when he died in 1633, 5000 armed followers and
friends attended his funeral, for all of whom there would be
entertainment provided.'[8]

'The diet of the Scots,' writes Chamberlayne, who visited
the country in 1708, 'is agreeable to their estates and qualities. No people eat better, or have greater varieties of flesh,
fish, wild and tame fowl, than the Scots nobility and gentry

---

[1] When.   [2] Law.   [3] Abundance.   [4] Sport.   [5] Remedy.   [6] Fixed.
[7] Ancient Cantus preserved in Wyntoun's *Orygnale Cronykill of Scotland.*
[8] Anderson: *History of the Frasers.*

in their own country, where they can furnish their tables with ten dishes cheaper than the English can provide three of the same kinds; and of their wines, the French themselves did not before the Union drink better, and at very easy rates. The tradesmen, farmers and common people are not excessive devourers of flesh, as men of the same rank are in England. Milkmeats and oatmeal, several ways prepared, and kale and roots dressed in several manners, is the constant diet of the poor people (for roast meat is seldom to be had but on gaudy-days); and with this kind of food they enjoy a better state of health than their southern neighbours, who fare higher.' And Captain Burt, who accompanied General Wade to Scotland in 1724, writes in his *Letters from the North of Scotland* that while in some parts he found no decent food, in others he was surfeited with delicacies – grouse, partridge, salmon, trout, and excellent honey. There was wine and brandy of fine quality, but 'the glory of the country was Usky'.[1]

On the whole, the remark of the French traveller, Estienne Perlin, in 1552, 'Nothing is scarce here but money', is substantially true of Scotland throughout her history.

In eighteenth-century Edinburgh, street vendors were everywhere in evidence.

'Buy my sonsie peeryorries! Saxpence a peck and awa they go!'

'Neeps like succar! Wha'll buy neeps?'

(Two girls often carried a clothes-basket of turnips between them.)

'Four bunches a penny, the bonnie caller radishes!'

'Leddies, leddies, here are cresses,
A' the wey frae Loudon Burn!'

'Wall cresses and purpey!'

And the children's rhyme survives:

'Wha'll buy syboes, wha'll buy leeks,
Wha'll buy the bonnie lass wi' the red cheeks?'

---

[1] Whisky (Gael. *uisge beatha*, water of life).

'Hot peas and beans!'

(These were carried in pitchers and measured out in a small cup.)

'Potatoes all hot, all hot!'

(The vendor carried in front of him, by means of a strap over his shoulder, a hot grill for his wares. He was superseded by the hot-chip man.)

Fruit, too, appeared in season.

'Sonsie cherries! Wha'll buy my bonnie cherries, twenty for a bawbee and ane to the mense o't!'

'Ripe strawberries!'

'Grossets, green grossets, a penny the basket!'

'Buy my fine pears, the queens o' beauty, the queens o' beauty! Only a penny the pund and awa they go!'

'Here's your fine rosy-cheekit Carse o' Gowries! The tap o' the tree, the tap o' the tree!'

('Hurlies' full of apples were pushed along the causeway.)

And the exotic 'Cocky-nit, cocky-nit, a ha'penny the bit, bit, bit!' was also in evidence.

The autumn fruits were in due course replaced by oranges. On Hogmanay, the sides of every street that led to the Tron Kirk – the great rallying-place for the communal welcome given by the people of Edinburgh to the New Year, was lined with hawkers and their barrows of fruit. These served as a modest Hogmanay handsel.

'Oranges! Braw oranges! Only a penny the piece!'

Fish and shellfish, too, appeared in their season.

'Caller herrin'! Ca-a-a-ller herrin'!'

'Rug-a-rug o' the caller haddies! Rug-a-rug o' the caller cod!'

'Haddies, caller haddies, fresh and loupin' in the creel!'

'Garvie herrin', a penny the plate!'

'Caller ou!' 'Caller partans!' 'Cockles and wulks!' 'Caller dulse and tangle!' – these were all familiar cries in our coastwise towns.

In Edinburgh, the vendors of shellfish had their stances throughout the Old Town. Each had an improvised table – often an orange box – on which were placed saucers of shellfish with the necessary condiments. They were patronized by all classes. (One or two still linger, though the women no longer cry their wares.)

The piemen, too, sold their wares 'pipin' and reekin''; so, too, the vendors of black and white puddings. Cheese was sold in cuts.

'Goudy! Finest Goudy!'

and during the summer months there was a lively response to the cries,

'Soor dook, a penny the pint!'

and 'Curds and whey! Curds and whey!'

Sonsie, of pleasant appearance; *peeryorries*, potatoes; *neeps*, turnips; *succar*, sugar; *caller*, fresh; *purpey*, purslane; *syboes*, young onions; *to the mense o't*, for good measure; *grosset*, gooseberry; *hurlie*, a handcart; *Carse o' Gowries*, apples from that region, noted for quality; *loupin'*, leaping; *garvies*, the local name for sprats (from the island in the Forth near which they were caught); ou, oysters; *partans*, the large edible crabs; *wulks*, whelks; *buckies*, periwinkles; *goudy*, Dutch Gouda cheese; *soor dook*, buttermilk.

The clamour was incessant.

The cries appear to have continued unabated into the sixties and seventies of the last century, and not a few survived into the present one.

The old economy persisted well into the nineteenth century, though in the 'big houses' the home produce was increasingly supplemented by luxuries from the South.

Writing in 1812, Elizabeth Grant of Rothiemurchus tells us that 'at this time in the Highlands, we were so remote from markets that we had to depend very much on our own produce for the necessaries of life. . . . We brewed our own beer, made our bread, made our candles; nothing was brought from afar but wine, groceries and flour, wheat not ripening well so high above the sea. Yet we lived in luxury; game was plentiful, red-deer, roe, hares, grouse, ptarmigan and partridge; the rivers provided trout and salmon, the different lochs pike and char; the garden abounded in common fruits and common vegetables; cranberries and raspberries ran over the country, and the poultry-yard was ever well furnished. The regular routine of business, where

45

so much was done at home, was really a perpetual amusement. I used to wonder when travellers asked my mother if she did not find her life dull.'[1]

In the cottage homes, too, the diet became less frugal, if no less wholesome. Mrs. Katherine Grant, writing of her corner of Argyll (Appin), where the men usually had a trade and worked the croft in their spare time, tells us that the ordinary diet was porridge or potatoes with milk, eggs, cheese, scones and oat cakes, with an occasional potful of broth or cock-a-leekie. A night's fishing or a feast of shellfish provided a welcome change. After the harvest, preparations were made for the winter months. A kitful of salted butter had been gathered, little by little, and now a store of dried ling and cod was laid up, with a barrel of Loch Fyne herring and a quantity of rock-dried saithe.

But 'it was when the mutton barrel was being filled that the rarest opportunity came for displaying the most brilliant feats of housewifery. The husbands, of course, saw to the procuring of the meat, and they broke it up and salted it; but the wives had by far the busiest time. . . . There was the tripe to be cleaned and apportioned for different methods of preparation. There was the suet, which must needs yield so many dozen candles, and the remaining portion of which was to go into white puddings. Nothing was allowed to go to waste. It was a time of general feasting on fragrant haggis, delicious potato soup made with tripe, toothsome hashes, sheep's head barley broth and – next to haggis in deliciousness – fine mince patties, fit for an epicure.[2] Then followed the rolling of home-fed bacon and the making of sausages. A nice quantity of lard was yielded in the process, which served many purposes, and with this the storing of winter provision was complete.'[3]

In Osgood Mackenzie's delightful book, *A Hundred Years in the Highlands*, which covers the nineteenth century,

[1] *Memoirs of a Highland Lady.*
[2] 'We are convinced that the art of preparing cheap dishes is much better understood by the intelligent poor than by those who assume the task of instructing them.'
— Meg Dods.

[3] *Myth, Tradition and Legend from Western Argyll.*

there is a description (by an uncle) of his grandmother's larder at Conan House, in Ross-shire:

'The room was shelved all round with moveable frames for holding planks, on which unimaginable quantities of dried preserved edibles reposed till called for. There were jam pots by the hundred of every sort, shelves of preserved candied apricots and Magnum Bonum plums that could not be surpassed in the world; other shelves with any amount of biscuits of all sorts of materials, once liquid enough to drop on sheets of paper, but in time dried to about two inches across and half an inch thick for dessert. Smoked sheep and deer tongues were there also, and from the roof hung strings of threaded artichoke bottoms, dried, I suppose, for putting into soups. In addition, there were endless curiosities of confectionery brought north by Kitty's talents from her Edinburgh cookery-school, while quantities of dried fruit, ginger, orange-peel, citron, etc., from North, Simpson and Graham of London, must have made my dear mother safe-encased in armour against any unexpected and hungry invader. Then every year she made gooseberry and currant wines, balm ditto, raspberry vinegar, spruce and ginger beer. I remember they were celebrated, and liqueurs numberless included magnums of camomile flowers and orange peel and gentian root bitters for old women with indigestion pains.'[1]

With the growth of industry, the whole business of brewing and distilling, of preserving and pickling, was gradually transferred from the stillroom to the factory, but happily in not a few of our country-houses and farmhouses the old skills are maintained.

[1] See p. 309.

III

THE RENASCENCE OF COOKERY
IN SCOTLAND

'Mere hunger, which is the best sauce, will not produce cookery, which is the art of sauces.'

Cookery aims, of course, at much more than merely supplying the necessities of nutrition. Its development is dependent on an increasing refinement of taste, which, in turn, is dependent on a certain degree of wealth and general culture. And if, as we have said, the art of a nation has its roots in the soil, it is equally axiomatic that external influences are necessary to foster its growth.

In cookery, as in all the arts, there is a continuous give-and-take among the nations. The Greeks, through their contact with Asia, added a touch of oriental splendour to their banquets;[1] the Romans, forsaking their old simple ways, borrowed in turn from the Greeks. Then come the Dark Ages of Cookery, as of all culture, and not till the Renascence – then, too with Italy as the starting-point – does the history of modern cookery begin.[2] Hitherto, sophisticated European cookery had remained 'Gothic' in character – abundant, costly and over-elaborate. Now began the transition from elaboration to elegance. Herbs and spices, for instance, were used no longer to disguise, but to enhance the natural flavour of a dish. This was indeed a gastronomic revolution.

The development of the art of cookery in France appears (judging by references in Montaigne) to owe much to Catherine de Medici (1519–89), wife of Henri II of France,

---

[1] 'In Greece the arts of cookery and medicine were associated, and were studied by physicians' of the greatest eminence.' – W. C. Hazlitt: *Old Cookery Books*.

[2] Most of the sixteenth-century dishes, the recipes of which survive, whilst interesting as museum pieces, would be instantly rejected by the modern gourmet. – F. M. McN.

48

who brought Italian cooks to Paris and introduced there a cultured simplicity hitherto unknown. (Ices, incidentally, were an Italian innovation.) The seed was sown on fertile soil. The French rapidly became masters of the art, and have retained their supremacy to this day. The spread of cosmopolitan hotels and restaurants has acquainted the whole civilized world with the type. The French Revolution dealt a severe blow to the art, as to so much else in the *ancien régime*; but it recovered, and in 1804, in the lifetime of Brillat-Savarin, the *Almanach des Gourmands* was started – 'the first sustained effort at investing gastronomy with the dignity of an art'.[1]

Scottish cooking has been aptly described as 'a pastoral cooking, brightly influenced by old ties with France'.

In the days of the Auld Alliance,[2] the fashions of living

---

[1] The names of its principal exponents are known the wide world over: Béchamel, for example, maître d'hôtel to Louis XIV, celebrated for his sauce; Vatel, the great Condé's cook, the story of whose suicide in despair at the tardy arrival of the fish is so touchingly told by Madame de Sévigné; the chef of the Prince of Soubise, whose name is borne by an onion sauce; and Richelieu, to whom is ascribed the mayonnaise. See *Enc. Brit.*, art. *Cookery*.

[2] Legend attributes to Charlemagne the
          Weill keipit ancient alliance
    Maid betuix Scotland and the realme of France.*
Its authentic beginnings, however, go no farther back than the twelfth century. Later, when England, led by her Norman conquerors into a series of wars of aggression, had subdued Wales and partially subdued Ireland, she turned to Scotland and France, who were thus drawn to make common cause against a powerful enemy, and it was by this means that Scotland was able to maintain the national independence asserted at Bannockburn in the fourteenth century. The Scottish archers fought with distinction during the Hundred Years' War, one of their leaders, the Earl of Buchan, being created Constable of France. In recognition of their services, Charles VII appointed as Royal bodyguard the famous Scots Guard of France, which consisted of a hundred gendarmes and two hundred archers.† Twenty-four of their number were told off as the special protectors of the Royal person. Louis XIV was reported to trust no other creatures of human make, and history shows that their motto, In omni modo fidelis (*Ever Faithful*), was well merited.

According to the old courtly creed of France, the privileges of the Scots Guard had 'an eminence that partook of sacredness'. Its captain was a high officer of state, the first we know of being John Stewart, Lord of Aubigny, founder of a great Scots house in France; many of its members – scions of distinguished houses such as Douglas, Stewart, and Hamilton – received titles and lands from successive French monarchs; and Scottish nobles were as much at home at the French court as at their own.

Conversely, during the regency of Albany in the sixteenth century, French troops were garrisoned in Scotland, and when the Regent was absent in France, he left the Sieur de la Bastie as guardian within the boundaries of Lothian and the Merse.

* Sir David Lyndsay: *Deploration of the Death of Queen Magdalene*.

† 'The institution of the Scots Guard was an acknowledgement of the service the Scots rendered to Charles VII in reducing France to his obedience, and of the great loyalty and virtue he found in them.' – Louis XII: 'Letters of General Naturalization

49

of the Scottish nobility were much influenced by the French Court, and the early Stuart kings vied with their continental contemporaries in the magnificence of their banquets.

Hector Boece[1] laments the 'extreme diligence' with which his contemporaries searched 'so mony deligat courses that they provoke the stomach to ressave more than it may sufficiently digest', and attributes this deviation from the simpler ways of an earlier generation to the nobility, who introduced them 'efter the fassione quhilke they have seen in France'.

In those days, poverty and love of adventure drove many young men of family or 'parts' abroad as soldiers of fortune or scholars, as later they went to London, India, and the Dominions, so that we had a cosmopolitan instead of, as today, an anglicized aristocracy.[2] It is, therefore, not surprising that in the earliest Scottish cookery-books we learn to dress cod in the Dutch way, lobsters in the Italian way,

for the Whole Scottish Nation in France.' (See Daniel's *Histoire de la Milice Française*, Vol. II.)

After the Union of the Crowns of England and Scotland in 1603, the native element in the Scots Guard was gradually thinned, but the Guard persisted as part of the pageantry of the French court until the latter went down, with all its pomps and vanities, in the maelstrom of the French Revolution.

Scott's *Quentin Durward* gives a picture of the life of a member of the famous Guard.

The prolonged intercourse between the two countries naturally led to numerous alliances between their royal and noble houses. William the Lion and Alexanders II and III had French wives, and James V had two in succession – the frail Magdalene, whom he married in Notre Dame and buried two months later in Holyrood Abbey, and Mary of Lorraine, the mother of Mary Stuart. Almost beneath the walls of Craigmillar Castle, on the outskirts of Edinburgh, there nestled the hamlet of Little France, the residence of such of Mary's attendants as could not find accommodation in the castle, and it is said that French sorrel grows freely in the neighbourhood. In the little historic garden at Croft-an-Righ, there grows another plant introduced from France – *archangelica officinalis*, which is used for purposes of confectionery. It has been in cultivation since 1568, a year or two after Queen Mary's return from France, and is believed to grow nowhere else in the United Kingdom.

The Auld Alliance has left traces in almost every department of Scottish national life, notably in her legal and ecclesiastical systems, and in the common speech. (See Appendix I: *Franco-Scottish Domestic Terms.*) The strong sentiment which still persists is crystallized in the flourishing Franco-Scottish Society. – F. M. McN.

[1] A fifteenth-century Scottish historian and friend of Erasmus.

[2] 'Then it was that the name of Scot was honourable over all the world, and that the glory of their ancestors was a pass-port and safe-conduct for any traveller of that country. . . . I have heard it related [of James (the Admirable) Crichton] . . . that after his peregrination of France, Spaine, and Italy, and that for speaking some of these languages with the liveliness of the country accent they would have had him pass for a native, he plainly told them, without making bones thereof, that truly he thought he had as much honour by his own country, which did contrevalue the riches of those nations by the valour, learning, and honesty wherein it did parallel, if not surpass them.' – Sir Thomas Urquhart of Cromarty (*c*. 1605–60: *Ekskybalauron*).

a nowt's tongue in the Polish way, and so forth, as well as numerous dishes *à la française*.[1]

We learn from the Exchequer Rolls that James I kept a French cook, and it is not unlikely that his successors did likewise. During the reign of James IV, the Scottish court was regarded as the most romantic and brilliant in Europe.[2] Its praises were sung by the Italian poet Ariosto, and it is the subject of a finely painted frieze in Siena. It was ornamented by a galaxy of poets[3] who virtually alone illumine the barren period in English literature that separates Chaucer from Spenser; knights from all over Europe took part in its jousts, and even negroes from Morocco arrived at Leith[4] in Scottish ships. James was as mindful, too, of the elegance of the table as of the splendours of the tournament.[5] Alas that so much chivalry and talent should have been blotted out on Flodden Field!

In the sixteenth century Mary of Lorraine, the wife of James V, introduced to Edinburgh the perfected civilization

[1] 'We of Scotland,' said Winterblossom [apropos of soup], 'probably owe our superiority in this department to our long and close alliance with that nation which has ever been most profoundly skilled in the mysteries of the soup-pot. That Scotland is indebted to France for even the slender proficiency she has attained in cookery, is abundantly evident from the culinary phraseology of the nation. Kitchen – cuisine – the word with us comprehends every kind of viand or preparation which may add to the relish of the coarse cake, and decoction of oatmeal and coleworts, which formed the staple of the daily meal. A peasant's butter, cheese, fish, meat and so forth, all are "kitchen". Then we have the hachi – the soup Lorraine and à la Reine, the veal Flory, or Florentine pie – our broche and our turn-broche, and our culinary adage, "hunger is good kitchen".' – *Annals of the Cleikum Club.*

[2] 'During the sixteenth century, all the leading powers of Europe found it their interest to court the goodwill of Scotland.' – P. Hume Brown: *Life of John Knox.*

[3] Henryson, Dunbar, Gavin Douglas, Sir David Lyndsay, and among lesser lights, Sir Gilbert Hay, chamberlain to Charles VI of France, who made several translations of the works of French authors.

[4] Here, in 1511, James IV 'buildit the *Michael,* ane verrie monstruous great ship, whilk tuik sae meikle timber that schee waisted all the woodis in Fyfe, except Falkland wood, besides the timber that cam out of Norroway'. – Pitscottie.

[5] In his *Dirige to the King at Stirling,* Dunbar invites James to return to the festive halls of Holyrood:

> To eit swan, cran, pertrik* and plever,†
> And every fische that swymis in rever;
> To drynk with ws the new fresche wyne,
> That grew upon the rever of Ryne,
> ffresche, fragrant clairettis‡ out of France,
> Of Angerss and of Orliance,
> With mony ane courss of grit dyntie:
>   Say ye amen, for cheritie.
>   * Partridge.   † Plover.   ‡ Claret.

51

of France.[1] James himself, according to Buchanan, was temperate in diet and seldom drank wine, but this apparently had no effect on the customs of the day, for at the Earl of Atholl's Buchanan was entertained 'with all sich delicious and sumptuous meattis as was to be had in Scotland, for fleschis, fischis, and all kinds of fyne wyne, and spycis, requisit for ane prince'. Under Mary Stuart, during whose girlhood at the French Court the Italian influence was just beginning to be felt, the supremacy of French fashions was maintained.[2] Knox, indeed, makes special reference to the extravagant banqueting of the queen and nobles: 'The affairis of the kytcheing were so gryping that the mynesteris stipendis could nocht be payit.'

This prolonged period of high living resulted at last in an actual shortage of food, and in 1581 a law was passed against 'superfluous banquetting'.

Dishes and courses were regulated according to rank, and transgressors not only were fined, but also suffered moral punishment, being stigmatized as men 'given to voluptuosity, and not for the weal of their person and the common weal of this realm'. Exemption was granted, however, in favour of certain high-days and holidays, including Yule and Pasch;[3] special occasions such as weddings; and banquets given officially to strangers from other countries; but no Scotsman was to make banquets to any other Scotsman 'but in the manner aforesaid'.

---

[1] In the sixteenth century much French and Flemish furniture and plate was imported.

[2] They say wyfis are sa delicat
In feiding, feisting, and bankat,*
  Some not content are with such cheir
As weill may suffice thair estate;
  For newfangilness† of cheir and geir.‡

And some will spend mair, I heir say,
In spyce and droggis on ane day
  Than wad thair mothers in any yeir,
Whilk|| will gar§ mony pak¶ decay,
  When they sa vainlie waste thair geir.
            – Sir Richard Maitland (1496–1586):
                Satire on the Toun Ladyes.

* Banquet.   † Novelty.   ‡ Possessions. || Which.   § Make.   ¶ Fortune.
[3] Christmas and Easter.

Other and severer acts followed, professedly occasioned by the prevailing dearth.[1]

The French dessert was introduced to Scotland in the sixteenth century,[2] the table being disserved or cleared, and the fruits and sweets which followed being served in another room.[3] A Scottish house had 'fyne lame pottis for desertis' and 'lyttil new plaitis for disertis' as early as 1594. And James VI, when visiting New College, St. Andrews, to hear a disputation between the 'Bischope' and Andrew Melville, passed to the College Hall, 'where was prepared a banquet of wat and dry confectiones, with all sortes of wyne,[4] wharat His Majestie camped verie merrilie a guid whyll'.

It does not appear, however, that French influences ever extended far beyond Edinburgh and Court circles. Fynes Moryson, for example, who visited Scotland in 1598, writes:

'Myselfe was at a Knight's House who had many servants to attend him, that brought in his meate with their heads covered with blew caps, the Table being more than half furnished with great platters of porredge[5] each having a little bit of sodden[6] meat; and when the Table was served, the servants did sit down with us,[7] but the upper messe,

---

[1] To some extent their influence was felt down to the eighteenth century. In 1744, at a meeting held in Portree to discourage the use of foreign luxuries, the Skye chiefs – Sir Alexander Macdonald of Macdonald, John Mackinnon of Mackinnon, Norman Macleod of Macleod, and Malcolm Macleod of Raasay – agreed to discontinue and discountenance the use of brandy, tobacco, and tea, whilst at the University of St. Andrews the bursars, so long as they continued to dine in the common hall, were restricted on three days of the week to fish and eggs, and to broth and beef on the other four. – F. M. McN.

[2] In England, the word dessert does not come into use until the middle of the following century.

[3] 'During the old *régime*, the French moved from table to the ante-room to refresh their lips and fingers immediately after the substantial part of their repast. Madame the Comtesse de Genlis appears to consider the abandonment of this practice and the introduction of finger-glasses as one of the most flagrant innovations of *parvenu* manners.' – Meg Dods: *Manual*, Note.

[4] One still reads in newspaper reports of municipal or other social gatherings in Scotland of a 'banquet' of cake and wine.

[5] Pottage, broth.   [6] Boiled.

[7] 'Till within this last (nineteenth) century, the farmers, even of a respectable condition, dined with their work-people. The difference betwixt those of high degree was ascertained by the place of the party above or below the salt, or sometimes by a line drawn with chalk on the dining-table. Lord Lovat, who knew well how to feed the vanity and restrain the appetites of his clansmen, allowed each sturdy Fraser who had

insteede of Porredge, had a Pullet with some prunes in the broth.[1] And I observed no Art of Cookery, or furniture of Household stuff, but rather rude neglect of both, though ... we were entertained after their best manner. .... They drink pure Wines, not with sugar as the English, yet at Feasts they put comfits in the Wine, after the French manner, but they had not our Vinteners' fraud to mix their Wines. .... [They] vulgarly eat hearth-cakes of oats, but in cities have also wheaten bread, which, for the most part, is bought by courtiers, gentlemen, and the best sort of citizens.'

The Reformation in Scotland was in fact a revolution, in many ways analogous in its effects to the French Revolution that succeeded it.[2] Drastic ills require drastic remedies, and drastic remedies, that benefit the system in one direction, have inevitably a baneful effect in another. In Scotland there began a praiseworthy cult of mind and character, but the arts declined. Beauty became suspect – she ministered, it was alleged, to the senses, not to the soul – and from the ancient trinity of Beauty, Goodness, and Truth, whose essential oneness it is the aim of civilization to demonstrate, she was ruthlessly expelled.[3] Her natural beauties, her love

the slightest pretensions to be a duinhé-wassel* the full honour of the sitting, but at the same time took care that his young kinsmen did not acquire at his table any taste for outlandish luxuries. His Lordship was always ready with some honourable apology why foreign wines and French brandy – delicacies which he conceived might sap the hardy habits of his cousins – should not circulate past an assigned point on the table.'
– Scott: *Waverley*, Note.

* (Approximately) gentleman.

[1] Cock-a-leekie.

[2] Democratic principles were understood and applied in Scotland long before England or Continental countries, though it was not in Parliament, but in the General Assembly of the Kirk, that the voice of the people made itself felt. It has been said with truth that Burns's *A Man's a Man for a' that* has done more for the growth of democracy than a thousand lectures and pamphlets. – F. M. McN.

A distinguished Frenchman, after seeing Sir David Lyndsay's *Satyr of the Thrie Estatis* at the Edinburgh Festival expressed his astonishment on finding that democratic ideas which were thought to be the last word in political thought at the time of the French Revolution had been freely circulating in Scotland two centuries earlier.
– F. M. McN.

[3] The above statement I must qualify in this, the revised edition of my book. Like so many others, I had long accepted uncritically the view here expressed; but, as Ian Finlay points out in his book, *Scotland*, the case for the destructive influence of Calvinism upon the arts in Scotland has been too plausibly argued, 'not only by Catholics, but by others looking for a ready explanation of the austerity and repression so marked in certain aspects of Scottish life.' These are, in fact, national characteristics

of literature, and her wealth of folk-music saved the country from aesthetic starvation. Presbyterian Scotland produced, indeed, a Raeburn, a Rennie, and the Adam brothers; but her Knox, her Carlyle, and her Livingstone were more truly representative of the rule of the Kirk.[1] Every depart-

that long pre-date the Reformation, and he refutes Calvin's critics with Calvin's own words:

'Forasmuch as carving and painting are the gifts of God, I require that they be both pure and lawfully used.'*

It was not, then, the arts that Calvin condemned, but what he considered to be their abuse in the churches of the Roman faith. At the same time he warned the new men of the Renaissance against the danger of mere sensuality, while exulting with them in the beauty of creation.†

'Is this the vandal,' asks Mr. Finlay, 'who brought a blight upon Scotland?'

'. . . In the Low Countries, where Calvin's influence was most intense, a great art of the people and of landscape grew up. In France, the Huguenots were master-craftsmen whose exile enriched countries from England to South Africa. In Scotland, craftsmanship was rooted more precariously, but the Reformation certainly did not blight it. . . . The Reformation, indeed, had little immediate cultural effect one way or the other. . . . Certainly, pictures and ornaments were removed from the churches, in accordance with Calvin's teaching. Much plate was taken by the fleeing priests themselves; that from Glasgow Cathedral went to the Scots College in Paris. . . . By the end of the sixteenth century this somewhat overwrought silver had begun to be replaced by chaste Communion cups of exquisite proportions and grace made within Scotland, some of them among the most perfect examples of the silversmith's art. At last Scotland was producing her own craftsmen, instead of relying upon foreigners.'

Painting came later, and in Scotland, no less than in Flanders, to which our painters owe practically everything, the art developed untrammelled.

'The fine arts,' says Mr. Finlay, 'naturally, received no direct encouragement from the Kirk, as an institution; but the men and women who were the Kirk showed themselves as eager patrons, within the limits of their purses, as their counterparts across in the Low Countries.'

Only towards the theatre was active hostility shown; but however much we may regret its arrested development, considering the quality of the average play and of the average player, there is at least some excuse for the popular attitude. – F. M. McN.

* *Institutes of the Christian Religion.*

† 'The flesh lusteth against the spirit.' – St. Paul.

The attempts to suppress secular music and dancing made by ministers of the smaller and narrower sects, like those made by the Puritans in England, were not characteristic of the nation as a whole. Few nations, if any, in fact, have preserved so rich a store of song and dance as the Scots, and this is largely a living, not a resuscitated heritage.

– F. M. McN.

[1] 'Banks . . . are in their modern form a Scottish invention. Besides those that sprang up in Scotland itself, the national banks of England and France owed their origin to two Scotsmen. A system of life insurance represented the provident habits and business talents of the nation. Adam Smith shares with the French economists the honour of founding political economy as the science of the wealth of nations. Mental philosophy became a favourite study, and a distinctively Scottish school produced thinkers who deeply influenced the later systems of the Continent. The history not of Scotland only, but of England and of some portions of Europe was written by Scotsmen. . . . The dawn of the scientific era of the nineteenth century was foreshadowed by Scotsmen of science, the founders of modern geology, chemistry, anatomy, physiology, and the practice of medicine. In Scotland was made the first of the great line of discoveries in the practical application of science by the use of steam as a motive power.' – H. S. Williams, LL.D.: *The Historian's History of the World,* Vol. XXI (New York and London).

ment of the national life was affected, not excepting the kitchen. This radical change was, as T. F. Henderson expresses it, the result 'partly of the severance of intercourse with France, partly of the Puritanism of the Reformers,[1] and partly of the increasing insufficiency of the supplies of meat. . . . In the austerer years of the seventeenth and eighteenth centuries, French influence was chiefly discernible in the ingenuity displayed in making the most of nothing.'

But even during the troublous Stuart and Jacobite periods, the connection with France was to some extent maintained, notably by the old Highland families who were proscribed after the Fifteen and the Forty-five.[2] There is,

In the domain of art – music (in its higher forms), the drama (practically non-existent before Barrie), and painting, literature alone being excepted – the achievement of Scotland is far less distinguished. The assertion, so freely made, that Presbytery is inimicable to aesthetic development contains probably as much truth, but certainly no more, as the assertion, equally freely made, that the rule of Rome is inimicable to intellectual development. A virile nation, Protestant or Catholic, will burst through any ecclesiastical strait-jacket. (Today it would appear that whilst Protestant Scotland grows steadily less Puritan, Catholic Ireland grows steadily more so.) That the Scottish churches are no longer indifferent, much less hostile to the fullest development of the arts (not excepting the drama), and that modern Presbytery is quite as catholic in outlook as Episcopacy, Roman or Anglican, there is ample evidence. – F. M. McN.

[1] In many devout Presbyterian households, cookery was looked on askance as pandering to the grosser appetites.

'Whilst on Sunday the Presbyterian gentleman took a sparing refection of bread and an egg or cold beef, between sermons, merely to allay the acute pangs of hunger, reserving his energies and carnal appetite for the supper, the (Episcopalian), after going to his meeting-house, had a substantial meal at midday, having no scruples. Hence it was a common saying that "if you would live well on Sunday, you must take an Episcopalian dinner and a Presbyterian supper".'

– H. Grey Graham: *Social Life in Scotland in the Eighteenth Century.*

In 1778, the cooks and cook-maids of Edinburgh went on strike because they had long been subjected to 'the profane practice of dressing meat on the Lord's Day'.

[2] In his introduction to *Letters from the North of Scotland*, by Capt. Burt, an English officer of Engineers who was sent to the Highlands as a contractor about 1730, Dr. Jamieson writes:

'From the state of the country, the political bias of the Highlanders, and the *éclat* which they acquired under Montrose and Dundee, the eyes of all Europe were turned towards them as the only hope of the house of Stewart. Their chiefs were courted by, and had frequent personal intercourse with the friends of that family who were of most note, both in Scotland, England, and Ireland, and on the continent. Studying to accomplish themselves for the part they had to act, and always received with the greatest distinction in the best society, they became statesmen, warriors, and fine gentlemen. Their sons, after passing through the usual routine of the schools and Universities of Scotland, were sent to France to finish their education. As the policy of the whigs was to crush and destroy, not to conciliate, and they found neither countenance nor employment at home, they entered into the French or Spanish service, and in these countries were, from political views, treated with a distinction suitable, not to their pecuniary circumstances, but to their importance in their own

56

indeed, a certain affinity between the Gaelic and Gallic races, which cannot be entirely explained by the long association of their aristocracies, and which can be traced even in the kitchen.[1] French influences appear to have persisted in Edinburgh throughout the eighteenth century. 'At the best houses,' says an English visitor, 'they dress their victuals after the French manner.' Burns, too, appears to have become acquainted there with French and other foreign survivals, for in his *Address to a Haggis* he asks:

> Is there that owre his French *ragout*,
> Or *olio* that wad staw a stew,
> Or *fricassee* wad make her spew
>   Wi' perfect scunner,
> Looks down wi' sneerin', scornfu' view
>   On sic a denner?

The merging of the Scottish and English crowns and the removal of James VI and his court from Edinburgh to London, mark the end of the Auld Alliance, and with it the waning of French and the waxing of English influences, social as well as political, in Scotland.[2] These influences,

country. Great numbers of the more promising youth of their clans joined them, and in order that the luxurious indulgences of a more favoured climate might not render them unfit or unwilling to settle in their own country, at the end of two or three years they returned for a time to their relations, with all their accomplishments in knowledge and manners, and, with their relish for early habits still unimpaired, resumed the quilted plaid and bonnet, and were replaced in their regiments abroad by another set of young adventurers of the same description. Thus, among the gentry, the urbanity and knowledge of the most polished countries of Europe, were added to a certain mental and moral civilization, good in its kind, and peculiar to themselves. At home, they conversed with the lower classes in the most kindly and cordial manner, on all occasions, and gratified their laudable and active curiosity in communicating all they knew. This advantage of conversing freely with their superiors, the peasantry of no other country in Europe enjoyed, and the consequence was that in 1745 the Scottish Highlanders of all description, had more of that polish of mind and sentiment which constitutes real civilization, than in general the inhabitants of any other country we know of, not even excepting Iceland.'

[1] 'Scottish and French cooking have a great deal in common,' writes one of the contributors to this collection, a Colonsay woman who became familiar with French methods in the service of a great Highland chief, 'the way we cook up meat and vegetables together, and go in so much for braising and stewing. I often think their charcoal stoves are very like our peat embers that keep the broth boiling so gently and bake the potatoes on the top.'

[2] From a purely cultural point of view, Scotland lost more than she gained by the Union of the Crowns. She lost the old close contact with the most highly civilized nation in the world, and established a new close contact with a nation for whom efficiency, not culture; comfort, not elegance; manufacture, not art, were paramount things. She lost her reigning family – and the Stuarts, whatever their shortcomings as

however, were reciprocal, and, relatively to her size, Scotland gave more than she got. As regards cookery, Scottish dishes were very soon popularized in Court circles.[1] King Jamie always enjoyed his native fare.

'Nobody among these brave English cooks,' says Laurie Linklater in *The Fortunes of Nigel*, 'can kittle up his Majesty's most sacred palate with our own gusty Scottish dishes. So I e'en betook myself to my craft, and concocted a mess of Friar's Chicken for the soup, and a savoury hachis,[2] that made the whole cabal coup the crans.'[3]

In the same volume George Heriot, goldsmith to James VI and I, who followed his royal patron to London, and later bequeathed his fortune to charities still flourishing in Edinburgh, thus invites his young compatriot, Lord Glenvarloch, to dine with him:

'"For the cheer, my Lord, a mess of white broth, a fat capon, well larded, a dish of beef collops for auld Scotland's sake, and it may be a cup of right old wine . . ." Besides the Scottish fare promised, the board displayed beef and pudding, the statutory dainties of old England.'

There was, however, no general amalgamation of Scottish and English cookery, and even in London Scottish influences were limited to narrow, if high circles. It was not, indeed,

rulers, were genuinely aristocratic in temperament (in contradistinction to the Houses of Tudor and Hanover) and devoted to the arts; she lost her nobility, who forsook the Canongate for Mayfair; she lost her Parliament; and finally she lost her intelligentsia. Consequently the brilliant capital of the early Stuarts has sunk steadily into semi-provincialism. Today she is a proud but saddened beauty, living on her memories, yet not entirely without hopes of better things – a hope quickened by the life and colour that permeate her grey streets when the Court sits at Holyrood and, more recently, by the International Festival. – F. M. McN.

[1] In food, as in other matters, there is an influence emanating from the Court that continuously modifies taste and custom.
In the time of Charles I and his Queen, Henrietta Maria, who had a fastidious palate, a more delicate note was introduced into the Royal Kitchens, and later a cultivated taste not only in food, but in wine, was encouraged by Queen Anne, in whose reign many splendid cellars were laid down; but the 'heavy Germanic influence' of the earlier Georges had a baneful effect on the Royal table that was not effectively counteracted until the arrival of the great Carême, chef to George IV. It was Carême who introduced the modern dinner menu and the setting and service of meals.
Both Queen Victoria and Edward VII and I favoured long, elaborate meals, and it is to George V and Queen Mary that we owe the comparative simplicity of the Royal table today – a simplicity that has been maintained by their successors. – F. M. McN.
[2] *Hachis*, haggis.
[3] *To coup the crans*, to go to rack and ruin, like a pot on the fire when the cran (iron tripod or iron instrument) which supports it is upset.

until the nineteenth century, when the magic wand of Sir Walter Scott had dispelled the hostility and mutual suspicion bred by centuries of feud, that the middle classes of the two countries borrowed freely from each other in this domain. Today our Scots porridge and barley broth and scones and orange marmalade are as popular south of the Tweed as are ham and eggs, Bath buns, and Yorkshire pudding in the north. But native dishes have a habit of deteriorating on alien soil and, despite their similarity to a casual observer, the cuisines of the two countries remain, in many respects, curiously distinctive.

IV

THE PLENISHING OF THE KITCHEN

'The ingle-neuk,* wi' routh† o' bannocks and bairns!'
– *Old Scottish toast or sentiment.*

In most countries, even today, one finds the rudest forms of
art coexisting with the highest, the earliest stage of civilization with the most advanced. It is not, therefore, surprising that while the banqueting halls of Linlithgow and
Holyrood vied in elegance with any in Europe, elsewhere in
the kingdom the most primitive methods of cookery prevailed.

'I have been assured,' writes Burt, in the early eighteenth
century, 'that in some of the Islands the meaner sort of
People still retain the Custom of boiling their Beef in the
Hide, or otherwise, being destitute of Vessels of Metal or
Earth, they put Water into a Block of Wood, made hollow
by the help of the Dirk and burning, and then with pretty
large Stones heated red-hot, and successively quenched in
that Vessel, they keep the Water boiling till they have
dressed their Food.'

This was a survival of conditions once universal in the
Highlands.

In *The Fair Maid of Perth* Scott describes an *al fresco*
kitchen on the shores of Loch Tay. The period is the fourteenth century, the occasion the funeral feast of a Highland
chief.

'The Highlanders, well known for ready hatchet men,
had constructed a long arbour or sylvan banqueting-room
[in which] the most important personages present were
invited to hold high festival. Others of less note were to
feast in various long sheds, constructed with less care;
and tables of sod, or rough planks, placed in the open air,

* Fireside.   † Plenty.

60

were allotted to the numberless multitude. At a distance were to be seen piles of glowing charcoal or blazing wood, around which countless cooks toiled, bustled, and fretted, like so many demons working in their native element. Pits, wrought in the hillside and lined with heated stones, served for stewing immense quantities of beef, mutton, and venison;[1] wooden spits supported sheep and goats, which were roasted entire; others were cut into joints and seethed in cauldrons made of the animals' own skins, sewed hastily together and filled with water; while huge quantities of pike, trout, salmon, and char were broiled with more ceremony on glowing embers.'

A similar scene from real life is described by Taylor, the Thames Water-Poet, who, in 1618, accompanied the Earl of Mar and a distinguished company on a shooting expedition into the Highlands, where they put up in temporary lodges called *lonchards*. 'The kitchin was alwayse on the side of a banke, many kettles and pots boyling, and many spits turning and winding, with great variety of cheere, as venison, bak't, sodden, rost and steu'de beefe, mutton, goates, kids, hares, fresh salmon, pidgeons, hens, capons, chickens, partridges, moor-cootes, heath-cocks, capperkellies,[2] and termagents;[3] good ale, sacke, white, and cleret, tent (or allegant)[4] with most potent *aquavitae*. Thus a company of about fourteen hundred was most amply fed.'[5]

[1] 'The Scottish Highlanders in former times had a concise mode of cooking their venison, or rather of dispensing with cooking it, which appears greatly to have surprised the French whom chance made acquainted with it. The Vidame of Chartres, when a hostage in England, during the reign of Edward VI, was permitted to travel into Scotland, and penetrated as far as the remote Highlands (*au fin fond des Sauvages*). After a great hunting party, at which a most wonderful quantity of game was destroyed, he saw these *Scottish Savages* devour a part of their venison raw, without any further preparation than compressing it between two batons of wood, so as to force out the blood, and render it extremely hard. This they reckoned a great delicacy; and when the Vidame partook of it, his compliance with their taste rendered him extremely popular.'

– Scott: *The Lady of the Lake*, Note.

[2] Capercailzie or mountain cock (Gael, *capull coille*).
[3] Ptarmigan (Gael. *tarmachan*).   [4] Alicant.
[5] In the following century, Prince Charlie, according to the Jacobite song, was regaled with much the same fare:

> Come o'er the stream, Charlie, dear Charlie, brave Charlie,
> Come o'er the stream, Charlie, and dine with Maclean;
> And though you be weary, we'll make your heart cheery,
> And welcome our Charlie and his loyal train.

The Scottish baronial kitchen, with its great fireplace designed to roast an ox whole, differed little from the corresponding types in other countries. The nation, after all, dwells in the cottage, and it is in the cottage that one finds all that is most truly characteristic of the nation.

The plenishing of a sixteenth-century kitchen of the humbler sort is minutely described in *The Wowing of Jok and Jynny*, one of the oldest surviving Scottish songs.[1] Jynny's mother recites her daughter's 'tocher-gud':[2]

'My berne,' scho sayis, 'hes of hir awin,
　　Ane guss, ane gryce,[3] ane cok, ane hen,
Ane calf, ane hog,[4] ane fute-braid sawin;[5]
　　Ane kirn,[6] ane pin,[7] that ye weill ken,
　　Ane pig,[8] ane pot, ane raip[9] thair ben,[10]
Ane fork, ane flaik,[11] ane reill,[12] ane rok:[13]
　　Dischis and dublaris[14] nyne or ten:
Come ye to wow our Jynny, Jok?

'Ane blanket, and ane wecht[15] also,
　　Ane schule,[16] ane scheit, and ane lang flail,
Ane ark,[17] ane almry,[18] and laidills two,
　　Ane milk-syth[19] with ane swine taill,[20]
　　Ane rowsty whittil[21] to scheir[22] the kaill,[23]
Ane wheill, ane mell[24] the beir[25] to knok
　　Ane coig,[26] ane caird wantand ane naill:[27]
Come ye to wow our Jynny, Jok?

'Ane furme,[28] ane furlet,[29] ane pott, ane pek,[30]
　　Ane tub, ane barrow, with ane wheil-band,

　　　　We'll bring down the track deer,
　　　　We'll bring down the black steer,
The lamb from the bracken and doe from the glen;
　　　　The salt sea we'll harry,
　　　　And bring to our Charlie
The cream from the bothy and curd from the pen.
　　　　　　　– James Hogg: *Come O'er the Stream, Charlie.*
　　　　　　　Air: *The Maclean's Welcome.*

[1] In the Bannatyne MS. (8568), this poem was assigned to Clark, whom Dunbar commemorates for his 'balat-making and tragide', but the name was deleted by the transcriber.

[2] Gael. *tocher*, a dowry.　　[3] A young pig.　　[4] Two-year-old sheep.　　[5] Corn to sow a foot-breadth.　　[6] Churn.　　[7] Skewer.　　[8] Earthen vessel.　　[9] Rope.
[10] In there.　　[11] Hurdle.　　[12] Reel.　　[13] Distaff.　　[14] Large dishes, as tureens.
[15] Instrument for winnowing corn.　　[16] Shovel.　　[17] Meal-chest.　　[18] Cupboard.
[19] Milk-strainer.　　[20] Corruption of seying-tale, sifting-measure (for milk).
[21] Rusty gullie.　　[22] Cut.　　[23] Colewort.　　[24] Mallet.　　[25] Barley.　　[26] Large wooden vessel.　　[27] A carding-comb with a nail missing.　　[28] Bench.
[29] Fourth of a boll.　　[30] Sixteenth of a boll.

Ane turs,[1] ane troch,[2] and ane meil-sek,
   Ane spurtill[3] braid[4] and ane elwand.'[5]

Jok contributes, in addition to a lengthy list of outdoor implements, 'ane trene truncheour,[6] ane ramehorn spoon,[7] . . . ane maskene-fatt',[8] together with

'Ane pepper-polk[9] made of a padill,[10]
Ane sponge, ane spindall wantand ane nok,[11]
Twa lusty lippis to lik ane laiddill,
To gang togidder, Jynny and Jok.'[12]

Here is a description (drawn from an existing inventory) of another sixteenth-century kitchen, that of the Manse of Stobo, which stood at the head of the Drygate of Glasgow.

'There are but two pieces of furniture, one a "weschell almerie", which was probably a plainly made kitchen dish-press, and the other a "dressing-burd", in other words a table on which meat and other articles of food were dressed. No form or stool or other kind of seat is provided, nor is there any other concession to comfort. There are cauldrons, kettles, "mekle"[13] pots and "litel" pots, frying-pans, goose-pans, roasting-irons, fish "skimmers", "mekle" speits and "litel" speits, stoups,[14] pitchers, and "piggis",[15] besides the special paraphernalia of the bake-house and brew-house.[16] A capon cave shows that poultry were kept, and the supply of provisions is on a scale that suggests that the household was given to what a contemporary calls "large tabling and belly cheer". There are, for example, eight marts, or salted carcases of beef; a pipe of salmon, containing eight dozen; a pipe of Loch Fyne herring; an ark containing eighty bolls of meal; six stone of butter and a "kebboc" or cheese

[1] Truss.   [2] Trough.   [3] Porridge-stick.   [4] Broad.   [5] Instrument for measuring an ell.   [6] Wooden platter.

[7] In olden times, each man had his horn spoon, which he carried at his side, or fastened to his bonnet, to sup the kail, porridge, or sowans. The old horn spoons had a whistle at the end of the handle. 'Better the suppin' end nor the whistle end,' says the proverb.

Before the introduction of glass, drinking-vessels were commonly made of horn, the better articles being silver-rimmed. Hornware is an old Scottish craft, still extant.

– F. M. McN.

[8] Brewing vessel.   [9] Bag.   [10] Pedlar's wallet.   [11] Notch.   [12] For Jenny and Jock to marry on.   [13] Big.   [14] Deep and narrow vessels for holding liquids.   [15] Earthen vessels.

[16] 'Dishes were commonly pewter, and drinking-cups were of tree with pewter or silver bases or pedestals. The Protector, Somerset, on landing at Leith, was astonished at the elegance of the table appurtenances, which included some of the best continental craftsmanship.' – C. Rogers: *Social and Domestic Scotland.*

weighing twenty-two pounds . . . and his barn is well stored
with wheat, oats, "beir", peas, and hay.'

In *Marmion*, Scott describes the kitchen of an inn in the
Lammermoors in the early sixteenth century.[1]

> Soon, by the chimney's merry blaze,
> Through the rude hostel might you gaze;
> Might see, where, in dark nook aloof,
> The rafters of the sooty roof
>   Bore wealth of winter cheer;
> Of sea-fowl dried, and solands store,
> And gammons of the tusky boar
>   And savoury haunch of deer.
> The chimney arch projected wide;
> Above, around it, and beside,
>   Were tools for housewives' hand;
> Nor wanted, in that martial day,
> The implements of Scottish fray,
>   The buckler, lance, and brand.
> Beneath its shade, the place of state,
> On oaken settle, Marmion sate,
> And viewed around the blazing hearth.
> His followers mix in noisy mirth;
> Whom, with brown ale, in jolly tide,
> From ancient vessels ranged aside,
> Full actively their host supplied.

The typical Scottish home of later times is the but-and-
ben, or two-roomed cottage. The furniture of the but, or
kitchen-end, consisted of an aumry[2] (cupboard) generally
placed opposite the window, where milk and provisions
were kept, and above it the skelf[3] (a wooden frame containing shelves) on which the 'pigs'[4] (crockery) and utensils
were arranged; a kist (chest) containing the family wardrobe;
a box-bed, built into the interior wall, with shelves at the

---

[1] 'The accommodations of a Scottish hostelrie, or inn, in the sixteenth century, may
be collected from Dunbar's admirable tale of *The Friars of Berwick*. Simon Lawder,
"the gay hostler", seems to have lived very comfortably; and his wife decorated her
person with a scarlet kirtle, and a belt of silk and silver, and rings upon her fingers;
and feasted her paramour with rabbits, capons, partridges, and Bordeaux wine.'
                                                              – Note to *Marmion*.

[2] Fr. *armoire*.   [3] Gael. *sgealp*.

[4] Pig (Gael. *pige*) is the common Scots word for a crock or earthenware jar.
        O there's eelie-pigs and jeelie-pigs
        An' pigs for hauden butter. – Old Song.
Eelie-pigs, oil-jars; *jeelie-pigs*, jam-jars; *hauden*, holding. A 'pig in the bed' is a
hot-water bottle. 'Pigs in the chimney' are chimney-pots.

head and at the foot, on which part of the apparel was deposited; a muckle chair (a wooden chair with arms) for the man, and stools or creepies for the woman and children There were also a plunge-churn, a spinning-wheel, a barrel of oatmeal and another of salt fish, and (before the introduction of the modern lamp) a crusie, with a supply of oil and dried pith of rushes. In addition there was the cottage library, consisting of not less than three volumes – the Bible, the *Pilgrim's Progress*, and (ever since his day) Burns.

All the cooking was done on the wide, open hearth. Over the fire, by means of a jointed iron arch with three legs, called the clips, was suspended whatever utensil was in use, the end of the clips being hooked to hold it fast. The clips were again hooked upon the end of a chain, called the crook, which was attached to an iron rod or beam commonly called the roof- or rantle-tree,[1] and this, in turn, was fixed across the chimney-stalk at some distance from the fire.

The ordinary cottage bread, consisting mainly of barley and mashlum,[2] bannocks and oatcakes, was baked on the girdle, a round thin plate of malleable or cast-iron, with a semicircular handle.[3] An equally indispensable utensil was the kail-pot, a round iron pot with three legs (evolved from the primeval tripod), and a close-fitting convex lid, in which broth or porridge was cooked. It served too as a rude oven, being on such occasions buried in burning peat.

Oatcakes were 'finished' on a toasting-stone[4] on their removal from the girdle. The quern sometimes served this purpose.

---

[1] In Orkney, amer- or emmer-tree.   [2] Mixed grain.

[3] 'In Roman times, hearth-cakes of oats were the bread of the savage natives, who baked them on stones round the fire. These stones the native Gaels named *greadeal*. They formed a ring round the fire, and hence the peculiar significance of the word girdle in the Scots vocabulary.' – T. F. Henderson: *Old-World Scotland*.

In the fourteenth century, Froissart tells us, the equipment of the Scottish soldier included a *flat plate of metal* and a wallet of oatmeal, for the purpose of making oatcakes. In the cottages, the plate was probably placed on a tripod over the peat embers.

The modern girdle was invented and first made in the little burgh of Culross, in Fife. In 1599, James VI granted to the Culrossians the exclusive privilege of its manufacture, and this was confirmed by Charles II in 1666. The girdle-smiths of Culross were hammered out of existence in the mid-eighteenth century when the Carron Iron-works began turning out cast-iron girdles in large quantities. – F. M. McN.

[4] One of the primitive toasting-stones is preserved, with other old Scottish domestic utensils, in the National Museum of Antiquities, Edinburgh.

In simple homes the kitchen was always the living-room, the focus and core of family life, and its praises have been sung by many of our vernacular poets. Here are glimpses of some typical kitchens:

THE MILLER'S KITCHEN

Merry may the maid be
    That marries the miller:
For foul day and fair day
    He's aye bringin' till her;
He's aye a penny in his purse
    For dinner and for supper;
And gin she please, a good fat cheese
    And lumps o' yellow butter.

Behind the door a bag o' meal,
    And in the kist was plenty
Of good hard cakes his mither bakes,
    And bannocks were na scanty.
A good fat sow, a sleeky cow
    Was standin' in the byre;
While lazy puss with mealy mouse
    Was playing at the fire.

In winter, when the wind and rain
    Blows o'er the house and byre,
He sits beside a clean hearth-stane
    Before a rousing fire;
With nut-brown ale he tells his tale,
    Which rows him o'er fu' nappy.
Wha'd be a king – a petty thing,
    When a miller lives sae happy?

SIR JOHN CLERK OF PENNICUIK (1684–1755).

THE FISHERMAN'S KITCHEN

And are ye sure the news is true?
    And are ye sure he's weel?
Is this the time to think o' wark?
    Ye jauds, fling bye your wheel!
Is this a time to think o' wark,
    When Colin's at the door?
Rax[1] me my coat, I'll to the quay,
    And see him come ashore.

[1] Reach.

Rise up and mak' a clean fireside,
    Put on the muckle[1] pot;
Gie little Kate her cotton gown,
    And Jock his Sunday coat;
And mak' their shoon as black as slaes,
    Their hose as white as snaw;
It's a' to please my ain gudeman:
    He likes to see them braw.[2]

There's twa fat hens upon the bauk,[3]
    Been fed this month and mair;
Mak' haste and thraw[4] their necks about,
    That Colin weel may fare.
And spread the table neat and clean,
    Gar[5] ilka[6] thing look braw,[7]
For wha can tell how Colin fared
    When he was far awa'?

        – There's Nae Luck About the House.[8]

THE FARMER'S KITCHEN

The gudeman, new come hame, is blyth to find,
    When he out o'er the halland[9] flings his een,
That ilka[10] turn is handled to his mind,
    That a' his housie looks sae cosh[11] and clean:
For cleanly house looes he, tho' e'er sae mean.

Weel kens the gudewife that the pleughs[12] require
    A heartsome meltith[13] and refreshing synd[14]
O nappy[15] liquor o'er a bleezin' fire:
    Sair wark and poortith[16] dinna weel be join'd.
Wi' buttered bannocks now the girdle reeks;
    I' the far nook the bowie[17] briskly reams;[18]
The readied kail[19] stands by the chimley cheeks,[20]
    And hads the riggin'[21] het wi' welcome steams
Whilk[22] than the daintiest kitchen[23] nicer seems.

    ROBERT FERGUSSON (1750–74): *The Farmer's Ingle.*

---

[1] Big.   [2] Well dressed.   [3] Roosting-beam.   [4] Twist.   [5] Make.
[6] Every.   [7] Fine.
[8] This song has been claimed for Jean Adams (1710–65) and for William Julius Mickle (1734–88). According to Burns, with whom it was a favourite, it came first on to the streets as a ballad about 1771 or 1772. It is included in Herd's collection (1776).
[9] An inner wall built between the fire-place and the door to screen the interior from draughts.   [10] Every.   [11] Snug.   [12] Ploughs.   [13] Meal.   [14] Drink.   [15] Strong.
[16] Poverty.   [17] A small barrel.   [18] Froth.   [19] Broth.   [20] The stone pillars at the side of the fire.   [21] Ridge.   [22] Which.   [23] Relish.

THE COTTER'S KITCHEN

At length his lonely cot appears in view,
    Beneath the shelter of an aged tree;
Th' expectant wee things, toddlin', stacher[1] through
    To meet their dad, wi' flichterin'[2] noise and glee.
His wee bit ingle,[3] blinkin' bonnily,
His clean hearthstane, his thriftie wifie's smile,
    The lispin' infant prattling on his knee
Does a' his weary kiaugh[4] and care beguile,
And makes him quite forget his labour and his toil.

      ROBERT BURNS (1759–96): *The Cotter's Saturday Night*.

THE SHEPHERD'S KITCHEN

Then round our wee cot though gruff winter should roar,
And poortith[5] glower[6] in like a wolf at the door;
Though our toom[7] purse had barely twa boddles[8] to clink,
    And a barley meal scone were the best on our bink,[9]
Yet he wi' his hirsel,[10] and I wi' my wheel,
    Through the howe o' the year[11] we would fen'[12] unco weel.[13]

      THOMAS PRINGLE (1789–1834): *The Ewe-buchtin's[14] Bonnie*.

Dorothy Wordsworth, in her *Recollections of a Tour Made in Scotland* (1803), describes the kitchen of a primitive Highland cottage, with the fire in the middle of the floor and a hole in the roof in place of a chimney:

'The good woman had provided, according to her promise, a better fire than we had found in the morning; and indeed when I sate down in the chimney corner of her smoky biggin' I thought I had never been more comfortable in my life. Coleridge had been there long enough to have a pan of coffee boiling for us. . . . We caressed our cups of coffee, laughing like children at the strange atmosphere in which we were: the smoke came in gusts, and spread along the walls and above our heads in the chimney, where the hens were roosting like light clouds in the sky. We laughed and laughed again, in spite of the smarting of our eyes, yet had a quieter

---

[1] Stagger.   [2] Fluttering.   [3] Fire (Gael. *aingeal*).   [4] Anxiety.
[5] Poverty.   [6] Stare.   [7] Empty.   [8] A small copper coin.   [9] Shelves fixed to the wall for holding plates, etc.   [10] A flock of sheep.   [11] The depth of winter.   [12] Fend.
[13] Very well.   [14] Folding of the ewes.

pleasure in observing the beauty of the beams and rafters gleaming between the clouds of smoke. They had been crusted over and varnished by many winters, till, where the firelight fell upon them, they were as glossy as black rocks on a sunny day cased in ice. When we had eaten our supper we sate about half an hour, and I think I had never felt so deeply the blessing of a hospitable welcome and a warm fire.'

Modern ranges and modern factory-made furniture and utensils have been gradually introduced into the cottage homes of Scotland today, but the old simple ways linger in the Highlands. A hundred years after Dorothy Wordsworth's visit, Mrs. Kennedy-Fraser was entertained in a kitchen of precisely the same type on the tiny island of Eriskay, in the Outer Hebrides.

Her hostess 'sat me down on a low three-legged stool by the peat-fire, which was burning brightly on the floor, and seated herself on another. I had learned by the experience of semi-suffocation to prefer those low stools to the high deal chair which was always politely brought from behind the partition for the stranger's use. On the low stool one was free from the smoke, which, when it reached a certain height, wandered at its own sweet will and escaped as best it might by the chinks in the "dry-stane" walls or the crevices in the roof. The interior of the old hut was really beautiful in the morning light, which slanted down from the small, deep-set windows on the dear old woman by the fire.' And in a neighbouring cottage 'a little clean sanded kitchen, with its tiny home-made dresser, adorned with fine old painted bowls and jugs, its two wooden benches along the walls with accommodation below for peats, its barrel of flour topped with the baking-board (serving as a kitchen table), and its bag of oatmeal by the fire, was the recognized rendezvous of the island'.

Though the Gael[1] does not sing the praises of his kitchen

---

[1] To speak of the Highlander as a Gael in contradistinction to the Lowlander is a mere *façon de parler*, for it is now generally accepted that *racially* the basis of the whole Scottish race is Celtic. *Culturally*, however, there is a real distinction, as even these few extracts indicate. Morley has spoken of Gladstone as a Highlander in the custody of a Lowlander; may not the modern Scot be described as a Celt in the custody of a Saxon?

in the simple homely way of the vernacular poets, he has a store of songs which are identified with the various domestic tasks. In the *Songs of the Hebrides*, Mrs. Kennedy-Fraser and Kenneth Macleod have preserved for us some of the ancient churning, quern-grinding, and waulking songs, each composed in a measure suited to the rhythmic motion of the body at work, and in his collection, *Carmina Gadelica*, Alexander Carmichael gives us some old runes and incantations associated with the ritual of domestic life, for to the Highlander the secular and the spiritual were inextricably blended. Very characteristic is the *Beannachadh Beothachaidh*, the Blessing of the Kindling:[1]

> I will kindle my fire this morning
> In presence of the holy angels of Heaven,
> In presence of Ariel of the loveliest form,
> In presence of Uriel of the myriad charms,
> Without malice, without jealousy, without envy,
> Without fear, without terror of anyone under the sun,
> But the Holy Son of God to shield me.
> Without malice, without jealousy, without envy,
> Without fear, without terror of anyone under the sun,
> But the Holy Son of God to shield me.
>
> God, kindle thou in my heart within
> A flame of love to my neighbour,
> To my foe, to my friend, to my kindred all,
> To the brave, to the knave, to the thrall,
> O Son of the loveliest Mary,
> From the lowliest thing that liveth,
> To the Name that is highest of all.
> O Son of the loveliest Mary,
> From the lowliest thing that liveth,
> To the Name that is highest of all.[2]

There are, however, indications (notably in the Scottish Renascence Movement) of a healthy reaction, and the increasing influence of *An Comunn Gaidhealach* (the Highland Association) testifies that the Scot no longer views with indifference that threatened extinction of Gaelic, but is awakening to the fact that were the ancient tongue to perish, with it would perish a great spiritual heritage. – F. M. McN.

[1] 'The people look upon fire as a miracle of divine power provided for their good – to warm their bodies when they are cold, to cook their food when they are hungry, and to remind them that they, too, like the fire, need constant renewal mentally and physically.' – A. C.

[2] BEANNACHADH BEOTHACHAIDH

Togaidh mi mo theine an diugh,
An lathair ainghlean naomha neimh,

In districts where wood is unattainable, the fire is *smoored* (smothered or subdued) with ashes that it may smoulder all night. The process was beautiful and symbolic, the woman chanting the while:

Smaladh an Teine.	Smooring the Fire.
An Tri numh	The sacred Three
A chumhnadh,	To save,
A chromhnadh,	To shield,
A chomraig,	To surround
A tula,	The hearth,
An taighe,	The house,
An taghlaich,	The household,
An oidhche,	This eve,
An nochd,	This night,
O an oidhche,	O this eve,
An nochd,	This night,
Agus gach oidhche,	And every night,
Gach aon oidhche.	Each single night.
Amen.	Amen.

An lathair Airil is ailde cruth,
An lathair Uiril nan uile sgeimh,
Gun ghnu, gun tnu, gun fharmad,
Gun ghiomh, gun gheimh roimh neach fo'n ghrein,
Ach Naomh Mhac De da m'thearmad.
    Gun ghnu, gun tnu, gun fharmad,
    Gun ghiomh, gun gheimh roimh neach fo'n ghrein,
    Ach Naomh Mhac De da m'thearmad.

Dhe fadaidh fein na m'chridhe steach
Aingheal ghraidh do m'choimhearsnach,
Do m'namh, do m'dhamh, do m'chairde
Do'n t-saoidh, do'n daoidh, do'n traille,
A mhic na Moire min-ghile,
Bho'n ni is isde crannachaire,
Gu ruig an t'Ainm is airde.
    A mhic na Moire min-ghile,
    Bho'n ni isde crannachaire.
    Gu ruig an t'Ainm is airde.

V

THE TABLE: SOME TYPICAL MEALS

'Cha'n fhiach cuirm gun a còmhradh' (A feast is worth nothing
without its conversation). – Gaelic Proverb

In the early Scots kitchen the fare consisted of game or
fish boiled or seethed in primitive fashion over the peat
embers; barley bannocks and oatcakes baked on the ancient
greadeal; cheese and butter; wild fruit, wild herbs, and the
honey of the wild bee. In the Highlands, in particular, the
ancient parsimony was long preserved. 'The great heroes of
antiquity,' says Sir John Sinclair, 'lived chiefly on broth. The
water in which a piece of mutton or venison was boiled,
thickened with oatmeal and flavoured with wild herbs,
formed the morning and evening meal in the hall of a Highland chief.'[1]

Sacheverell, who visited Mull and Iona in 1688, comments:
'They bound their appetites by their necessities, and their
happiness consists not in having much, but in coveting little';
and about the same time Martin Martin writes of the people
of Skye:

'Their ordinary diet is butter, cheese, milk, potatoes,
coleworts, *brochan*, i.e. oatmeal boiled with water. The latter,
taken with some bread, is the constant food of several
thousands of both sexes in this and other islands during
winter and spring, yet they undergo many fatigues both by
sea and land, and are very healthful. This verifies what the
poet saith: *Populis sat est Lymphaque Ceresque*, Nature is
satisfied with bread and water.'

The same frugality prevailed in the Lowlands. An English
visitor in 1704 remarks that at Lesmahagow, a village in
Lanarkshire, he found the people living on cakes made of
pease and barley mixed. 'They ate no meat, nor drank any-

[1] 'Among the peculiarities of Highland manners is an avowed contempt for the
luxuries of the table. A Highland hunter will eat with a keen appetite and sufficient
discrimination, but were he to stop in any pursuit because it was meal-time, to growl
over a bad dinner or visibly exult over a good one, the manly dignity of his character
would be considered as fallen for ever.' – Mrs. Grant of Laggan (1807).

thing but water, and the common people go without shoes or stockings all the year round. I pitied their poverty, but observed the people were fresh and lusty, and did not seem to be under any uneasiness with their way of living.'

Over and over again, in our proverbs and poetry, the virtue of frugality[1] is lauded:

> Mickle[2] meat, mony maladies.
> Surfeits slay mair than swords.
> He that eats but ae[3] dish seldom needs the doctor.
> Licht suppers mak lang life.

Allan Ramsay writes:

> For me, I can be weel content,
> To eat my bannock on the bent,[4]
> And kitchen't[5] wi' fresh air;
> O' lang kail I can mak' a feast,
> And cantily[6] haud up my crest
> And laugh at dishes rare.

In *The Cotter's Saturday Night*, Burns describes the simple fare on which he was nurtured:

> But now the supper crowns their simple board,
> The halesome[7] parritch,[8] chief of Scotia's food;
> The soupe their only hawkie[9] does afford,
> That yont the hallan[10] snugly chows her cood:
> The dame brings forth, in complimental mood,
> To grace the lad, her weel-hained[11] kebbuck,[12] fell;[13]
> And aft he's pressed, and aft he ca's it gude.
> The frugal wifie, garrulous, will tell
> How 'twas a twalmont[14] auld, sin' lint was i' the bell.

And elsewhere he writes:

> What though on hamely fare we dine,
> Wear hodden grey[15] an' a' that?
> Gie fools their silks, an' knaves their wine –
> A man's a man for a' that!

[1] Scottish frugality is, of course, proverbial. But so, too, is Scottish hospitality. Thus even the table illustrates what Gregory Smith calls 'the Caledonian antisyzygy', 'the contrasts which the Scot shows at every turn, in his political and ecclesiastical history, in his polemical restlessness, in his adaptability, . . . in his practical judgment'. The Aberdonian, in whom both virtues are highly developed, and who has the rare gift of being able to laugh at himself, delights the world with a constant stream of jests based on the former attribute, but, characteristically, leaves the stranger to discover the latter for himself. – F. M. McN.

[2] Much. [3] One. [4] In the open. [5] Give it relish. [6] Cheerily.
[7] Wholesome. [8] Porridge. [9] Cow. [10] Inner wall (corr. of Gael. *an talan*, a wooden partition). [11] Well-preserved. [12] Cheese (Gael. *cabag*). [13] Strong.
[14] Twelvemonth. [15] Grey homespun.

Because of that, Fergusson would say:

> On siccan[1] food[2] has mony a doughty deed
>   By Caledonia's ancestors been done;
> By this did mony a wight fu' weirlike[3] bleed
>   In brulzies[4] frae the dawn to set o' sun;
> 'Twas this that braced their gardies[5] stiff and strang,
>   That bent the deadly yew in ancient days,
> Laid Denmark's daring sons in yird[6] alang,
>   Gar'd[7] Scottish thistles bang the Roman bays:
> For near our crests their heads they doughtna[8] raise![9]

In the old song, *The Blythesome Bridal*,[10] we have a complete exposition of the kitchen of the humbler classes in Scotland in the seventeenth century.

> And there'll be lang kail[11] and pottage
> And bannocks[12] o' barley meal,
> And there'll be guid saut herrin'
> To relish a cogue[13] o' guid yill.[14]

· · · · · · · · · · · ·

[1] Such. [2] i.e. bannocks and kail. [3] War-like. [4] Broils. [5] Arms (Gael. *gairdean*).
[6] Earth. [7] Caused. [8] Dared not.

[9] *The Farmer's Ingle*. Centuries ago, English military commanders, surveying the battlefield where lay the Scottish and English dead, commented on the fine physique of their fallen adversaries.

A remarkable tribute to the physique of the Scots was paid by Eckermann, when Goethe and he were discussing the physical degeneration consequen* on a city life. He describes the Highlanders as he saw them that June day on the field of Waterloo, stepping forth erect and powerful on their brawny limbs, so physically perfect, he says, that they look like 'men in whom there is no original sin.'

– See J. P. Eckermann: *Gespräche mit Goethe in den Letzten Jahren Seines Lebens*.

'The farm hands (in Scotland) . . . still lived principally on oatmeal, milk, and vegetable broths. This was due, in no small measure, to the survival of the primitive system of providing the men working on the estate with food in part payment of their wages. As a result, the Scottish labourers were men of much finer physique than the Southerners. Frank Buckland, at one time medical officer to the Guards, described the weedy condition of the English recruits compared to the hardy and well-built men from the Scottish farms.'

– J. C. Drummond and Anne Wilbraham: *The Englishman's Food*.

Army statistics show that in the 1860s the average Scot was an inch taller than the average Englishman, but by the end of the century there was a marked deterioration, and the physical standard among our recruits now fell well below the English standard.

'An imperial race,' wrote the fifth Lord Rosebery, 'cannot be raised in a slum'; and our cities, notably Glasgow, were now notoriously slum-poisoned. Much has been done in recent years, but we are still grappling with the evil caused by our grossly culpable negligence. Now that the national consciousness has been thoroughly aroused, however, it is safe to prophesy that we shall not abate our efforts until the old basis of health and decent living is restored to the whole population. – F. M. McN.

[10] Attributed to Sir Robert Semphill of Beltrees, Renfrewshire (*c*. 1595–1660) or his son Francis.

[11] Colewort. [12] Round flat cakes. [13] A drinking-vessel. [14] Ale.

Wi' siybows[1] and rifarts[2] and carlines[3]
That are baith sodden[4] and raw.

There'll be tartan,[5] dragen,[5] and brochan,[5]
And fouth[6] o' guid gabbocks[7] o' skate,
Powsowdie,[8] and drammock,[10] and crowdie,[10]
And caller nowt-feet[11] on a plate.
And there'll be partans[12] and buckies,[13]
And speldins[14] and haddocks enew,[15]
And singit sheep heads and a haggis,
And scadlips[16] to sup till ye're fou.[17]

There'll be lapper-milk kebbucks,[18]
And sowens,[19] and farls,[20] and baps,[21]
Wi' swats[22] and well-scrappit paunches,[23]
And brandy in stoups[24] and in caups;[24]
And there'll be meal-kail[25] and custocks,[26]
Wi' skink[27] to sup till ye rive,[28]
And roasts to roast on a brander
O' flouks[29] that were taken alive.

Scrapt haddocks, wilks, dulse,[30] and tangle,[30]
And a mill[31] o' guid sneeshin'[32] to prie;[33]
When weary wi' eatin' and drinkin'
We'll rise up and dance till we dee.

Note the abundance of fish and the variety of preparations
of oatmeal.

Tartan or tart-an-purry (purée) is a kind of pudding
made of chopped kail and oatmeal; brochan is a gruel or
porridge, occasionally flavoured with onions and grated
cheese; drammock is made of raw meal and water. Crowdie
is a thicker variety of the same, sometimes with the addition
of butter; or it may be made with buttermilk or with whipped
cream. There is no beef except 'nowt-feet', and no mutton
except 'singit sheep heads', tripe, and the pluck contained
in the haggis.

In *The Bride of Lammermoor* (period 1700), Scott gives
us an aristocratic dinner menu. The worthy Caleb seeks to

[1] Young onions.   [2] Radishes.   [3] Peas.   [4] Boiled.   [5] Preparations of oatmeal.
[6] Abundance.   [7] Mouthfuls.   [8] Sheep's-head broth.   [9] [10] Preparations of meal.
[11] Fresh ox-feet.   [12] Crabs.   [13] Winkles.   [14] Small fish split and dried.   [15] Enough.
[16] Thin broth with barley.   [17] Full.   [18] Sour-milk cheeses.   [19] Flummery.
[20] Oat-cakes.   [21] Rolls.   [22] New Ale.   [23] Tripe.   [24] Drinking-vessels.   [25] Kale
brose.   [26] Cabbage stalks.   [27] A soup.   [28] Burst.   [29] Flounders.   [30] Edible
seaweeds.   [31] Box.   [32] Snuff.   [33] Taste.

hide by a ruse the impoverished state of the young Master of Ravenswood's larder, and thus describes the imaginary feast he is about to prepare:

'First course, capons in white broth – roast kid – bacon with reverence;[1] second course, roasted leveret – buttered crabs – a veal florentine;[2] third course, blackcock, plum-damas,[3] a tart, a flam,[4] and some nonsense sweet things – an' that's a' – forbye the apples and pears.' Later, describing the imaginary accident that has ruined the feast: 'The good vivers lying a' aboot – beef, capons, and white broth – florentine and flams – bacon wi' reverence – an' a' the sweet confections wi' whim-whams.'[5]

In the same book we read of the preparations made in a Lowland hamlet for the arrival of the Master and the Marquis of A.:

'Never had there been such slaughtering of capons, and fat geese, and barn-yard fowls, never such boiling of reested[6] hams; never such making of car-cakes[7] and sweet scones, Selkirk bannocks, cookies, and petticoat-tails - delicacies but little known to the present generation.'

At a ceremonial dinner (eighteenth century) at Lord Stair's, the menu was more elaborate, the first course consisting of Scotch broth, turbot, broiled salmon, mutton-collops, pigeon pie, boiled chicken, boiled ham and French beans; the second, of mushrooms, peas, lobsters, goose, cherry tart, cream loaves; the dessert being a 'fairy feast' of cream, jellies, strawberries, cherries, sweetmeats, almond-cream and lemon-cream.

(The custom of loading the table with a variety of dishes persisted, even in Jane Austen's England, well into the nineteenth century, when the new fashion was introduced of serving a series of courses with only one kind of dish at a time.)

In 1784, the French traveller, Faujas de St. Fond, tells us, 'at the Duke of Argyll's table, the different courses and the

[1] With its garnishings.   [2] A kind of pie.   [3] Prunes.   [4] Fr. *flan.*
[5] A variety of sweet.   [6] Smoked.
[7] Small cakes made with eggs and eaten on Fastern's E'en (Shrove Tuesday): probably a kind of pancake. Car, from *keren*, to turn or toss. – Jamieson.

after-meats were all done as in France, and with the same variety and abundance. We had delicate water-fowl, excellent fish, and vegetables which did honour to the Scotch gardeners.

'At the dessert, the cloth and napkins disappeared, and the mahogany table was covered with brilliant decanters filled with the most exquisite wines, vases of porcelain and crystal glass containing comfits, and beautiful baskets replete with choice fruits, which could scarcely have been expected in this cold climate, even with every assistance from art. . . .

'In the drawing-room, tea and coffee were served; but the latter is always weak, bitter, and destitute of its fine aroma.'[1]

Dr. Samuel Johnson was astonished at the high standard of living in the Hebrides. 'I forgot to inquire,' he writes, 'how they were supplied with so much exotic luxury. Perhaps the French may bring them wine for wool, and the Dutch give them tea and coffee at the fishing-season, in exchange for fresh provision. Their trade is unconstrained; they pay no customs, for there is no officer to demand them; whatever there is made dear only by impost, is obtained here at an easy rate.'

The Inverness merchants could have explained the 'exotic luxury'. One of these, John Steuart, a bailie of Inverness, left a record of his life in letters, written mostly to his agents, from 1715 to 1752. He is described as 'a man of dignity and good education, very much at ease in the social life of the Highlands.' Apart from a considerable home trade in oatmeal and other provender, Steuart exported quantities of cured fish[2] to France and Spain, Italy, Holland and Sweden, and in return imported a variety of goods, from timber, glass and iron to silk and muslin, tea and coffee, raisins and spices, oranges and lemons, and precious casks of brandy and wine. These last he supplied in exchange for herring to many of the Highland lairds and gentry. One

[1] *Voyage en Angleterre et en Ecosse* (1797).
[2] An interesting entry is 'cod fish muded (mudded)' so as to carry in barrels without pickle.

order to his agent is for 'two quarts of the best eating florence oyl'; another dated January 10, 1732, to Alex. Rose, Mercht. of Inverness, at Liverno, runs:

'If he comes to Cadiz to load, to ship six half butts best Cherrie Seck . . . with 2000 white raisins in 20 barrell, and 6 chests lemones, and 2 of bitter Orringes, besides what I ordered from Liverno formerly. But if he load salt at Lisbone, in that case you'll ship 4 half hogsheads white Lisbone wine, and 8 chests lemones, and orringes as above.'

In eighteenth-century Edinburgh there were many haunts, such as Johnie Dowie's,

> where ye can get
> A crum o' tripe, ham, dish o' pease,
> An egg, or, cauler[1] frae the seas,
> A fluke[2] or whiting.

> A nice beef-steak; or ye may get
> A guid buffed[3] herring, reisted[4] skate,
> An' ingins,[5] or (though past its date)
> A cut o' veal.[6]

'The principal taverns of our Old City,' we read in the *Annals of the Cleikum Club*, 'used to be called Oyster-Taverns, in honour of their favourite viand.'

Oysters are, of course, in season in those months that have an R in their name, and it was when the evenings were drawing in that the oyster-wives set out to climb the long hill from Newhaven and Musselburgh to Edinburgh.

'I like to see their weel-shaped shanks aneath their short yellow petticoats,' remarks the Shepherd in *Noctes Ambrosianae*. 'There's something hertsome in the creak o' their creashy creels on their braid backs, as they gang swingin' up the stey streets wi'out sweetin', wi' their leather belts atower their mutched heids.'

The women took up their stances in various busy corners of the town, preferably under a street-lamp, and, attracted by their cry, 'Caller Ou!' (fresh oysters) – the most beautiful

---

[1] Fresh. [2] Flounder. [3] Pickled. [4] Smoked. [5] Onions. [6] Chambers: *Minor Antiquities.*

of all the old Edinburgh street cries – their customers gathered round them.[1]

'How many celebrated wits and bon-vivants, now quite chop-fallen,' said Winterblossom, 'have dived into the dark defiles of closes and wynds in pursuit of this delicacy, and of the wine, the wit, the song that gave it zest. I have heard my learned and facetious friend, the late Professor Creech – for it was rather before my day – say that before public amusements were much known in our Presbyterian capital an Oyster-ploy, which always included music and a little dance, was the delight of the young fashionables of both sexes.'

The principal oyster-parties took place in Lucky Middlemass's tavern in the Cowgate (where the south pier of the bridge now stands). It was the resort of Fergusson and his fellow-wits, and received the poet's tribute:

> Whan big as burns the gutters rin,
> Gin ye hae catcht a droukit skin,
> To Lucky Middlemist's loup in,
> An' sit fu' snug
> Owre oysters and a dram o' gin,
> Or haddock lug.[2]

[1] 'The municipal authorities of Edinburgh were wont to pay considerable attention to the "feast of shells", both as regarded the supply and the price. . . . At the commencement of the dredging-season, a voyage was boldly taken to the oyster-beds in the Firth of Forth by the public functionaries, with something of the solemnity of the Doge of Venice wedding his Adriatic bride.' – Meg Dods: *Manual of Cookery*, Note.

The fishermen of the Forth used to sing as they trailed the dredging-nets; for, as Scott tells us,

> The herring loves the merry moonlight,
> The mackerel loves the wind.
> But the oyster loves the dredging-song,
> For he comes of gentle kind.

'The apparent superstition of having to sing to the oyster to woo it into the net has a rational explanation. The dredge had to be pulled very steadily by rowing over the oyster-beds, otherwise it would tip up and miss the oysters. It was found that this could be best achieved by means of a rowing-song. The songs were mostly improvised except one or two which seem to have become stylised. One of these is in the repertoire of the Newhaven Fisherwives' Choir.' – Francis Collinson in a letter to the author.

Each boat had five men, one of whom was a recognized leader of song.

> Wha'll dreg a buckie?
> I'll dreg a clam,
> I'll dreg a buckie,
> And I'll be lucky,
> And I'll no be lang. – Quoted by Peter McNeill, Tranent.

Dreg, dredge.

[2] *Droukit*, drenched; *Lucky*, Mistress, Goody; *loup in*, dash in; *haddock lug*, the flesh nearest the ear (a tit-bit).

'"No spot on earth once," said Mr. Touchwood, "like the Old Flesh Market Close of Edinburgh, for a spare-rib steak;[1] and I believe it has not yet quite lost its ancient celebrity. I never ate one in perfection but there": and the old beau related, with much vivacity, the adventures of a night on which he had accompanied to this resort the eccentric Earl of Kellie, and a party of Caledonian bon-vivants of the last age. "But the receipt?" inquired Redgill, with grave earnestness corresponding to the magnitude of the subject. "O! neither more nor less than that those taverns were, and are kept by butchers' wives, so that the primest of the meat found its way there. In the darksome den into which we dived – Luckie Middrit's of savoury memory – hungry customers consumed beef-steaks by wholesale, at all hours of the night and day, or rather of the perpetual night. The coal-fire always in prime condition, and short way between the brander and the mouth, Doctor, . . . before the collop-tongs had collapsed in the hands of the cook, in rushed the red-legged waiting-wench with the smoking wooden platter. . . . Ay, this is to eat a steak in perfection."'[2]

In his *Elegy on Lucky Wood*, Allan Ramsay has immortalized the landlady of his favourite resort in the Canongate.

> She gae us aft hale legs o' lamb,
> And didna hain[3] her mutton-ham;
> Then aye at Yule whene'er we cam',
>   A braw goose-pye:
> An' wasna that good belly-baum?[4]
>   Nane dare deny.

It is doubtful if oysters were obtained anywhere with so little trouble as at Hopetoun House, the Earl of Hopetoun's seat, a few miles from Linlithgow, in the eighteenth century.

'This fine Palace and Garden lies in the middle of a spacious Park, well stocked with Deer and environed with a Stone Wall. To the South of the great Avenue lies the Kitchen-Garden; and joining to it a House and Walk for Pheasants and a Plantation for other Fowls and Beasts; and under his great Terras is a Bed of Oysters, from whence his Kitchen is supplied all the Year round, in the greatest Quantities.'

– John Mackay: *A Journey through Scotland* (1722–3).

[1] 'In England, the best steaks are cut from the middle of the rump. In Ireland, Scotland, and France, steaks that are thought more delicate are oftener cut, like chops, from the sirloin or spare-rib, trimming off the superfluous fat, and chopping away the bone.' – Meg Dods.

[2] *Annals of the Cleikum Club.*   [3] Spare.   [4] Fare.

80

Lucky Flockhart,[1] of the Potter's Row, and other eighteenth-century vintners, used to provide a savoury chop-steak stew, known as a *soss*,[2] for their customers who had not been able to breakfast on account of the previous evening's conviviality, and who felt hungry during the forenoon; Dawny Douglas's Tavern[3] in the Anchor Close was noted for its suppers of tripe and rizzared[4] haddocks, minced collops and hashes, which never cost more than sixpence a head; and we read how Professor R. Simpson, Dr. Cullen, and Adam Smith were lured from the tavern where they could have their much loved banquets of hen broth, composed of two or three howtowdies,[5] a haggis, a crab pie, with ample punch.[6]

In 1769, David Hume, philosopher and gastronome, returned to Edinburgh from Paris, where he had been the idol of the salons, and announced to his friends that he intended to devote the remaining years of his life to what he

---

[1] 'Mrs. Flockhart, better known as Luckie Fykie, . . . seems to have been the Mrs. Flockhart of *Waverley*. . . . She was a neat, little, thin woman, usually habited in a plain striped blue gown, and apron of the same stuff, with a white *mutch*, having a black ribbon round the head, and lappets brought down along the cheeks and tied under the chin. . . . Her customers were very numerous and respectable, including Mr. Dundas, afterwards Lord Melville – Lord Stonefield – Lord Braxfield – Sheriff Cockburn – Mr. Scott, father of Sir Walter – Mr. Donald Smith, banker, and Dr. Cullen. The use and wont of these gentlemen, on entering the shop, and finding Mrs. Flockhart engaged with customers, was to salute her with "Hoo do ye do, mem?" and a *coup de chapeau*, and then walk *ben* to the room, where, upon the bunker-seat of the window, they found three bottles, severally containing brandy, rum, and whiskey, flanked by gingerbread and biscuits. They seldom sat down, but after partaking of what bottle they chose, walked quickly off.'
　　　　　　　　　　　　　　　　　　　　　　　– R. Chambers: *Traditions of Edinburgh*.

[2] O. Fr. *sausse*.

[3] Mentioned in *St. Ronan's Well*.

'The guests, before getting to any of the rooms, had to traverse the kitchen – a dark, fiery pandemonium, through which numerous ineffable ministers of flame were constantly flying, like the devils in a sketch of the Valley of the Shadow of Death, in the *Pilgrim's Progress*. Close by the door of the kitchen sat Mrs. Douglas, a woman of immense bulk, dressed out in the most splendid style, with a headdress of stupendous grandeur, and a coloured silk gown having daisies flowered upon it like sunflowers, and tulips as big as cabbages. She never rose from her seat upon the entry of the guests, either because she was unable from fatness, or that by sitting, she might preserve the greater dignity. She only bowed to them as they passed, and there were numerous waiters and slip-shod damsels, ready to obey her directions. . . . The genius and tongue of his wife had evidently been too much for [Dauniel] for she kept him in the most perfect subjection, and he acted only as a sort of head waiter under her.'
　　　　　　　　　　　　　　　　　　　　　　　– R. Chambers: *Traditions of Edinburgh*.

[4] Sun-dried.　　　　　[5] Pullets.

[6] See Henry Grey Graham: *Social Life in Scotland in the Eighteenth Century*.

81

frankly called 'my great Talent for Cookery'. He had collected several recipes in France, but was nevertheless devoted to many of our Scottish traditional dishes.

'I have just now lying on the Table before me,' he writes, 'a Receipt for making *Soupe à la Reine*, copy'd with my own Hand. For Beef and Cabbage (a charming dish) and old Mutton and old Claret, nobody excels me. I also make Sheep's Head Broth in a manner that Mr. Keith speaks of it for eight days after, and the Duc de Nivernois would bind himself Apprentice to my Lass to learn it.'

Hume's elegant dinners and select suppers became a feature of the social life of the city, being unsurpassed for the quality of the food, the wine and, not least, the talk.

Two notable Edinburgh hosts in the time of Sir Walter Scott were the brothers Ballantyne. James entertained his guests with 'an aldermanic display of turtle and venison, with the suitable accompaniments of iced punch, potent ale and generous Madeira'. John's dinners, on the other hand, 'were in all respects Parisian, for his wasted palate disdained such John Bull luxuries as were all in all with James. The piquant pastry of Strasburg or Perigord was never to seek; and even the *pièce de résistance* was probably a boar's head from Coblentz, or a turkey ready stuffed with truffles from the Palais Royal'.

Ambrose's Tavern was the scene of the lively debates and hearty feasting of Christopher North's *Noctes Ambrosianae* (1825–35).[1]

How Edinburgh folk in a humbler walk of life fared we learn from James Bertram (1824–92) who, while training with Tait, the proprietor of *Tait's Edinburgh Magazine*, encountered many men of letters, including Scott and de Quincey.

'Many a time (as an apprentice) did I indulge in a boiling-hot pennyworth of black-pudding, confectioned in a small shop close to Tweeddale Court, where the firm (Oliver and Boyd) then, as now, carried on business. . . . Another gastro-

---

[1] (Demolished in 1864, its traditions are carried on in a modernized style by the Café Royal, with its Oyster Bar.)

nomic treat was to indulge in one of Spence's hot pies in his tavern in Hunter Square, a favourite haunt of apprentices like myself. . . . My own allowance for the midday meal was twopence halfpenny *per diem*, and I never asked for more; for in the well-known eating-house in the east end of Rose Street kept by kindly Jenny Anderson, it provided a substantial meal – say, excellent sheep's-head broth, a savoury trotter and a penny loaf.'

Mrs. Anderson kept two dining-rooms – 'one for those who had a cut from the joint of the day, the other for the "kail-suppers", as Jenny's servant called his mistress's humbler customers. . . . But there were apprentices who could not even attain to the luxury of sheep's head broth. One sturdy boy used to bring with him to the shop a handful of oatmeal, which, by the aid of boiling water, a pinch of salt and a spoon, he made into brose, and ate gladly for his dinner.'

Tripe suppers were very popular. The best were to be had at the Guildford Tavern – a haunt of de Quincey in his Edinburgh days – where the tripe was 'smothered in a thick white sauce richly stocked with thin slices of well-boiled onions'.

Kirsty Bell, of the Rainbow Tavern, was famous for her 'devils', and Paterson's – a humbler house – for its 'potted heid', a plateful of which, with mashed potatoes and a bottle of Prestonpans table beer, was considered 'cheap and filling' at sevenpence.

A special treat in Bertram's apprentice days was a walk on Saturday afternoon to Newhaven, to enjoy one of Mrs. Clarke's famous fish-dinners. 'She provided several courses of well-cooked fish, including perhaps a dozen oysters to each person as an *hors d'œuvre*, which cost tenpence a head; so that for about sixteen pence one could not only dine, but accompany the dinner with a modicum of ale, and spare a penny besides to the waitress.'

At one period, he tells us, there were more than fifty places where refreshments could be had in the vicinity of the city, and on Sundays they were often crowded with working-folk and children. 'A strawberry feast, a "feed of gooseberries", or a basin of curds and cream were usual refreshments. . . . In the King's Park, on a fine Sunday, I have counted as many as fifty dealers in curds and cream.'[1]

Supper had a very special place in Edinburgh's Golden Age. It was an intimate and informal meal, with plenty of good, simple fare, good wine, a good fire and an incessant flow of good talk.

'Early dinners,' says Lord Cockburn, 'begat suppers. But suppers are so delightful that they have survived long after dinners have become late. . . . Almost all my set, which is perhaps the merriest, the most intellectual, and not the most severely abstemious in Edinburgh, are addicted to it. . . . Supper is cheaper than dinner; shorter; less ceremonious; and more poetical. The business of the day is over; and its still fresh events interest. It is chiefly intimate associates that are drawn together at that familiar hour, of which night deepens the sociability. If there be any fun or heart or spirit in a man at all, it is then, if ever, that it will appear.'

Edinburgh was a small society. People knew one another well. Everyone could be 'placed', both geographically and genealogically, and cousins to the fortieth degree were freely acknowledged.[2] 'It was impossible to maintain social pretensions, to "put on an act". There was a wholesome freedom from money snobbery. It was, in fact, an unpretentious and truly civilized way of life, and the supper-party was one of its most delightful features.'

Southern visitors, it is true, often failed to relish our national dishes.

'When shall I see Scotland again?' writes Sydney Smith,

---

[1] *Memories of Books, Authors and Events* (1893).

[2] 'Amongst the social organizations of the world, perhaps none has so captured the imagination of the world as the Scottish clan system. The reason is not difficult to find, for it has carried down, into the modern world, the great principle of Tribality and Inheritance, from which people elsewhere have so often strayed, but to which the human race ever returns for inspiration.' – Sir Thomas Innes of Learney: *The Clans, Septs and Regiments of the Scottish Highlands*.

It used to be said that when a young man's engagement to an unknown fair was announced, in Scotland the first question asked was, 'Who is she?'; in England, 'What has she?'; and in Ireland, 'What is she like?'; meaning, 'Is she pretty?' (Of course all sensible people ask, 'What is she like?' in the wider sense.) – F. M. McN.

the witty English divine, who spent five years (1798–1803) in Edinburgh. 'Never shall I forget the happy days I spent there amidst odious smells,[1] barbarous sounds,[2] *bad suppers*,[3] excellent hearts, and the most enlightened and cultivated understandings.'

This view was shared by the average peninsular Englishman.[4] One anonymous writer tells us that he was so disgusted at the mere sight of haggis and sheep's head that he could not bring himself to taste them. True, the 'honest sonsy face' of the haggis is hardly calculated to inspire an appetite in the uninitiated (though it did inspire Burns to an ode), and a singed sheep's head, to the eye, is no lovesome thing, God wot (though we have Dorothy Wordsworth's word that 'Coleridge and I ate heartily of it');[5] but Dr. Johnson's comment is more sagacious:

'Their more elaborate cookery, or made dishes, an Englishman, at the first taste, is not likely to approve, but the culinary compositions of every country are often such as become grateful to other nations only by degrees.' And George Saintsbury,[6] another Englishman, and a distinguished critic of food and wine, as well as of letters, writes:

'Generally speaking, Scotch ideas on food are sound. The people who regard haggis and sheep's head as things that the lips should not allow to enter them, and the tongue should refuse to mention, are, begging their pardon, fools.'[7]

---

[1] In former days Edinburgh was a by-word among cities all more or less dirty and smelly. Her congested system of housing – which lingers in the tall grey *lands* of the High Street – greatly intensified the evil, and the snell winds that blew up from the Firth were a badly needed antidote to the prevalent stench. It was doubtless the very intensity of the evil that drove her to her sewerage experiments and eventually made her a pioneer in public sanitation. – F. M. McN.

[2] Dunbar in the fifteenth and Fergusson in the eighteenth century complain of the turmoil caused by the street traders, crying their wares.

[3] The italics are mine. – F. M. McN.

[4] In *Humphry Clinker*, an English visitor to Edinburgh remarks: 'I am not yet Scotchman enough to relish their singed sheep's head and haggis.'

Dean Ramsay, in his *Reminiscences of Scottish Life and Character*, relates how old Lady Perth, offended with a French gentleman for some disparaging remark on Scottish dishes, answered him curtly, 'Weel, weel, some fowk like parritch, and some like puddocks.'

[5] *Recollections of a Tour made in Scotland* (1803).

[6] For many years Professor of English in the University of Edinburgh.

[7] 'But,' he adds, 'I cannot forgive them for making sandwiches of mutton.'

— *A Second Scrap Book.*

Until well into the nineteenth century our inns, and particularly those of the Highlands, met with much adverse criticism from English travellers – most of it only too well deserved; for in comparison with English inns ours were, generally speaking, very primitive and, at their worst, miserably poor and dirty. But it is interesting to note that whatever abuse the accommodation receives, there are few complaints about either food or drink. At Moffat, in 1705, Joseph Taylor 'met with good wine, and some mutton pretty well dressed, but looking into our beds, found there was no lying in them'. John Wesley writes, 'We were most surprised at the entertainment we met with in every place, so far different from common report. We had all things good, cheap, in great abundance, and remarkably well dressed.' At Elgin, Dr. Samuel Johnson could not eat the dinner set before him but, he says, 'This was the first time and, except one, the last, that I had found any reason to complain of a Scottish table.' Of the inn at Dalmally, Faujas de St. Fond says, 'We were astonished at its elegance in so desert a place. . . . Our supper consisted of two dishes of fine game, the one of heathcock, the other of woodcock, a creamy fresh butter, cheese of the country, a pot of preserved *vaccinium* (blaeberries), a wild fruit which grows on the mountains, and port wine – all served up together. It was a luxurious repast for the country.' The Wordsworths, again (according to Dorothy) encountered one thoroughly bad meal – 'some sorry soup made of barley and water, for it had no other taste,' and 'a shoulder of mutton so hard that it was impossible to chew the little flesh that may be scraped off the bones,' but were compensated elsewhere with an excellent meal of 'fresh salmon, a fowl, gooseberries and cream, and potatoes,' – and were agreeably surprised at the lowness of the reckoning. Lastly, of a meal at the inn at Dalwhinnie, Elizabeth Grant of Rothiemurchus writes, 'All the accessories of the dinner were wretched, but the dinner itself, I remember, was excellent: hotch-potch, salmon, fine mutton, grouse, scanty vegetables, bad bread but good wine.'[1]

[1] 'Here (in Scotland) we find that cooks are born, not made, and they have the same

86

In Victorian times, dinner in the well-to-do Scottish home appears to have been as elaborate as in its English counterpart, whilst retaining much of its national character. General Sir Ian Hamilton describes in his autobiography[1] the laird's table at his Argyllshire home – Hafton, on the Holy Loch – in his boyhood in the eighteen-sixties.

'In the kitchen, a huge sirloin of beef, or, at least, a gigot from a four-year-old black-faced sheep, late of the far-famed Hafton flock, would be revolving slowly on the main spit before an immense fire. . . . Game or fowls would be gaily roasting at a higher number of revolutions on another lesser spit; below these two spits was a metal tray sloping downwards towards the centre so as to let the gravy collect into a deep, rich, brown, oily pool.

'As to the output of that kitchen, a few years ago my brother Vereker, wishing to refresh his memory, asked my Aunt Camilla (who at the time happened to have another very old lady staying with her) – "Wasn't it the case that at dinner there were always four covered dishes laid, one at each corner of the table, as well as those at the top and bottom?" Both the old ladies held up their hands and exclaimed with one voice – "*And* the side dishes!" Yes, there were the side dishes. That made eight dishes in all. Today it will seem to be too strange to be true, but it is true, though some of them may have held only vegetables. Always there was either haggis or sheep's head at the foot of the table; that was *de rigueur*; and always one of the corner dishes was curry and rice. A turkey, a goose, or a haunch of roe-deer venison, or some such flea-bite was somewhere for sure. There were no such things as *hors d'œuvre*, but before the heavy stuff, there had been, of course, soup and fish – real fish – none of your flabby stuff from off the ice at the

instinctive knowledge of cookery which we admire in the French and Italian house-wives, be they peasants or *grandes dames*.' – Countess Morphy: *English Recipes*.

'Our palates are rather French (or anyhow, European) than Yorkshire, and our own native ways of preparing our native products for gustation are decidedly not English. Some, such as the milk-meats and oatmeal dishes mentioned by Chamberlayne, are manly as Cossack cookery. Others show a delicate discrimination (proved long ago by our discovery of braxy mutton) which presupposes the true culinary instinct.'
              – Donald and Catherine Carswell: *The Scots Week-end.*
[1] *When I Was a Boy* (1939).

fishmonger's, but freshly caught in sea or river by the estate fishermen, great heroes and friends to us children. After this came eight sweets. Cream was handed round with all the sweets, which had to be eaten with a spoon and not with a fork as in England.[1] Now-a-days the cream custom has spread.

'. . . After, not before the jellies and puddings, came the game, according to its season, as to which I very specially and fondly remember the toast which underlay the grouse. . . . The toast was laid down very thickly buttered under the grouse on the spit. Then it was basted and basted and basted with the drip from the birds themselves. The result was a tit-bit as unknown today as a fresh-laid egg from a dodo.

'How did the ancients put it all away? I really can't think. As to where, that was more understandable. When my Grandpapa Gort came to pay us a visit and I as a child saw him walk side by side with my Grandpapa Hamilton across the hall, I am reported to have exclaimed, "Tiens, Henriette, mes grandpères portent tous deux le même grand coeur," meaning thereby that the two tummies were as like one another and as round as two peas.'

Not dinner, however, but breakfast, is the meal upon which we particularly pride ourselves.

'In the breakfast,' says Dr. Johnson, 'the Scots, whether of the Lowlands or mountains, must be confessed to excel us. The tea and coffee are accompanied not only with butter, but with honey, conserves, and marmalades. If an epicure could remove by a wish in quest of sensual gratification, wherever he had supped, he would breakfast in Scotland.'[2]

Sir Walter Scott had, happily, a lively interest in the table

---

[1] 'This custom,' he tells us, 'was considered in both England and Ireland to be barbarous and very surprising, so much so that when Admiral O'Grady (my mother's maternal grand-uncle) came to stay, his wife laid a complaint that he had awakened her in the middle of the night merely to murmur in her ear, "Susan, the next time they offer you cream with calf's foot jelly, take it!" '

(Calf's foot jelly with whipped cream has long been a popular dish in the West of Scotland. – F. M. McN.)

[2] 'Brother, let us breakfast in Scotland, lunch in Australia and dine in Paris.'
– Henry Kingsley.

and with his aid we may easily trace the evolution of the Scottish breakfast.

First, a feudal breakfast from *Old Mortality*:

'The breakfast of Lady Margaret Bellenden no more resembled a modern *déjeuner*, than the great stone hall at Tillietudlem could brook comparison with a modern drawing-room. No tea, no coffee, no variety of rolls, but solid and substantial viands – the priestly ham, the knightly sirloin, the noble baron of beef, the princely venison pasty; while silver flagons, saved with difficulty from the claws of the Covenanters, now mantled, some with ale, some with mead, and some with generous wine of various qualities and descriptions.'

In 1729, Mackintosh of Borlum laments the sadly changed times:

'When I come to a friend's house of a morning, I used to be asked if I had had my morning draught yet. I am now asked if I have had my tea. And in lieu of the big quaigh[1] with strong ale and toast, and after a dram of good wholesome Scots spirits, there is now the tea-kettle put to the fire, the tea-table and silver and china equipage brought in, and marmalade and cream.'

In *Waverley* there are two descriptions of the Highland breakfast, of diverse types. The period is the eighteenth century.

'Waverley found Miss Bradwardine presiding over the tea and coffee,[2] the table loaded with warm bread, both of flour, oatmeal, and barley-meal, in the shape of loaves, cakes, biscuits, and other varieties, together with eggs, reindeer ham, mutton and beef ditto, smoked salmon, marmalade, and all the other delicacies which induced even Johnson himself to extol the luxury of a Scotch breakfast above that of all other countries. A mess of oatmeal porridge, flanked by a silver jug, which held an equal

[1] Gael. *cuach*, a cup or bowl.
[2] Coffee, according to a venerable tradition, was transplanted in some dim and distant age from Abyssinia, its *pays d'origine*, to Arabia, and was first popularized in Europe by a Turkish ambassador at the court of Louis XIV. It probably made its first appearance in Britain during Cromwell's Protectorate.

mixture of cream and buttermilk, was placed for the Baron's share of this repast.'

Then an *al fresco* breakfast from the same book:

'Much nearer to the mouth of the cave he heard the notes of a lively Gaelic song, guided by which, in a sunny recess shaded by a glittering birch-tree, and carpeted with a bank of firm white sand, he found the damsel of the caravan, whose lay had already reached him, busy, to the best of her power, in arranging to advantage a morning repast of milk, eggs, barley bread, fresh butter and honeycomb. . . . To this she now added a few bunches of cranberries, gathered in an adjacent morass. . . . Evan and his attendant now returned slowly along the beach, the latter bearing a large salmon-trout, the produce of the morning's sport. . . . A spark from the lock of his pistol produced a light, and a few withered fir branches were quickly in flame, and as speedily reduced to hot embers, on which the trout was broiled in large slices. To crown the repast, Evan produced from the pocket of his short jerkin a large scallop-shell, and from under the folds of his plaid a ram's horn full of whiskey. Of this he took a copious dram.'

Neither tea nor coffee appears on the Highland breakfast-table described by Tobias Smollett in *Humphry Clinker*:

'One kit of boiled eggs; a second, full of butter; a third, full of cream; an entire cheese made of goat's milk; a large earthen pot, full of honey; the best part of a ham; a cold venison pasty; a bushel of oatmeal, made into thin cakes and bannocks; with a small wheaten loaf in the middle, for the strangers; a stone bottle full of whisky; another of brandy, and a kilderkin of ale. There was a ladle chained to the cream-kit, with curious wooden bickers to be filled from this reservoir. The spirits were drank out of a silver quaff (quaich), and the ale out of horns. Great justice was done to the collation by the guests.'

In 1784, at the house of Maclean of Torloisk, on the island of Mull, Faujas de St. Fond found the breakfast-table 'elegantly covered with the following articles: Plates of smoked beef, cheese of the country and English cheese,

fresh eggs, salted herrings, butter, milk, and cream; a sort
of *bouillie* of oatmeal and water, in eating which, each spoonful is plunged into a basin of cream; milk worked up with
yolks of eggs, sugar, and rum; currant jelly, conserve of
myrtle, a wild fruit that grows among the heath; tea, coffee,
three kinds of bread (sea biscuits, oatmeal cakes, and very
thin and fine barley cakes); and Jamaica rum.'

'The breakfast!' exclaims Dr. Redgill in Susan Ferrier's
Marriage, after vigorously abusing the Scottish dinner, 'that's
what redeems the land – and every county has its peculiar
excellence. In Argyllshire you have the Lochfyne herring,
fat, luscious, and delicious, just out of the water, falling
to pieces with its own richness – melting away like butter
in your mouth. In Aberdeenshire, you have the Finnan
haddo' with a flavour all its own, vastly relishing – just
salt enough to be piquant, without parching you up with
thirst. In Perthshire there is the Tay salmon, kippered, crisp
and juicy – a very magnificent morsel – a *leetle* heavy, but
that's easily counteracted by a teaspoonful of the Athole
whiskey. In other places you have the exquisite mutton of
the country made into hams of a most delicate flavour;
flour scones, soft and white; oatcakes, thin and crisp;
marmalade and jams of every description.'[1]

Smoked breakfast delicacies, from solan geese to finnan-
haddies and mutton-hams, were a speciality of our forefathers, who were highly skilled in what has been called
'this most fascinating and poetic branch of cookery'.

'Smoked Solan geese are well-known,' says Meg Dods, 'as
contributing to the abundance of a Scottish breakfast,
though too rank and fishy-flavoured for unpractised palates.
They are eaten as whets, or relishes.'

In 1618, Taylor, the Water-Poet, who was regaled with
this dish in Edinburgh, writes:

'Amongst our viands that we had there, I must not forget

[1] 'Besides the ordinary articles of eggs, broiled fish, pickled herrings, Sardinias,
Finnans, beef, mutton, and goat hams, reindeer's and beef tongues, sausages, potted
meats, cold pies of game, etc., a few stimulating hot dishes are, by a sort of tacit
prescription, set apart for the *déjeuner à la fourchette* of the gourmand and sportsman.
Of this number are broiled kidneys, calf's and lamb's liver with fine herbs, and mutton
cutlets *à la Vénitienne*. – Meg Dods.

the soleland goose, a most delicat fowle, which breeds in great abundance in a little rock called the Basse, which stands two miles out into the sea. It is very good flesh, but it is eaten in the forme as wee eate oysters, standing at a side-board, a little before dinner, unsanctified without grace; and after it is eaten, it must be well liquored with two or three good rowses of sherrie or Canarie sacke.[1]

'The lord or owner of the Basse doth profit at the least two hundred pound yeerly by those geese.'

Although, doubtless owing to the pork taboo, Scotland lagged far behind England and Ireland in the curing of bacon and ham, she produced excellent mutton, beef and venison hams. But her special pride was the curing of fish, of which more anon.

Breakfast, like supper, was commonly a social occasion – a custom that has by no means died out. James Bertram, who describes in his *Memories* the social and intellectual life of Edinburgh in the mid-nineteenth century, writes:

'At the opening of the Court of Session, the judges and high officials are always entertained at breakfast by the President. . . . The Lord High Commissioner to the General Assembly of the Church of Scotland entertains the ministers at "breakfasts" during the sittings of the Church Court. The Moderator does the same, and many of the hospitably inclined citizens of Edinburgh entertain country clergymen and other members of Assembly at breakfast, as well as at dinner. For Professors of the University to entertain their students was, and still is, a recognized custom, happily so, for many of the hungry lads who in my young days, at all events, seldom had another opportunity of making a square meal'.

'Literary and other travellers,' he goes on, 'used to be surprised and delighted with the tables liberally supplied with an appetite-provoking variety of fish, flesh and fowl,

<hr />

[1] 'There is only one more Island in the West of Scotland, called Ailsey (Ailsa Craig), where these Geese do breed; and from these two Places the Country is furnish'd with them during the months of July and August. . . . They leave the Island in September, and where they retire is not known.'
    – John Mackay: *A Journey through Scotland* (1722–3).

hot and cold; with rolls, scones, coffee, delicious cream, and especially with a condiment described by an old-time tourist, "a bitter-sweet but most delightful compound of orange skins and juices, called "marmalade", which we never see in England".'

Two more brief descriptions – the first by Mrs. Walford, *née* Colquhoun of Luss.

'I can see my parents' breakfast-table yet: the many and varied dishes, hot and cold, the dark and light jellies (black currant and white currant – what has become of white currant jelly? – one never sees it now): then such potato scones, barley scones, and scones that were just 'scones' and nothing else, each kind nicely wrapped up in its snowy napkin, with the little peak that lifted and fell back, falling lower and lower as the pile was diminished; the brown eggs that everyone prefers to white – and why? – the butter, sweet, old yellow butter framed in watercress.'

Lastly, a modern Highland breakfast, pre-war. The guests are awakened by the skirling of the pipes. The family piper walks round the house playing the rouse, 'Hey Johnnie Cope, are ye wauken yet?' Breakfast is set in the hall, where a fire of peat and logs is burning. Through the open window comes the scent of pine and heather. The air is like wine. A long day on the hill lies ahead.

Bill of Fare

Porridge and Cream
Grilled trout   Finnan-haddie with poached egg
Ayrshire bacon and mushrooms   Boiled eggs
Cold venison pasty   Potted grouse
Smoked mutton ham
Baps   Girdle Scones   Oatcakes
Heather Honey   Butter   Marmalade
Toast, brown and white
Tea   Coffee
Fresh Fruit

Afternoon tea evolved naturally out of the 'four-hours', which was long regarded as a necessary refreshment by all classes in Scotland. Originally ale and claret were the sole beverages served.

Tea appears to have been introduced to Scotland by the beautiful and gracious Mary of Modena, wife of James VII and II, who, while Duke of York, held court at Holyrood in 1681 as Lord High Commissioner.[1] It was denounced by both medical men and clergy, and its acceptance was slow; but by 1750 its conquest of the womenfolk was complete, and wine was reserved for gentlemen.[2]

The introduction of afternoon tea gave a great impetus to the national flair for baking, among both amateurs and professionals.

'When I was a boy,' writes Henry Mackenzie (*The Man of Feeling*) (b. 1745), 'tea was the meal of ceremony and we had fifty-odd kinds of teabread. One Scott made a little fortune by his milk-bakes. His shop in Forrester's Wynd was surrounded at five o'clock by a great concourse of servant maids. . . . A similar reputation was enjoyed by the rolls of one Symington, a baker of Leith.'

The cake-baxters, too, made their contribution.

Tea in England seems to have been a much simpler affair. In the early nineteenth century, 'In the vera best houses,' writes Mrs. Pringle from London to her friend, Miss Nancy Eydent, in Ayrshire, 'what I principally notised was, that the tea and coffee is not made by the lady of the house, but out of the room, and brought in without sugar or milk or servors, everyone helping himself, and only plain, flimsy loaf bread and butter is served – no such thing as shortbread, seed-cake, bun, marmlet or jeely to be seen, which is an okonomical plan, and well worthy of adoption in ginteel families with narrow incomes, in Irvine or elsewhere.'[3]

During the nineteenth century, the Scottish tea-table reached as high a point of perfection as the breakfast-table.

---

[1] Doubtless tea had been drunk in Scotland before this date, but this was its formal introduction.

[2] 'In 1705 green tea was advertised and sold at 16*s*. and Bohea at 30*s*. a pound by George Scott, goldsmith, Luckenbooths.' – Chambers: *Traditions of Edinburgh*.

[3] John Galt: *The Ayrshire Legatees*.

Cakes apart, visitors are surprised at the variety of scones and light teabread.

'The ideal setting for tea' – I quote from my own *Scots Cellar* – 'is a cosy interior on a grey winter day. The tea equipage on a low table beside a glowing fire – the delicate china on the finely embroidered tea-cloth, the polished silver reflecting the dancing flames – the hot buttered toast, freshly baked scones and tempting home-made cakes – for many of us these made the tea hour the pleasantest hour of the day.

'And the farmhouse tea! How one used to tuck in after a long tramp over the hill! There is no tea like it, plain or high, with its oatcakes, its variety of scones, its velvet-textured sponges spread with strawberries (or other berries in season) and whipped cream, or with home-made jam, or fresh lemon curd; its chunks of thick, crisp shortbread; its rich almond-studded fruit cake (known to the world as Dundee); its small crystal dishes of jams and jellies, red, green and amber; and the big brown teapot – as couthie and comforting as any tappit-hen[1] – the very symbol of feminine conviviality.'

People who normally dine late – that is, broadly speaking, those above a certain income level – are apt to look down on high tea as a bourgeois affair – as indeed it is. But what of it? We are not Russians to shudder (if they still do so) at the word *bourgeois*. The fame of French cooking emanates not from her cosmopolitan hotels, but from the kitchens of the *bourgeoisie* – sensible folk who make an intelligent use of the natural products of their country. It is true that the Scottish high tea, at its worst, is a heavy, unpalatable and indigestible meal, but any man, be he peer or ploughman, with an appetite sharpened by the open air, will sit down with a sigh of content to the high tea provided by the average Scottish farmhouse, country inn, or intelligent housewife. Thanks to the domestic revolution of post-war years, high tea is no longer regarded as incompatible with high life.

The birthplace of the modern tea-room is Glasgow; its pioneer, Catherine Cranston (Mrs. Cochrane), the daughter

---

[1] A pewter quart measure of ale or claret.

of an hotel proprietor, who has earned a place of honour in our social history. Although the coffee-house flourished throughout Britain during the eighteenth and nineteenth centuries, the tea-room dates only from the 1880s; yet this is not surprising when one recalls that the coffee-house was the monopoly of the male sex, and that women entertained exclusively at home – until Miss Cranston appeared upon the scene.[1] In Neil Munro's words, 'Miss Cranston, clever, far-seeing, artistic to her finger-tips, and of a high, adventurous spirit, was the first to discern in Glasgow that her sex was positively yearning for some kind of afternoon distraction that had not yet been invented.' In 1884, she rented a half-shop in Aitkin's Hotel, in Argyle Street, and soon afterwards acquired the whole building, which she re-fashioned as the Crown Lunch and Tea Rooms. Later she opened premises in Ingram Street and Buchanan Street.

This was the period when the 'Glasgow School' of painting was burgeoning in the grey city of the West, and Miss Cranston's tea-rooms were, in fact, an off-shoot of that movement. She herself had a keen love of beauty, and she had also the imagination to employ two gifted, but as yet obscure young artist-architects – George Walton (brother of E. A. Walton, R.S.A.) and Charles Rennie Macintosh (who was to achieve European fame) with the latter's wife, Margaret Macdonald, a decorator of great originality.

'Together,' says William Power, 'the designers produced something which was at once severely simple and strikingly original, a varied harmony which was based on the square and the straight line, with black and white, grey and brown, as the leading shades, relieved by small sections of rose and emerald green, and by fresh flowers chosen by Miss Cranston herself.'[2]

[1] Like practically all pioneers, Miss Cranston had a modest forerunner.
'The original Glasgow tea-room, according to well-established tradition, was the back parlour of an unpretentious shop near the corner of Argyle Street and the Broomielaw. Here the shopkeeper's wife, a kindly body, used to refresh her husband's country customers with a cup of tea – at first, for love, but eventually, on their insistence and as the numbers who desired tea increased, at a penny a cup.'
– *The Scots Cellar.*
[2] Three times a week, a donkey cart, driven by a boy in green livery, delivered flowers from Miss Cranston's own garden with precise instructions for their display.

In 1904, Miss Cranston opened the most distinguished of all her establishments – the Willow Tea-Room in Sauchiehall Street. With this, Macintosh was given a free hand, and he designed not only the building, but the furniture, the cutlery and even the earlier menu cards. Although Glasgow's buildings are rich in classical and Renaissance detail, Macintosh's building has not a single historic feature.

Sauchiehall Street takes its name from the Sauchie Haugh (the marsh land where saughs or willows grow) on which it was built, and Macintosh used the willow theme throughout. The heavy silk curtains in the dining-room downstairs were embroidered with a tree motif by Margaret Macdonald. On the staircase, the uprights of the banister rose to the roof, where they curved downwards and, hung with large glass beads, formed stylized trees. Then, set in the glass of the charming bow-window were tiny mirrors, cut in the shape of willow leaves, that glittered as they caught the light. The Room de Luxe upstairs had unusual charm and dignity with its grey carpet, white walls and purple upholstery, its lovely chandelier – a cluster of crystal balls and spheroids hung on silver chains – and the appearance of the whole interior has been described as 'rich, glittering and jewel-like.'[1]

The daintiness and variety of the fare and the excellence of the service, together with the beauty and originality of the decoration, brought the Glasgow tea-room of the early twentieth century a wide renown.[2]

Glasgow is the home not only of the tea-room, but also

[1] The Willow Tea-Room inspired panegyrics from Continental critics; indeed the sole complete record is to be found in the pages of the German art magazine, *Die Kunst*.

[2] 'The total result of Miss Cranston's achievement was a complete breakaway from the Victorian drawing-room, the "gilded saloon," and the glorified pub. The tea-rooms were a refreshing note in Glasgow life. They re-acted upon the tastes of the people, with the result that many a humble home in Glasgow is more beautiful than a Mayfair mansion. . . . It is curious that Miss Cranston's methods have never been adopted in London, or even in Edinburgh.' – William Power.

The idea of the tea-room, however, spread like wildfire, and in a few years encircled the globe.

Miss Cranston's own tea-rooms are now, alas, only a memory. The façade of the Willow Tea-Room remains, but is swallowed up by Daly's drapery store.

of the snack bar, of which both the American cafeteria and the London sandwich bar are descendent.[1] Its pioneer was William Lang (b. 1820) who, about the middle of the century opened a little eating-house in Queen Street on a site which, though later greatly extended, he occupied all his life.

Lang's was the subject of a eulogy written in the 1860s by Shirley Brooks, then editor of *Punch*:

'In a handsome apartment you find ... such varied arrangements for supplying your wants as I have seen nowhere else. Mr. Lang is the Napoleon of sandwiches and announces, I am told, that he has a hundred different kinds of Lord S.'s invention. Among the ordinary show I observed sandwiches of the usual meats, of frizzled bacon, of lobster, salmon, grouse, blackcock, partridge, pheasant, herring and shrimp, and others of all the potted meats that Crosse and Blackwell could supply. Then there were oysters, taken from their shells and placed, with their liquor, in delicate little glass vases, a silver fork by each; there was coffee made in the Napier invention so popular in the North; claret, in neat casks; milk, which was drunk by bearded men and did not, I daresay, do them any harm; beer and porter; spirits of the primest quality.'

Another notable *Punch* contributor – none other than Thackeray – visited Lang's, which he described as a place where he had discovered 'fifty separate ways of spoiling one's dinner'.[2]

If our dinners and suppers remain more distinctive than distinguished, we can reflect with satisfaction that our breakfasts and teas, at their best, are nowhere surpassed.

[1] The 'Sandwich Bars' later established in London by Mr. Kenelm Foss were admittedly an inspiration from Glasgow, for it was here that Mr. Foss, while acting as producer to the Scottish Repertory Company, first encountered the 'perpendicular repast' – a discovery which induced him, on his return to London, to renounce the stage for a more lucrative career.

[2] 'When Mr. Lang introduced the "payment by honour" principle, now universal in Glasgow tearooms, he was regarded as taking serious risks, but he soon proved that the moral sense of his customers in very few cases broke down when they were left to help themselves to food or drink, and made up the addition for themselves.

In this respect, the Glasgow quick-lunch type of bar seems inimitable – no other city that I know of manifests such confidence in the integrity of its customers.'
– William Power in *The Daily Record*, April 6, 1929.

VI

HOSPITALITY

I saw a stranger yestreen;
I put the food in the eating place,
Drink in the drinking place,
Music in the listening place;
And, in the sacred name of the Triune,
He blessed myself and my house,
My cattle and my dear ones.
And the lark said in her song,
    Often, often, often,
Goes the Christ in the stranger's guise;
    Often, often, often,
Goes the Christ in the stranger's guise.

– Old Gaelic Rune recovered by Kenneth Macleod.

Among the ancient Scots it was deemed infamous in a man to have the door of his house shut, lest, as the bards express it, 'the stranger should come and behold his contracted soul'. The free and open hospitality which characterizes a primitive condition of society survived much later in Scotland, and particularly in the Highlands,[1] than in the more highly civilized countries of Europe. Fynes Moryson, a graduate of Cambridge, who visited Scotland in 1598, tells us that he noticed no regular inns with signs hanging out, but that private householders would entertain passengers on entreaty or where acquaintance was claimed. The last statement is interestingly corroborated in the account of his journey to Scotland which that eccentric genius, John Taylor, the Thames waterman (commonly known as the Water-Poet), printed in 1618. In the course of what he terms his 'Pennyless Pilgrimage, or Moneyless Perambulation', he claims to have depended entirely on private hospitality. Everywhere, indeed, in his progress through Scotland, he

[1] Hospitality was one of the virtues emphasized in the rule of Iona. Martin records that in the isle of Barra all strangers were obliged by the natives to eat 'ocean-meat' on coming off the sea, however recently they might have eaten.

appears to have been feasted sumptuously, and liberally supplied with money by hospitable gentlemen who probably found his witty conversation ample recompense. 'So much of a virtue comparatively rare in England, and so much plenty in a country which his own people were accustomed to think of as the birthplace of famine, seems,' Chambers comments, 'to have greatly astonished him.'

Defoe (1706–8) and Bishop Pococke (1760) add their testimony; and Pennant, who visited Scotland in 1769 and again in 1772, writes of the Highlanders:

'As for the common people, they were chiefly characterized by good manners, pride, inquisitiveness, and a *genius for hospitality* and religion.'[1]

Dr. Johnson, in 1776, was amazed at the scale and magnificence of the hospitality he enjoyed – 'veal in Edinburgh, roasted kid in Inverness, admirable venison and generous wine in the castle of Dunvegan'. 'Everywhere,' he writes, 'we were treated like princes in their progress.'[2]

'The last act of manorial hospitality,' Scott reminds us in a note to *The Pirate*, 'was enacted upon the lawn. On each, in front of the mansion, was a platform of masonry – the loupin'-on stone. Here gentlemen mounted their horses, and were supplied with the doch-an-doruis or stirrup-cup.[3]

---

[1] Lest they might have under their roof an enemy to whom the laws of hospitality equally applied, it was customary in olden times never to ask the name and business of a stranger until a year and a day had elapsed – an extraordinary effort, says Hugh Miller, for a people so naturally inquisitive.

[2] The lavish hospitality of the Highland chiefs was equalled only by their vanity.

'A great hero was Clanranald,' said the old folk. 'He would have seven casks of the ruddy wine of Spain in his stable, and if a stranger asked what that was for he would be told that that was the drink for Clanranald's horses. One of the MacNeill chiefs, however, went one better than that. Each evening, after dinner, he sent a trumpeter up to his castle-tower to make the following proclamation: Ye kings, princes, and potentates of all the earth, be it known unto you that MacNeill of Barra has dined – the rest of the world may dine now.'

– Kenneth Macleod: Note to *The Songs of the Hebrides*.

[3] 'A glass of ardent spirits, or draught of ale, given by the host to his guests when about to depart.' – Scott: *Guy Mannering*.

'The Poculum Potatorium of the valiant Baron, his blessed Bear, has a prototype at the fine old Castle of Glammis, so rich in memorials of ancient times; it is a massive beaker of silver, double gilt, moulded into the shape of a lion, and holding an English pint of wine. The form alludes to the family name of Strathmore, which is Lyon, and, when exhibited, the cup must necessarily be emptied to the Earl's health. The author ought perhaps to be ashamed of recording that he has had the honour of swallowing the contents of the lion; and the recollection of the feat served to suggest the story of the Bear of Bradwardine. In the family of Scott of Thirlstane (not Thirlstane in the

100

Drunk from a quaich (a timber bowl with two ears), it was otherwise known as a bonalay.'

It was precisely because the tradition of private hospitality was so strong that the development of the inn was so long retarded. The Wordsworths, on their Highland tour in the autumn of 1803, had no Boswell to arrange hospitality, nor did they choose to claim it like the adventurous Water-Poet; and, save in one or two Lowland halting-places, the fastidious Dorothy found the standard of cleanliness and comfort considerably lower than in English inns.[1]

Two pictures of Highland hospitality, both from real life. The first is from Boswell's *Tour to the Hebrides* (1786).

'"Mr. McQueen's compliments to Mr. Boswell, and begs leave to acquaint him that, fearing the want of a proper boat, as much as the rain of yesterday, might have caused a stop, he is now at Skianwden with *Macgillichallum's*[2] carriage, to convey him and Dr. Johnson to Rasay, where they will meet with a most hearty welcome, and where Macleod,[3] being on a visit, now attends their motions." . . .

'It was past six o'clock when we arrived.[4] Some excellent brandy was served round immediately, according to the custom of the Highlands, where a dram is generally taken every day. They call it a *scalch*.[5] On a sideboard was placed for us, who had come off the sea, a substantial dinner

Forest, but the place of the same name in Roxburghshire) was long preserved a cup of the same kind, in the form of a jack-boot. Each guest was obliged to empty this at his departure. If the guest's name was Scott, the necessity was doubly imperative.' –
– Scott: *Waverley*, Note.

[1] All that is long since altered. For better and for worse, the Highlands are becoming rapidly 'civilized'. 'A generation ago,' the writer was told by the proprietrix of a Hebridean inn, 'a Highland maid-servant would blush with shame on being offered a tip. Now she looks for it as a matter of course.'

The virtue of hospitality is being systematically extirpated in the Highlands by the powers that be. A man who has paid a sum running into four figures for a few weeks' deer-stalking naturally objects to having his day's sport ruined by the appearance of a couple of pedestrians at the moment his gun is levelled at the stag. Therefore in many districts the crofters are not merely discouraged from giving hospitality, but are forbidden under threat of eviction. Thus not only the material but even the spiritual well-being of the native race is sacrificed to the great god Sport. – F. M. McN.

[2] The Highland expression for the Laird of Raasay, a chieftain of the Clan Macleod.

[3] *The* Macleod: chief of the clan.

[4] 'We were introduced into the house, which one of the company called "the *Court* of Rasay", with politeness which not the Court of Versailles could have thought defective.'
– Dr. Samuel Johnson: *Letters*.

[5] Usually skalk (Scott). From Gael. *sgailc*.

and a variety of wines. Then we had coffee and tea. I observed in the room several elegantly bound books and other marks of improved life. Soon afterwards a fiddler appeared, and a little ball began. *Rasay* himself danced with as much spirit as any man, and Malcolm bounded like a roe. Sandie Macleod, who has at times an excessive flow of spirits, . . . made much jovial noise. Dr. Johnson was so delighted with this scene that he said: "I know not how we shall get away." . . . We had a company of thirty at supper, and all was good humour and gaiety, without intemperance.'

The second is by Alexander Carmichael, who describes an experience when collecting material for his *Carmina Gadelica* (published in 1900) in the Outer Hebrides:

'The house was clean and comfortable, if plain and unpretending, most things in it being home-made. There were three girls in the house, young, comely, and shy, and four women, middle-aged, handsome, and picturesque in their homespun gowns and high-crowned mutches. Three of the women had been to the moorland pastures with their cattle, and had turned in here to rest on their way home.

'"Hail to the house and household," said I, greeting the inmates in the salutation of our fathers. "Hail to you, kindly stranger," replied the housewife. "Come forward and take this seat. If it be not ill-mannered, may we ask whence you have come today? . . . May the Possessor keep you in his own keeping, good man! You have left early and travelled far, and must be hungry." With this the woman raised her eyes towards her daughters standing demurely silent, and motionless as Greek statues, in the background. In a moment the three fair girls became active and animated. One ran to the stack and brought in an armful of hard black peats, another ran to the well and brought in a pail of clear spring water, while the third quickly spread a cloth, white as snow, upon the table in the inner room. The three neighbour women rose to leave, and I rose to do the same. "Where are you going, good man?" asked the housewife in injured surprise, moving between me and the door. "You must not go till you eat a bit and drink a sip.

That indeed would be a reproach to us that we would not soon get over. . . . Food will be ready presently, and in the meantime you will bathe your feet and dry your stockings which are wet after coming through the marshes of the moorland." Then the women went down upon her knees and washed and dried the feet of the stranger as tenderly as a mother would those of her child. . . .

'In an incredibly short time I was asked to go "ben" and break bread. . . . The table was laden with wholesome food sufficient for several persons. There were fried herrings and boiled turbot fresh from the sea, and eggs fresh from the yard. There were fresh butter and salt butter, wheaten scones, barley bannocks, and oat-cakes, with excellent tea and cream. The woman apologized that she had no "aran coinnich" – moss bread, that is loaf bread – and no biscuits, they being simple crofter folk far away from the big town.

'"This," said I, taking my seat, "looks like the table for a 'reiteach' (betrothal), rather than for one man."'

Burns, who made a tour of the Highlands in 1787, leaves an enduring tribute to the virtue of hospitality in the race to which he was bound by blood and sentiment:

> When death's dark stream I'll ferry o'er –
> A time that surely shall come –
> In heaven itself I'll ask no more
> Than just a Highland welcome.

RECIPES

A Grace*

Soli Dei Honor et Gloria

'This was the fashionable grace-before-meat at the tables of the Scottish nobility in the reign of Queen Mary. . . . This legend was carved over many doorways in old Edinburgh.' – R. Chambers: *Traditions of Edinburgh*.

The Covenanter's Grace

Some hae meat that canna eat,
And some wad eat that want it;
But we hae meat, and we can eat,
And sae the Lord be thankit.

* These lines, repeated by Burns when he dined with the Earl of Selkirk, and generally considered his own, were, according to Chambers, current in the south-west of Scotland before the poet's time, and were known as the Covenanter's grace.

SOUPS

'Sir, I am above all national prejudices; and, I must say, I yield the Scots the superiority in all soups – save turtle and mulligatawny. An antiquarian friend of mine attributes this to their early and long connection with the French, a nation eminent in soups.' – Dr. Redgill, in the *Annals of the Cleikum Club*.

Barley-Broth or Scotch Broth

'The bland, balsamic barley-broth of Scotland.' – Meg Dods.

[In Aberdeen] 'At dinner, Dr. Johnson ate several plates of Scotch broth, with barley and peas in it, and seemed very fond of the dish. I said, "You never ate it before?" – Johnson, "No, sir; but I don't care how soon I eat it again." '
        – Boswell: *Journal of a Tour to the Hebrides with Samuel Johnson* (1786).

(Traditional Recipe)

Neck or shoulder of mutton (or runner of beef, or a good marrow bone), barley (pot or pearl), peas, onion, leek, cabbage, turnip, carrot, parsley, salt, pepper, water

Wash two ounces of dried peas and soak overnight. Wipe and trim a piece of mutton of one and a half to two pounds, and put it into the broth-pot with two quarts of water, two ounces of barley and the soaked peas. Add salt. Bring to the boil and skim. While it is boiling gently, dice about a breakfastcupful of turnip and another of carrot, and cut up a leek or an onion (or a small onion and the white part of a leek), and when the soup has boiled for about an hour add the vegetables. When fresh peas are in season, add a teacupful, in place of the dried peas. Allow to simmer for at least two hours longer. Ten minutes before serving add half a small white heart of cabbage, finely shredded. Skim off the fat, season to taste, and just before serving add a tablespoonful of chopped parsley. Serve very hot.

If the meat is to be served separately, put into boiling water and cook according to weight, allowing one hour for the first pound and twenty minutes for each additional pound. Remove when ready and re-heat at the last. Garnish with blocks of carrot and turnip cooked in the broth, and serve with caper or nasturtium seed sauce.

Turnips, carrot and parsley have an affinity with mutton. With beef the vegetables may be varied a little – e.g. kail or greens, may be used in place of white cabbage and a stick or two of celery in place of parsley; and more leek may be added.

Hodgils (q.v.) or suet dumplings may be boiled with the beef.

In the making of broth there are endless minor variations.

'This is the comfortable *pot au feu* of Scotland, which still furnishes the Manse and the farmhouse dinner and the pot-luck of homely and hearty old-world hospitality.'
– Meg Dods.

The old-style pot barley was always considered preferable to the processed 'pearl' and 'patent' barley. – F. M. McN.

'Turkey beans, stripped of their blackening outer husk, are admirably adapted for lithing[1] barley broth.' – Meg Dods.

Enough is usually made for two days. The second day's broth used to be known as cock-crown kail.

'Do not season till near the end, then add some cream or the yolk of an egg and stir, but do not let it boil again. Some people leave a turnip in whole, remove it when soft, mash it and put it back.

'Much time and trouble will be saved when making this or any other of the vegetable broths, if the vegetables are only roughly sliced to start with. Then, when they are soft, if the broth is poured through a colander, the vegetables can be quickly and easily cut up small while still in the colander by using two knives, one in each hand and working with them crosswise. A lump of sugar and another of butter should be added to all the barley broths, the sugar at the beginning, the butter at the end.'
– The Carswells in *The Scots Week-end.*

The ingredients given in a two-hundred-year-old recipe are: a chopped leg of beef, a fowl, carrots, barley, celery, sweet herbs, onions, parsley, and *a few marigolds*! See *A New and Easy Method of Cookery*, by Elizabeth Cleland (Edinburgh, 1759).

In the eighteenth century, Faujas de St. Fond was regaled in Mull with 'a large dish of Scots soup, composed of broth of beef, mutton, and sometimes fowl, mixed with a little oatmeal, onions, parsley, and a considerable quantity of peas. Instead of slices of bread as in France, small slices of mutton and giblets of fowl are thrown into this soup.'

In Caithness and elsewhere, *Shilling Broth* was made from shilled corn, i.e. freed from the husk (Gael. *sileanan*, seeds of corn).

Hen Broth. – Barley-Broth made with a fowl in place of meat.

Kate sits i' the neuk, suppin' hen broo.
– Robert Burns: *Gudee'en to you, Kimmer.*

Chacklowrie. – Mashed cabbage mixed with barley-broth (Aberdeenshire).

'Like the Russians, we believe in the kailyard school for our broth, and if everybody in Scotland were to stick to the old custom, still preserved by French peasants and bourgeois and Russian workers, of relishing every day a pint of liquid containing the innumerable salts of the commonest greenstuff, Scotland would be the better for it.'
– *The Scots Week-end.*

[1] *To lithe:* to thicken or mellow. A.S. *lith-ian,* to mitigate. – Jamieson. A Scottish culinary term.

Powsowdie[1] or Sheep's Head Broth

(*Meg Dods's Recipe*)

Sheep's head and trotters, mutton, barley, peas, carrot, turnips, onions, parsley, salt, pepper, water

Choose a large, fat, young head. When carefully singed by the blacksmith, soak it and the singed trotters for a night, if you please, in lukewarm water. Take out the glassy part of the eyes, scrape the head and trotters, and brush till perfectly clean and white; then split the head with a cleaver, and lay aside the brains, etc., clean the nostrils and gristly parts, split also the trotters, and cut out the tendons. Wash the head and feet once more, and let them blanch till wanted for the pot.

Take a large cupful of barley, and about twice that quantity of soaked white, or old, or fresh green peas, with a gallon or rather more of water. Put to this the head, and from two to three pounds of scrag or trimmings of mutton, perfectly sweet, and some salt. Take off the scum very carefully as it rises, and the broth will be as limpid and white as any broth made of beef or mutton. When the head has boiled rather more than an hour, add sliced carrot and turnip, and afterwards some onions and parsley shred. A head or two of celery sliced is admired by some modern gourmands, though we would rather approve of the native flavour of this really excellent soup. The more slowly the head is boiled, the better will both the meat and soup be. From two to three hours' boiling, according to the size of the head and the age of the animal, and an hour's simmering by the side of the fire, will finish the soup. Many prefer the head of a ram to that of a wether, but it requires much longer boiling. In either case the trotters require less boiling than the head. Serve with the trotters and sliced carrot round

[1] From *pow*, the head, and *sowdie*, sodden or boiled.

109

the head. Sheep's head, not too much boiled, makes an excellent ragout or hash of higher flavour than calf's head ragoût.

To singe the head at home, hold it over the fire, and as the wool singes scrub the burnt wool off with a knife; then hold the head over the fire and repeat until all the wool has been singed and rubbed off. Finally, go over the whole head carefully with a hot iron or poker until no trace of wool is left.

It is said that the reason why the head was so tender in the old days was that the blacksmith's boys played football with it!

The decay of the smiddy has sadly reduced the popularity of this excellent soup.
– F. M. McN.

'The reviewer of the first edition of this work* in *Blackwood's Magazine* suggests that there should be two heads and eight trotters, which admirable emendation certainly more than doubles the value of the receipt.' – M. D.

* Meg Dods's *Manual*.

Powsowdie is mentioned by Scott in *The Antiquary*.

'This national preparation was wont to be a favourite Sunday dinner dish in many comfortable Scottish families. Where gentlemen "killed their own mutton", the head was reserved for the Sunday's broth; and to good family customers, and to *victuallers*, a prime *tup's* head was a common Saturday's gift from the butchers with whom they dealt. By the way, nationally speaking, we ought to say fleshers, as our countrymen would, till very lately, have been mortally offended at the designation of "butcher".'
– M. D.

'It needs little watchin', and disna gang wrang wi' owre lang boiling. Cleek it on (suspend it from the chain above the fire) an' let it het richt through the boil; then cleek it up (on a higher link) so as it'll no boil owre and pit oot the fire, and ye may lock the door and gang a' to the kirk.' – A Housewife.

This, we may assume, is why powsowdie was the favourite Sunday dinner soup.

'What although it be seen at the British Coffee-house, London? There it lacks the true accent.' – Christopher North.

'Sheep's head broth is reckoned medicinal in certain cases; and was frequently prescribed as an article of diet by the celebrated Dr. Cullen.' – M. D.

Hotch-Potch or Hairst Bree

> Then here's to ilka kindly Scot:
> Wi' mony gude broths he boils his pot,
> But rare hotch-potch beats a' the lot,
> It smells and smacks sae brawly.
> – Sheriff Bell.

'A truly delicious soup, quite peculiar to Scotland, but worthy of being introduced into the very first leaf of the *Almanach des Gourmands*.'
– J. G. Lockhart: *Peter's Letters to his Kinsfolk*.

Hotch-Potch, known also as Hairst Bree (Harvest Broth) is made only when the kail-yard is in its prime, and the soup is fragrant with the juices of young growing things. Where possible, go out with a basket to select your vegetables within an hour or so before starting to prepare them. – F. M. McN.

(Traditional Recipe)

Neck of lamb or a good marrow bone, young carrots, turnips, cauliflower, lettuce, green peas, broad beans, spring onions, parsley, salt, pepper, water

Put three pounds of neck of lamb or a good marrow bone into the broth-pot with three quarts or less of cold water and a little salt. Bring to the boil and skim carefully. Shell a pint and a half of fresh green peas; shell and skin half a pint of young broad beans; pare six young turnips, scrape six young carrots and cut both into dice; prepare and slice or chop a few spring onions – up to a dozen according to size. Retain half a pint of peas and put the rest, along with the other prepared vegetables, into the boiling liquor. Lower the heat and simmer very gently for three or four hours or longer. It can hardly be cooked too slowly or too long.[1] Meanwhile put a cauliflower and a lettuce into water with a little salt and let them lie for half an hour; then break the cauliflower into small sprigs and chop the lettuce. Add these, along with the rest of the peas, to the soup, and to simmer for half an hour longer. Just before dishing up, add a small handful of chopped parsley. The soup should be almost as thick as porridge. (Nowadays it is usually rather less substantial.) When ready, remove the mutton, season the soup and serve in a heated tureen.

This makes a famous hot dish after a long day on the hill.

The excellence of this soup depends mainly on the meat, whether beef or mutton, being perfectly fresh, and the vegetables being all young, and full of sweet juices, and boiled till of good consistence. The sweet white turnip is best for hotch-potch, or the small, round, smooth-grained yellow kind peculiar to Scotland, and almost equal to the genuine *navet* of France. – Meg Dods.

Almost any other young vegetables in season may be added to this soup – e.g. shredded heart of white cabbage, which takes less time than the cauliflower to cook. 'Be generous with your onions,' says one housewife. Some people like the inclusion of a very little mint. – The meat may be cut up and served in the soup, but this is seldom done nowadays. Some cooks add the mutton, cut into chops, an hour and a half before serving. – With the omission of meat and the addition of a little butter you have an excellent *maigre* soup.

It is related of Prince Albert that when on board a Highland loch steamer he was lured to the galley by the delicious odour of hotch-potch.
'How is it made?' he asked the cook, who failed to recognize him.
'Weel, there's mutton intill't and neeps intill't and peas intill't——'
'But what's intill't?'
'I'm tellin' ye, there's mutton intill't and neeps intill't and——'
'Yes, but what's *intill't*?'
'Gudesake, man, am I no thrang tellin' ye what's intill't! There's mutton intill't——'
The timely arrival of a member of the Prince's suite put an end to the confusion. He explained that 'intill't' meant 'into it' and nothing more. – F. M. McN.

[1] 'Eight hours is not too much,' – Lady Harriet St. Clair.

Skink: An Old Scots Stew Soup

'A spoonfu' o' stink will spoil a patfu' o' skink.
(One ill weed will spoil a mess of pottage.)
– Old Scots Proverb.

(*Meg Dods's Recipe*)

Beef, mixed vegetables, water, pepper, and salt

Take a leg of beef, put it on with a gallon of water; let it
boil for six hours, taking care to skim the soup well all the
time, as the gravy should be very clear and bright; then
strain the liquor from the meat, take the sinewy part of the
meat and lay it aside till your soup is ready to serve up. Cut
the sinews about an inch long. Have some vegetables cut,
such as carrots, turnips, leeks, onions, celery, lettuce,
cabbage shred small, and green peas, when to be had.
Blanch the whole in boiling water for ten minutes. Put the
whole into the soup and boil till quite tender. Serve up the
sinews in the tureen with the soup. Season the soup with salt
and pepper before dishing it.

'Herbs may be used in these soups; and white peas (boilers) are by many thought an
improvement. Both are cheap and excellent family dishes.' – M. D.

The Old Scots Brown Soup

(*Meg Dods's Recipe*)

Beef, meat trimmings, carrot, celery, onions, leek, turnip,
water, catsup, salt, pepper, cayenne, sippets

Have eight pounds of a shin of beef chipped across in two
places, and a knuckle of veal or a scrag or some shanks of
mutton with any fresh trimmings the larder can furnish,
and a piece of ham, if the ham flavour is admired. Heat and
rub hard a nicely tinned stew-pot; melt in it some butter, or
rub it with marrow. Let the meat, with a slice of carrot, a
head of celery, onions, the white part of two leeks, and a
turnip, sliced, *catch*, but not burn, over a quick fire (let it
be nicely browned); then add four quarts, or better, of soft
water. Carefully skim. When it is once skimmed, throw in a
pint of cold water to refresh it, and take off what more

scum is detached till it become quite limpid. Let the stew-pot simmer slowly by the fire for four hours, without stirring it any more from the bottom, till all the strength is obtained, but not so long as to cause the soup to become ropy. Take it off and let it settle; skim off the fat, and strain off gently what flows freely through a fine search. When ready, put to it two pounds of rump-steaks, cut rather small and nicely browned in the frying-pan, but drained from the frying-fat. Simmer the steaks in the soup for an hour; strain it; add a small glassful of catsup, with salt, pepper, and cayenne; slip toasted sippets into the tureen and skimming off the filmy fat, serve the soup with the steaks in it. Without the steaks, which one now rarely sees, this is plain *brown soup*.

The Old Scots White Soup or Soupe À La Reine

(*Meg Dods's Recipe*)

Veal, fowl, bacon, lemon-thyme, onions, carrot, turnip, celery, peppercorns, mace, macaroni or vermicelli or French roll, water

Take a large knuckle of the whitest veal, well broken and soaked, a white fowl skinned, or two chickens, a quarter-pound of well-coloured lean undressed bacon, lemon-thyme, onions, carrot, celery, and a white turnip, a few white peppercorns, and two blades of mace. Boil for about two hours; skim repeatedly and carefully during that time. When the stock is well tasted, strain it off. It will form a jelly. When to be used, take off the saucepan fat, clear off the sediment, and put the jelly into a tin saucepan or stew-pan well tinned; boil for half an hour, and serve on a couple of rounds of a small French roll; or with macaroni, pre-viously soaked, and stewed in the soup till perfectly soft, or vermicelli. This is plain white soup.

'This soup was introduced, or rather revived in Scotland by Hume the historian, after his residence in Paris; see his letters to Adam Smith on his culinary experiments in Burton's *Life of Hume*.' – Meg Dods: *A Manual of Cookery*, Note.

'Last night, guests of the University of Edinburgh celebrated the 250th anniversary of the death of David Hume by drinking cups of soup . . . *Soupe à la Reine*.'
– *Edinburgh Evening Dispatch*, May 9, 1961.

Lorraine Soup[1]

(Meg Dods's Recipe)

The old Scots white soup (q.v.), sweet almonds, eggs, cold roast fowl, bread-crumbs, lemon-peel, nutmeg, cream

The old Scots white soup is raised to Lorraine soup as follows: Take a half-pound of sweet almonds, blanched (that is, scalded and the husks rubbed off), the hard-boiled yolks of three eggs, and the skinned breast and white parts of cold roast fowl; beat the almonds to a paste in a mortar with a little water to prevent their oiling; mince very finely the fowl and eggs and some bread-crumbs. Add to this hash an English pint or more of the stock, lemon-peel, and a scrape of nutmeg; bring it to the boil and put to it a pint of boiling sweet cream and the rest of the stock. Let it be for a considerable time on the very eve of boiling that it may thicken, but take care it does not boil, lest the cream curdle. Strain through a sieve. Yolks of eggs will do for half the cream.

Potage À La Reine *(The Fashionable White Soup)*

(Meg Dods's Recipe)

Fowls, veal, veal-broth, parsley, bread-crumbs, almonds (sweet and bitter), egg yolks, cream

Take a couple of large or three small fat pullets; clean and skin them; take also two pounds or more of veal cut into pieces; put these together into a very nicely tinned stewpan with parsley, and moisten them with clear boiling veal-broth. Let this stew softly for an hour; then soak in the broth the soft part of a penny loaf; cut the flesh off the breasts and wings of the chickens; chop and pound it in a mortar

[1] This soup would appear to be named after Mary of Lorraine, or Guise, wife of James V and mother of Mary Stuart. Victor Maclure, however, thinks it is properly *Potage à la Reine Margot* (Marguerite de Valois) who has been confused with Mary of Lorraine.

The French have a *Crème Marie-Stuart*, which is a chicken *velouté* with barley cream, garnished with a *printanière* of vegetables and diced carrots. – F. M. McN.

114

with the hard yolks of four eggs, the soaked crumbs, ten sweet almonds and three bitter, all blanched. Rub the compound into the soup; strain the whole, and add gradually a quart of sweet cream brought to boil by itself; the beat yolks of three or four eggs may be substituted for two-thirds of the cream. Cow-heel or calf's feet will make a good white soup. Rabbits may be economically substituted for chickens, and lean beef for the veal.

Friar's Chicken[1]

'A dish invented by that luxurious body of men.' – Sir John Sinclair.

(Mrs. Dalgairns's[2] Recipe)

Chicken, veal, eggs, salt, pepper, parsley, water

Put two pounds of knuckle of veal into a pan with some water; boil for two hours; strain; cut a young fowl into joints, skin it, and add it to the boiling broth; season with white pepper and salt; let it boil for a little, then add a tablespoonful of chopped parsley. When the chicken is boiled tender, add three well-beaten eggs; stir them quickly into the broth one way, and remove immediately from the fire.

Friar's chicken is served (old style) with the carved chicken in the soup. Meg Dods recommends the addition of a little mace, and adds: 'The stock may be simply made of butter, and the meat may be nicely browned in the frying-pan before it is put to the soup. Rabbits make this very well. Some like the egg curdled, and egg in great quantity, making the dish a sort of *ragout* of eggs and chicken.' Another old recipe gives a flavouring of cinnamon. – F. M. McN.

Feather Fowlie (*A Luncheon Soup*)

(Lady Clark of Tillypronie's Recipe)

Fowl, ham, celery, onion, thyme, parsley, mace, salt, eggs, cream

Take a fresh fowl; joint and let the pieces soak for half an hour in cold water to which you have added a dessert-

[1] Mrs. Glasse (a Londoner) calls it *Scots Chicken* in her *Art of Cookery* (1747), and adds 'This is also a very pretty dish for sick people, but the Scotch gentlemen are very fond of it.'
[2] From *The Practice of Cookery*, by Mrs. Dalgairns (Edinburgh, 1829).

115

spoonful of salt, then wash it well under the tap and put it into a stewpan with a slice of ham, a stick of celery cut small, a sliced onion, thyme, parsley, and a bit of mace. Cover with a quart of cold water, put the lid on, and bring it to the boil; then draw it to the side and let it cook gently for an hour and a half; strain, and immediately clear off all the grease with paper. Put it into another stew-pan and add a dessertspoonful of chopped parsley and a ladleful of first stock. Let it heat up for fifteen minutes and add the minced white meat of the fowl. Remove from the fire, stir in three strained yolks of egg and a dessertspoonful of warmed cream. Pour into a heated tureen.

Lady Clark suggests that the name is a corruption of *œufs filés*. I think it more likely that *fowlie* is a corruption of *volaille* – the more so as the soup bears a strong resemblance to the French *velouté de volaille*. The soup may well be a legacy of the Auld Alliance. – F. M. McN.

Cock-A-Leekie

> I've supped gude bree i' mony a howff
>   Wi'in Auld Reekie,
> But nane wi' siccan a gusty gowff
>   As cock-a-leekie.
>   – Anon.

Bree, soup; *howff*, tavern; *Auld Reekie*, Edinburgh; *siccan*, such; *gusty gowff*, savoury taste.

The King (James VI and I): 'Come, my lords and lieges, let us all to dinner, for the cocky-leeky is a-cooling.' – Scott: *The Fortunes of Nigel*, last line.

(Traditional Recipe)

A cock or plump fowl, leeks, prunes, Jamaica pepper, salt veal or beef stock or water

Cut off the roots and part of the heads of two or three bunches of leeks and wash thoroughly. Truss the fowl and place in a large pot with three or four of the leeks, blanched and chopped, and two quarts of good stock. Bring to the boil and cook gently for two hours or longer, until the fowl is tender, when it should be removed. Clear off all the grease with paper. Add the remainder of the leeks, blanched (if old and strong) and cut into inch lengths, which may be split, with more salt if required, and Jamaica pepper to

116

taste. Simmer very gently until the leeks are tender. Half an hour before serving, add a dozen or so of prunes, unbroken. A little minced fowl may be added to the soup.

If water is used in place of stock, add a clove, a blade of mace, a sprig of parsley and six peppercorns tied in muslin, and remove along with the fowl.

'The soup must be very thick of leeks, and the first part of them must be boiled down into the soup until it become a lubricous compound.' – Meg Dods.

'The leek is one of the most honourable and ancient of pot-herbs. It is called *par excellence* the herb, and learned critics assert that our word porridge or pottage is derived from the Latin *porrus*, a leek. The leek is the badge of a high-spirited, honourable and fiery nation – the Ancient Britons. In the old poetry of the northern nations, where a young man would now be styled the *flower*, he was called "the *leek* of his family, or tribe", an epithet of most savoury meaning.' – Ibid.

'*Shepherd:* Speakin' o' cocky-leekie, the man was an atheist that first polluted it with prunes.
'*North:* At least no Christian.
'*Shepherd:* Prunes gie't a sickenin' sweetness till it tastes like a mouthfu' o' a Cockney poem.' – Christopher North: *Noctes Ambrosianae.*

'At a formal banquet given by the late Lord Holland, Talleyrand, who was as celebrated for gastronomy as for diplomacy, inquired "earnestly" of Lord Jeffrey the nature of Cock-a-leekie, and wished particularly to know if *prunes* (French plums) were essential to its concoction. Mr. Jeffrey was unable to give the Ex-Bishop and Prince any satisfactory information; and the sagacious diplomat, with his usual tact, settled for himself that prunes should be boiled in the famous historical soup, warmly patronised by "gentle King Jamie", but taken out before the *potage* was sent to table. . . . Cock-a-leekie *à la Talleyrand* is worthy of trial, especially as conservative English cooks still affirm that this is the practice in Scotland.'
 – Meg Dods: *Manual of Cookery*, Note.

Personally, I am all for the addition of prunes, to be served one in each plate.
 – F. M. McN.

'I will always give the preference in the way of soup to their (the Scots') Cock-a-Leekie, even before their inimitable Hotch-Potch.'
 – Alexis Soyer (quoted in the *Encyclopedia of Practical Cookery*).

In the days of cock-fighting, a *fugie* (defeated bird) made into cock-a-leekie was the popular Fastern's E'en supper in the Lowlands.
 – See T. Wilkie in Proc. Berwickshire Naturalist Club (1916).

Nettle Kail (*Highlands and Hebrides*)

'This simple but delicious soup is associated specially with the month of March, when nettles are young and fresh and the black March cockerel is exactly a year old, with young and tender flesh.[1] The nettles were picked commonly on the old drystone dykes or the walls of the drystone-built "black" houses, now rapidly vanishing. In the old days, March time was tonic time, and it was believed that nettle kail, taken three times during the month – sometimes on three consecutive days – purified the blood,

---

[1] In *Rob Roy*, Sir Walter Scott tells us that it was once customary to force nettles for early spring kail, and describes how Andrew Service, the old gardener of Loch Leven, raised nettles under glasses for this purpose.

cleared the complexion,[1] and, in general, ensured good health during the ensuing year. Shrove Tuesday was a very special night for a nettle kail supper. All the members of the family were expected to be present, and a blessing was invoked on the spring work.' – Rachel Macleod, Barra, in a letter to the author, accompanying the recipe.

A year-old cockerel, young nettles, oat or barley meal, butter, salt, pepper, wild garlic or onion or mint, water

Gather a sufficient quantity of young nettles from the higher part of the wall, where they are clean. (It is advisable to wear gloves.) Strip off the young, tender leaves at the top[2] (discarding the coarser ones), and wash in several changes of salted water. Dry in a clean cloth and chop finely, unless the leaves are very small. Put the dressed and stuffed bird into the kail-pot with two quarts of cold water. Bring slowly to the boil, and add the nettles – about three-quarters of a pint – and a handful of oat or barley meal, stirring well. Add salt to taste, a good pat of butter, and a little wild garlic, onion or mint, as preferred. Simmer until the bird is tender, then season the kail to taste.

For the stuffing, rub a piece of butter into twice its weight in oatmeal or barley meal, or substitute finely chopped suet for the butter. Season with salt, pepper and a little wild garlic or mint (fresh or powdered). Mix the ingredients well and stuff the bird. Insert a skewer in the opening.

In some districts whole barley is substituted for meal, but it should then be put on in cold water.

Nettles make an excellent substitute for spinach in early spring.

'In Scotland I have eaten nettles, I have slept in nettle sheets and I have dined off a nettle tablecloth. . . . The stalks of the old nettles are as good as flax for making cloth. I have heard my mother say that she thought nettle cloth more durable than any other species of linen.'
  Thomas Campbell (the poet), quoted by Mrs. Grieve in *A Modern Herbal*.

Scottish paper manufacturers have experimented with nettles successfully. A green dye is extracted from the leaves and a yellow dye from the roots. – Ibid.

[1] I daresay the infusion of nettle leaves proved more efficacious than washing their faces in May dew, a rite to which our lassies were likewise much addicted. – F. M. McN.
[2] 'We used to go out and gather the nettles – just the four or five most delicate young leaves, of course.' – Maria S. Stewart (in a letter to the author).

Nettle Soup

Nettles, milk, water, butter, pepper, salt, potato- or cornflour

Prepare the nettles as above and steam in a little water. Add milk, a small piece of butter, pepper and salt, and thicken with cornflour, potato-flour, or a little mashed potato.

Bawd Bree or Scots Hare Soup

(*Traditional Recipe*)

> 'Hare soup, sir, I will candidly own, is only understood in Scotland.'
> – Dr. Redgill: *Annals of the Cleikum Club.*

A hare, shin of beef, turnip, carrots, onions, parsnip (optional), celery, a pot-posy (bouquet garni), cloves, black peppercorns, cayenne pepper, salt, butter, flour or rice flour or arrowroot, mushroom ketchup, port wine

Skin and clean the hare thoroughly, holding it over a large basin to catch all the blood, which contains much of the flavour of the animal. Add a teaspoonful of vinegar to the blood and set it aside. Wipe the hare carefully with a damp cloth to remove any small hairs that may adhere to it. Cut a dozen or so very small steaks from the back, shoulders and rump, and put aside.[1] Cut two pounds of shin or neck of beef into small pieces. Put the beef into a pot with all that remains of the hare, and add four quarts of cold water. When it comes to the boil, add salt, a small turnip, a small parsnip (optional), two medium-sized carrots, three sticks of celery with foliage (all sliced or cut up), two medium-sized onions each stuck with two cloves, a teaspoonful of black peppercorns, a pot-posy consisting of two sprigs of parsley, two bay leaves, a sprig of thyme and a blade of mace. Simmer for three hours and strain, rubbing the vegetables through the colander.

[1] 'You may lay aside as much of the fleshy part of a good hare as will make a handsome dish of hare cakes, minced collops, garnished with sippets, or as will make forcemeat balls for the soup.' – Meg Dods.

Flatten the hare steaks by beating with a meat bat or rolling-pin. Season with salt and pepper, dredge with flour and brown nicely in hot butter or bacon fat (about one and a half ounces). Add to the strained stock. Bring to the boil and simmer very gently for an hour and a half.

Strain the blood and rub it with two ounces of flour, or rice flour or arrowroot, as if making starch, add a little more hot soup and stir into the remainder of the soup, which must be kept just below boiling-point (lest the blood curdle), for ten minutes. (It may be placed over boiling water and stirred occasionally, for that period.) Meanwhile pound the parboiled liver in a mortar with the pieces of hare boiled for stock, and rub this through a hair sieve. Stir a little of the soup into this, and when thick and creamy stir it back into the pot of soup. Add a spoonful or two (according to taste) of mushroom ketchup, and/or a gill of port wine, with any further seasoning required.

The hare steaks are served (old style) in the tureen, and a boiled potato for each person is served separately.

A knuckle of veal, or a veal bone and a ham bone, may be substituted for beef.

In the farmhouse, hare soup is often thickened with oatmeal – an excellent practice. Instead of thickening the blood with flour, stir about four ounces of oatmeal (medium quality) into the strained stock and simmer for an hour.

For a simpler soup, omit the beef, herbs and wine, and reduce the quantity of vegetables.

The white mountain hare is good only for soup. There is too much rich meat on the brown hare to use exclusively for soup, and the best parts should be jugged or treated as Meg Dods suggests. – F. M. McN.

Red wine, in the proportion of a quarter-pint to a tureen of soup, is reckoned an improvement by some gourmands, and those of the old school still like a large spoonful of currant jelly dissolved in the soup.

Dr. Alexander ('Jupiter') Carlyle (1722–1805) insisted on having currants in his hare soup – apparently an eighteenth-century fashion.

Poacher's Soup (*Or Soupe à la Meg Merrilies*)

'Of the ruder and more national form (which is also, I think, the best) of grouse soup, the celebrated stew whereof Meg Merrilies made Dominie Sampson partake was probably a variety, though the authority said that moor-game were not the only ingredient of that soup or broth or stew. (See p. 164.) . . . For the really hungry man, this is, no doubt, the best way of all, but as a dinner dish it is perhaps, as has been hinted, too solid for the mere overture to which we have now reduced soup. In the days of our ancestors they ate it late instead of early in the order of dishes, and I am not certain that they were wrong.' – George Saintsbury.

(*Megs Dods's Recipe*)

Venison, beef or mutton, game, celery, carrots, turnips, potatoes, cabbage, onions, parsley, peppercorns, spices, salt, red wine, mushroom catsup, water

This savoury and highly relishing new stew-soup may be made of any or everything known by the name of game. Take from two to four pounds of the trimmings or coarse parts of venison, shin of beef, or shanks or lean scrag of good mutton – all fresh. If game is plenty, then use no meat. Break the bones and boil this with celery, a couple of carrots and turnips, four onions, a bunch of parsley, and a quarter-ounce of peppercorns, the larger proportion Jamaica pepper. Strain this stock when it has boiled for three hours. Cut down and skin a blackcock or woodcock, a pheasant, half a hare or a rabbit, a brace of partridges or grouse, or one of each (whichever is obtained most easily), and season the pieces with mixed spices. These may be floured and browned in the frying-pan; but as this is a process dictated by the eye as much as the palate, it is not necessary in making this soup. Put the game to the strained stock with a dozen small onions, a couple of heads of celery sliced, half a dozen peeled potatoes, and, when it boils, a small white cabbage quartered, black pepper, allspice, and salt to taste. Let the soup simmer till the game is tender, but not overdone; and, lest it should, the vegetables may be put in half an hour before the meat.

'This soup may be coloured and flavoured with red wine, and if two spoonfuls of mushroom catsup is mixed should not be salted till that ingredient is added, as catsup contains so much salt itself.' – M. D.

'The Club were at variance on [Meg Dods's] receipt. Jekyl declared for the simple racy flavour of the rude sylvan cheer; Winterblossom liked the addition of forcemeat-balls and catsup; and the Doctor – hovering between the tureens like Macheath between his rival charmers – laid his ears deeply in both, but when compelled to decide, from an habitual reverence to soups as they are, voted for the plain soup, as originally swallowed with so much unction by Dominie Sampson.' – *Annals of the Cleikum Club*.

Grouse Soup

'But oh! my dear North, what grouse soup at Dalnacardoch! You smell it on the homeward hill, as if it were exhaling from the heather.'
— Christopher North: *Noctes Ambrosianae*.

Grouse, celery, peppercorns, juniper berries (optional), salt, cayenne pepper, butter, oatmeal, beef stock, port wine or red wine and whisky or cream

Slightly under-roast two old birds and remove all the flesh from the carcases. Set aside two breasts and pound the remaining flesh in a mortar. Put the bones into a goblet with a quart of good stock. (Failing stock, use water with a marrow bone or three or four rashers of streaky bacon.) Bring to the boil and skim. Add salt, six black peppercorns, two white peppercorns and, if liked, six or eight juniper berries, slightly crushed, with two sticks of celery. Simmer for two hours and strain.

Melt two ounces of butter and fry two ounces of coarse oatmeal to a warm brown. Add a little stock to make it of the consistency of cream, then stir into the rest of the stock. Add the pounded flesh of the birds and simmer for twenty minutes longer. Dice the breast fillets, fry in butter and add to the soup. Lastly add a tablespoonful of red wine with a teaspoonful of whisky, or substitute some thick fresh cream.

'Grouse, pheasant, partridge, hare and rabbit soups are all better in Scotland than elsewhere. But those who want hare or rabbit soup usually know how to make it, and those who can come by the game birds have usually come also by some attendant who can dress them for the tureen. The bird soups are improved, if thick, by a final addition of cream; if thin, by a glassful of sherry or red wine. A bouquet of herbs is absolutely necessary.* Brown breadcrumbs cast upon the soup at the last are correct, but some people prefer sago, as brown bread may make the liquid curdle. The sago must be added an hour before serving, and must be carefully stirred. Unlike oatmeal, it has no virtue in its knots.' — *The Scots Week-end.*

Other game soups may be made in this way. Ptarmigan soup is excellent. As with black game and capercailzie, the old birds are nearly hopeless except as soup.
— F. M. McN.

* This may be used in the stock. No strong-scented herbs, however.

Superlative Game Soup

(*Meg Dods's Recipe*)

Game, venison or rabbits, ham, onions, carrots, parsnips, celery, parsley, Jamaica pepper, cloves, veal or beef stock

This soup is made of all sorts of black or red game, or of venison or wild rabbits. Skin the birds, carve and trim them neatly, and fry the pieces along with a few slices of ham, sliced onions, carrots, and parsnips, a little of each. Drain and stew this meat gently for an hour in good fresh veal or beef stock-broth, with a head of celery cut in nice bits, a little minced parsley, and what seasonings you like. Very small steaks of venison may be fried, as the birds, and stewed in the broth; and if the stock is made of any venison trimmings, it will be an advantage both in flavour and strength.

'Jamaica pepper and cloves are suitable seasonings; celery, from its nutty flavour, is a proper vegetable for hare and game soups. Take out the ham before dishing.' – M. D.

Red Pottage

Haricot beans, onion, celery, beetroot, tomatoes, butter, salt and pepper, meat or bone stock or water

Rinse and drain eight ounces of haricot beans, leave overnight to soak in cold water to cover, then drain well. Slice a medium-sized onion, a stick of celery or a piece of parsnip, a small boiled beetroot (peeled) and four medium-sized tomatoes. Melt an ounce of butter in a saucepan, add the beans and vegetables, and fry gently for five minutes, stirring occasionally. Add the stock and season to taste. Bring to the boil, skim if necessary, and simmer gently for three hours or longer. Remove the beetroot and pass all the rest through a sieve. Re-heat and serve garnished with chopped mint.

Lentils may be substituted for haricot beans.

123

Fish and Shellfish Soups

'These are among the best and most characteristic that Scotland has to offer, and are rarely to be met elsewhere in the British Isles outside of the most expensive restaurants for French fare.' – *The Scots Week-end.*

Plain Scots Fish-And-Sauce

(*Meg Dods's Recipe*)

Haddock or other fish, green onions, parsley, chives, pepper, butter, flour, catsup

This is, in fact, just a fish soup. Make a stock of the heads, points of the tails, fins, etc., or where fish is cheap and fresh, cut down one or two to help the stock. Boil green onions, parsley, and chives in this, and some whole pepper. When all the substance is obtained, strain it. Thicken with butter kneaded in browned flour, but only to the consistency of a soup, and put in the fish (generally haddock), cut in three or divided. Boil the fish ten minutes, add catsup, and serve them and the sauce together in tureen or soup dish.

Salmon Soup

'This is provided in Heaven for good Scots.
– *The Scots Week-end.*

The trimmings and a small slice of fresh salmon, the bones of one or two fresh whiting, carrot, turnip, onion, celery, parsley, brown breadcrumbs, potato-flour or mashed potato, water

Put into your fish kettle the head, bones, fins and skin of the salmon, along with the bones of the whiting (these make all the difference) and the prepared vegetables – a small carrot, a small turnip, a small onion and a stick of celery. Cover amply with cold water, bring to the boil, add salt, and boil gently for at least an hour. Strain and remove all the fat and oil. Thicken with a little potato-flour or cooked and mashed potato. Add some scallops of uncooked salmon, a tablespoonful of chopped parsley and some brown breadcrumbs. As soon as the salmon is cooked, the soup is ready.

Cullen Skink

(A Cottage Recipe from the Shores of the Moray Firth)

Finnan-haddie, onion, mashed potatoes, butter, milk, pepper and salt

Skin a Finnan-haddie, and place it in a pan with sufficient boiling water to cover it (no more). Bring to the boil and add a chopped onion. When the haddock is cooked, take it out and remove all the bones. Flake the fish and return all the bones to the stock. Boil for one hour. Strain the stock and again bring to the boil. Boil about a pint of milk separately and add it to the stock with the flaked fish and salt to taste. Boil for a few minutes. Add enough mashed potato to make the soup a nice consistency, with a tablespoonful of butter, and pepper to taste, and serve.

Partan Bree[1] *(Crab Soup)*

(Lady Clark of Tillypronie's Recipe)

Crabs, rice, white stock, salt, pepper, anchovy, cream

Pick all the meat from two cooked crabs and set aside that from the large claws. Boil five or six ounces of rice in milk till soft and pass it with the crab-meat through a tammy into a basin. Stir it with a wooden spoon till perfectly smooth and add to it, very gradually, sufficient white unseasoned stock for a party of twelve or fourteen people. Do not make it as thick as a purée. Season with salt, white pepper, and anchovy. Put it all into a pan and stir it over the fire until quite hot, but do not let it boil. Add pieces of meat from the claws, and, just before serving, stir in half a pint of cream.

[1] From Gael. *partan*, a crab.

Mussel Brose

At Musselbrough and eke[1] Newhaven
The fisher-wives will get top livin
When lads gang[2] oot on Sunday's even
    To treat their joes,[3]
An' tak o' fat pandours[4] a prieven[5]
    Or mussel brose.
        – Robert Fergusson.

(*Traditional Recipe*)

Mussels, oatmeal, stock or milk-and-water

Wash the shells in several waters, scraping them well, then put them into a colander and run cold water on them until it runs away quite clear and free of sand, after which put them to steep for two hours. Drain them, put them on the fire in an iron stew-pan, closely covered, shake them occasionally until the shells open, and remove immediately from the fire. Strain the liquor into a basin, take the mussels out of the shells, and remove the beards and black parts. Put the liquor on with some fresh fish stock or some milk-and-water. Bring to the boil, add the mussels, and make hot, but do not cook. Have some oatmeal toasting before the fire. Put a handful or so in a bowl and dash a cupful of the mussel bree over it. Stir up quickly so as to form knots, return to the pan for a minute or two, and serve very hot.

Cockles may be used in the same way.

Mussels, 'the oyster's poor relation', were conceivably consumed in the burgh of that name as early as the Roman period, for this was originally a Roman station, and owes its name to the shellfish. – F. M. McN.

Winkle Soup (*Hebrides*)

Winkles, oatmeal, fish stock or milk, water

Gather a small pailful of winkles on the rocks at low tide. Put them into a pot, cover them with water, and bring them to the boil. Take out the winkles (reserving the liquor) and pick the fish out of the shells with a long pin. Strain care-

---

[1] Also.   [2] Go.   [3] Sweethearts.
[4] Pandours or pandores, 'an esteemed variety of oyster found near Prestonpans on the Firth of Forth' (Chambers).
[5] Tasting.

fully the water they were boiled in, as it is often sandy, and return it to the pot. It will probably be too salt, so it is an advantage to use equal proportions of the liquor and water in which fresh fish has been boiled; but if this is not available, a little milk and fresh water will do. When it comes to the boil, add enough oatmeal to make it of the consistency of thin gruel. The meal should be allowed to fall in a steady rain from the left hand, whilst you stir it with a porridge stick or wooden spoon. When the oatmeal is nearly cooked (which takes about twenty minutes), put back the winkles and boil for ten minutes longer.

Shellfish Soup (*Hebrides*)

Cockles, mussels, or razor-fish, fresh fish stock, milk, cornflour, butter, pepper, salt

Proceed as for winkle soup, adding milk to part of the liquor. Put in a morsel of butter, thicken with cornflour, and season to taste. Use plenty of pepper. Razor-fish should be chopped small before being added.

'As much of the flavour of delicate shell-fish is lost in washing them free of sand, the washings may be kept, strained repeatedly, and put to the stock; but where shell-fish are in plenty this is idle.' – Meg Dods.

BROSE AND KAIL

Fat Brose

The Monks of Melrose made fat brose
On Fridays when they fasted. – *A Godly Song.*

Ox head, cow heel or hough (shin of beef), oatmeal, salt, water

Put half an ox head or heel or a good piece of hough into a goblet with water to cover amply. Boil until an almost pure oil floats on the top. Put a handful of lightly toasted oatmeal into a bowl with a pinch of salt, dash upon it a

ladleful of the fat broth, and stir it up quickly so as to form
knots. Return to the pot for a minute or two to re-heat; then
stir well and serve.

'A fat pot boiling, popples and glances on the tap, like as mony broun lammer[1]
beads.' – Meg Dods.
  Yule Brose. – In olden times, all, gentle and simple, had fat brose on Yule Day
morning. – Scott.

Kail Brose

> When I see our Scots lads,
>   Wi' their kilts and cockades,
> That sae aften hae lounder'd our foes, man;
>   I think to mysel',
>   On the meal and the *yill*,
> And the fruits o' our Scottish kail brose, man.
>   – Andrew Shirrefs (1762–1800): *A Cogie o' Yill.*
>
>   *Loundered*, beaten severely.   *Yill*, ale.

This is identical with Fat Brose, save that when the fat
floats on the top, a good stock of kail, well washed and
chopped, is added and boiled until tender.

Neep Brose (*Aberdeenshire*)

*Turnips, oatmeal, butter, salt, pepper, a marrow bone, milk,
water*

Wash and pare six Swedish turnips and cut into small dice.
Place in a pot with the marrow bone, add water to cover and
a little salt. Bring to the boil and cook gently until the turnips
are soft and richly yellow. Put three tablespoonfuls of oatmeal into a bowl. Add a walnut of butter and a little salt
and pepper. Strain the turnip bree (stock) into a small
saucepan and bring to the boil. Pour a little over the prepared oatmeal and stir until the brose forms small knots.
Add the remainder of the liquid gradually, and serve the
brose piping hot.

The turnips may be made into a purée.

[1] *Lammer*, amber.

Green Kail[1]

(*Old Cottage Recipe*)

Greens, oatmeal, pepper, salt, cream, water

Put into a pot as much water as will cover your greens.
Remove the strong shanks (this is 'ribbing' them) and put
them in when the water is boiling. Boil till tender, leaving
them uncovered. Take them out, squeeze them free of the
liquor, and chop them finely or squeeze them through a sieve.
Sprinkle with oatmeal and put back into the pot with the
stock. Add a little warmed cream, with pepper and salt to
taste. Stir, boil up for a few minutes, and serve with thin
oatcakes.

Muslin Kail[3]

'A purely vegetable soup, without animal ingredients of any
kind, and composed of shelled barley, greens, onions, etc.'
                    – C. Mackay.

Water Kail

A soup made without meat, of greens and grolls (oats
stripped off the husk in the mill).

[1] Called also Pan Kail and Lenten Kail.
[2] Faill was a small monastery in the parish of Tarbolton, near Mauchline, Ayrshire.
[3] Meslin or mashlum (mixed).

129

Barley Kail

(*Old Cottage Recipe*)

Hough, barley, kail, pepper and salt, water

Put two pounds of hough and a teacupful of barley into a goblet with about three quarts of cold water. Bring it to the boil and remove the scum. Let it boil for three hours. Have ready a cullender full of kail, which you have washed carefully, and picked down very fine with the fingers. Boil till tender. Add salt and pepper to taste. Serve with oatcakes.

Two or three leeks sliced, may be added with the greens.

Kilmeny Kail (*Fife*)

Rabbit, pickled pork, greens, salt, water

Take a rabbit, clean it well, and cut it into pieces. Put them into a pot with a piece of pickled pork and sufficient cold water to cover them. Take two heads of greens, pick down with the fingers, and wash free from sand. Add to the broth and boil for three hours. If the pork is very salt, do not add more salt. Serve with oatcakes.

DISHES OF FISH

Fish, as we have seen, have always played an extremely important part in the national diet.

As a nation, we have long been skilled in the curing of fish. White fish are apt to be insipid, but instead of sauces and seasonings, our fisherfolk rely mainly upon the use of the elements to give them *goût*.* Thus, after being slightly salted, they are variously 'rizzared', or sun-dried; 'blawn' or wind-blown – that is, hung up in the wind, but out of the sun, or in a passage with a current of air; rock-dried, being sprayed with sea-water during the process; or, as with skate, earth-dried – that is, left on the grass for a day or two with a grassy sod reversed on them. Sometimes, again, they receive a touch of the forest, being smoked over oak or silver birch sawdust, to which a few juniper twigs or pine cones may be added.

The kippering of herring is carried out mainly on the west coast, the 'wastlin' ', or west coast herring being the pick of the market. On the east coast, they specialize in the curing of haddock and other white fish. In the mid-nineteenth century there were three main cures – the Moray Firth or Buckie cure, the Auchmithie or Arbroath cure, and the widely renowned Findon cure. The once popular 'bervie' (derived from Inverbervie, in the Mearns) has fallen into disuse, but spelding, which are rock-dried and not smoked at all, are still popular in the north-east.

Most of our overseas and foreign visitors delight in our smoked fish, whether a plump Loch Fyne kipper, a buttercup-yellow finnan-haddie, a pale 'Moray Firth', a copper-coloured Arbroath 'smokie', or a slice of pinkish brown smoked salmon.

It was the Rev. Dr. Folliott in Thomas Love Peacock's *Crotchet Castle* who averred that this skill was our 'single eximious virtue', and that he was content to learn nothing of us but 'the art and science of fish for breakfast'.

* *Scotticé*, goo.

To Dress A Cod's Head And Shoulders (*Scots Fashion*)

(*Meg Dods's Recipe*)

Cod, lobster, oyster, eggs, bread-crumbs, lemon, pepper, salt, flour, butter, parsley, vinegar, stock, Madeira or sherry

This was a great affair in its day. It is still a formidable, nay, even a respectable-looking dish, with a kind of bulky magnificence which appears imposing at the head of a long board. Have a quart of good stock ready for the sauce, made of beef or veal, seasoned with onion, carrot, and turnip. Rub the fish with salt over night, taking off the scales, but do not wash it. When to be dressed wash it clean, then quickly dash hot water over the upper side, and with a blunt knife remove the slime which will ooze out, taking great care not to break the skin. Do the same to the other side of the fish; then place it on the strainer, wipe it clean, and plunge it into a turbot-kettle of boiling water with a handful of salt and a half-pint of vinegar. It must be entirely covered, and will take from thirty to forty minutes' slow boiling. Set it to drain, slide it carefully on a deep dish, and glaze with beat yolks of eggs, over which strew fine bread-crumbs, grated lemon-peel, pepper, and salt. Stick numerous bits of butter over the fish and set it before a clear fire, strewing more crumbs, lemon-peel, and minced parsley over it and basting with the butter. In the meanwhile thicken the stock with butter kneaded in flour and strain it, adding to it half a hundred oysters nicely picked and bearded, and a glassful of their liquor, two glasses of Madeira or sherry, the juice of a lemon, the hard meat of a boiled lobster cut down, and the soft part pounded. Boil this sauce for five minutes and skim it well; wipe clean the edges of the dish in which the fish is crisping, and pour the half of the sauce around it, serving the rest in a tureen. Garnish with fried oysters, small fried flounders, and pickled samphire, or slices of lemon.

'Cod's head is also dressed with brown sauce made of the stock with butter nicely browned, and a little mushroom-catsup. This sauce is generally made more piquant than white, by the addition of a few boned anchovies.' – M. D.

This Scots mode of dressing cod is nearly the same as the French *Cabillaud à la Sainte Menehould*, only the cod is then stuffed with either meat or fish forcemeat. Cod may be par-boiled and finished in the oven with the above sauce. Oysters, mussels, or cockles may take the place of lobster. – Id.

Cabbie-Claw[1]

'Cod-fish salted for a short time and not dried in the manner of common salt fish, and boiled with parsley and horseradish. They eat it with egg-sauce, and it is very luscious and palatable.' – Capt. Topham, an English visitor to Edinburgh (1774–5).

I have been unable to find the precise details for the preparation of this old Scottish dish, but give here a modern reconstruction. – F. M. McN.

A codling, parsley, horseradish, salt, pepper, water, egg sauce

Take a freshly caught codling (freshness is essential) of about three and a half pounds in weight; clean and skin it, and wipe

[1] In the Shetland dialect, a young cod is a *kabbilow*. cf. Fr. *cabillaud* and Dutch *kabeljaauw*. – F. M. McN.

132

it dry. Rub the fish inside and out with salt, and let it lie for twelve hours; then hang it up in the open air. If it is a windy day, so much the better; but the fish should be kept out of the direct rays of the sun. Leave for from twenty-four to forty-eight hours, according to the degree of 'highness' desired. Place in a saucepan with sufficient water, heated to boiling-point, to cover. Add three or four sprigs of parsley and a tablespoonful of grated horseradish. Simmer very gently until the fish is cooked, but do not over-cook. Remove the fish, skin, lift all the flesh from the bone, and divide neatly into small pieces. Arrange a border of hot mashed potato on a heated ashet, place the fish in the centre, and cover with egg sauce made with milk and fish stock in equal parts. Serve very hot.

To Dress And Keep Dry Salted Tusk, Ling,[1] Or Cod Fish

(*Mrs. Dalgairns's Recipe*)

Cut in square bits, or put one large piece in water over-night; wash it clean in fresh water, and put it on to boil in cold for one hour and a half; then cool the water, so that the fish may be easily handled; take it out of the saucepan and pick out the loose bones and scrape it clean without taking off the skin. Put it on in boiling water, and if the fish is too fresh add a little salt with it and let it boil gently from one hour to one and a half. The very thick part will take this time, the thin bits less, to dress. When dished, garnish with hard-boiled eggs and parsley.

Plain boiled parsnips and a butter tureen of egg sauce are served with it.[2]

When the fish is put on the second time some people prefer boiling it in milk and water. To keep any of this sort of fish for winter use it ought to be cut or sawed in pieces,

---

[1] There is a Gaelic saying that ling would be the beef of the sea if it had always salt enough, butter enough, and boiling enough.

[2] In Morayshire, dried fish were served with home-made mustard, the seeds, freshly gathered in the cottage garden, being pounded in a mortar.

and when perfectly dry, laid in a small cask or wooden box with oatmeal, oatmeal seeds, or malt dust between each layer.

Dried Fish Pudding

(*Mrs. Dalgairns's Recipe*)

Fish, potatoes, milk, butter

Boil the fish, take off the skin and take out the bones, pound it, and add to it an equal quantity of mashed potatoes moistened with good milk and a bit of butter;[1] put it in a dish, smooth it with a knife, and stick here and there little bits of butter and brown it in a Dutch oven; serve it with egg sauce.

Whiting In The Scots Way

(*Lady Harriet St. Clair's Recipe*)

Whiting, flour, butter, parsley, green onions or chives, broth, cream

Choose small, perfectly fresh fish; rub them in flour till it adheres; lay them in a frying-pan with a good bit of butter; sauté them very slowly. They should not be dry or coloured. Mince some parsley and green onions or chives very finely; put them into some good broth and about two tablespoonfuls of cream; mix it well together and pour it over the whiting before they are quite finished cooking; move them about very gently, not to break them, till they are done. They are very delicate and excellent done in this way, which, though simple, requires great care. No butter should be used but what is required to fire them.

[1] A teaspoonful or more of made mustard may be added. – F. M. McN.

Blawn (Wind-Blown) Fish

(Traditional Method)

Obtain the fish – whiting, haddock or other white fish – as
fresh as possible, clean and skin them, take out the eyes,
cover the fish over with salt, immediately after which take
them out and shake off the superfluous salt, pass a string
through the eye-holes, and hang them up to dry in a passage,
or some place where there is a current of air; the next morning take them off, just roll them lightly in a little flour,
broil them gently over a slow fire, and serve very hot, with
a small piece of fresh butter rubbed over each, or serve quite
dry, if preferable.

When I was a child in Orkney, this was my favourite breakfast dish. Many years
later, I was much gratified to find the following passage in a cookery book by the great
Soyer:

'Of all the modes of preparing and dressing whitings for breakfast I cannot but
admire and prize the system pursued by the Scotch, which renders them the most light,
wholesome, and delicious food that could possibly be served for breakfast.'

The small whiting, hung up with its skin on, and broiled without being rubbed in
flour, is excellent. A wooden frame, called a *hake*, is used for drying fish. In Orkney
cuiths (which in Shetland they call piltocks and in the Hebrides cuddies) are prepared
in this way, care being taken that the fish are perfectly fresh, newly gutted, and
thoroughly cleaned, and that the salt is rubbed well in along the bones from which the
guts have been removed. They may be either boiled or brandered – if boiled, they are
eaten with butter, melted. They are particularly good with buttered bere bannocks or
wheaten-meal scones and tea. – F. M. McN.

Haddock In Brown Sauce *(An Excellent Scots Dish)*

> Haddies, caller haddies,
> Fresh an' loupin' in the creel!
> – *Old Edinburgh Street Cry.*

> 'A January haddock an' a February hen
> Are no' to be marrowed in the ither months ten.
> – *A Moray Saying.*

(Megs Dods's Recipe)

Clean, cut off the heads, tails, and fins, and skin from six to
eight medium-sized haddock. Take the heads, tails, and
trimmings, with two or three of the fish cut down, and boil
them in a quart of water or broth, with a couple of onions,
some sweet herbs, and a piece of lemon-peel; thicken with

135

plenty of butter and browned flour, and season highly with mixed spices and mushroom catsup; strain the sauce, and when it boils and is skimmed, put in the fish cut into neat pieces, and, if you choose, previously browned in the frying-pan. If there be too little sauce, add some good beef-gravy; put in, if you like, a quarter-hundred of oysters and a glass of their liquor, or some mussels and a little wine. Take out the fish, when ready, with a slice, and pour the sauce, which should be brown, smooth, and thick, around them.

Earth-Dried Skate

'Skate are placed on the damp grass and covered with sods for a day or two. They are too tough if eaten fresh, but seasoned for just the right time they are the most excellent breakfast dish I know. And they make very good soup. . . . Skate must be fried or baked and served with the skin on, never boiled.' – Mortimer Batten.

For breakfast, cut the fish small and fry in butter or bacon fat. – F. M. McN.

Skate are said not to take salt. They are frequently hung up unsalted and eaten 'high' – an acquired taste – as in the Island of Lewis. – Id.

Tatties An' Herrin'

(Traditional But-and-Ben Dish)

'The other day, landing from our boat, we went into a cottar's house just as the gudewife was preparing the family dinner. A pot of new potatoes was boiling on the fire. Looking now and again into the pot, and listening with inclined ear to the sound, actually musical in such a case, of its boiling and bubbling, she was ready at the proper instant to snatch it off the fire, and carrying it to the corner of the kitchen she poured off the water and immediately re-hung it over the fire, shortening the chain by which it was suspended by a link or two, that the fire might not, now that it was water-less, have too much effect upon it. She then got some half-dozen fresh herrings, caught early that morning – herrings large, beautiful, and as silvery-scaled as a salmon – and drying them nicely with a cloth, she placed them flatwise, side by side, on the top of the potatoes in the pot, the lid of which she was careful to fit tightly by means of a coarse kitchen towel, which served at once to cover the contents and to cause the lid to fit so tightly that the steam was effectually retained.

'During quarter of an hour, perhaps, the wife kept an attentive eye on the pot, never once lifting the lid, however, but from time to time raising or lowering a link in the chain as in her judgment was necessary. All being ready at last, she took the pot off the fire and set it on a low stool in the middle of the floor. She then lifted the lid and the cloth, and the room was instantly filled with a savoury steam that made one's mouth water merely to inhale it.

'Occupying each a low chair, we were invited to fall to, to eat without knife, or fork, or trencher, just with our fingers out of the pot as it stood. It was a little startling, but only for a moment. After a word of grace we dipped our hand into the pot and took out a potato, hot and mealy, and with another we took a nip out of the silvery flank of the herring nearest us. It was a mouthful for a king, sir!' – Rev. Alexander Stewart: *Nether Lochaber* (1883).

To Fry Herring (*Scots Fashion*)

> Wha'll buy my caller herrin'?
> They're bonnie fish and dainty fairin'.
> Wha'll buy my caller herrin',
>   New drawn frae the Forth?
>   – Lady Nairne: *Caller Herrin'*.

Fresh herring, oatmeal, pepper, salt, dripping

Cleanse, dry and trim the herring. Score across slantwise in two or three places on each side. Sprinkle with pepper and salt and toss in coarse oatmeal on a sheet of kitchen paper until they are thoroughly coated. An ounce of oatmeal and the same quantity of dripping should be allowed for every two herring. Make the dripping smoking hot in a frying-pan

137

and brown the herring nicely on both sides, allowing them from ten to fifteen minutes. Drain on paper and serve very hot. They may be garnished with parsley and cut lemon.

Another way is to split and bone the herring, flatten them with care and proceed as above. Cook for seven minutes or longer.

In Buchan, vinegar and oatcakes are considered the perfect accompaniment to this dish.

Potted Herring

> Though the casual Govan herring
> Warns us by a sense unerring
> That the dead need but interring –
> *Pisces Benedicte.*
>
> Taken fresh and all unspotted,
> Rolled in vinegar and potted,
> O, it tickles the parotid –
> *Pisces Benedicte.*
>   – Parvus[1] (in Glasgow University Magazine):
>   *Sistette to Fish.*

Fresh herring, salt, peppercorns, cloves, bay leaf, blade of mace, onion (optional), white vinegar, water

Skin, cleanse and head-and-tail six plump medium-sized herring; then split lengthwise. Remove the backbone by lifting one end and prising it away from the flesh with a knife. Sprinkle the fillets with salt and mill black pepper over them. Roll tightly, skin outside, beginning at the tail, and pack into a pie dish or shallow casserole. Distribute the spices – six peppercorns, two cloves, a small bay leaf and a blade of mace – among the fillets. (Some housewives add a small shredded onion.) Pour over just enough vinegar and water – half and half, or rather more vinegar than water – to cover the fish. Cover the dish with a buttered paper or lid, and bake in a slow oven for fully an hour,[2] then uncover and bake for twenty minutes longer. Serve cold with potato salad.

The spices used vary considerably. Some add only a bay leaf. Perhaps the best potted herring I ever tasted were very fresh and very plump Lochfynes, to which nothing but salt and pepper, vinegar and water was added. – F. M. McN.

[1] The late Rt. Hon. Walter Elliot, M.P.
[2] Mrs. McIver (1773) says: Pot herring for four hours in a slow oven.

138

Pickled Herring

(*Mrs. Dalgairns's Recipe*)

Salt herring, onions, brown sugar, pepper, salt, vinegar

Take half a dozen Lochfyne herring out of brine. Split them down the back and soak them in cold water overnight. In the morning clean them nicely and cut them crosswise into strips of half an inch in width. Put them into a deep dish with six onions sliced thin. Sprinkle them with pepper and salt and three tablespoonfuls of brown sugar. Pour on enough vinegar to cover them. They will be ready to use in time for supper, and will keep for a week or more in a cool place.

To Dress Red Herring, Sardinias, And Buffed (Pickled) Herring

(*Meg Dods's Recipe*)

Red herring, oil or butter

Skin, open, and trim red herring. If old and dry, pour some hot small beer or water over them and let them steep a half-hour, or longer if hard. Broil them over a clear fire at a considerable distance, or before the fire; rub them with good oil or fresh butter while broiling, and rub on a little more when they are served. Serve them very hot with cold butter, or with melted butter and mustard, and mashed potatoes or parsnips.

'Steep pickled herrings from one to two days and nights, changing the water if they be very salt. Hang them up on a stick pushed through the eyes, and broil them when wanted. These are called *buffed* herrings in Scotland, and are used at breakfast or supper.' – M. D.

Herring, in the form of the heavily salted and heavily smoked red herring, were long the staple diet of the masses. They did not always please. The sixteenth-century poet, Alexander Montgomery, writes:

> This is no life that I lead up a land
> On raw reid herring reisted in the reek.[1]

The red herring is the forerunner of the kipper, which is split before curing. The development of mildly smoked fish was brought about by quick railway transport.

[1] *Reisted in the reek*, smoke-dried.

139

To Boil Salmon

(Meg Dods's Recipe)

Scale or clean the fish without any unnecessary washing or handling, and without cutting it too much open. Have a roomy and well-scoured fish-kettle, and if the salmon be very large and thick, when you have placed it on the strainer and in the kettle, fill up and amply cover it with cold spring water, that it may heat gradually. Throw in six ounces of salt to a gallon of water. If only a jole or quarter is boiled, it may be put in with warm water. In both cases take off the scum carefully, and let the fish boil slowly, allowing ten minutes to the pound; if the piece is not heavier than five or six pounds, then the time must be less; but it is even more difficult to fix the time that fish should boil than the length of time that meat requires. Experience, and those symptoms which the eye of a practised cook alone can discern, must fix the point, and nothing is more disgusting and unwholesome than underdone fish. It may be probed. The minute the boiling of any fish is completed, the fish-strainer must be lifted and rested across the pan, to drain the fish. Throw a soft cloth or flannel in several folds over it. It would become soft if permitted to soak in the hot water. Dish on a hot fish-plate with a napkin under.

'Besides the essences to be used at discretion, which are now found on every sideboard of any pretension, shrimp, anchovy and lobster sauce are served with salmon; also plain melted butter; and where the fish is not fresh, and served in what is esteemed by some as the greatest perfection – crisp, curdy, and creamy – it is the practice to send up a sauce tureen of the plain liquor in which it was boiled. Fennel and butter are still heard of for salmon, but are nearly obsolete. Sliced cucumber is often served with salmon, and indeed with all boiled fish. Mustard is considered an improvement to salmon when over-ripe – beginning to spoil, in short; salmon may then be boiled with horse-radish. *Garnish* with a fringe of curled green parsley and slices of lemon. The carver must help a slice of the thick part with a smaller one of the thin, which is the fattest and the best liked by those in the secret. *Carême* skins salmon – a bad practice.'
– M. D.

'Bantrach Choinnich Eachainn's (Kenneth Hector's widow's) boiled salmon tasted better than that of anyone else. Her recipe was to boil the salmon overnight and leave it all night in the water it was boiled in. In the morning each slice was encased in its own jelly.' – Osgood Mackenzie: *A Hundred Years in the Highlands.*

'When I boiled salmon in the island of Mull, I always did it in sea-water, so that shows how much salt it can stand.' – Mrs. Lily Macleod.

Salmon and trout in prime condition need no *court-bouillon.* With hot salmon serve Hollandaise sauce; with cold, mayonnaise.

'*Shepherd:* Tibbie was for cuttin't in twa cuts, but I like to see a sawmon served up in its integrity.

'*Tickler:* And each slice should run from gill to tail.

'*Shepherd:* Alang the shouthers and the back and the line, in that latitude, for the thick; and alang the side and the belly and the line, in that latitude, for the thin; but nae short-curd till in the mouth. . . . The kyeanne pepper – the mustard – the vinegar – the catshop – the Harvey sass – the yest – the chovies! Thank ye, Dolly, my dear. Mair butter, Tickler. North – put the mashed potatoes on the part o' my plate near the saut – and the roond anes a bit ayont. Tappy – the breid; and meanwhile, afore yokin' to our sawmon, what say ye, sirs, to a bottle o' porter?'

– Christopher North: *Noctes Ambrosianae.*

'A kettle of fish is a fête-champêtre of a particular kind, which is to other fête-champêtres what the piscatory eclogues of Brown or Sannazaro are to pastoral poetry. A large cauldron is boiled by the side of a salmon river, containing a quantity of water, thickened with salt to the consistence of brine. In this the fish is plunged when taken, and eaten by the company *fronde super viridi.* This is accounted the best way of eating salmon by those who desire to taste the fish in a state of extreme freshness. Others prefer it after being kept a day or two, when the curd melts into oil, and the fish becomes richer and more luscious. The more judicious gastronomes eat no other sauce than a spoonful of the water in which the salmon has been boiled, together with a little pepper and vinegar.' – Scott: *St. Ronan's Well,* Note.

'The river Beauly is famous for its salmon fishing. . . . As Kilmorack is at the head of the run, and only a short distance from the sea, the pool below the Fall is thronged with fish, and the curious may here, as at Glenmoriston, witness the frequent and arduous attempts of the fish to leap the rock and pass the Fall. They sometimes light upon the rock and are captured. This suggested to the former Lairds of Lovat the well-known feat with which they used to regale their visitors: a kettle was placed upon the flat rock beside the fall, and kept full of boiling water. Into this the fish sometimes fell, in their attempts to ascend, and being boiled in the presence of the company, were presented to dinner. This was a delicacy in the gastronomical art unknown to Monsieur Ude.' – R. Carruthers: *The Highland Note-Book.*

Salmon Fritters

(*Mrs. Dalgairns's Recipe*)

Salmon, potatoes, cream, egg, lard or beef dripping

Cut small some cold boiled salted salmon; pound some boiled potatoes, moistened with cream and the yolk of an egg beaten; mix them together and make it into small fritters and fry them of a light brown in fresh lard or beef dripping; serve them with hard-boiled eggs, cut in quarters. For sauce, melt two ounces of butter with a little cream and flour mixed, and add, when it is hot, a dessert-spoonful of soy and two of mushroom catsup.

Mrs. Macleod's Salmon Steaks

Salmon, flour, salt, pepper, cayenne, thick cream, anchovy essence, dry sherry

Cut two nice-sized steaks in half lengthwise and dip in seasoned flour, to which should be added a dusting of cayenne pepper. Lay them in a well-buttered flat fire-proof dish. Mix two tablespoonfuls of thick cream with a teaspoonful of anchovy essence. Add pinches of salt and pepper and a tablespoonful of dry sherry. Pour the mixture over the steaks and bake in a moderate oven about twenty-five minutes. Serve in the dish.

Tweed Kettle (*Salmon Hash*)

Fresh salmon, shallot or chives, parsley, salt, pepper, mace wine vinegar or white wine, water

Cut a pound of fresh salmon, freed from skin and bone, into one-inch cubes. Season with salt, pepper and a tiny pinch of mace, and place in a fish-kettle or saucepan with a minced shallot or a tablespoonful of chopped chives. Add half a cup of water and a quarter cup of wine vinegar or white wine, bring to the boil and simmer very gently for about thirty-five minutes. Add a tablespoonful of chopped parsley shortly before dishing up.

A few small mushrooms, chopped and cooked in butter for ten minutes, may be added, or a few cooked shrimps, or one or two chopped hard-boiled eggs. Another variant has a dash of anchovy sauce.

Serve hot with fresh girdle scones or a border of creamed potatoes, or cold garnished with cress and cucumber.

In Edinburgh, in the mid-nineteenth century, 'in a house down a stair in Broughton Street, much frequented by booksellers' clerks, one might obtain, at the modest charge of sevenpence, a liberal helping from a succulent dish called "salmon hash", better known as "Tweed Kettle", and it could be obtained all day long, hot or cold to taste.

'Shocking to relate, it could be got all the year round and always excellently cooked. The landlady, being a Kelso woman, was familiar with the fish and its capabilities.'
                                    – James Bertram: *Books, Authors and Events.*

Pickled Salmon

(*Mrs. Dalgairns's Recipe*)

Salmon, pepper, salt, allspice, mace, vinegar, water, sweet oil

Cut the salmon into pieces, boil it as for eating, and lay it on a dry cloth until the following day. Boil two quarts of good vinegar with one of the liquor the fish was boiled in, one ounce of whole black pepper, half an ounce of allspice, and four blades of mace. Put the salmon into something deep and pour over it the prepared vinegar when cold. A little sweet oil put upon the top will make it keep a twelve-month.

Spiced Salmon

(*Mrs. Dalgairns's Recipe*)

Salmon, salt, pepper, cinnamon, vinegar, water

Mix together, in the proportion of one-third of salt-and-water to one pint of vinegar, one ounce of whole black pepper, and one ounce of cinnamon. Cut the salmon into slices and boil it in this; when cold pack it close in a pan and pour over it the liquor it was boiled in, with the spices, so as to cover it completely; cover the pan closely to exclude the air.

Potted Salmon Roe

(*Old Tweedside Recipe*)

Salmon roe, milk, water, salt, saltpetre, spirit of nitre, lard

Take the roe from a fish as nearly spawning as possible. Wash the roe well in milk-and-water, and then in cold water, till it come clean off. Afterwards put the roe in a sieve and

143

drain fifteen minutes. To salt them take eight ounces of salt to three pounds of spawn and let them lie in the brine forty-eight hours. Lay them on a board about three-fourths of a yard from the fire, letting them remain there about half a day. Bruise them well with a roller, then put them into a pot and press them well down. Put on them in the proportion of eight drops of spirit of nitre and as much saltpetre as will lie upon a sixpence to every pound of spawn. Cover them with a piece of writing-paper upon which lay a coating of hog's lard as cold as it will spread, then tie over all a piece of dressed sheepskin, and keep in a warm place summer and winter.

'This recipe was got from Easton, Hawick, one of the best fishers in the south of Scotland, who prepared and sold salmon roe at a high price.' – Meg Dods.

Smoked Cod's Roe may be prepared in the same manner.

Friar's Fish-In-Sauce

(*Meg Dods's Recipe*)

Red or other trout, or carp, or perch; salt, mixed spices, onions, cloves, mace, black and Jamaica peppercorns, claret or Rhenish wine, anchovy, lemon, cayenne, flour, butter, stock

Clean the fish very well; if large, they may be divided or split. Rub them inside with salt and mixed spices. Lay them in the stew-pan and put in nearly as much good stock as will cover them, with a couple of onions and four cloves stuck in them, some Jamaica and black peppercorns, and a bit of mace; add when the fish have stewed a few minutes, a couple of glasses of claret or Rhenish wine, a boned anchovy, the juice of a lemon, and a little cayenne. Take up the fish carefully when ready, and keep them hot. Thicken the sauce with butter kneaded in browned flour; add a little mushroom catsup and a few pickled oysters, if approved; the sauce, though less piquant, is more delicate without catsup. Having skimmed and strained, pour it over the fish.

'Meg Dods states that a fish boiled in the pickling-kettle, when, perhaps, some dozens of cut fish are preparing for the London market, is superbly done, meltingly rich, and of incomparable flavour. Such a treat is to be procured only at the fishing-stations; at which, Mrs. Dods slyly remarks, assizes and presbyteries are always held.'
                                        – R. Carruthers: *The Highland Note-Book.*

Burn Trout

'Butter and burn trout are kittle meat for maidens.' – Old Saying.

Burn trout are improved in flavour when slightly salted and allowed to lie overnight. Next day, wipe them, sprinkle again with salt and a little pepper, dip in milk and roll in coarse oatmeal. Cook very quickly in smoking hot lard, browning them on both sides, and serve with lemon and butter.

An Angler's breakfast: Plump burn trout fried in oatmeal, accompanied with fried tomatoes and thick slices of brown bread and turnip-yellow butter.

On a wild spot within the Ballochiebuie Forest, with Lochnagar towering above it, stands one of the most delightful of the Royal Shiels, once a favourite picnic site of Queen Victoria when in residence at Balmoral. Close by flows the Garbh Allt, where John Brown often fished. The Queen records, 'When we came back to the little Shiel, after walking for an hour, we had tea. Brown had caught some excellent trout and cooked them with oatmeal, which the dear Empress (Eugénie) liked extremely, and said would be her dinner.'
                    – *Leaves from a Journal of Our Life in the Highlands* (1846–61).

Home-Smoked Fish

'Home-smoked fish are best because the fish are perfectly fresh when they go into the shed, instead of being the remnants of what has not been sold fresh. As we don't intend to keep them longer than three or four days, we neither over-salt nor over-smoke them.

'Fresh out of the sea, our fish go into a brine bath – a saturated solution of herring-salt diluted with twice its own volume (of water). If the fish has been cut open or skinned so that the water penetrates it more quickly, it remains only about an hour in this solution. Herrings, trout and flat fish go into the brine just as they leave the water and are not "drawn" until they come out of it, five or six hours, according to the weather. They are then hung by the tails till drained and ready for smoking in the old damp stable.[1]

'The only wood available is the silver birch, which gives the sweetest and best flavour. All the sawdust is kept from the wood-yard and thoroughly dried. It is spread about four inches deep on a flag on the cobbled floor, and having been set going by the use of a drop of methylated spirit, it smoulders for hours. A damp smoke and no heat is needed, and the fish, hung from the roof, are soon a rich golden-brown.

'A few green birch chips, a handful of peat, and one or two fir cones sprinkled over the sawdust, improve the flavour. This process occupies from twelve to thirty-six hours, according to your tastes.' – Mortimer Batten.

To Kipper Herring

(*Traditional Recipe*)

Kippers are taken while fresh, and split up. They are then cleaned and thrown into vats with plenty of salt, where they are allowed to lie for a few minutes. Finally they are spread out on tenterhooks or racks, and hung up for eight hours' smoking.[2]

'Some years ago, when staying at a fishing-port on Lochfyneside, I used to watch the herring-boats sail in at dawn and unload their cargo, which was run straight up to the kippering-sheds. Here the fish were plunged into a brine bath and thereafter hung up to smoke over smouldering oak chips, while their colour changed slowly from silver to burnished copper. We ate them, fragrant and succulent, for breakfast next morning, with buttered baps, crisp oatcakes and hot tea.

'I sent a box of these "white" (lightly smoked) kippers to a friend in London. "Gold would not buy these here," she wrote in acknowledgment.' – F. M. McN.

To Dry Herring without Salt (Old Hebridean Method). 'The Natives preserve and dry their Herring without Salt, for the space of eight months, provided they be taken after the tenth of September; they use no other art in it, but take out their Guts, and then, tying a rush about their Necks, hang them by pairs upon a rope made of Heath, cross a House, and they eat well, and free from Putrefaction.'
 – Martin: *Description of the Western Islands* (1703).

[1] 'I have never found a wooden shed successful.' – M.B.
[2] Kippers are excellent grilled, fried, or lightly poached, or made into savouries.

To Smoke Finnan Or Aberdeen Haddock

(Mrs. Dalgairns's Recipe)

> The Buchan bodies throu' the beech
> Their bunch o' Findrums cry,
> An' skirl out baul', in Norland speech,
> 'Guid speldings fa' will buy?'
>   – Robert Fergusson: *Leith Races*

Clean the haddock thoroughly and split them, take off the heads, put some salt on them, and let them lie two hours, or all night, if they are required to keep more than a week; then, having hung them two or three hours in the open air to dry, smoke them in a chimney over peat or hardwood sawdust.

When there is not a chimney suitable for the purpose they may be done in an old cask open at both ends, into which put some sawdust with a red-hot iron in the midst; place rods of wood across the top of the cask, tie the haddock by the tail in pairs, and hang them on the sticks to smoke; the heat should be kept as equal as possible, as it spoils the fish to get alternately hot and cold; when done, they should be of a fine yellow colour, which they should acquire in twelve hours at furthest. When they are to be drest, the skin must be taken off. They may be boiled or broiled, and are generally used for breakfast.

'When kept above twenty-four hours, they lose much of their delicacy.' – Meg Dods.

Findon (pronounced Finnan) is a fishing-hamlet in the Mearns, about six miles south of Aberdeen. It stands on an exposed hillside, looking out to the North Sea and a rocky coastline. Here the now widely renowned finnan-haddie originated. The fish-wives cured their husbands' catches of inshore fish, some for home consumption and some to be packed and dispatched by stage-coach to Edinburgh. In the eighteenth century, the hard, salty, peat-cured haddock were known as Findrums. In the early nineteenth century they were modified to the finnans we know today. The inauguration of trawling led inevitably to a drift from Findon to Torry, now a part of the city of Aberdeen and its main fisherfolks' quarter. Now (in the mid-twentieth century) besides the ruins of old cottages some dozen blue-slated houses remain and the population is only about forty, many of whom travel to work in Torry. – F. M. McN.

'A Finnan haddock dried over the smoke of the sea-weed and sprinkled with salt-water during the process, acquires a relish of a very peculiar and delicate flavour, inimitable on any other coast than that of Aberdeenshire. Some of our Edinburgh philosophers tried to produce their equal in vain. I was one of a party at a dinner where the philosophical haddocks were placed in competition with the genuine Finnan-fish. These were served round without distinction whence they came; but only one gentleman out of twelve present espoused the cause of philosophy.'
       – Sir Walter Scott: Note to Boswell's *Tour to the Hebrides.*

'A Findon Haddock, skinned, rubbed with butter, broiled and served with pats of fresh cold butter is the kind of English (sic) fare which no chef, however gifted he may be, can hope to match on the Continent.' – André Simon: *Basic English Fare.*

Arbroath Smokies

Smokies, pepper, butter

Heat the fish on both sides (it has already been cooked in the long smoking process), open it out, remove the backbone, mill black pepper over the fish, spread with butter, close up and heat for a few minutes in the oven or under the grill. (In the old days it was brandered.) Serve piping hot.

The smokie, like the finnan-haddie, makes an excellent savoury.

The Arbroath smokie originated in the near-by fishing-hamlet of Auchmithie. Day after day, during the season, the men set out with baited lines after the haddock.

'With the setting of the sun,' writes a native, 'the boats come home and in the back-houses the lamps are lit. Up the brae come the creels of fish, and soon every woman and child is gutting, cleaning and salting. Little sticks of wood are stuck into the haddocks gills, and two by two, tied tail to tail, they are hung on little wooden spits high up in the old-fashioned lums (chimneys) . . . curing in the smoke of the fire; then they are taken down, grey black and sooty – but once remove the skins and what a delicious sight you see! Crisp, golden outer flesh paling into pure whiteness near the bone.'

In their picturesque fisher-dress the 'luckies' (gudewives) went round the countryside with their creels strapped to their shoulders.

As the demand grew, 'smoke-pits' were sunk in the ground and the fish were hung over halved whisky barrels and smoked over chips of some special wood. (Oak and silver birch are commonly used in smoking fish.)

Near the beginning of the nineteenth century, a community of Auchmithie fisherfolk settled in Arbroath and continued to practise their ancient craft; but it was not until near the end of the century that the industry as we know it today began to develop, and the name *Auchmithie* gave place to *Arbroath*.

Whereas the finnan-haddie is split and cured to a golden-yellow, the Arbroath smokie is closed and is smoked to a sooty copper. – F. M. McN.

To Kipper Salmon

(A Modern Method)

A fresh salmon, herring-salt, Demerara sugar, olive oil, rum or whisky

Cut the salmon in half lengthwise, remove the backbone and wipe the fish carefully with a dry cloth. Lay the halves side by side on a suitable tray and cover entirely, above and below, with herring-salt. Leave for twenty-four hours. Wipe off the surplus salt and hang the sections to drip in a still, cold atmosphere for, say, six hours. Replace them on the clean tray, smother them with olive oil and leave for five or six hours; then drain carefully and rub off the oil with a cloth soaked in rum or whisky. Cover them with Demerara sugar as you did previously with salt and leave for the same time or longer. (This removes the salt and also helps to cure.) Wipe off the sugar, hang the fish again to drain and treat once more to the olive oil process. Wipe off completely with the spirit-soaked cloth, and the fish is ready for smoking.

The salmon may be smoked in an ordinary kiln. The fire should be set with peat, oak chips and oak sawdust, and lit about 6 p.m. on two successive evenings. During the day, when the fire has gone out, the fish should be left hanging in the kiln. After two firings, the fish is ready for the table.

Some connoisseurs hold that with a proportion of juniper wood as fuel the fish acquires a delicate flavour.

Smoked trout is equally good.

'It sounds a lengthy process and rather an expensive one, but in both respects it sounds more formidable than it is. It means that instead of having to give that salmon away, you have a beautiful side-table dish which will keep from two to three weeks if taken ordinary care of (i.e. not kept continuously in a centrally heated room).'
Mortimer Batten.

'A chunk of smoked salmon is an excellent thing to take on the hill, though normally one slices it tissue-thin (as one should slice smoked roe-deer venison). – Id.

'A salmon-bone, with some rough pickings left, makes an admirable grill. The bone cut out of a kippered salmon should be left rough for this purpose. Seasoned with pepper and salt, broiled and buttered, it is quite an epicure's breakfast morsel.'
– Meg Dods.

'These fish, dried in the turf smoke of their cabins, or shielings, formed a savoury addition to the mess of potatoes mixed with onions, which was a principal part of their winter food.' – Scott: *Guy Mannering*.

Kippered salmon is mentioned in the Household Book of James V (1513–42).

'As for her (Kate Archy's) kippers, who nowadays could settle like her the exact quantities of salt, sugar and smoke each dried salmon and grilse required, to suit the date of their consumption, whether immediate or deferred, confidentially imparted to her by the dear calculating mother? Until salmon close time ended the family was never disgraced through being out of salmon or wonderful kipper, not to mention venison and venison hams.'
– Osgood Mackenzie: *A Hundred Years in the Highlands*.

'We caught it one summer's day when the world was a kaleidoscope of azure sky and peat-brown water and the dancing green of silver-birch leaves. It was a fighting fish caught on light tackle, and it took the better part of an hour to land. I forget exactly what it weighed, but it was around a dozen pounds, and we were mighty pleased with ourselves. . . . Discreet inquiries led us to the little man.[1] . . . (He worked up a stair in a back street and he was a great expert in the smoking of salmon.) . . . A week later we got our fish back. It was smooth, stiff, succulent, its pinky-brown flesh just ripe for cutting in not-too-thin slices and wolfing with a squeeze of lemon juice and a touch of red pepper. I have never known smoked salmon taste so good.'

– Gastrologue in *The Scotsman* (March, 1959).

To Dress Smoked Haddock

(From an old coverless book on Cottage Cookery)

Findon, Aberdeen, and St. Andrews highly smoked split haddock: broil over or cook in front of a quick clear fire; when ready rub butter well into them and serve piping hot.

Arbroath and Auchmithie highly smoked closed haddock: heat on both sides, open them out, take out the backbone, spread with butter, close up, place in the oven a few minutes, and serve.

Eyemouth and Montrose lightly smoked haddock: cook in a frying-pan with bacon or smoked pork and a little water, with a lid on to keep in the steam.

Finnan-Haddie *(Fisherwife's Fashion)*

Skin a finnan-haddie, and cut it into pieces. Lay these in a stew-pan with a dessertspoonful of butter. Put on the lid closely and steam for five minutes. Now break a teaspoonful of cornflour with a little milk and add more milk – about a breakfastcupful in all. Pour over the fish and butter, bring it to the boil, and cook for a few minutes. Take out the pieces of fish, lay them nicely on a dish, and pour the sauce over them.

[1] In Edinburgh.

Ham And Haddie

A smoked haddock, thin slices of smoked ham, pepper

The pale (lightly smoked) Moray Firth haddie is specially suitable for this dish. Skin a good-sized fish (first heating and clapping the skin) and cut into neat pieces. Fry the ham, then remove and keep hot while you fry the fish in the ham fat, adding a little butter if required, and turning once. Season with pepper, and serve the ham round the haddie.

Another way is to cook the haddie along with the ham or bacon and a little water under a close-fitting lid.

'It is altogether delectable. . . . It was worth coming to Glasgow to discover such a dish. . . . The combination of fried smoked ham and haddock is perfect, perfect as the wedding of bacon and egg.' – L. S. Gulliver: *So This is Glasgow.*

To Fry Sillocks

(*Sillocks are the fry of the saith or coal-fish, a variety of cod.***)**

Sillocks, salt, oatmeal, butter

'The perfect dish of sillocks must be caught and cooked by the consumers. When the moon rises on a late summer's night, you must fish far out on a sea moved only by the slow, broad Atlantic swell. And the little mountain of sillocks, the reward of cold but exciting hours, must be "dite" (cleaned) in a moonlit rockpool. Then home at cockcrow.

'Around the kitchen fire, while the rest of the household sleep, come the happy rites of cooking and eating. Each tiny, headless fish, wrapped in a stout jacket of salted oatmeal, is popped into a pan of hot butter. There they bounce and spit while the fishers, ringed round pan and fire, exquisitely thaw. At last, richly browned and curled into fantastic shapes, and so tender they almost fall to pieces, they are dished.

'Sillock-eating at the kitchen table dispenses with knives and forks. You lift a sillock gently between thumb and forefinger, snip off the tail, press the plump sides – and the backbone shoots forth! The delicious morsel left – hot, crisp

151

oatmeal and sweet, melting fish – you eat on buttered "bere" bread, a darkly brown, flatly sour scone.'

Note. – This recipe won a prize many years ago in a competition in *Everyman*.

Crappit Heids[1]

(*North-East*)

Formerly a favourite supper dish all over Scotland. It is mentioned in *Guy Mannering*.

'Run up to Miss Napier's upo' the Squaur, and say I wad be sair obleeged till her gin she wad len' me that fine receipt o' hers for crappit heids.' ...
– George MacDonald: Robert Falconer.

(*Meg Dods's Recipe*)

Heads of haddock, forcemeat

The original Scots farce was simply oatmeal, minced suet or butter, pepper, salt, and onions made into a coarse forcemeat for stuffing the heads of haddock and whiting. Modern crappit heads are farced with the fleshy parts of a boiled lobster or crab, minced, a boned anchovy, the chopped yolk of an egg, grated bread or pounded biscuit, white pepper, salt, cayenne, a large piece of butter broken down into bits, with beat eggs to bind, and a little oyster liquor. A plainer and perhaps as suitable stuffing may be made of the roe of haddock or cod parboiled, skinned, and minced, mixed with double its bulk of pounded rusks or bread-crumbs, a good piece of butter, shred parsley, and seasonings, with an egg to cement the forcemeat. Place the crappit or stuffed heads on end in the bottom of a buttered stew-pan, pour the fish-soup gently over them, cover and boil a half-hour.

(*Isle of Lewis*)

The heads and livers of fresh haddock, oatmeal, pepper, salt, milk

Chop the livers, which must be perfectly fresh, mix them with an equal quantity of raw oatmeal, add pepper and salt, and

[1] 'To *crap*: to fill, to stuff. Teut. *kroppen*.' – Jamieson. Called also *Stappit Heids*.

bind with milk. Stuff the heads with this mixture, and boil them with the fish. The liquor makes good stock for fish soup.

A similar stuffing is made with cods' livers, but the body, not the head, is stuffed, through the gullet.

Cropadeu[1]

Oatmeal, water, haddock liver

Take oatmeal and water, make a dumplin; put in the middle a haddock's liver, season it well with pepper and salt; boil it well in a cloth as you do an apple dumplin. The liver dissolves in the oatmeal and eats very fine.

Cod-Liver Bannock (*Bonnach Grùan*)

(*Isle of Barra*)

A cod's liver, pepper, salt, baking-soda

Take the liver of a fair-sized cod, fresh from the sea, and let it lie overnight in salted water. Mince roughly, or, better, tear up with the fingers, removing all the stringy bits. Mix in a bowl with a tablespoonful of oatmeal, add a pinch of baking soda, and season with pepper and salt. Form into a bannock (a flat round), put it on a plate, and place in a pot of boiling water. Put the fish over it, and let it cook slowly till ready. Or the cod's gullet may be stuffed with the mixture.

In Skye this dish is called *Bonnach Donn* (Brown Bannock). A recipe obtained there adds 'a small onion chopped', but omits baking-soda, and the liver is not steeped overnight, but merely washed well.

[1] A Scots dish from Mrs. Glasse's *Art of Cookery* (Edinburgh, 1747).

153

Shetland Fish Liver Dishes

The livers, which must be perfectly fresh, make a rich and nourishing stuffing. (Cod liver is richest in oil.) In Shetland, where they are much used, a special utensil called a panna-brad (Isl. *panna*, kettle, and *brad*, melting) is used for melting fish livers, and the oil obtained is stored for winter use.

Haggamuggie: A sort of piscatorial haggis. Wash the muggie (stomach) of a fish, tie the small end tightly with fine string, fill two-thirds full with a stuffing made by breaking up the liver with the fingers, mixing it with an equal quantity of lightly toasted, fine oatmeal, and seasoning with salt and pepper. Tie the open end about an inch down so that it does not slip off. Plunge into boiling salted water and boil for twenty-five or thirty minutes. Drain and serve with hot potatoes. The muggie is eaten along with its contents.

Stap: Wash some haddock livers and dissolve slowly (for about an hour) in a small earthenware crock set in a pan of boiling water. Add the flaked flesh from the heads of the boiled haddock, season and serve with the fish.

Slot: Beat together a cod's roe (skinned) and quarter of a ling liver. Add salt and pepper and sufficient barley meal to bind (three or four ounces), making it not too stiff. Drop in spoonfuls into boiling fish stock, cook for twenty or twenty-five minutes and serve with fresh boiled fish.

Liver Burstin: Dissolve sillock livers as for stap, and mix to a soft consistency with burstin (see p. 273). Season and serve hot.

Gree'd Fish: Melt the livers of any fresh white fish, remove any sediment and strain over the cooked fish. Sprinkle with salt and pepper and serve hot.

Kroppen or *Krappin:* Fish liver and meal thoroughly mixed and seasoned, stuffed into a fish head, and boiled. cf. *Crappit Heids.*

Krus or *Liver-krus:* A piece of dough (oatmeal and water, with a pinch of salt) made in the shape of a cruse (small earthenware bowl), filled with livers, and baked on the hearth. cf. *Cropadeu.*

Liver-flakki: 'Two speldit, suket piltiks,[1] laid together with livers between them and roasted on the hearth.'

Mugildens: 'Piltiks or silliks roasted with their livers inside them.'

Sangster: 'A *brüni* (bannock) made of sillik livers and bere burston.'
— From *A Glossary of the Shetland Dialect*, by J. S. Angus.

Kiossed Heids (*Shetland*)

These are fish heads rolled in a cloth and put into the crevice of a stone wall, where they are left until they acquire a gamey flavour. They are then cooked – usually roasted – and are eaten with butter and potatoes.

[1] Split, partially dried coal-fish in their second year.

Oysters Stewed In Their Own Juice (*Scots Fashion*)

(*Lady Harriet St. Clair's Recipe*)

> Come prie,[1] frail man, for gin[2] thou'rt sick,
> The oyster is a rare cathartic
> As ever doctor patient gart[3] lick
> To cure his ails;
> Whether you ha'e the head or heart ache.
> It aye prevails.
>
> – Robert Fergusson.

Oysters, salt

This is an excellent method of dressing them. Take the largest you can get; wash them clean through their own juice; lay them close together in a frying-pan; sprinkle them with a little salt. Do not put one above another. Make them a fine brown on both sides. If one pan is not sufficient, do off more. When they are all done, pour some of their liquor into the pan, mixing it with any that may be left from their cooking. Let it boil for a minute or two. Pour it over the oysters and serve very hot.

Lobster, Haut Goût

(*Supplied to the Cleikum Club by H. Jekyl, Esq.*)

Lobster, white pepper, cayenne, mace, cloves, nutmeg, salt, gravy, butter, soy or walnut catsup or vinegar, red wine

Pick the firm meat from a parboiled lobster or two and take also the inside, if not thin and watery. Season highly with white pepper, cayenne, pounded mace, and cloves, nutmeg, and salt. Take a little well-flavoured gravy – for example, the jelly of roast veal – a few tiny bits of butter, a spoonful of soy or walnut catsup, or of any favourite flavoured vinegar, and a spoonful of red wine. Stew the cut lobster in this sauce ıor a few minutes.

'This is one of those delicate messes which the gourmand loves to cook for himself in a silver dish held over a spirit-lamp, or in a silver stew-pan; the preparation of the morsel being to him the better part of it.' – H. J.

[1] Taste.   [2] If.   [3] Caused.

Partan Pie

(*Meg Dods's Recipe*)

Partan (*crab*), *salt, white pepper, nutmeg, butter, bread, vinegar, mustard* (*optional*)

Pick the meat out of the claws and body; clean the shell nicely and return the whole meat into it,[1] first seasoned with salt, white pepper, and nutmeg; with a few bits of fresh butter and some bread-crumbs. A half-glass of vinegar, beat and heated up with a little made mustard, may be added, and a small quantity of salad-oil substituted for the butter. Brown the meat when laid in the shell with a salamander.

Limpet Stovies (*Isle of Colonsay*)

Limpets,[2] *potatoes, water, pepper, salt, butter*

Gather two quarts of limpets on the rocks at low tide. Put them in a pot, cover them with water, and bring to the boil. Take out the limpets, remove them from the shells, and remove the eyes and the sandy trail. Take three times their quantity of peeled potatoes, put a layer in the bottom of a large round three-legged pot, add a layer of limpets, season with pepper and a little salt, and repeat the operation until they are all used up. Then add two cupfuls of the liquor in which the limpets were scalded and put pieces of butter

---

[1] Flake the claw flesh finely and mix with the soft part. – F. M. McN.

[2] *Limpets:* 'Unattractive rockfish of real gastronomic merit. In many dishes in which cooked oysters appear they could easily and advantageously be replaced by limpets.'
– André Simon.

The contributor of the Limpet Stovies recipe, who is a native of Colonsay, writes: 'I have never seen or heard of the above but in Colonsay, nor have I tasted anything better. They also used to have a dish of fancy seaweed, but the recipe was a secret. I never found out, but a Colonsay woman used to make it for some club in Edinburgh.'

'The Limpet being parboil'd in a very little quantity of water, the Broth is drank to increase Milk in Nurses, and likewise when the Milk proves astringent to the Infants. The Broth of the Black Periwinkle is used in the same cases. It is observed that limpets being frequently eaten in June, are apt to occasion the Jaundice. . . . The tender yellow part of the Limpet which is next to the Shell, is reckoned good nourishment and very easie of digestion.' – Martin: *Description of the Western Islands* (1703).

over the top, using about half a pound for that quantity.
Cover it all with a clean white cloth well rolled in round the
edges, bring to the boil, and hang it high up on the crook
above a peat-fire. Let it simmer slowly for at least an hour.

To Dry Sillocks

Clean the sillocks, which must be perfectly fresh, wash them
well in salt water, and hang them up on a fish-hake outside,
in bunches. Leave them until they are quite hard. They are
eaten uncooked, and are very popular with the school-
bairns of Ultima Thule as a relish with their midday 'piece'
of buttered bere bannock or oatcake.

DISHES OF GAME AND POULTRY

To Roast Red Deer Or Roe

(An Old Holyrood Recipe, supplied to the Cleikum Club by P. Winterblossom, Esq.)

'This was one of those original receipts on which our old beau plumed himself not a little. This mode of dressing venison, he said, had been invented by the Master of the Kitchen to Mary of Guise, and had been ever since preserved a profound secret by the noble family of M——, till the late Earl communicated it to himself.'
– *Annals of the Cleikum Club*.

Venison, spices, claret, vinegar or lemons, butter, walnut catsup

Season the haunch highly by rubbing it well with mixed spices. Soak it for six hours in claret and a quarter-pint of the best vinegar or the fresh juice of three lemons; turn it frequently and baste with the liquor. Strain the liquor in which the venison was soaked; add to it fresh butter melted, and with this baste the haunch during the whole time it is roasting. Fifteen minutes before the roast is drawn remove the paper, baste with butter, and dredge lightly with flour to froth and brown it.

For sauce. – Take the contents of the dripping-pan, which will be very rich and highly flavoured, and a half-pint of clear brown gravy, drawn from venison or full-aged heath mutton. Boil them up together, skim, add a teaspoonful of walnut catsup, and pour the same round the roast. Instead of the walnut catsup, lemon juice or any of the flavoured vinegars most congenial to venison, and to the taste of the gastronome, may advantageously be substituted.

Rob Roy's Pleesure *(Braised Haunch of Venison)*

I first came across this romantically named dish at a dinner given not far from the scene of the exploits of this, the most famous of Highland caterans. Whether cattle-raiding in the fertile 'laigh countrie', or chasing the wild deer in the hills, it was un-

158

thinkable that the redoubtable Rob Roy should return with his followers lacking the wherewithal for a feast.

A traditional prayer or grace on the night of a foray runs:

> He that ordained us to be born,
> Send us mair meat for the morn.
> Come by right or come by wrang,
> Christ, let us not fast owre lang,
> But blithely spend what's blithely got.
> Ride, Rowland, hough's i' the pot!

Whether hough of beef or haunch of venison, the succulent piece would be pot-roasted in a capacious three-legged iron pot, or braised with whatever vegetables and wild herbs lay to hand.

This is a sophisticated version of a dish enjoyed by generations of hunters and raiders. – F. M. McN.

A small haunch of venison, carrots, onions, celery, a pot-posy (bouquet garni), *cloves, salt, pepper, beef or mutton or venison stock, cayenne, claret*

Arrange in the bottom of a casserole or braising-pan two sliced onions stuck with three cloves, three medium carrots sliced, three or four sticks of celery, chopped, a pot-posy (a sprig of thyme, two or three sprigs of parsley, a small dried bay leaf and a blade of mace tied together), and a pint and a half of rich beef or mutton stock, or stock made from the bones and trimmings of the venison. Add salt to taste. Trim the haunch and lay it on the bed of vegetables. The casserole should just hold it. Cover closely, placing a buttered paper between the lid and the meat. Bring to the boil, then cook on the top of the stove or in a moderate oven for three hours, basting the haunch with the juice from time to time. When nearly ready, add pepper and half a pint of claret. When done, remove the haunch to a buttered baking-dish, and spoon over it a little of the juice of the braise. Brush the surface with glaze. Strain the remainder of the juice, add a saltspoonful of cayenne pepper and a little brandy or port, thicken by reducing, and pour over the haunch just as it goes to table.

Mealy potatoes and grilled tomatoes, braised celery, or a purée of chestnuts may be served with the dish. Also rowan jelly.

'The Highlanders of Lochaber, as the saying goes, "pay their daughters' tochers[1] by the light of the Michaelmas moon". Then it was that they were wont to come over the

[1] *Tochers*, dowries.

seven hills and seven waters to help themselves to our cattle when the same were at their fattest and best. It would be a scurry of bare knees down pass and brae, a ring of the robbers round the herd sheltering on the bieldy side of the hill or in the hollows among the ripe grass, a brisk change of shot and blow if alarm arose, and then hie! over the moor by Macfarlane's lantern.[1]

'. . . "It's no theft" (Elrigmore) would urge, "but war on a parish scale: it takes coolness of the head, some valour, and great genius to take some fifty or maybe a hundred head of bestial hot over hill and moor".' – Neil Munro: *John Splendid.*

Venison varies greatly in quality. 'The high ground in summer gives the sweetest pickings, and stags that dwell habitually among the stony tops make incomparably the best venison.' – Alan Gordon Cameron: *The Wild Red Deer of Scotland.*

'A deer would be killed . . . and the venison would be hung up in the spray of a great waterfall, which entirely prevented any blue flies getting at it.'
— Osgood Mackenzie: *A Hundred Years in the Highlands.*

'With venison Burgundy goes as naturally as cold punch with the turtle and with far more obvious reason. The bouquet of the one and the savour of the other were evidently predestined to make a happy love-match.
— Alexander Innes-Shand in *The Fur and Feather Series.*

To Fry Venison Collops

(Supplied to the Cleikum Club by P. Winterblossom, Esq.)

Venison, gravy, lemon or orange, claret, pepper, salt, cayenne, nutmeg

Cut oblong slices from the haunch, or slices neatly trimmed from the neck or loin. Have a gravy, drawn from the bones and trimmings, ready thickened with butter rolled in lightly browned flour. Strain into a small stew-pan, boil, and add a squeeze of lemon or orange and a small glass of claret, pepper to taste, a saltspoonful of salt, the size of a pin's head of cayenne, and a scrape of nutmeg. Fry and dish the collops hot, and pour this sauce over them.

'A still higher goût may be imparted to this sauce by eschalot wine, basil wine, or Tarragon vinegar, chosen as may suit the taste of the eater. If those flavours are not liked, some old venison-eaters may relish a very little pounded fine sugar and vinegar in the gravy, and currant jelly may be served in a sweetmeat glass. Garnish with fried crumbs. This is a very excellent way of dressing venison, particularly when it is not fat enough to roast well.' – P. W.

'The learned in cookery dissent from the Baron of Bradwardine, and hold the roe venison dry and indifferent food, unless when dressed in soup and Scotch collops.'
— Scott: *Waverley*, Note.

[1] On Lochlomondside, the country of the Macfarlanes, who were notorious creagh-lifters, 'Marfarlane's lantern' was a synonym for the moon. – F. M. McN.

'My father was a good hand at breakfast, being especially fond of smoked salmon and venison collops, at which none alive could match Kate Archy (his cook).'
                    – Osgood Mackenzie: *A Hundred Years in the Highlands.*

Venison Pasty

'The princely venison pastry,' – Scott: *Old Mortality*

(*Meg Dods's Recipe*)

Venison, gravy, pepper, salt, mace, allspice, claret or port, eschalot vinegar, onions (optional), pastry

A modern pasty is made of what does not roast well, as the neck, the breast, the shoulder. The breast makes a good pasty. Cut into little chops, trimmings off all bones and skins. Make some good gravy from the bones and other trimmings. Place fat and lean pieces of the meat together, or, if very lean, place thin slices from the firm fat of a leg or a neck of mutton along with each piece. Season the meat with pepper, salt, pounded mace, and allspice. Place it handsomely in a dish and put in the drawn gravy, a quarter-pint of claret or port, a glassful of eschalot vinegar, and, if liked, a couple of onions very finely shred. Cover the dish with a thick crust.

VENISON PASTY CRUST

Flour, butter, eggs, hot water

Make a paste in the proportion of two pounds of flour to more than a pound of butter, with six beat eggs and hot water. Roll it out three times, double it, and the last time let the part intended for the top crust remain pretty thick.

'This is a dish in which ornament is not only allowable but is actually expected. The paste decorations are, however, matters of fancy. Before the pasty is served, if the meat be lean, more sauce made of a little red wine gravy, mixed spices, and the juice of a lemon, may be put in hot. A common fault of venison pasty is being overdone. An hour and a half in a moderate oven is fully sufficient for baking an ordinary-sized pasty – an hour will do for a small one.' – M. D.

Gillie's Venison

(Recipe from the daughter of a gamekeeper in Wester Ross)

Venison, salt, pepper, flour, bacon fat or beef dripping

Cut the meat into one-inch cubes and dip into seasoned flour. Melt plenty of fat in a strong iron pot or earthenware casserole – two inches is a good depth – put in the venison and keep turning until browned all over. Sprinkle with salt and pepper, cover closely, and cook gently for an hour or until the meat is tender. Dish the meat, pour off any superfluous fat, and make gravy in the usual way, thickening it with flour.

This is perhaps the simplest and (say the gillies) certainly the best way of cooking venison, as it completely counteracts the natural dryness of the meat. The recipe may be varied in several ways. One or two sliced onions may be browned in the fat before the venison is put in. One or two chopped rashers of bacon may be added. A few chestnuts, peeled and scraped, may be cooked with the meat. And the laird adds a glass of port wine.

Red blaeberries or jam made from them are good with venison because of their sweet acidity. Serve in a glass dish.

Note. – In most European countries, venison is regarded as a great delicacy, and it is difficult to understand why in Scotland, where it is plentiful and comparatively cheap – cheaper, in fact, than beef – it is so little valued by the urban population. It is true that when shot at the wrong season and, as too often, badly cooked, the flesh of the deer can be rank, tough and unpalatable; but when shot at the right season and cooked with knowledge and care, it is an admirable dish. Only prime venison is worth handling, and what is needed, above all, is a close season to protect the deer. What is also needed is closer co-operation between the sportsman, the butcher, and the customer, so that this desirable food should be available in season to every Scottish housewife.

– F. M. McN.

'From October 21 this year the Red Deer in Scotland have been given legal Close Season . . . for stags from October 21 to June 30, and for hinds from February 16 to October 20.' – *The Scotsman*, October 27, 1962.

To Prepare Grouse

Of the varieties of grouse – wood grouse (capercailzie), black grouse, red grouse, and white grouse (ptarmigan) – the red has the most exquisite flavour. It weighs about nineteen ounces, and should hang for from three to ten days, according to its age and the weather.[1] Young birds do not keep so well as old ones. Soft, downy plumes on the breast and under the wings, pointed wings and rounded spurs are signs of youth.

Pluck the birds carefully so as to avoid breaking the delicate skin, do not wash them, but draw and wipe inside and out with a damp cloth.

'The grouse exists naturally in certain parts of the North of England, but its true home is Scotland. . . . All attempts to use this splendid little game-bird on the Continent of Europe, even in Norway, have failed. The grouse pines away and dies outside of Scotland.' – Moray Maclaren.

'Here is a bird as noble in the eating as any that flies, in which, being indigenous to our shores, we have a monopoly; a remarkable bird which has created a railway traffic of its own, and constrains Parliament to adjourn before the Twelfth of August in order that members may be free to shoot it untrammelled by cares of State. Who can think of the delicately flaking, peat- and ling-scented black flesh of a plump grouse unmoved?' – P. Morton Shand: *A Book of Food*.

'While nearly all the game-birds are good, and some eminently good, grouse seems to me to be the best, to possess the fullest and at the same time the least violent flavour – to have the best consistency of flesh, and to present the greatest variety of attractions in different parts.' – George Saintsbury.

Roast Grouse (*Scots Fashion*)

Prepare as directed above. Put an ounce or two of butter, into which you have worked a little lemon-juice, pepper, and salt, into each bird, but not in the crop. Some cooks stuff the birds with red whortleberries or cranberries, which bring out the flavours well and keep them as moist as butter does. It is essential to avoid dryness. Wrap the birds well with fat bacon and enclose this with greaseproof paper till ten minutes before serving; then remove the wrappings, flour the birds, and brown. Or the bacon and greaseproof paper may be omitted, and the birds basted frequently and freely with butter. The time allotted is twenty to thirty minutes, according to the size and age of the birds. (Pheasant and partridge must be well done, wild duck, solan goose,

[1] 'It was the custom of a hospitable friend of mine in Scotland, who was equally good with rod and gun, to keep a supply of grouse hanging till he could accompany them with salmon caught in a river which was by no means a very early opening one, and I never found birds taste better'. – George Saintsbury.

etc., underdone, but grouse must be removed in the nick of time – neither over nor actually underdone.)

Boil the livers for ten minutes and pound them in a mortar with a little butter, salt, and cayenne, and spread this on pieces of toast large enough to hold a bird. Place this toast under each bird during the last few minutes of roasting, but do not put it into the fat in the pan to get sodden. Serve with fried bread-crumbs, but without gravy in the dish.

The usual accompaniments are chip potatoes, watercress, French beans, mushrooms, and clear gravy. Bread, nut or fruit sauce, and melted butter[1] are also occasionally served. Cranberry or rowan jelly goes very well with grouse, and so do pickled peaches. So does claret.

Roast grouse à la Rob Roy. – Prepare as above, wrapping each bird in slices of fat bacon and sprigs of heather, to be removed before browning.

'M. Soyer wraps the birds when to be roasted in sprigs of heather moistened with a glass of whisky.' – Meg Dods.

'Grouse forms a better solid than anything else I know to finish a fish dinner with – there is some subtle and peculiar appropriateness in its special earthy and dry savour as a contrast to the fishiness.' – George Saintsbury.

'I have always deeply regretted that I did not preserve a French book on game and its cookery which passed through my hands some years ago. The author frankly admitted that grouse do not live in France . . . but, as he very justly observed, some of his friends might have a brace or more sent him by an English friend, and he gave with great pride a recipe for *Grouse à la Dundy*. Dundy, I remember, he defined as being not only the gamiest, *la plus giboyeuse*, city of Scotland, but also renowned for every refinement of taste and luxury – superior, in short, to Peebles itself. And the way they cooked grouse in Dundy was – but that is exactly what I have forgotten.' – Id.

Meg Merrilies Stew

(From 'Guy Mannering')

'Meg, in the meanwhile, went to a great black caldron that was boiling on a fire on the floor, and, lifting the lid, an odour was diffused through the vault which, if the vapours of a witch's caldron could in aught be trusted, promised

---

[1] 'It must be confessed that the thing is still done (the trimming being actually poured over the birds) in Scotland, where they certainly understand cookery, and where they ought to understand that of grouse in particular. But it seems to me an abomination, and it must be remembered that if Scottish cookery, admirable as it is, has a tendency to sin, that tendency is in the direction of what is delicately called "richness", and that this may be an instance. No doubt the counter tendency of the grouse to the original sin of dryness has also to be considered.' – George Saintsbury.

better things than the hell-broth which such vessels are usually supposed to contain.[1] It was, in fact, the savour of a goodly stew, composed of fowls, hares, partridges, and moor-game, boiled in a large mess with potatoes, onions, and leeks, and from the size of the caldron, appeared to be prepared for half a dozen people at least.

'"So ye hae eat naethin' a' day?" said Meg, heaving a large portion of this mess into a brown dish, and strewing it savourily with salt and pepper.

'"Nothing," answered the dominie, "scelestissima! – that is – gudewife!"

'"Hae then," said she, placing the dish before him; "there's what will warm your heart. . . . There's been mony a moonlight watch to bring a' that trade thegither," continued Meg; "the folks that are to eat that dinner thought little o' your game-laws."' – Sir Walter Scott.

'To the admirers of good eating, gipsy cookery seems to have little to recommend it. I can assure you, however, that the cook of a nobleman of high distinction, a person who never reads even a novel without an eye to the enlargement of the culinary science, has added to the Almanach des Gourmands a certain *Potage à la Meg Merrilies de Derncleugh*, consisting of game and poultry of all kinds, stewed with vegetables into a soup, which rivals in savour and richness the gallant messes of Camacho's wedding, and which the Baron of Bradwardine would certainly have reckoned among the *Epulae lautiores*.' – *Blackwood's Magazine*, April, 1817.

'The artist alluded to in this passage is Monsieur Florence, cook to Henry and Charles, late Dukes of Buccleugh, and of high distinction in his profession.'
– (Note to *Guy Mannering* in the Border Edition of the Waverley novels.)

On Dressing Poultry

'MEG'S sauce for fowls was either the national "drappit egg", egg-sauce, parsley and butter, or, if the fowls were of a dark complexion, liver-sauce, as a veil of their dinginess. TOUCHWOOD chose celery-sauce for fowls, and oyster-sauce for turkey; JEKYL preferred lemon-sauce, but often enjoined the Nabob. The best sort of stuffing or forcemeat for poultry was the cause of many disputes. MEG long stood out for sweet stuffing for her turkeys, orthodox apple-sauce

[1] In *Macbeth*, Act IV, Sc. 1, Shakespeare supplies us with a complete recipe for hell-broth in the best manner of the Scottish witches.

for her goose, and a sweet pudding in the belly of her suckling pig. After a feud which lasted three days, the belligerents came to a treaty on the old basis of the *uti possidetis*, though the best stuffing for boiled or roasted poultry or veal was agreed to be – "Crumbs of stale bread, two parts; suet, marrow, or fresh butter, one part; a little parsley, boiled for a minute, and very finely shred; the quarter of a nutmeg grated, a teaspoonful of lemon-peel, grated, allspice and salt – the whole to be worked up to a proper consistence, with two or three yolks of eggs well beat." If for roasted or boiled turkey, pickled oysters chopped, ham or tongue grated, and eschalot to taste may be added. MEG'S sweet stuffing was made by discarding the parsley, ham, oysters, and tongue, and substituting a large handful of currants, picked, rubbed, and dried, as for puddings.'
– *Annals of the Cleikum Club*.

A Stoved Howtowdie,[1] With Drappit Eggs

(*Meg Dods's Recipe*)

A pullet, butter, button onions, spices, herbs (optional), water or broth, eggs, spinach, gravy

Prepare and stuff with forcemeat a young plump fowl.[2] Put it into a yetling concave-bottomed small pot with a close-fitting lid, with button onions, spices, and at least a quarter-pound of butter. Add herbs, if approved. When the fowl has hardened and been turned, add a half-pint or rather more of boiling water or broth. Fit on the lid very close and set the pot over embers. A cloth may be wrapped round the lid if it is not luted on. An hour will do a small fowl, and so in proportion. Have a little seasoned gravy, in which parboil the liver. Poach nicely in this gravy five or six small eggs. Dress them on flattened balls of spinach round the dish, and serve the fowl, rubbing down the liver to thicken the

[1] O. Fr. *hutaudeau*, a pullet.
[2] 'Take the fattest and youngest eerocks (yearlings),' says Meg, 'and the whitest.'

gravy and liquor in which the fowl was stewed, which pour over it for sauce, skimming it nicely, and serving all very hot.

'This is a very nice small Scotch dish. Mushrooms, oysters, forcemeat balls, etc., may be added to enrich it; and celery may be put to the sauce; the spinage may be and often is omitted. Slices of ham may be served round the fowl, or two young boiled or stewed fowls with a small salted tongue between them will make a nice family dinner dish.' – M. D.

'A common and an approved smuggling way of boiling a pullet or howtowdie in Scotland, was in a well-cleaned haggis bag, which must have preserved the juices much better than a cloth. In the days of Popery and good cheer – and they were certainly synonymous, though we do not quite subscribe to the opinion of Dr. Redgill, that no Presbyterian country can ever attain eminence in Gastronomy – in those days of paternosters and venison pasties, stoups of untaxed clarets and oral confession, a pullet so treated was, according to waggish legends, the secret regale provided for Mess John by his fair penitents. *Vide* Allan Ramsay's *Monk and Miller's Wife*, or *Friars of Berwick*; also *Traditions of the Cleikum*, and *Bughtrigg's Wife's Receipt for 'Ane capon stewed in brews'*. Butter, shred onions, and spice were put in the bag along with the fowl, and formed the sauce, or else oysters with their liquor strained.'
– *Annals of the Cleikum Club*.

A *Stoved Howtowdie wi' Drappit Eggs* and *Wee Grumphie* (sucking-pig) *wi' Neeps* (turnips) were two dishes that delighted Penelope in *Penelope's Experiences in Scotland* (Kate Douglas Wiggan) in late Victorian times.

Mince-Fowl

Chicken or fowl, mushrooms, flour, butter or bacon fat, parsley, chives, or spring onion, salt, pepper, nutmeg, lemon juice, cream (optional), chicken or veal stock

Measure one and a half to two cups of the minced white meat of a cooked fowl and half a cup or more of mushrooms, peeled and minced. Stew the minced mushrooms in butter or, better, bacon fat, in a covered pan for about fifteen minutes. Melt one and a half tablespoonfuls of butter, add two ounces of flour and stir till smooth; stir in a cup of stock gradually and cook, stirring, for ten minutes. Season with salt, pepper and a very little grated nutmeg. Add the diced chicken and the mushrooms with the butter in which they were cooked. Add a dessertspoonful of chopped parsley, another of chopped chives, a few drops of lemon juice and two tablespoonfuls of cream. Make thoroughly hot.

If spring onions or shallots are used instead of chives, slice or chop them and cook with the mushrooms.

Serve with a border of creamed potato or rice boiled in chicken stock and garnish with hot buttered peas; or serve with scrambled eggs as an accompaniment.

'Harvest-Homes were scenes of happy mirth and much food. There were roasted fowls, *mince-fowl*, apple-pie, haggis, singed sheep's head and trotters, black and white puddings, sowens and curds, and plenty of whisky.'
 – Elizabeth Haldane: *The Scotland of Our Fathers.*

Scots Chicken Fillets

Breast of chicken, chicken broth, egg sauce (see p. 199)

'Poach fillets of chicken in well-flavoured chicken broth and coat with egg sauce.'

From Henry Smith's *Classical Recipes of the World.*

Chicken Stovies (*Highlands*)

A plump chicken or fowl, potatoes, onions or shallots (optional), butter, salt, pepper, water

Prepare the bird and cut up neatly. Peel two pounds of potatoes and cut up roughly. Slice an onion or two shallots. Arrange in a pot alternate layers of potatoes, onion and chicken, sprinkling each layer with salt and pepper and dotting liberally with butter. Add about three gills of water and cover tightly. Simmer very gently for two or three hours, or until the chicken is tender. If necessary, add a little hot water occasionally to prevent burning.

This was long a popular dish at Highland rural weddings. Known formerly as Stoved Hens, it is mentioned by Dr. Norman Macleod in his *Reminiscences of a Highland Parish.* – F. M. McN.

Kingdom Of Fife Pie

(*Traditional Recipe*)

Rabbit, pickled pork, nutmeg, pepper, salt, forcemeat, gravy, white wine (optional), egg (optional)

Skin a rabbit, cut it into joints, and let it lie for an hour in cold water. Make a gravy with the carcass and liver. Cut into slices a pound of pickled pork, season with grated nutmeg, pepper, and salt. Make forcemeat balls as below, pack rabbit, pork, and balls into a dish with a sliced hard-boiled egg, if liked, and a teacupful of good gravy. The old recipes advise the addition of three tablespoonfuls of white wine, but this is often omitted. Cover with a puff paste. It is advisable to make three holes in the paste, as a rabbit pie needs plenty of ventilation. Bake for an hour. It may be eaten hot or cold.

FORCEMEAT

Rabbit liver, bread-crumbs, fat bacon, minced parsley, pepper and salt, lemon thyme, grated nutmeg (optional), egg

Mince the liver, chop the bacon, and beat the egg. Mix the dry ingredients and bind with the egg. Form into small balls.

Scots Rabbit Curry

(Meg Dods's Recipe)

Rabbit, streaky bacon, onions, butter, flour, curry-powder, mushroom-powder, celery (optional), coconut (optional), salt and cayenne, stock

Choose a fat, fresh rabbit. (To test it, examine the kidney.) Cut it into at least twelve pieces; brown these in butter, with onions. When browned, if you wish delicate cookery, pour off the butter and add three-quarters of a pint of well-seasoned stock, one large spoonful of curry-powder and one of flour, six ounces of streaky bacon cut into half-inch cubes, and also half a dozen button onions. Season with a teaspoonful of mushroom-powder. Simmer this slowly for half an hour at least, stirring it. Add what more seasoning you think required, as cayenne, a little tumeric, or some acid. Pile up the pieces of rabbit and pour the sauce, which should be thickish as in all curry dishes, over them. Serve with plain boiled rice in a separate dish.

Fresh coconut is an excellent ingredient in mild curries. Rasp and stew it the whole time: we do not like *green* vegetables in curries though they are sometimes used. Mushrooms are an enrichment, celery is good, and onion indispensable.

DISHES OF MEAT

Haggis

> Fair fa'[1] your honest, sonsie[2] face,
> Great chieftain o' the puddin race!
> Aboon them a' ye tak your place,
>   Painch,[3] tripe, or thairm.[4]
> Weel are ye wordy o' a grace
>   As lang's my airm.
>
>   – Burns: *Address to a Haggis.*

The name haggis was commonly thought to derive from the French *hachis*, which is the form used by King James's Scottish cook in *The Fortunes of Nigel*, but a more likely derivation, as we now know, is simply *hag*, from hack, to chop.[5] The name was presumably converted into French in the same way as Ayrshire embroidery became *broderie anglaise* (sic).

The theory that the haggis is one of the nobler legacies of France may in any case be dismissed. The composition of the dish alone disproves the assumption, and the French themselves allude to the haggis, which appears to have been commonly sent to Scots in exile in the days of the Auld Alliance, as *le pain bénit d'Ecosse*. In a modern menu, it appears as *Puding de St. André*!

The haggis is, in fact, simply a super-sausage, or, as Burns describes it, the 'great chieftain o' the puddin (sausage) race', and like the sausage, it was once common to many lands. Of course, the contents must have varied as much as do those of the sausage in our own time. To such as still 'look down wi' sneerin', scornfu' view on sic a denner', we would point out that the most aesthetic of nations, the ancient Greeks, had a haggis of their own, which was immortalized by Aristophanes in *The Clouds*. Strepsiades entertains Socrates with a personal experience:

> Why, now the murder's out!
> So was I served with a stuffed sheep's paunch I broiled
> On Jove's day last, just such a scurvy trick;
> Because, forsooth, not dreaming of your thunder,
> I never thought to give the rascal vent,
> Bounce goes the bag, and covers me all over
> With its rich contents of such varied sorts.[6]

A pity we don't know what was 'intill't!' We are luckier with the ancient Romans, for a recipe has been preserved in the work of Apicius Coelius, *De Arte Coquinaria* (All About Cooking). The ingredients are chopped pork, suet, egg yolks, pepper, lovage, *asa foetida*, ginger, rue, gravy and oil. The manner of stuffing, cooking and pricking is identical with our own.

Why everybody except the Scots stopped stuffing the paunch whilst they went on stuffing the intestines, the annals of gastronomy do not reveal. And why so many people furth of Scotland regard the haggis as an uncivilized dish and the sausage as a civilized one is another mystery.

[1] Good befall.   [2] Comely.   [3] Paunch, a variety of tripe.   [4] Intestines
[5] The Scottish National Dictionary.
[6] A similar incident is related with much gusto by Christopher North in the *Noctes Ambrosianae*. The uninitiated are advised to note the danger of a too sudden attack on the 'chieftain'. Some carvers begin by carefully cutting a St. Andrew's Cross (×) on the top, and then turn the flaps over to make an aperture.

The choice of the haggis as the supreme national dish of Scotland is very fitting. It is a testimony to the national gift of making the most of small means; for in the haggis we have concocted from humble, even despised ingredients a veritable *plat de gourmets*. It contains a proportion of oatmeal, for centuries the national staple grain, whilst the savoury and wholesome blending of the cereal with onion and suet (met with in its simplicity in such dishes as Mealy Puddings, the Fitless Cock, and Skirl-in-the-Pan) is typically Scottish. Further, it is a thoroughly democratic dish, equally available and equally honoured in castle, farm and croft. Finally, the use of the paunch of the animal as the receptacle of the ingredients gives that touch of romantic barbarism so dear to the Scottish heart.

There are many references to the haggis in our literature. Here are a few:

> The gallowis gaipis eftir thy graceless gruntill
> As thou wald for ane haggies.
>   – William Dunbar (?1460–?1520): *The F'yting of Dunbar and Kennedy.*

> A haggis fat,
> Weel tottl'd in a sything-pat.
>   – Robert Fergusson: *To the Principal and Professors of the University of St. Andrews on their Superb Treat to Dr. Samuel Johnson.*

> As sure as I'm a Scot,
> A redshank Norland haggis-eater.
>   – J. Halliday: *Rustic Bard.*

> 'A gallimaufray of offal.'
>   – W. E. Henley.

(At Blair Castle, the home of the Dukes of Atholl), 'there were several Scotch dishes, two soups and the celebrated "Haggis", which I tried last night and really liked very much. The Duchess was delighted with my taking it.'
  – Queen Victoria: *More Leaves from a Journal of our Life in the Highlands.*

Gaipis, gapes; *gruntill*, snout; *wald*, would; *tottl'd*, boiled, simmered; *sything-pat*, seething-pot; *redshank*, a contemptuous name for a Highlander, from his bare legs; *Norland*, North Country.

(*Traditional Cottage Recipe*)

'In the peasant's home it was set in the centre of the table, all gathering round with their horn spoons, and it was "deil tak' the hindmost".'
  – T. F. Henderson: *Old-World Scotland.*

The large stomach bag of a sheep, the pluck (including heart, lights and liver), beef-suet, pin-head (coarse) oatmeal, onions, black pepper, salt, stock or gravy

Brown and birstle (dry or toast) a breakfastcupful of oatmeal before the fire or in the oven. Clean the great bag thoroughly, washing it first in cold water and then, after turning it inside out, scalding and scraping it with a knife; then let it soak overnight in cold salted water. In the morning put it aside with the rough side turned out. Wash the pluck well and put on to boil covered with cold water, letting the windpipe hang over the side of the pot to let out any impurities. Let it boil for an hour and a half, then take it out and cut away the pipes and any superfluities of gristle. Mince the heart and lights and grate half the liver. (The rest of the liver is not required.) Put them into a basin with half a pound of minced suet, two medium-sized onions finely chopped, and the toasted oatmeal, and season highly with black pepper and salt. (A pinch of cayenne, say some housewives, 'makes all the difference'.) Over the whole pour, preferably when cold, as much of the liquid in which the pluck was boiled (or, better still, good stock) as will make the mixture sappy.

Fill the stomach bag rather more than half full – say five-eighths – as it requires plenty of room to swell. Sew it up securely and place it on an enamel plate in a pot of boiling water (to which half a pint of milk is often added), or, better still, boil it in stock. As soon as it begins to swell, prick it all over with a large needle to prevent its bursting. Boil steadily, without the lid, for three hours, adding boiling water as required to keep the haggis covered. Serve very hot without any garnish.

The usual accompaniments are mashed potatoes and mashed turnips, or, better still, the two mashed together with pepper and a good piece of dripping (see the recipe for Clapshot).

A little lean mutton may be substituted for the lights.

Should the haggis be made some time before it is wanted, re-heat by putting it into a pot of boiling water and letting it simmer (uncovered for an hour or longer, according to size).

To keep, store in the oatmeal girnel or bury in oatmeal in a large jar.

The smaller or knight's hood bag is sometimes boiled and minced along with the pluck.

Some cooks shake a little flour into the haggis bag before filling. Some add a little nutmeg or a pinch of dried herbs.

Mrs. Alan Breck's Ingredients. A sheep's pluck, two teacupfuls of oatmeal, a large teacupful of suet, two teaspoonfuls of salt or more, half a teaspoonful of white pepper, half a teaspoonful of Jamaica pepper, a quarter teaspoonful black pepper, a quarter of a nutmeg grated, a pint of stock.

'The best haggis I ever tasted is made by my mother-in-law. I cannot tell how she does it, for like all good artists she has subordinated technique to her personal intuition. There is no niggling about so many ounces of this or cupfuls of that; when it looks as if more liver is needed, in more liver goes, with another pinch of Prestonpans salt and a carefree twist of the pepper-mill. I do know, however, that she insists on stone-ground oatmeal.' – Gastrologue in *The Scotsman*.

Haggis in a jar. The haggis may be put into a buttered jar or basin instead of the bag, and steamed for four hours. It should not be too moist.

Haggis-in-the-pan. Both bag and jar may be dispensed with, and the haggis may be cooked like a stew in a saucepan. It has to be stirred occasionally, and kept sufficiently moist to prevent its sticking to the bottom of the pan.

Two or three small haggises may be made in place of one large one by cutting up the great bag, wrapping some of the mixture in each piece and sewing it up. Always allow room to swell.

Meg Dods's Haggis

'The exact formula by which the Prize Haggis was prepared at the famous Competition of Haggises held in Edinburgh, when the Cleikum Haggis carried the stakes, and that of Christopher North came in second.' – Meg Dods.[1]

'*Tickler:* A dozen of us entered our haggises for a sweep-stakes – and the match was decided at worthy Mrs. Ferguson's, High Street. My haggis (they were all made either by our wives or cooks at our respective places of abode) ran second to Meg Dods's. The Director General's (which was what sporting men would have called a roarer) came in third – none of the others was placed.'

– Christopher North: *Noctes Ambrosianae*.

Sheep's pluck and paunch, beef-suet, onions, oatmeal, pepper, salt, cayenne, lemon or vinegar

Clean a sheep's pluck thoroughly. Make incisions in the heart and liver to allow the blood to flow out, and parboil the whole, letting the windpipe lie over the side of the pot to permit the discharge of impurities; the water may be changed after a few minutes' boiling for fresh water. A half-hour's boiling will be sufficient; but throw back the half of the liver to boil till it will grate easily; take the heart, the half of the liver, and part of the lights, trimming away all skins and black-looking parts, and mince them together. Mince also a pound of good beef-suet and four or more onions. Grate the other half of the liver. Have a dozen of small onions peeled and scalded in two waters to mix with this mince. Have ready some finely ground oatmeal, toasted slowly before the fire for hours, till it is of a light brown

[1] *Shepherd:* Tell me about the Haggis-Feast.

colour and perfectly dry. Less than two teacupfuls of meal will do for this quantity of meat. Spread the mince on a board and strew the meal lightly over it, with a high seasoning of pepper, salt, and a little cayenne, first well mixed. Have a haggis bag (i.e. a sheep's paunch) perfectly clean, and see that there be no thin part in it, else your whole labour will be lost by its bursting.

Some cooks use two bags, one as an outer case. Put in the meat with a half-pint of good beef gravy, or as much strong broth as will make it a very thick stew. Be careful not to fill the bag too full, but allow the meat room to swell; add the juice of a lemon or a little good vinegar; press out the air and sew up the bag, prick it with a large needle when it first swells in the pot to prevent bursting; let it boil slowly for three hours if large.

'This is a genuine Scotch Haggis; the lemon and cayenne may be omitted, and instead of beef-gravy, a little of the broth in which the pluck is parboiled may be taken. A finer haggis may be made by parboiling and skinning sheeps' tongues and kidneys, and substituting these minced for the most of the lights. and soaked bread or crisped crumbs for the toasted meal. There are, moreover, sundry modern refinements on the above recipe – such as eggs, milk, pounded biscuit, etc. – but these, by good judges, are not deemed improvements. Some cooks use the small fat tripes, as in making lamb's haggis.' – M. D.

Haggis Royal

'We find the following directions for Haggis Royal in the Minutes of Sederunt of the Cleikum Club.' – Meg Dods.

Mutton, suet, beef-marrow, bread-crumbs or oatmeal, anchovies, parsley, lemon, pepper, cayenne, eggs, red wine

Three pounds of leg of mutton chopped, a pound of suet chopped, a little, or rather as much beef-marrow as you can spare, the crumb of a penny loaf (our own nutty-flavoured browned oatmeal, by the way, far better), the beat yolks of four eggs, a half-pint of red wine, three mellow fresh anchovies boned, minced parsley, lemon grate, white pepper, crystals of cayenne to taste – crystals alone ensure a perfect diffusion of the flavour – blend the ingredients well, truss them neatly in a veal caul, bake in a deep dish, in a quick oven, and turn out. Serve hot as fire, with brown gravy, and venison sauce.

'Mr. Allan Cunningham, in some of his Tales, orders the parboiled minced meat of sheep's head for haggis. We have no experience of this receipt, but it promises well.'
– *Annals of the Cleikum Club.*

Deer Haggis

(From the Kitchen of a Highland Chief)

Deer's heart, liver, and suet, coarse oatmeal, onions, black pepper, salt, paste

Boil the heart and a piece of the liver of a deer. When cold, mince the heart very fine and grate a teacupful of the liver. To these add a teacupful of coarse oatmeal, previously toasted in the oven or before the fire, half a pound of finely minced suet, three finely chopped onions, a tablespoonful of salt, and a strong seasoning of black pepper. Mix all well together. Put into a pudding-basin, cover with paste as for a beef-steak pudding, and boil for four hours. Serve in the basin, very hot.

Collops-In-The-Pan

(Meg Dods's Recipe)

Rump beef (sliced), butter, onions, salt, pepper, oyster-pickle or walnut ketchup

Cut the meat rather thinner than for broiling; make the butter hot and place the collops in the pan, with about the proportion of a couple of middle-sized onions sliced to each half-pound. If the butter be salt, pepper is used, but no additional salt. Cover the pan with a close lid or plate reversed. When done, the collops may be drawn aside, and a little oyster-pickle or walnut ketchup and boiling water added to the onion-gravy sauce in the pan. Dish and serve hot. Ten minutes will dress them.

Above A catch of herring
Below Old water-mill at Milngavie

Old domestic utensils

Left Wooden luggie ;
Fro'-stick ; Plump-churn

Below Three-legged pot ;
Brander ;
Spurtle or Porridge-stick ;
Toasting-stone ;
Bannock-spathe ;
Girdle

Above The breakfast
Below Grace Before Meat
from the painting by Sir David Wilkie

A fishing community in St Andrews, 1890

'This national dish possessed rather too much gusto for Jekyl; but the Doctor admired it exceedingly, and even suggested that, independently of the collops, this was an excellent method of preparing onion gravy, which only required the addition of a little red wine and lemon-juice, to those who like an acid relish, to be a complete sauce.'
– *Annals of the Cleikum Club.*

Mince or Minced Collops

(An everyday Scottish dish)

Minced steak, bread-crumbs or oatmeal or barley (optional), dripping, onion, mushroom ketchup (optional), beef gravy and/or water, pepper and salt

Take a pound of steak, which should be carefully minced with a small proportion of fat. Melt a tablespoonful of dripping in a stew-pan, and when it is smoking hot put in a finely chopped onion. Let it cook for a few seconds and add the minced steak. Brown it carefully, beating it well with a wooden spoon to keep it free from lumps. Add salt, half a teacupful of gravy, and water as required. Simmer very gently for at least an hour. Then add a handful or more of bread-crumbs (which will absorb any liquid fat), or a dessertspoonful of oatmeal (which gives a very agreeable flavour) or of barley, with a seasoning of pepper. A table-spoonful of mushroom ketchup may be added. Cook it a few minutes longer and serve on a hot ashet garnished with sippets of toast or fried bread and slices of hard-boiled egg, or with a border of mashed potatoes.

Minced collops may be baked in the oven, or first stewed and then baked. They will keep for some time, if packed in a jar and covered like potted meats.

Hare, venison, and veal collops are made as above, with the seasonings appropriate to each. Mrs. Dalgairns recommends Jamaica pepper and port wine for hare.

'Mince and Mashed' is said to be to the Glaswegian what 'Sausages and Mashed' is to the Londoner.

Scots Kidney Collops

(Meg Dods's Recipe)

Kidney, flour, butter, eschalot or young onions, salt, pepper, parsley, vinegar or mushroom ketchup

Cut a fresh kidney in slices of the size of very small steaks, or into mouthfuls. Soak the slices in water and dry them well. Dust them with flour and brown them in the stew-pan with fresh butter. When the collops are browned, pour some hot water into the pan, a minced eschalot, or the white of four young onions minced, with salt, pepper, shred parsley, and a spoonful of plain or eschalot vinegar, or of onion-pickle liquor. Cover the stew-pan close and let the collops simmer slowly till done. If flavoured vinegar is not used, a spoonful of mushroom ketchup put in before the collops are dished will be a great improvement. Thicken the gravy. Garnish this dish like liver with fried parsley.

'Some good cooks season this dish with an anchovy and lemon-pickle; others add made mustard.' – M. D.

Highland Beef Balls

(From the Highland Feill Cookery-book)

Beefsteak, suet, saltpetre, black pepper, Jamaica pepper, sugar, ginger, cloves

Mince finely two pounds of lean beefsteak and one pound of suet. Add to these a dessertspoonful of black pepper, the same of Jamaica pepper, one and a half dessertspoonfuls of salt, a teaspoonful apiece of saltpetre, sugar, and ginger, and half a teaspoonful of ground cloves. Mix well, roll into balls, and cover these with melted suet. When well covered with fresh suet they will keep for a week or ten days. When they are required for table, fry them a rich brown in deep fat.

This preparation can be put into ox-skins and tied into links.

This is an excellent breakfast or supper dish.

Smoked Scots Sausages (*To Keep and Eat Cold*)

(*Meg Dods's Recipe*)

Beef, suet, pepper, salt, onion, ox-gut

Salt a piece of beef for two days and mince it with suet. Season it highly with pepper, salt, onion, or eschalot. Fill a large well-cleaned ox-gut, plait it in links, and hang the sausage in the chimney to dry.[1] Boil it as wanted, either a single link or altogether. No onion if to keep.

Inky-Pinky

(*Meg Dods's Recipe*)

Cold roast beef, carrots, onion, vinegar, flour, pepper, salt

Slice boiled carrots; slice also cold roast beef, trimming away outside and skins. Put an onion to a good gravy (drawn from the roast beef-bones, if you like), and let the carrots and beef slowly simmer in this; add vinegar, pepper and salt. Thicken the gravy – take out the onion and serve hot, with sippets, as any other hash.

Forfar Bridies[2]

(*As made by Mr. Jolly, a baker in the Back Wynd (now Queen Street), Forfar, in the mid-nineteenth century*)

Steak, pepper, salt, onions (optional), flour, water

Take a pound of the best steak. Beat it with the paste roller, then cut it into narrow strips, and again cut these into inch lengths and season with salt and pepper. Divide into three portions. Mince finely three ounces of suet. Make a

---

[1] 'Some of these sausages used to be made when a Mart was killed; they formed an excellent article of supply for the hill, or moor, or the boat; and in the Hebrides and remote parts of the Highlands they still hold a favourite place in the wide open chimney.' – M. D.

[2] These are mentioned by Barrie in *Sentimental Tommie*. Sir James was, of course, a native of Kirriemuir (Thrums), a village in Angus (Forfarshire).

stiff dough with flour, water, and a seasoning of salt[1] and roll out thin into three ovals. Cover the half of each oval with the meat; sprinkle with the suet and a little minced onion if desired; wet the edges, fold over, and crimp with finger and thumb; nip a small hole on top of each. Bake for about half an hour in a quick oven and they will come out golden-brown dappled beauties, fit for a king's supper.

The bridies may be baked in a hot oven until the paste begins to colour, then at a reduced (moderate) temperature until the steak is tender when tested with a skewer. They should be eaten hot.

'In the normal pre-war "siccy" or sixpenny bridie, you used to get one-sixth of a pound of stewing steak and kidney diced by hand. The crust was made by mixing two pounds of lard with a peck (eight pounds) of flour. A hole was made in the paste to let off steam. If you got a bridie with two holes, it had onions in it.

'Of a Saturday, the hardy, granite-cheeked lads of Angus used to line up in the back court of Jolly, the baker, and order three at a time. Once a lanky loon from Padanaram created something of a local record by eating eight, wiping his mouth, and saying, "Ay, they're fine. If they werena sae dear, I'd hae made my supper o' them." '

– An Old Forfarian.

Potted Head (*Or Scots Brawn*)

(*Old Family Recipe*)

Ox head, ox foot, salt, pepper, cayenne, mustard, bay leaf, mace, cloves or allspice or nutmeg, water

Soak half an ox head and a foot for a few hours. Break them up into several pieces. Remove from the foot as much of the fat and marrow as possible. Scald head and foot with boiling water and, when cool enough, scrape and clean them thoroughly. Put them into a large saucepan, plentifully covered with cold water, and add two tablespoonfuls of salt. Bring this very slowly to the boil, skim carefully, and let it simmer for three hours. Take out the head and foot and remove all the best meat from them. Return the bones to the pan, adding more water if there is not enough to cover them. Add a bay leaf, a blade of mace, and a very few

[1] The fatless crust, which was rolled out very thin, was primarily a receptacle for the meat. (See note to Black Bun: huff paste.) Nowadays rough puff or short paste is commonly used. – F. M. McN.

cloves, if liked. Let this simmer for two or three hours longer. Strain into a basin and put aside till it gets cold. There should be at least eight breakfastcupfuls of liquid. Next day (or sooner) remove all the fat from the top of the stock, which should now be a jelly. Trim and chop the meat and put it into a clean saucepan with the stock. Let this simmer for fifteen or twenty minutes. Add half a teaspoonful of mustard, the same of allspice or nutmeg if cloves have not been used, and season rather highly with pepper and cayenne. Pour into wetted moulds and put in a cool place to set. Turn out, and serve with salad.

A Glasgow School of Cookery recipe dated 1888 lists the following ingredients: One ox head, 100 (say ½ oz.) peppercorns, 25 allspice berries, 8 cloves, 4 blades of mace, 4 bay leaves, 4 sprigs of parsley, 4 sprigs of thyme, 4 sprigs of marjoram, 2 small onions and salt to taste – all to be put on with the bones after the meat has been removed.

Some cooks add nothing more than salt, pepper and a tablespoonful or two of ketchup or Worcestershire sauce.

A good-sized head yields approximately sixteen pounds.

Potted Hough

(*Old Cottage Recipe*)

Hough (shin of beef), water, pepper, salt

Take the nap end of hough, about three pounds or so, make the butcher break it through, put it into a saucepan and nearly cover it with water. Put it on the fire at night, bring it almost to boiling-point, then place it on the hob and let it simmer gently all night; don't let it boil. In the morning the meat will fall from the bones. Mince the meat pretty small, and put it in the saucepan again; add a little boiling water if required, and pepper and salt to taste, and let it boil for ten minutes, no longer. Put it into bowls or moulds and set aside to cool. It will have a rich taste, far before the common way of cooking it.

White Collops

(*Meg Dods's Recipe*)

Veal, butter, broth or water, lemon, ketchup or lemon-pickle, mace, pepper, salt, egg, bread-crumbs

Cut small slices of equal thickness out of veal, and flour and brown them over a brisk fire in fresh butter. When enough are browned for your dish, put a little weak veal-broth or boiling water to them in a small close stew-pan, adding, when they are nearly ready, the juice of a lemon, a spoonful of ketchup, or the same of lemon-pickle with mace, pepper, and salt to taste. Thicken and strain the sauce and pour it over the collops. They may be egged and dipped in crumbs. Serve curled slices of toasted bacon, or mushrooms if in season.

Veal Flory (*Florentine Pie*)[1]

(*Meg Dods's Recipe*)

Veal, bacon, spices, herbs, gravy, forcemeat, eggs or sweetbread, truffles, morells or mushrooms, paste

Cut chops from the back-ribs or breast of veal. Trim off the bones and season the chops highly with mixed spices and such minced herbs as you choose. Add a few slices of lean bacon, forcemeat balls, and boiled yolks of eggs; or a scalded sweetbread cut into bits, and truffles, morells, or mushrooms as is convenient or approved. Add a little gravy drawn from the trimmings, and cover the pie.

'You may put in oysters, yolks of hard eggs, and artichoke bottoms.' – Mrs. McIver.

[1] This ancient and once honoured dish (mentioned by Scott in *The Bride of Lammermoor*) is a legacy of the Auld Alliance and may conceivably have come to us via Paris from Florence, as the name suggests. Certainly two French queens, Catherine and Marie, both of the famous Florentine family of Medici, exercised much influence on the French cuisine of their day, and through Mary, Queen of Scots, that influence was felt in Scotland. – F. M. McN.

To Boil A Gigot With Turnip (*A Scottish National Dish*)

(*Meg Dods's Recipe*)

A leg of mutton – the gigot of the French and Scottish kitchen – may be kept from two days to a week before boiling. The pipe, as it is technically called, must be cut out, and the mustiness which gathers on the surface and in the folds and soft places rubbed off occasionally. It is whitest when quite fresh, but most delicate when hung a few days in the larder, though not so long as to allow the juices to thicken and the flavour to deteriorate. Mountain wether mutton, from four to five years old, is far the best, whether for boiling or roasting. Choose it short in the shank, thick in the thigh, and of a pure, healthy, brownish red. Chop but a very small bit off the shank; if too much is taken off the juices will be drained by this conduit in the boiling. If you wish to whiten the meat, blanch it for ten minutes in warm water or put it in a floured cloth if you like. Boil in an oval-shaped or roomy kettle, letting the water come very slowly to boil. Skim carefully. Boil carrots and turnips with the mutton, and the younger and more juicy they are the better they suit this joint. Be sure never to run a fork or anything sharp into the meat, which would drain its juices. *All meat ought to be well done*, but a leg of mutton rather under than over, to look plump and retain its juices. About two hours of slow boiling will dress it. Garnish with slices of carrot. Pour caper sauce over the meat and serve mashed turnip or cauliflower in a separate dish.

'This joint, above all others, should be boiled slowly to eat well. . . . The best balmy, mellow barley or rice broth may be made of what remains.' – M. D.

'There is an adaptation, a *natural affinity*, to borrow a learned phrase, between certain vegetables and roots, and certain pieces and kinds of meat. A cook who would excel in her profession, ought, day and night, to study this doctrine of coherence and natural affinity. Who but a fool would dissever from the round of salted beef the greens or cabbage which become part and parcel of it as soon as it reaches the pot?' – Id.

'*To grow a shoulder or leg of mutton.* – This art is well known to the London bakers. Have a very small leg or shoulder; change it upon a customer for one a little larger, and that upon another for one better still, till by the dinner-hour you have a heavy excellent joint grown out of your original very small one.'
– P. Touchwood in the *Annals of the Cleikum Club*.

'A Nor'-loch trout was formerly a familiar name in Edinburgh for a roast of beef or a leg of mutton. There was a club of citizens who used to meet in a tavern in one of the closes between the High Street and the Nor' Loch. The invitation to join the company was generally thus: "Will ye gang and eat a Nor'-loch trout the day?" The reason of the designation was obvious. This was the only species of *fish* which the Nor' Loch, on which the shambles were situated, could supply.'
– Hislop: *Book of Scottish Anecdote.*

The Nor'-loch, in Princes Street Gardens, was drained to make room for the railway.

Poor Man Of Mutton

This Scottish dish is the blade-bone grilled or cooked before the fire.

'There is a traditional story of Lord ――, after a long and severe fit of illness with which he was seized in London, horrifying his landlord by whining forth from behind his bed-curtains when urged to choose and eat, "I think I could tak' a snap o' a Puir Man".' – *Annals of the Cleikum Club.*

To Dress A Sheep's Head

O Lord, when hunger pinches sore,
   Do Thou stand us in stead
And send us, from Thy bounteous store
   A tup or wether head.
      – Robert Burns: *A Grace.*

A gude sheep's heid,
Wha's hide was singeit, never fleed.[1]
      – Robert Fergusson.

The head, after singeing, should be boiled long and gently, as for powsowdie (q.v.) along with the trotters. It is then split and laid flat in a large ashet, with the trotters around it, the tongue, sliced, and, if liked, balls of yolk of egg. The dish is garnished with sliced vegetables – carrots, turnips and onions – that have been cooked in the broth. Parsley or brain sauce may be served with it.

'The sauces ordered for boiled mutton and cow-heel are well adapted to this dish, if sauce must be had where so little is required. For ragoût, a sauce may be made of the broth thickened with butter and flour.' – Meg Dods.

'This dish has furnished whole pages to Joe Miller and his right witty contemporaries. In one of the most pleasing pieces of biography that ever was written, "The Life of Lady Grizel Baillie", there is an amusing "sheep's head anecdote", which at once affords a glimpse of the simplicity of the national manners, and of the dexterity and good sense of the affectionate and very juvenile heroine. Her father, Sir Patrick Home,

[1] Flayed, skinned.

184

proscribed after the Restoration, was hidden near his own mansion – his lady and his
daughter Grizel being alone privy to his place of concealment. It was the duty of this
young girl, not only to carry food to her father during the night, but to abstract these
supplies from the dinner-table, so that neither the servants nor younger children might
be aware that there was an invisible guest to feed. Her inordinate appetite and strata-
gems to procure food became the cause of many jokes at table; and one day, when a
sheep's head – a favourite dish with Sir Patrick – was produced, she had just conveyed
nearly the whole into her lap, when her young brother, afterwards Earl of Marchmont,
looked up and exclaimed, "Mother, Mother, look at Grizel; while we have been taking
our broth, she has eaten up the whole sheep's head!"

'The consternation of young Home could not, however, exceed that of a learned
gentleman, who at present fills a chair in Edinburgh University upon a somewhat
similar occasion. Before filling his present honourable situation, Professor —— was
for some years a professor in S—— College; and, as might be surmized, in the
lapse of those years of exile, experienced a natural and national longing for that
savoury food which, to a Scotsman, is like his mother's milk. A sheep's head was
accordingly procured by his orders, and sent to the blacksmith's to be singed. The hour
of dinner arrived; the chops of the learned professor watered with expectation when
lo! to his disappointment and horror, the fleshless skull was presented; and, doubly
worse, accompanied with the sauce of a bill, setting forth, "To polishing a sheep's
head for Professor ——, one shilling and four pence"! – thus making the unfortunate
philosopher come down with sixteen shillings, Scots money, for being deprived of the
exquisite pleasure which he had anticipated in polishing the skull himself.'
                                   – Meg Dods: *Manual of Cookery*, Note.

'The village of Duddingstone was long celebrated for "sheep's head", and was
consequently a favourite resort of the frugal citizens of Edinburgh. Sheep's head clubs
were not infrequent throughout the country, and the "Tup's Head Dinner" about
Michaelmas-day is still a high and solemn festival with the official dignitaries in certain
of our Scottish Royal burghs. This was before the days of Reform. They may, alas!
have changed all that now.' – Id.

'Every Wednesday,'[1] Neil Munro tells us, 'Glasgow solemnly goes through the
curious rite of eating mutton-heads and trotters.' He failed, after an intensive search,
to discover the origin of this long-established custom, or why Wednesday.'
                                   – *The Looker-On*, edited by George Blake.

A singed sheep's head used to be a special dish on St. Andrew's Night.

Jellied Sheep's Head

*A sheep's head (with tongue), salt, peppercorns, cloves,
parsley, thyme, gelatine, water*

Thoroughly clean the head and soak overnight in cold salted
water. Drain and place in a pot with cold water to cover. Add
six black peppercorns, two cloves, two sprigs of parsley and
one of thyme. Bring slowly to the boil, skim thoroughly
and simmer for from two to three hours according to size
and age. When the meat can be detached easily from the

[1] In pre-war days.

185

bone, take out the head and boil the stock until reduced to about a pint. Remove all the meat from the head, skin the tongue and mince both very finely. Dissolve a tablespoonful of gelatine in the stock, then strain into a basin. Stir in the meat and tongue. When just about to set, stir again and pour into a wetted mould.

Half a pound of bacon may be boiled in the stock and minced with the meat and tongue.

When the head has been singed in the old style, as for powsowdie, no seasoning other than pepper and salt is required.

' "Gellied sheep's heid" was for centuries a favourite dish among all classes in Scotland. It appeared at the court of successive kings, and could be procured at almost any hostelry throughout the land.' – F. M. McN.

Small Mutton Pies[1]

> Maimed Hepburn from the croft gate cries,
> 'Come buy my hot and tottling pies!
> Fine mutton pies, fat piping hot,
> One for a penny, four for a groat!'
> – Charles Spence: *Errol Winter Market.*

(Traditional Recipe)

Mutton, gravy, pepper, salt, mace or nutmeg, crust, flour, salt, dripping, milk or water

Remove the skin, bone, and gristle from three-quarters of a pound of lean mutton. Cut the meat into small pieces, and season with salt, pepper, and, if liked, a little mace or nutmeg.

[1] These pies were praised by Dr. Johnson. In his *Reminiscences*, Professor James Stuart pays tribute to Mrs. Gillespie, the pie-wife of his St. Andrews schooldays. Delightful as were her pigeon- and apple-pies, 'her chef-d'œuvre . . . was a certain kind of mutton-pie. The mutton was minced to the smallest consistency, and was made up in a standing crust, which was strong enough to contain the most delicious gravy. . . . There were no lumps of fat or grease in them at all. . . . They always arrived piping hot. . . . It makes my mouth water still when I think of those pies.'

Glasgow, about the same period, had her 'Granny Black', who was famed far beyond the city limits for her Twopenny Pies.

'When I was a boy,' writes a reminiscent Glaswegian in 1929, 'her establishment in the Candleriggs was a favourite resort of the farmers and the farmers' wives among whom I was brought up, and it was always considered a great treat when one visited Glasgow to call there and have a sixpenny tea.'

For six pies make a crust as follows: Put four ounces of fresh beef dripping into a saucepan with half a pint of water. Bring this to the boil, but do not let it reduce in quantity. Sieve a pound of flour into a bowl and add to it half a teaspoonful of salt. Make a well in the centre and pour in the hot liquid. Mix at first with a spoon or knife, but when cool enough use the hands and mix quickly into one lump. Turn out on a floured board and knead lightly till free from cracks. Put aside nearly a third of the paste to keep warm and divide the rest into six pieces. With these line six small ring tins or form them with the hand into small cases. (This may be done round a tumbler.) Fill the cases with meat, just moisten with water or gravy. Cut rounds from the remainder of the paste, wet the edges, and lay over the pies with the wetted side down, and press the two edges of paste firmly together. Trim round with a pair of scissors, make a small hole in the centre of each pie, and brush them with a little milk or beaten egg. Bake for from thirty to forty minutes in a moderate oven. Remove the pies from the tins, fill them up with a little hot gravy, and serve very hot.

Slices from the leg, diced small, are best.

'A little py of cocks' combs' figures in one of Lady Grisell Baillie's menus.

'The Pious Club was composed of decent, orderly citizens who met every night, Sundays not excepted, in a pye-house. . . . The agreeable uncertainty as to whether their name arose from their *piety*, or the circumstance of their eating *pies*, kept the Club hearty for many years.' – R. Chambers: *Traditions of Edinburgh.*

'Soutar's clods, and other forms of bread fascinating to youngsters, as well as penny pies of high reputation, were to be had at a shop which all Edinburgh people speak of with extreme regard and affection – the Baijen Hole – situated immediately to the east of Forrester's Wynd, and opposite to the old Tolbooth. The name – a mystery to later generations – seems to have reference to the Baijens' or Baijen[1] Class, a term bestowed in former days upon the junior students in the college.' – Id.

In *Guy Mannering*, Scott tells us how his hero, 'after threading a dark lane or two, reached the High Street, then clanging with the voices of oyster-women and the bells of piemen.'

[1] 'Fr. *béjaune*, a novice, from *bec jaune*, "yellow beak", a term used for a fledgling or unfledged bird.' – Jamieson.

First-year students in the Universities of Aberdeen and St. Andrews are still commonly designated 'bejants'. – F. M. McN.

Glasgow Tripe

(Meg Dods's Recipe)

Tripe, knuckle of veal, pepper, salt, water

When well cleaned and blanched, cut the tripe into pieces; roll them up neatly, fasten with a thread and, with a marrow bone, or knuckle, or trimmings of veal, place them in a stoneware jar with pepper and salt. Place the closed jar in a pot of water, which keep full as it boils away. It will take eight hours at least. Keep the tripe in its own jelly in the jar, and dress it as it is wanted.

To Cure Ayrshire Bacon

A small side of home-fed pork, salt, saltpetre, moist brown sugar, white vinegar

Mix six ounces of salt, one ounce of saltpetre and eight ounces of moist brown sugar in a bowl. Bone the pork, and rub the mixture well into it, particularly on the cut side from which the bones have been removed. Place in a pickling-pan or crock and sprinkle over it any of the remaining pickle mixture. Leave in a cool place for three days, then sprinkle with a pint of white vinegar. Turn daily in the pickle for a month, then take it out and hang up to drain for twenty-four hours. Flatten it well on a board, then roll up tightly (the rind outwards) and secure with strong string. Hang up in a current of air and leave until quite dry. It may be boiled and served cold, or sliced and grilled.

'In the potato-growing and dairy districts of Cunningham and Kyle . . . are raised the swine that become Ayrshire bacon, clean-fed on the gleanings of the potato crop and churn milk. . . . The bacon has a really unmatchable flavour. The actual ham, salt and smoke cured, when properly boiled or otherwise cooked, compares very favourably with York ham. Westphalian ham, or the vaunted peach-fed ham of Virginia. Ayrshire bacon, like any other good bacon, is spoiled when fried. It should be grilled.'
– Victor MacClure: *Scotland's Inner Man.*

Meg Dods mentions with approval a Dumfriesshire ham.

Spiced Bacon

(A Farmhouse Recipe)

A fifteen-score pig, salt, brown sugar, Jamaica pepper, mixed spices, saltpetre

Remove all bones and cut the sides into halves. Take about two pounds of salt and half an ounce of saltpetre and rub the skin until it sweats. Rub the bacon on the flesh side with the remaining saltpetre, especially in the places from which the shoulder and loin bones have been removed. Cover the pork completely with salt, allowing about seven pounds to each piece, and lay it in the salting trough, one piece on top of the other. Leave for twelve days, turning every second day, and removing the top piece to the bottom each time. The salt should now be absorbed. Brush off any surplus and sprinkle with brown sugar, allowing half a pound to each piece. Leave for two days longer, when the bacon will be ready for rolling.

Put into a dredger two ounces of Jamaica pepper and two ounces of mixed spices, including a proportion of cloves, and sprinkle the bacon, allowing two ounces of the mixture to each piece. Roll up and tie with strong twine or cord (not too thin) at intervals of two and a half inches, leaving a strong loop to hang the rolls up by. Let them hang for at least a week before use.

'For regular picnic use, the best sandwich in the world, and the most filling, is made by slitting baps, buttering both inside pieces and closing them over a thick slice of spiced bacon which is a Scottish speciality of which we are justly proud.'
– Donald and Catherine Carswell: *The Scots Week-end.*

Beef-Ham

(Traditional Recipe)

Beef, salt, saltpetre, raw sugar, cloves, Jamaica and black pepper

For a rump of about twenty pounds take a quarter-pound of saltpetre, two pounds of salt, a quarter-pound of coarse raw sugar, half an ounce of cloves, an ounce of Jamaica and one of black pepper, ground. Mix all thoroughly, rub the beef all over, and stuff as much as possible into the bone. Let it lie for two or three days. Then add another pound of salt, rub it well, and turn it every other day. It will be ready in three weeks. Drain it from the brine and hang it up. If you want it smoked, hang it over a barrel in which you burn peat or turf. The smoke will soon taste it, if you turn it well on every part. Then hang it up to dry. Or it may be boiled when taken out of the pickle, and allowed to stand till cold in the water in which it was boiled, or it may be baked in a deep dish, covered with a coarse paste.

'The Natives are accustomed to salt their Beef[1] in a Cow's Hide, which keeps it close from Air, and preserves it as well, if not better than Barrels, and tastes they say best when this way used. This Beef is transported to Glasgow, a city in the West of Scotland, and from thence being put into Barrels there, exported to the Indies in good Condition.' – Martin: *Description of the Western Islands* (1703).

Mutton-Ham[2]

(*Traditional Recipe*)

Mutton, coarse salt, brown sugar, saltpetre, Jamaica and black pepper, coriander seeds

Cut a hind-quarter of good mutton into the shape of a ham. Pound an ounce of saltpetre with a pound of coarse salt and four ounces of brown sugar.[3] Add two ounces of Jamaica and black pepper and half an ounce of coriander seeds. Rub the ham well with this mixture, taking care to stuff some into the hole in the shank. Lay the ham in the trough, keep it carefully covered, and baste it with the brine every other day or even every day. Let it lie for a fortnight. Then take it out and press it with a weight for one day. Smoke it with

[1] 'Their Beef is sweet and tender as any can be; they (the cows) live upon Seaware in Winter and Spring, and are fatned by it, nor are they slaughtered before they eat plentifully of it in December.' – Id.

[2] Mentioned by Scott and other writers.

[3] 'A mutton ham is sometimes cured with the above quantity of salt and sugar, with the addition of half an ounce of white pepper, a quarter of an ounce of cloves, and one nutmeg.' – Mrs. Dalgairns.

190

sawdust[1] for ten or fifteen days or hang it to dry in the kitchen. In the Highlands, dried junipers are used in curing mutton-hams. 'No sort of meat,' says Meg Dods, 'is more improved by smoking with aromatic woods than mutton.'

If the ham is to be boiled soon after it is smoked, soak it for one hour, but if it has been smoked any length of time it will require to be soaked for several hours. Put it on in cold water, and boil it gently for two hours. It is eaten cold at breakfast, luncheon, or supper.

The Scottish Border is famous for the excellence of its mutton-hams. They are carefully pickled with salt, a little coarse sugar, and very little saltpetre, kept in the pickle for three weeks, and hung for months in shepherd's chimneys, where peat and wood are the only fuel. Without previous steeping, they are boiled quickly for an hour, or a little more, if large, and allowed to soak in the pot-liquor for twenty-four hours.
                                                                    – Meg Dods.

[1] 'Drive the end out of an old puncheon or cask. Invert it over birch or juniper branches, or a heap of sawdust of green hardwood (oak is best), in which sawdust a bar of red-hot iron is buried. Hang the tongues, hams, fish, etc.,* on sticks across the casks, and cover it to confine the smoke, giving a very little air below, that the material may smoke and smoulder slowly, but not burn.' – Meg Dods.

* 'In Caithness and elsewhere geese are still cured and smoked and are highly relishing.' – Id.

DISHES OF VEGETABLES

It must be freely owned that the Scots have shown very little ingenuity in the preparation of vegetables. Amongst the rural population they were long consumed almost entirely in the form of broth – and there is, in fact, no better way to preserve the precious juices that are so often discarded in more sophisticated cookery. They are also much used in stews, which have always been more popular in Scotland than in England.

The Scottish housewife at least knows how to boil a potato. Curiously, a perfectly boiled potato is a thing that is rarely to be had in the most expensive hotels and restaurants. They simply will not steam them dry.

Within the present century, salads, once rarely seen save on the tables of the well-to-do, are, happily, enjoying a wide popularity.

So long as we can produce good broths and good salads, we need not worry overmuch about our lack of elaborate vegetable dishes. – F. M. McN.

Buttered Peas

The buttered peas o' Lauderdale
Are better than the best o' kail
When Tammie's pith begins to fail.
– Old Rhyme.

Fresh green peas, spring onions or mint, salt, pepper, butter, water

Have a quart of peas, freshly picked and freshly shelled. (The smaller and younger the sweeter. When older and bigger, they are best used in soups.) Wash well and drain in a colander. Put into boiling water to cover, with one or two spring onions or a sprig of mint, a pinch of sugar, and salt to taste. Simmer for eight or ten minutes, until tender but not overcooked. Drain, turn on to a hot dish, toss in butter, and sprinkle, if liked, with chopped parsley or chopped chives.

Colcannon (*A Highland Dish*)

Cabbages, carrots, potatoes, turnips, salt, pepper, mignonette (optional), brown sauce, butter

Take two cabbages, two or three good red carrots, eight or ten potatoes, and two turnips, all well boiled. Chop the cabbages finely, mash the other vegetables. Melt a good piece of butter in a stew-pan, put in all the vegetables, and mix thoroughly. Season with salt, pepper, and mignonette, and add a spoonful of good brown sauce. Serve piping hot.

Kailkenny[1] (*Aberdeenshire and N.E.*)

> There's cauld kail in Aberdeen
> And custocks[2] in Strathbogie
> Where ilka lad maun ha'e his lass,
> But I maun ha'e my cogie.
> – Old Song.

Cabbage, potatoes, pepper, salt, cream

Mash equal quantities of boiled cabbage and potatoes. Stir in a cupful of cream, season with pepper and salt, mix thoroughly, and serve very hot.

Rumbledethumps (*Borders*)

Potatoes, cabbage, butter, pepper, salt

'*North:* May I ask, with all due solemnity, what *are* rumbledethumps?

'*Shepherd:* Something like Mr. Hazlitt's character of Shakespere. Take a peck of purtatoes, and put them into a boyne[3] – at them with a beetle – a dab of butter – the beetle again – another dab – then cabbage – purtato – beetle and dab – saut[4] meanwhile – and a shake o' common black pepper – feenally, cabbage and purtato throughither – pree,[5] and you'll fin' them decent rumbledethumps.'
            – Christopher North: *Noctes Ambrosianae.*

Use boiled potatoes and cabbage in approximately equal quantities. Chopped chives or cooked onions are often added. The mixture may be put into a pudding-dish covered with grated cheese, and browned in the oven. – F. M. McN.

[1] Probably a corruption of *colcannon*. – F. M. McN.   [2] Stems of colewort.
          [3] Large pot.   [4] Salt.   [5] Taste.

Lang Kail

With crowdy-mowdy they fed me,
Lang kail and ranty-tanty.
– Allan Ramsay: *Tea-Table Miscellany.*

Crowdy-mowdy, milk porridge; *ranty-tanty*, a kind of beverage distilled from heath and other vegetable substances.

Curly kail, butter, salt, pepper, water

Gather two or three stocks of crisp young green kail. Separate the blades from the stems, wash them well and boil in salted water till tender. Drain carefully, and beat up the blades with butter. Season with salt and pepper.

Serve with boiled beef, fresh pork or other meat.

Kail thrives all over Scotland, in the most exposed situations and in the coldest weather. It is improved by a touch of frost – indeed, the keener the frost, the more delicate the flavour.

Boiled beef and lang kail was a favourite dish with the curlers on Duddingston Loch, who enjoyed it at the Sheep's Heid Inn.

Kail and Knockit Corn (*Shetland*)

Kail an' k-nock, kail an' k-nock,
Kail an' knockit corn,
Tak' dee fill wi' hearty will
O' kail an' knockit corn.
– Old Shetland Song.

Knocked corn (groats) mixed with cabbage which has been boiled with a morsel of pork or reisted (smoked) mutton and well seasoned, was formerly a popular dish in the Northern Isles. The corn was prepared thus:

A few handfuls of well-dressed bere (the native type of barley) after being dried, were put into the knocking-stone, moistened with a little warm water and lightly bruised with a mallet in order to break the husks. The husks were then floated off by steeping in the water, and the grain was left round and whole. This was used in place of the pearl barley of today.

Neep Purry (*Stewed Turnips*)

(*Meg Dods's Recipe*)

Turnips, fresh butter, white pepper, salt, ginger

Pare off all that would be hard, woody, and stringy when boiled. Boil them in plenty of water for from three-quarters of an hour to nearly two hours, according to the age and size. Drain them and mash them with a wooden spoon through a colander. Return them into a stew-pan to warm, with a piece of fresh butter, white pepper, ginger and salt. When mixed well with the butter, place them neatly in the dish and mark in diamonds or sippets.

'The Cleikum Club put a little powdered ginger to their mashed turnips, which were studiously chosen of the yellow, sweet, juicy sort, for which Scotland is·celebrated – that kind which, in the days of semi-barbarism, were served raw, as a delicate whet before dinner, as turnips are in Russia at the present day. Mashed turnips to be eaten with boiled fowl or veal, or the more insipid meats, are considerably improved by the Cleikum seasoning of ginger, which, besides, corrects the flatulent properties of this esculent.' – M. D.

Clapshot (*Orkney*)

Potatoes, turnips, chives (optional), butter or dripping, pepper, salt

Mash together equal quantities of boiled potatoes and boiled turnips. Add some chopped chives, a good piece of dripping, and pepper and salt to taste. Mix thoroughly, and serve very hot.

Few people realize the difference it makes mashing the two vegetables together. Clapshot goes admirably with haggis.

Stovies (*Stoved[1] Potatoes*)

(*Lady Clark of Tillypronie's Recipe*)

Potatoes, butter, water, salt

Choose potatoes of a good quality, and put them into a pot

[1] Fr. *étuvé.*

with a very little water – just enough to cover the bottom and prevent burning. Sprinkle with salt, and add tiny bits of butter here and there. Cover closely, and simmer very gently till soft and melted.

(A Cottage Recipe)

Potatoes, onions, salt and pepper, dripping, water

The old-fashioned iron saucepan with a close-fitting lid is ideal for stovies. Peel eight or ten medium-sized potatoes (mealy for preference) and slice thickly. Peel three medium onions and slice thinly. Melt two tablespoonfuls of good beef dripping and fry the onions till lightly coloured. Add the potatoes, sprinkling them well with salt and pepper. Add about half a pint of water – no more – cover closely and cook very gently for an hour and a half, shaking the pan occasionally to prevent sticking. Serve alone, or as an accompaniment to cold meat.

This is a grand supper dish on a cold night.

'A cheap and delicious mess is furnished in summer to those healthy and happy children educated in what are called the *Maiden Hospitals* of Edinburgh. Good potatoes, boiled, peeled, and roughly broken, are boiled up with sweet milk, and a small proportion of butter.' – Meg Dods.

Scots Potato Pies

Potatoes, cooked scraps of meat, onion, pepper, salt, gravy, dripping

Pare very finely some large potatoes, choosing those of nearly equal size. Cut off the tops about half an inch thick and hollow out the centre, leaving the potato at least half an inch thick all over. Mince some cooked scraps of meat, mix with it some chopped parboiled onion, season with pepper and salt, and moisten with a little gravy. A few drops of ketchup may be added. Stuff the potatoes with this mixture, put on the tops, place in a greased baking-tin, and bake in a quick oven for at least an hour, basting occasionally with

196

melted dripping. Serve with a good gravy or hot tomato sauce poured round.

Banffshire Potato Pies: Cream an ounce of butter, beat in an egg yolk, add three ounces of breadcrumbs, a pinch of powered herbs, salt and pepper, and three-quarters of a gill of milk. Stuff the potatoes with this mixture.

Shetland Liver Koogs: Stuff the potatoes with seasoned fish livers. Formerly cooked among the hot peat 'brands' on the hearth, they are now baked in the oven until the potatoes are cooked and the livers dissolved.

Angus Potato Pies: Bake four large potatoes until quite soft. Cut off a top slice and scoop out all the potato. Mash well. Heat two cups of cooked and flaked finnan-haddie with two ounces of butter and milk to moisten. Add most of the potato with milk to make a smooth, creamy mixture. Season and pack into the potato shells. Pile high, put on the lid and heat through in the oven.

Scots Potato Fritters

(*Lady Harriet St. Clair's Recipe*)

Potatoes, bread-crumbs, eggs, ham, olive oil

Parboil half a dozen, or more if required, large kidney potatoes; cut them in slices about the thickness of a crown piece; beat up a couple of eggs with a tablespoonful of finely grated bread-crumbs, and an equal quantity of lean ham grated. Dip each slice of potato in this mixture, and fry in plenty of good olive oil.[1]

To Stew and Roast Onions

(*Meg Dods's Recipe*)

Onions, stock, white pepper, salt, butter, flour, mushroom ketchup

Scald and peel a dozen medium-sized, or two or three Spanish onions. If old and acrid, parboil them, and stew very slowly for nearly an hour in good veal or beef broth, with white pepper and salt; thicken the sauce with a little butter kneaded in flour, and, dishing the onions in a small hash-dish, pour it over them. A little mushroom ketchup may be added, and they may be browned.

[1] Meg Dods says: 'Fry in plenty of dripping, and serve with any sort of steak and chops, or alone as a supper dish. They may be dipped in small-beer fritter-batter.'

Onions are roasted before the fire in their skins, peeled, and served with cold butter and salt. They are eaten either alone or with roasted potatoes, or with red or pickled herring. In the latter case we would recommend mustard as well as butter.

Stewed and roasted onions used to be a favourite supper-dish in Scotland, and were reckoned medicinal. The onions were stewed (after parboiling) in a butter-sauce, to which cream was put. . . . Onions used to form the favourite *bon-bons* of the Highlander, 'who with a few of these and an oat-cake,' says Sir John Sinclair, 'would travel an incredible distance, and live for days without other food.' . . . The Scotch peasants season their *chappit tatties* (mashed potatoes) and sometimes their brose with shred onion. 'There is an admirable receipt for *gusty* chappit potatoes in an early volume of *Blackwood's Magazine*, the work which, in the mysteries of Comus, is wont to take the lead of all the periodicals of the day. The receipt to which we allude is after the practice of the pastoral inhabitants of Ettrick, Yarrow, and Teviotdale. Before calling the potato-beetle into operation, salt, pepper, and *an onion* finely shred are sprinkled over the potatoes, with a dash of sweet milk. The *onion* is the *bonne bouche*.' – Meg Dods.

SAUCES

As regards sauces, the Scots appear to have shown as little inventiveness as their neighbours across the Border. They have, however, contributed two standard sauces to Anglo-Celtic (usually misnamed Anglo-Saxon) civilization – Egg Sauce and Bread Sauce. The former is merely a variation of Béchamel; the latter is original.

Egg Sauce

'*Sauce Ecossaise:* Béchamel Sauce, into which is mixed finely-chopped hard-boiled egg.' – Henry Smith: *Classical Recipes of the World.*

For a plain egg sauce, to a pint of well-flavoured white sauce add two or more roughly-chopped hard-boiled eggs.

For a richer sauce, use a light Béchamel with finely chopped eggs.

For a coating sauce, add the chopped whites only, and grate the yolks over the coating.

A little finely minced parsley is sometimes added to the sauce.

Bread Sauce

'Mint Sauce with lamb and Bread Sauce for poultry and game, a Scottish discovery, I believe, are among the most glorious treasures of our national (British) fare.'
– P. Morton Shand: *A Book of Food.*

White bread-crumbs, shallot or onion, clove, mace, pepper-corns, salt, butter, milk, cream

Sieve from two to three ounces of freshly made bread-crumbs (according to thickness desired). Put into a small saucepan half a pint of milk, a shallot or small onion stuck with a clove, half a blade of mace and six peppercorns. Heat slowly to near boiling-point, then leave in a warm place to infuse for half an hour or longer. Strain the seasoned milk into another saucepan, add the crumbs and stir, keeping it just below simmering-point, until smooth and of a dropping consistency (about twenty minutes). Season. Remove from the heat and add a pat of fresh butter and some fresh cream – a quarter-ounce of butter and two tablespoonfuls of cream, or double the butter and half the cream. Serve in a heated sauce-boat.

The sauce, minus the cream, may be left, covered, until required, and reheated, without boiling, along with the cream, last thing.

Some gourmets prefer all butter, no cream, in the sauce.

Another method is to break up a stale slice of bread, put it into a saucepan with cold milk, leave to soak for an hour and then place in the bottom of the oven. It has various ingredients added, and is said to taste much better than when made in the ordinary way with boiling milk.

Christopher North's Sauce (*for Meat or Game*)

Brown sauce, game gravy, lemon juice, mushroom ketchup, port wine, castor sugar, salt, cayenne pepper

Measure into the upper part of a double saucepan a gill of brown sauce, two or three tablespoonfuls of game gravy, one of lemon juice, half of mushroom ketchup and a half a glass of port wine. Add fine sugar, salt and cayenne pepper to taste. Make very hot, but take care that it does not boil.

Sauce For Roast Grouse

(*Mrs. Lily Macleod's Recipe*)

Sediment from roasting-tin, brandy, thin cream, salt

Strain away the fat from the roasting-tin, but leave the sediment. Pour half a wineglass of brandy (for two birds) into the tin and set it alight. When the flame has died, pour in half a pint of thin cream. Add a pinch of salt. Stir over a gentle heat until the cream is hot, but not boiling. Pour this heavenly sauce over the birds and serve at once.

A Highland Fish-Sauce (*For the Store-room*)

'The Cleikum Club were favoured with this original recipe from an intelligent Highland lady, who has contributed several valuable original recipes to this volume.[1] This sauce boasts neither the name of Burgesse nor Harvey, but we would advise those who wish to combine economy with what is healthful and elegant, to make a fair trial of it.'

Red wine, vinegar, anchovies, horse-radish, onions, parsley, lemon-thyme, bay leaves, nutmeg, mace, cloves, black pepper, cochineal

To an English pint of red port (Burgundy or claret is better) add fifteen anchovies, chopped and prepared by steeping in vinegar in a close-covered vessel for a week; add to this a stick of horse-radish scraped, two onions, and a handful of parsley chopped, a dessertspoonful of lemon-thyme stripped of the stalks, two bay leaves, nutmeg, and six blades of mace roughly pounded, nine cloves, and a small dessertspoonful of black pepper bruised. Pour over these ingredients a large half-pint of port-wine vinegar, and simmer slowly in a silver or new block-tin saucepan, or earthen pipkin, till the bones of the anchovies are dissolved. Add a few grains of cochineal if the colour is not good. Strain the liquor through a hair sieve and, when cold, bottle it for use, securing the vials well with corks and leather. When to be used, shake the vials before pouring out the sauce; two tablespoonfuls will impart a high flavour to four ounces of beat butter, in which it must be simmered for a minute before it is served.

Heather Honey Sauce

Heather honey, orange or lemon, butter, egg, water

Heat half a pint of water and blend with it a cupful of heather honey. Add the juice and grated rind of half an orange or lemon, a teaspoonful of butter and a well-beaten

[1] Meg Dods's *Manual*.

egg. Cook in a double saucepan or in a small bowl placed in a saucepan of hot water, stirring constantly, for ten or fifteen minutes.

Note – One or two other sauces, attached to a particular recipe, will be found elsewhere.

SNACKS AND SAVOURIES

A Scots Rabbit

(Meg Dods's Recipe)

Cheese, porter, mustard, pepper, buttered toast

Pare the crust off a slice of bread cut smooth and of about a half-inch in thickness. Toast it, but do not let it wither or harden in the toasting. Butter it. Grate down mellow Stilton, Gouda, Cheshire, or good Dunlop cheese; and, if not fat, put to it some bits of fresh butter. Put this into a cheese-toaster which has a hot-water reservoir and add to it a glassful of well-flavoured brown-stout porter, a large teaspoonful of made mustard, and pepper (very finely ground) to taste. Stir the mixture till it is completely dissolved, brown it, and then, filling the reservoir with boiling water, serve the cheese with hot dry or buttered toasts on a separate dish.

'This is one of the best plain preparations of the kind that we are acquainted with. Some gourmands use red wine instead of porter, but the latter liquor is much better adapted to the flavour of cheese. Others use a proportion of soft putrid cheese, or the whole of it in that state. This is of course a matter of taste beyond the jurisdiction of any culinary dictator. To dip the toasts in hot porter makes another variety in this preparation.' – M. D.

Scots Woodcock

(Old Family Recipe)

Anchovy paste, eggs, cream, parsley, butter, cayenne, hot buttered toast

Take six small rounds of buttered toast, spread them with anchovy paste, arrange on a hot dish, and keep hot. Melt two tablespoonfuls of butter in a saucepan, put in three tablespoonfuls of cream and the raw yolks of three eggs, and stir over the fire until the mixture is a creamy mass. Add a little finely chopped parsley and a dash of cayenne. Heap on the rounds of toast and serve very hot.

Scots Eggs

(*Meg Dods's Recipe*)

Eggs, forcemeat, ham, anchovy, bread, spices, etc.

Five eggs make a dish. Boil them hard as for salad. Peel and dip them in beat egg and cover them with a forcemeat made of grated ham, chopped anchovy, crumbs, mixed spices, etc. Fry them nicely in good clarified dripping and serve them with a gravy-sauce separately.

Pork sausage meat is the more usual coating nowadays. Egg and crumb before frying. The eggs may be served cold with salad.

Nun's Beads

(*Mrs. Dalgairns's Recipe*)

Cheese, eggs, bread-crumbs, salt, puff paste, butter

Pound in a mortar four ounces of good cheese with a little salt, the beaten yolk of three eggs, and some crumbs of bread; roll them as large as walnuts, cover them with puff paste, and fry them in butter a light brown colour. Serve them in a napkin.

Scots Toasts

Of these are many varieties: finnan-haddie, Arbroath smokie, kippered herring or salmon, cooked, flaked, and done up with a little Béchamel sauce, melted butter or thick cream; soft herring roes; minced game moistened and seasoned – all piled on rounds of buttered toast or fried bread, and garnished as desired.

Herring-Roe Toasts: (1) Lightly fry the roes in butter; or dip in olive oil and grill; then coil each roe on a round of buttered toast, sprinkle with lemon juice and cayenne, and garnish with slices of lemon and crisply fried parsley.

(2) Poach the roes in water with salt, white peppercorns, a small bay leaf and a dash of vinegar; drain carefully; coil each roe on a round of buttered toast, dot with butter and broil for five minutes; sprinkle with lemon juice and minced parsley.

Finnan-Toasts: (1) To four ounces of flaked finnan add a little coralline pepper, an ounce of butter, two tablespoonfuls of thick cream and a dessertspoonful of chopped parsley. Heat, spread on buttered toast and sprinkle with chopped parsley and lobster coral or coralline pepper.

(2) Blend the flaked fish with thick white sauce flavoured with cheese and a few grains of cayenne. Spread on toast, sprinkle with grated cheese and crumbs and brown under the grill.

Grouse Liver Savouries: Simmer the livers in salted water for ten minutes. Drain thoroughly and pound with a small pat of butter or with grouse drippings. Season with salt and cayenne. Spread on fingers of buttered toast and garnish each with a button mushroom previously fried in butter.

Kipper Creams

Kippered herring, eggs, salt and pepper, thick cream or white sauce, parsley

Remove the skin and bone from a plump kipper and rub the flesh through a sieve. Add two egg yolks, pepper, little or no salt (if the fish is highly cured), two tablespoonfuls of thick cream or white sauce, and the well-beaten white of one egg. Mix well and turn into little paper cases. Bake in a moderate oven to a light golden brown. Sprinkle with finely chopped parsley and serve on fish paper, or turn on to small round oatcakes made hot and crisp in the oven and buttered.

Green Dumplings

Suet pastry, young and tender green buds, shoots, etc.

These dumplings are made only at the time of the year when
things are covered with their first budding greenness.

'The dumplings are made in the ordinary way with suet
and flour seasoned with pepper and salt, but they are green
with some of everything that grows in spring freshness,
which you gather unobtrusively during the day. Pick the
green buds of hawthorn, the succulent tips of nettles, grass
and other green things, remembering that in this condition
nothing is poisonous; include dandelion leaves, daisy stems,
shoots of young corn and turnip-tops or anything that tastes
sweet and harmless. Wash them and chop them fine. Work
them into your dough until it is green through and through.
For soup make small dumplings not more than an inch
across; for stews and meats make them larger so that they
can be cut up. They go with anything, are delicious and
play the part of a salad in wholesomeness.'

– From *The Scots Week-end.*

Angler's Omelette

*Fresh herring milts, smoked salmon, salt, cayenne, parsley,
chervil, chives, butter, an omelette* aux fines herbes

Sprinkle some milts with salt, cayenne, and a little finely
chopped parsley, chervil and chives. Wrap each milt in a
thin slice of smoked salmon and poach gently in butter.
Make your omelette and place the salmon rolls in the centre.
Roll up and serve immediately.

PUDDINGS AND PIES

In the earlier edition of this work, I wrote, 'Whilst sweets, pies and tarts are common to many countries, the true home of the pudding is England.' I should have said, Great Britain, for on further research I have found that puddings (differing, of course, in detail) appear more or less simultaneously on both sides of the Border, especially throughout the eighteenth and nineteenth centuries.

It is true that as a nation the Scots are soup-lovers rather than pudding-lovers (in England it is the other way about) and that until recently puddings appeared mainly on middle-class and upper-class tables (as did soup in England).[1] Yet Meg Dods's *Manual*, which was published shortly before Mrs. Beeton was born, contains a far greater number of recipes for puddings and sweets than does the first edition of that lady's immortal work; and the popularity of the pudding on 'genteel' tables in Scotland is testified by Elizabeth Grant of Rothiemurchus (b. 1797), who refers in her Memoirs to 'my mother's first cook, Nellie Grant, she who could make so many puddings, 99 if I remember aright'.

The Scottish custom of taking cream, custard, or other sweet sauce, with puddings accounts for the fact that our pudding-plates are shallow, like small soup plates, and not flat, as in England, where it is customary to eat puddings dry. Scottish brides who settle south of the Border usually make a point of taking their pudding-plates with them or, if they have been provided with an English dinner-set, send north to have it supplemented.

Aunt Mary's Pudding

(Mrs. Dalgairns's Recipe)

Bread-crumbs, brown sugar, suet, raisins, currants, apples, ginger, nutmeg, brandy, eggs

Of bloom raisins stoned, currants nicely cleaned, suet finely minced, bread grated, apples minced, and brown sugar, a quarter of a pound of each; four well-beaten eggs, a teaspoonful of pounded ginger, half a teaspoonful of salt, half a nutmeg grated, and one glass of brandy. Mix the ingredients well and boil in a cloth for two hours. Serve with a sauce of melted butter, a glass of wine, and some sugar.

[1] 'An English friend of mine said to his Scottish wife, "In Scotland, soup is a food; in England, it is a class distinction." ' – Gastrologue in *The Scotsman*.

Citron Pudding

(Mrs. McIver's Recipe)

Citron, sugar, sugar biscuits, eggs, spinach, wine or spirits, butter

Slice half a pound of citron thin and shred it very small with a knife; beat and sift half a pound of sugar; beat sugar and citron very well together in a marble mortar; have the yolks of ten or a dozen eggs cast till they are like a cream. Then mix them by degrees into the beat sugar and citron and cast them very well with a spoon or knife. You may mix in a very little sugar biscuit. Put in as much of the juice of spinach as make it of a fine green; mix all well together. When you are just about putting it in the oven put in a dram and oiled butter and mix it very well. In all fine baked puddings let the oiled butter be the last thing you put in. Let it not be too hot.

Holyrood Pudding

(D. Williamson's Recipe)[1]

Semolina, butter, sugar, salt, ratafia biscuits, marmalade, eggs, milk

Bring a pint of milk to the boil and stir in two ounces of semolina, with three ounces of castor sugar, two of ratafia biscuits, and one of butter. Let it boil for about five minutes, stirring all the time. Pour it into a basin and allow it to cool. Meanwhile switch the whites of three eggs to a froth and butter a pudding mould. Beat into the mixture the yolks of three eggs, one at a time; flavour with a dessertspoonful of orange marmalade, and, lastly, add the whites of the eggs, beaten to a stiff froth. Mix gently, pour into the buttered mould, and steam for an hour and a quarter. Turn out and serve with almond sauce.

[1] D. Williamson and Son were cooks, confectioners, caterers and teachers of cookery in Dundas Street, Edinburgh, in the mid-nineteenth century.

Egg, sugar, milk, ground almonds, orange-flower water

Mix together in a small saucepan one egg with one ounce of sugar, one gill of milk, one ounce of ground sweet almonds, and one tablespoonful of orange-flower water. Put it on over a slow fire and stir with a switch till it becomes like thick cream, but do not let it boil.

Scots Marmalade Pudding

(*Old Family Recipe*)

Bread, raw sugar, raisins, marmalade, eggs, milk

Grate six ounces of stale bread, pour over it three teacupfuls of boiling milk, and set it aside till nearly cold. While it is cooling, separate the yolks and whites of three eggs. Beat up the yolks with three ounces of sugar, add a good tablespoonful of marmalade, and stir into the bread and milk. Switch the whites to a stiff froth and stir lightly into the pudding. Butter a mould and ornament it with big raisins, stoned. Pour in the pudding mixture and put the mould immediately into a pan with boiling water that will just come up to the level of the pudding inside the mould. Draw the pan aside so that it may remain just under boiling-point, and let it cook thus for an hour and three-quarters. When ready, take it out of the water, lift off the lid, let it stand for five minutes or more, then turn out and serve with hot custard sauce.

Plum Porridge

(Meg Dods's Recipe)

*Shin of beef, veal (optional), raisins, currants, prunes, pepper,
mace, nutmeg*

Boil ten pounds of a shin for five hours in a gallon, or rather
more, of water. Skim carefully. Strain off the liquor and
put to it a piece of veal cut from the fillet. Soften the crumb
of a penny loaf in the soup and beat it smoothly. Thicken the
soup with this and put to it half a pound of cleansed stoned
raisins and half a pound of stoned prunes, a pound of currants well cleaned, and some pepper, mace, and grated
nutmeg. When the fruit is soft the dish is ready. A little more
bread may be used if greater consistency is wanted, and the
veal may be omitted. Nearly obsolete.

From the earliest times, our Celtic forefathers celebrated the winter solstice and the
return of the fructifying sun from the farthest point in its circuit with a ceremonial
cutting of the mistletoe, the bringing in of evergreens, and the supping of a festive
gruel which was the symbol of the inexhaustible Cauldron of Keridwen – a sort of
Celtic cornucopia – and the portent of future abundance. In the Highlands, this gruel
has always been a special kind of sowans; in the Lowlands, they used more commonly
a rich brose, known as the Yule Brose. In the Middle Ages (and long after), when
sugar, spices and dried fruits were increasingly imported from foreign lands, the more
prosperous classes celebrated the festival with plum pottage, or porridge.

In the early years of the eighteenth century, plum porridge mysteriously solidified
into plum pudding. Nobody knows just how, when, or where it happened. Possibly in
some household the porridge was accidentally allowed to boil dry, but was removed
before it got burned, and the participants decided that it tasted better that way – and
the idea caught on.

We are all apt to think of plum pudding as a characteristically English dish, but
according to Robert Chambers, the first recipe, 'at least under that name', appears
in a Scottish cookery-book. Just as nobody knows for certain whether whisky originated in Scotland or Ireland – there was so much going and coming between the two
countries, and especially between Antrim and Kintyre, in early times – we may never
know for certain on which side of the Border the original plum pudding came into
being. Curiously, in *The Household Book of Lady Grisell Baillie*, the menu for 'Sunday,
Christenmas 1715' includes both 'plum patage' and 'plum puden'. – F. M. McN.

Plum Pudding

(Meg Dods's Recipe)

Biscuit, flour, raisins, currants, suet, sugar, nutmeg, cinnamon, mace, salt, lemon and orange and citron peel, blanched almonds, eggs, milk, wine or brandy

Take four ounces of pounded pudding biscuit, or of good common biscuit, and two ounces of the best flour, a half-pound of bloom or muscatel raisins stoned, the same quantity of fresh Zante currants picked and plumped, and a half-pound of suet stripped of skins and filaments, and shred; a small teaspoonful of nutmeg grated, a quarter-pound of fine beat sugar, a dram of pounded cinnamon, two blades of mace, and a saltspoonful of salt; three ounces of candied lemon, orange, and citron peel sliced, and two ounces of blanched almonds roughly chopped. Beat four eggs well, and put to them a little sweet milk, a glass of white wine or brandy, and then mix in the flour and all the ingredients minced. Tie up the pudding firmly and boil it for three hours, keeping up the boil and turning the cloth. Serve with caudle sauce.

'Plum pudding will keep long, and re-warm when wanted, in slices, in the Dutch oven or frying-pan.' – M. D.

A sprig of berried holly is inserted in the middle. 'This,' says Meg Dods, 'is to keep away the witches.'

'Instead of one huge plum pudding, we prepare at The Cleikum a hen and chickens, putting the hen, of ten or twelve pounds, to boil a couple of hours before her chickens. We have the hen for Christmas or company, and a plum-chicken can be heated up any day.' – Id.

CAUDLE SAUCE *(For a Plum Pudding)*

(Meg Dods's Recipe)

Melted butter, wine, rum, sugar, lemon, cinnamon

A glass of white wine, a half-glass of brandy or old rum or rum-shrub, pounded sugar to taste, the grate of a lemon, and a little cinnamon, stirred into a little thickened melted butter; sprinkle a little cinnamon on the top.

Cloutie Dumpling

A great favourite with the bairns in our cottage homes; so called because it is boiled in a clout or cloth.

Oatmeal, flour, suet, sultanas, bicarbonate of soda, cinnamon or mixed spice, buttermilk or thick sour milk

Mix in a bowl three ounces of oatmeal and three of flour (or six ounces of either oatmeal or flour), three ounces of shredded suet and three of sugar, four ounces of sultanas (or two of sultanas and two of currants), one teaspoonful of ground cinnamon or mixed spices, and half a teaspoonful of bicarbonate of soda. Stir in enough buttermilk or thick sour milk to make a thick soft batter – about three-quarters of a cupful. Dip a pudding cloth into boiling water and dredge lightly with flour. Spoon in the batter. (If the cloth is held inside a bowl large enough to hold the batter, it will give the pudding a round shape.) Draw the fullness of the cloth evenly together and tie firmly with string, leaving room for the dumpling to swell. Place an old plate in the bottom of a large pot, lower the dumpling on to this, and pour over enough boiling water to cover. Simmer for two and a half hours, adding more boiling water as required. Turn out carefully on to a hot ashet and dredge with castor sugar. Serve with custard sauce.

Sweet puddings (sausages) were made by stuffing this or a similar mixture into tripe skins and proceeding as for white or mealie puddings.

A Bride's Pie (*A Scots Pie*)

(*Meg Dods's Recipe*)

Calves' feet, mutton suet, apples, currants, raisins, candied lemon and citron peel, cinnamon, nutmeg, mace, brandy, Madeira, puff-paste

This is just a very nice mince pie. Chop the meat of two calves' feet, previously boiled, a pound of mutton suet, and a pound of pared apples, all separately, till they are fine. Mix them and add to them a half-pound of picked and rubbed currants and the same quantity of raisins stoned and chopped. Season with a quarter-ounce of cinnamon in powder, two drams of grated nutmeg and pounded mace, an ounce of candied citron and double the quantity of lemon peel, both sliced thin, a glass of brandy, and another of Madeira. Line a thin pan which has a slip-bottom with puff paste, and put the minced meat, etc., into it. Roll out a cover for the pie, which usually has a glass or gold ring concealed somewhere in the crust, and should be embellished with appropriate ornaments and devices, as Cupids, turtles, torches, flames, darts, and other emblematic devices of this kind.

(At a wedding feast) ' "Isna that a gallant banquet?" said Watty. "Look at yon grand pastry pie wi' the king's crown on't. . . . Wad ye like to pree[1] it, doctor? I'll just nip off ane o' the perlies[2] on the crown to let ye taste how good it is." '
– John Galt: *The Entail.*

Scottish Flans: Flan À La Caleb Balderstone

(*Meg Dods's Recipe*)[3]

In *The Bride of Lammermoor*, a flam (flan) figures in the menu which the worthy Caleb Balderstone draws up for the Master of Ravenswood.

Puff-paste, preserved fruit, frangipane (optional)

Rub butter on a fluted tin flan mould with a loose bottom, and line it with good puff-paste. With a pastry-knife Vandyke the edge, and carve each Vandyke as a rose-leaf, veined. Bake 'blind'. Fill with any sort of preserved fruit, as cherries, apples, apricots or pears.

Creamed flans are made by preparing thick frangipane[4] into which six ounces of sweet and one of bitter almonds, blanched and finely chopped, are stirred.

'These delicate preparations, we have no doubt, were perfectly well known when Scotland's "Kings kept court in Holyrood". The art has lingered on, ever since, among old-fashioned pastry-cooks in Edinburgh; and we have seen the flan, most beautifully served with the green Gascon gooseberry, preserved as only Mrs. Frazer, a celebrated pastry-cook of the last generation, could preserve and flavour this delicate small gooseberry.' – M. D.

[1] *pree*, taste.   [2] *perlies*, pearls.   [3] Abbreviated.
[4] *Frangipane:* A rich custard, to which are added some crushed ratafias, grated lemon rind and a glass of rum or brandy. It may be flavoured with orange, coffee, vanilla, orange-flower essence, or anything suitable to the dish it is to be used with.

Mrs. Dalgairns's Scots Pudding

Eggs, loaf sugar, butter, lemon, puff-paste

Take eight well-beaten yolks and three whites of eggs, half a
pound of pounded loaf sugar, a quarter-pound of melted
butter, the grated peel and juice of a lemon. Mix all together
and bake it in a dish lined with puff paste. Turn it out to
serve and strew over the top grated loaf sugar.

Almond Flory (*Florentine Tart*)

A favourite sweet in Edinburgh's Golden Age

(*Mrs. Cleland's Recipe*)

*Almonds, currants, butter, sugar, cinnamon, nutmeg, candied
lemon and citron peel (optional), eggs, cream, brandy, puff
paste*

Blanch and beat very fine a pound of almonds with orange-
flower water; beat eight eggs, but half of the whites; mix
them with two gills of cream and half a gill of brandy,
half a pound of clarified butter, a pound of currants well
washed and picked; season it with sugar, cinnamon, and
nutmeg, all pounded fine; mix them all very well; put them
in a dish with puff paste under and over them. You may put
candied lemon and citron in thin slices in it if you please. A
little while bakes it.

Apple Flory: Filling: Slices of apples that have been
simmering for a little in a syrup of sugar and water and
flavoured with cinnamon and grated lemon rind, over which
is spread orange or quince marmalade.

Prune Flory: Filling: Prunes, stoned and cooked gently in
a syrup of sugar and water, to which is added a squeeze of
lemon and a spoonful or so of port wine.

214

Greengage Frushie (*Victorian*)

Frushie[1] is a variety of fruit tart long popular in the West of Scotland. It is a flat open tart with a trellis-work of pastry over the fruit, and is eaten with rich cream, which is usually served separately but is sometimes whipped and served on the tart.

Any suitable fruit may be used – apple most commonly. A Greengage Frushie appears on the menu (preserved and shown to me by her daughter) of the wedding breakfast provided for a Helensburgh bride in the 1870s. – F. M. McN.

Greengages, sugar, water, rich shortcrust, thick cream

Wash and dry a sufficient number of ripe greengages. Cut each in half and remove the stone, then cut into thin slices. Line an ashet or tart-dish with a thin layer of shortcrust, letting it hang half an inch over the edge all round. Roll the pastry for the top to the exact size of the dish, and cut into strips half an inch wide. Lay every other strip about an inch apart, one way across on a waxed paper, lay the remaining strips across the other way, and weave them in and out, beginning with the centre strips and working out to the sides. Now cover the lined ashet with the fruit, arranging the slices, slightly overlapping one another, in neat rows. Moisten with a little light sugar-and-water syrup and sprinkle with granulated sugar. Turn the lattice top over the filling; seal the ends to the pastry on the edge of the dish, turn the overhanging pastry back over the ends of the lattice strips, and build up a fluted or crimped edge. Brush the pastry lightly with milk and bake.

Apple Puddings in Skins

(*Meg Dods's Recipe*)

Apples, biscuit, sugar, suet, cinnamon, nutmeg, wine or other liquor

Mince apples and grate biscuit; take an equal weight to these of minced suet. Sweeten this with sugar, and season with cinnamon and grated nutmeg. Moisten the whole with

---

[1] *Frushie* is an old Scots word signifying brittle, friable or crumbly, and clearly refers to the pastry with which the tart is made. – F. M. McN.

215

wine or any well-flavoured liquor, and mix, and fill the skins, but not too full, as the bread swells. Boil, and serve hot.

'These will keep for a week or ten days and re-warm by boiling; they may be browned in the Dutch oven. Another kind of fine pudding is made of rice boiled in milk, with suet, currants, sugar, and seasonings. The suet in these puddings should not be shred too small, which makes it thaw and disappear, nor yet left in lumps.' – M. D.

Urney Pudding (*Victorian*)

Flour, butter, castor sugar, bicarbonate of soda, jam, eggs

Sift four ounces of flour. Beat two eggs. Cream four ounces of butter with two of sugar. Beat in the flour and eggs alternately. Add two tablespoonfuls of jam (strawberry for preference) and, lastly, mix half a teaspoonful of soda with a teaspoonful of milk. Mix thoroughly. Turn into a greased pudding-bowl (which should be little more than half full), cover with greased paper, and steam for an hour and a half.

Serve with arrowroot sauce or creamy custard.

SWEETS

'As we are disposed to give the Monks full credit for many of the best French dishes, and for our own antiquated preparations, so are the fair recluses of France and Italy entitled to the merit of much that is elegant in confectionery, of which they long had, and still have, tasteful exhibitions on festivals. To their leisure and taste we owe caramelled and candied fruits fruits *en chemise*, Chantilly, and caramel baskets, etc., etc., as really as we do the most delicate lace, needlework, and cut paper.' – Meg Dods.

'The most alluring delicacies of the genteel Scottish dinner-table were those half-forgotten delights, flummeries, possets and syllabubs, all members of one noble family.' – Marion Lochhead: *The Scots Household in the Eighteenth Century*.

One might add, flans and flories, berry creams and trifles. – F. M. McN.

Some of the dishes in this section – Whipt Sillabubs, A Hedgehog, A Floating Island, for example, are Scottish variations of dishes to be found in other countries. – Id.

A Crokain[1]

(Mrs. Cleland's Recipe)

Sugar, water, lemon

Take three-quarters of a pound of fine sugar, put it in a clear copper pan with two gills of water, put it on the fire, let it boil slowly, skim it, but don't stir it; put in the juice of half a lemon, then let it boil brown; then take a spoon and try if it ropes; oil your mould and spin it on as neatly as you can and let it be pretty thick at the bottom; when it is done take it off as gently as you can. You may put any creams or any red or green preserved apples or oranges under it.

Scots Flummery

(Mrs. Cleland's Recipe)

Milk, cream, eggs, rose-water, sugar, nutmeg, sack

Take a mutchkin (pint) of milk and one of cream; beat the yolks of nine eggs with a little rose-water, sugar, and nutmeg;

[1] From *Croqu'en bouche*.

put it in a dish, and the dish over a pan of boiling water covered close; when it begins to grow thick have ready some currants plumped in sack and strew over it. It must not be stirred while it is over the fire, and when it is pretty stiff send it up hot.

Whipt Sillabubs (*Scots Fashion*)

(*Mrs. Cleland's Recipe*)

Cream, white wine, lemon, sugar

Take a mutchkin (pint) of thick cream, put to it half a mutchkin of white wine, the juice of a lemon, and grate the rind in it; sweeten it to your taste, whisk it up well, skim off the top as you are whisking it, and put it on a sieve; then put wine in the glass, either white or red, and a little sugar; then send it to table with teaspoons about it.

In one of the menus in *The Household Book of Lady Grisell Baillie*, there appears 'a salver w^t jellies and sillie bubess'; in another (supper at Mr. Cockburn's), 'In the middle of the table a pirimide sillibubs and orange cream in the past(e), above it sweet meets dry and wet.'

A Hen's Nest

(*Mrs. Cleland's Recipe*)

Calves-foot jelly, blancmange, lemon peel, egg-shells

Take calves-foot jelly that is very strong and put it in a white bowl or a Turk's-cap, fill it near half-full of the jelly, let it be cold; take five eggs, make a hole in the narrow end of them that the yolks and whites may come out; then fill them with blamong; let them stand till they are cold, then take off the shells by pieces and take care not to break the blamong; then lay them in the middle of the jelly so that they don't touch one another; then pour more jelly on them when it is almost cold. Cut some lemon peel as straws and, when the jelly is stiff, strew it over it; then pour a little more jelly

218

over it. When all is cold and very stiff, dip the bowl in hot water. Have an ashet ready and put it on the top of the bowl and turn it out quickly. Don't let the bowl be a moment in the water.

A Floating Island (*Scots Fashion*)

'And for a Floating Island, or a Hedgehog, we could never pretend to ony sic grandery at the Cleikum.' – Meg Dods, in the *Annals of the Cleikum Club*.

Eggs, quince, raspberry or red currant jelly, cream, wine, sugar, lemon peel

Three spoonfuls of guava quince, or raspberry or red currant jelly and the whites of as many eggs; beat them together one way till the spoon will stand erect; pile it upon cream beaten up with wine and sugar and a little grated lemon peel.

A Hedgehog (*Scots Fashion*)

(*Mrs. Cleland's Recipe*)

Almonds, sack or orange-flower water, eggs, cream, butter, currants

Blanch and beat a pound of almonds very fine with a spoonful of sack or orange-flower water to keep them from oiling; make it into a stiff paste, then beat up six eggs and put two whites; sweeten it with fine sugar, then put in half a mutchkin (half-pint) of cream and a quarter of a pound of beat butter; set it on your stove and keep it stirring till it is so stiff that you can make it into the shape of a hedgehog, then stick it full of blanched almonds cut in straws; set them in like the bristles with two currants plumped for eyes, then place it in the middle of the dish and boil some cream; put in it the yolks of two eggs and sweeten it to your taste; put it on a slow fire and when it is scalding hot take it off; you must keep it stirring all the while; when it is cold put it about the hedgehog.

219

Whim-Wham[1]

(Mrs. Dalgairns's Recipe)

Cream, white wine, lemon, Naples biscuit, red currant jelly, candied citron and orange peel

Sweeten a quart of cream and mix with it a teacupful of white wine and the grated peel of a lemon; whisk to a froth, which drain upon the back of a sieve and put part into a deep glass dish; cut some Naples biscuit[2] as thin as possible and put a layer lightly over the froth and one of red currant jelly, then a layer of the froth and one of biscuit and jelly; finish with the froth and pour the remainder of the cream into the dish and garnish with citron and candied orange peel cut into straws.

Fairy Butter

(Mrs. Dalgairns's Recipe)

Butter, orange-flower water, eggs, sweet almonds, lemon peel, loaf sugar, Naples biscuits, white wine

Wash a quarter of a pound of fresh butter in orange-flower water and beat it with the pounded yolks of five or six hard-boiled eggs; blanch and pound to a paste with a little orange-flower water two ounces of sweet almonds; add a little grated lemon peel and pounded and sifted loaf sugar; mix all together and, with a wooden spoon, work it through a stone colander. Soak some Naples biscuits in white wine and put over them the fairy butter in heaps as high as it can be raised.

---

[1] 'Whim-whams' are mentioned by Scott in *The Bride of Lammermoor*.

[2] *(Mrs. Cleland's Recipe for Naples Biscuit):*
Take a pound of fine sugar pounded and sifted, a pound of fine flour; beat eight eggs with two spoonfuls of rose-water; mix flour and sugar, then wet it with the eggs and as much cold water as will make a light paste; beat the paste very well then put them (the biscuits) in papered tin pans.* Bake in a gentle oven.

* The correct Naples biscuit-tin is eight inches long, three wide, and one deep.

A Burnt Cream

(Mrs. Cleland's Recipe)

Cream, eggs, flour, sugar, cinnamon, orange

Boil a mutchkin (pint) of cream and thicken it with the yolks of eight eggs and a spoonful of flour; boil cinnamon and the rind of an orange in the cream; take care it is not curdled, sweeten it to your taste; take a quarter-pound of loaf sugar in a stew-pan and pour over it a gill of water; let it boil till it ropes and don't stir it till you take it off; then by degrees strew it over your ashet of cream; brown it with a salamander or in the oven.

(Aberdeenshire Recipe)[1]

Cream, eggs, castor sugar

Beat the yolks of four eggs in a basin. Heat a pint of cream, and, when boiling, pour it on to the yolks, stirring well. Pour the custard into the dish in which it is to be sent to the table. Allow it to become quite cold. Strew the surface thickly with castor sugar and brown it with a red-hot salamander or under a hot grill. The sugar should make a hard surface, like light brown ice, all over the top, about an eighth of an inch thick.

Scots Trifle

(Traditional Recipe)

Stale sponge cakes or rice cake, ratafias, raspberry or strawberry jam, lemon rind, sherry, brandy (optional), rich custard, cream, garnishing

Split six individual sponge cakes and spread thickly with

---

[1] 'It is amusing to remember that this recipe, which came from a country-house in Aberdeenshire in the (eighteen-) sixties, was offered to the kitchens of Trinity College, Cambridge, by an undergraduate, and rejected with contempt. When the undergraduate became a Fellow, just thirty years ago (i.e. in 1879), he presented it again. This time it was accepted as a matter of course. It speedily became one of the favourite dishes of May Week.' – Eleanor L. Jenkinson:* *The Ocklye Cookery Book* (1909).

* The sister of a former Cambridge University Librarian.

jam. Put together again and arrange in a shallow glass dish. Pound about eighteen ratafia biscuits and strew over the sponges. Sprinkle with the grated rind of half a lemon. Over this pour a gill of sherry (not too dry) and two tablespoonfuls of brandy, then three-quarters of a pint of rich custard. Allow to stand for at least an hour. Whip half a pint of cream, add sugar to taste and flavour with vanilla or Drambuie.[1] Pile this over the custard and garnish with crystallized rose petals (pink) or cherries and angelica; ratafias and pistachio nuts; pink sugar with a border of ratafias; harlequin comfits; or as desired.

Marsala, ginger wine, or fruit syrup, may be substituted for sherry.

Drambuie Cream

Eggs, milk, sugar, gelatine, cream, Drambuie, wine jelly, sponge fingers

Pour a gill of cool wine jelly into the bottom of a charlotte mould, and while still liquid, line the sides with sponge fingers. Leave to set. When set, pour Drambuie cream into the mould. Leave again to set. Unmould and decorate with whipped cream.

To make the Drambuie cream, scald three-quarters of a pint of milk. Blend three ounces of sugar and three-quarters of an ounce of powdered gelatine with two well-beaten eggs. Pour the milk over the egg mixture and return to the pan. Cook, but do not boil. Set aside to cool, but do not let it set. Whip half a pint of cream, adding four ounces of Drambuie. When the custard is cool, blend together and pour into the sponge-finger lined mould.

(This recipe was kindly given to the author by Mrs. Mackinnon, Chairman of the Drambuie Liqueur Company and guardian of its secret.)

Drambuie is excellent in a trifle, or sprinkled over strawberries in lieu of cream, or as a flavouring for whipped cream or ice cream.

[1] Meg Dods, in her recipe for *An Elegant Trifle*, writes, 'Beat the cream with sugar a glass of white wine, lemon juice and grate, and a few bits of cinnamon.'

Edinburgh Fog (*Modern*)

Cream, sugar, vanilla, ratafia biscuits, almonds

Beat half a pint of cream to a stiff froth with a little pounded sugar and vanilla flavouring. Mix thoroughly with a good handful of ratafia biscuits and some blanched and chopped almonds. Serve in a glass bowl or dish.

Custard For A Centre Dish (*Old Scots Style*)

Make a strong whip of sweetened cream. Heap it over a rich custard, and garnish with bright green and scarlet preserved fruits.

The custard may be spread with apricot jam.

Ideal for the Christmas table.

Caledonian Cream

(*Mrs. Dalgairns's Recipe*)

Orange marmalade, brandy, loaf sugar, lemon, cream

Mince a tablespoonful of orange marmalade; add it, with a glass of brandy, some pounded loaf sugar, and the juice of a lemon, to a quart of cream; whisk it for half an hour and pour it into a shape with holes in it, or put it into a small hair sieve with a bit of thin muslin laid into it.

Caledonian Ice (*Iced Stapag*)

Cream, vanilla, sugar, oatmeal

Whip some cream stiffly; sweeten it and flavour with vanilla; set it to freeze. When nearly frozen stir in coarse toasted oatmeal, well dried in the oven without being browned. Serve in a glass dish or in individual glasses.

Deer-Horn Jelly

A personal friend of the writer, whilst travelling recently in the Rannoch district, fell in with a young girl of the locality who was carrying a small deer horn. On inquiry, the girl explained that she was taking it home, and that when boiled for several hours the horn would make 'a delicious jelly'. Only the horn of a *young* deer is used.

This information having been received just as the book was going to press, it was impossible to obtain details of the mode of preparation.

Another correspondent, a native of Ballindalloch, recollects that her mother made some sort of oil from a deer's foot. – F. M. McN.

Deerfoot Jelly. This is made very much in the manner of calf's foot jelly. (See Margaret Fraser's *Highland Cookery Book.*)

BANNOCKS, SCONES, AND TEABREAD

The process of bread-making is basically the same in all countries and in all ages, but there are many variations in the final stage of the dough. In Scotland these have always been particularly numerous.

The bread *de luxe* was Mayne bread, which was made with the finest stone flour. It is mentioned in 1443, when, according to the Edinburgh records, it was decreed that it should be made only on 'Whitsunday, Sanct Geillis Mass (St. Giles Day, September 1), Yule and Pasch'. It appears to have been a rich kind of tea loaf containing sugar, butter, eggs and currants, which, as 'raysins of Corinth' were already imported in the fifteenth century. (It was also popular in England. Chaucer in one of his poems uses the simile, 'white as *paine de maine*', which suggests a French origin.)

In eighteenth-century Edinburgh, according to Henry Mackenzie (*The Man of Feeling*), there were more than fifty different kinds of teabread. A few are listed below.

'Today's enviable reputation derives from long years of skilled craftsmanship. The industry has a notable tradition which was founded and consolidated by the ancient Incorporation of Baxters, as the bakers were known in former centuries.

'Great changes in techniques and public taste have taken place since the early baxters worked from early morning in their individual bakehouses at the back of their shops, and what was originally a very localized trade has widened in scope enormously.'

If every Frenchwoman is born with a wooden spoon in her hand, every Scotswoman is born with a rolling-pin under her arm. There may be a divergence of opinion as to her skill in cooking, but it is certain that she has developed a remarkable technique in baking – not only in bannocks, scones and oatcakes, but also in the finer manipulations of wheat – in cakes, pastry and shortbread.[1] – F. M. McN.

Some Varieties Of Bread

In sixteenth-century Scotland there were four kinds of wheaten bread, the finest called *Manche*, the second *Cheat*, or trencher bread, the third *Ravelled*, and the fourth *Mashloch*. The Ravelled was baked just as it came from the mill, flour, bran, and all. From the Mashloch the flour was almost entirely sifted; a portion of rye was mixed with the bran, and this composition was used by poor people and servants. (See Arnot's *History of Edinburgh*.)

Breid o' Mane. A very light and savoury white bread. See above.

Breid o' Trayt. A superior kind of white bread.

Ankerstock. A large loaf of rye, oblong in shape. – Jamieson. 'The anker-stock was a round loaf made of rye flour, and seasoned with spice and currants, and used as New Year gingerbread.' – Hislop's *Scottish Anecdotes* (1875). 'A Musselburgh ankerstoke' is mentioned by D. M. Moir in *Mansie Waugh*. Ankerstock gingerbread is still sold by Edinburgh bakers. Probably from Dutch *anker*, a measure (the fourth part of a boll).

---

[1] 'If manipulation, delicate and deft, be one of the secrets of good, or fine cooking, there should be many good, or fine cooks among Scots housewives. So many of them can turn out scones and paste that are gossamer.'
                                                            – Victor MacClure: *Scotland's Inner Man.*

Bake, baik. A small cake, a biscuit. – Fergusson, Burns. Varieties: butter-bake, water-bake, wine-bake (a soft crumbly wine-biscuit), Hawick bake (flavoured with allopice), cappie-bake (shaped with a raised rim).

Bakin-Lotch. 'A species of bread, perhaps of an enticing quality.' – Jamieson.

Bawbee Raw. A ha'penny roll. – *St. Ronan's Well.*

Birlin. A small cake made of oatmeal or barley-meal. Cf. Gael. *builan*, a loaf.

Clod. A flat kind of loaf, made of coarse wheaten flour or pease-meal. *Clods.* Small raised loaves, baked of coarse flour, of which three were sold for five farthings. *Soutar's Clods.* A kind of coarse brown wheaten bread used in Selkirk, leavened and surrounded with a thick crust, like clods. – Jamieson. Mentioned by Scott in *Redgauntlet.*

'The Baijen Hole, a celebrated and very ancient baker's shop, . . . was famed for a species of rolls called Soutar's Clods, which were in great request among the boys of Edinburgh on account of their satisfactory dimensions.'
– R. Chambers: *Traditions of Edinburgh.*

Derrin. A broad thick cake or loaf of oat or barley-meal or mixed pease- and barley-meal, which is fired in the oven or on the hearth covered with hot ashes; Roxburghshire. 'This term is very ancient and is probably derived from the mode of preparation. Teut. *derren*, to dry or parch.' – Jamieson.

Fadge, fage. A large flat cake or loaf. Fr. *fouace*, a thick cake. – Allan Ramsay.

Foal. A bannock or cake; any soft, thick bread; soft gingerbread biscuits covered with sugar-coated caraway seeds. Sold at the Lammas Fair (Orkney).

Meldar. A salted cake. – Douglas. Isl. *malldr*, from *mal-a*, to grind. – Jamieson.

Nacket (Roxburgh). *Nockit* (Galloway), *Nackie* (Ayrshire). A small cake or loaf; a piece of bread eaten at noon; something to eat with wine. Sueo-Goth. *kneck*, globulous.
– Jamieson.

Snoddie. A thick cake or bannock baked among hot ashes (Orkney). Isl. *snad*, food.
– Jamieson.

Sod. A species of bread (Ayrshire).

Tivlach. A thick cake of oatmeal (Shetland).

Tod, Toddie. A small round cake of any kind of bread, given to children to keep them in good humour (Roxburgh), *Todgie* (Berwickshire), *Toly*, *Toddle* (Upper Clydesdale). Isl. *taata, placenta infantum.* – Jamieson.

Wafrans. Wafers, thin cakes. *Wafroun* (Lanarkshire). *Treas. Acts.*

Whig. A fine wheaten tea-bread. – Sir John Sinclair.

Wine-bake. A soft crumbly wine-biscuit.

Bannocks And Scones

In Scotland, amongst the rural population generally, the girdle until recent times took the place of the oven, the bannock of the loaf. – F. M. McN.

(General Directions)

The girdle should be put on to heat before the dough is mixed. To test the heat, sprinkle a little flour over it. If it browns at once the girdle is too hot; if it takes a few seconds to brown it will do. For scones and bannocks, sprinkle the girdle with flour, unless they are themselves sufficiently

226

floury to prevent sticking; but for Scots crumpets and drop scones grease the girdle very slightly – just enough to prevent sticking – with a piece of suet wrapped in a clean rag. In a word, the girdle is floured for dough and greased for batter.

The girdle should never be washed, but should be cleaned when hot by being rubbed with coarse salt and a piece of paper, and then dusted with a clean cloth.

Use only the best materials. The best baking-soda is to be had from the chemist. Use the finest flour and see that it is dry. Sift it at least once, allowing the air to get into it as much as possible, into a basin, or, better, straight on to the baking-board or marble slab. Mix the dry ingredients thoroughly and gather them into a heap in the centre of the board. Make a hole in the centre into which pour the milk. Then go round the edge of the pool of milk with a wooden spoon and toss the flour lightly in. Never stir in the centre.

The dough should be as soft as is compatible with its being lightly handled, and should be handled as little as possible. Roll out lightly, and fire slowly for about ten minutes on the one side, then turn and fire for about five on the other. Turn only once.

Buttermilk, with bicarbonate of soda, is always used for bannocks and girdle scones. It produces a much better scone – bulkier, softer, and moister-eating – than does sweet or sour milk. This is due to the softening or maturing or ripening action of the lactic acid it contains on the gluten of the flour, an action somewhat akin to that which takes place during fermentation.

A very fine scone can be obtained thus: Drop a spoonful of the dough on a heap of flour; flour the hands, lift the dough lightly with one hand and transfer it to the other, shaking off the loose flour in the transference. Pass the dough lightly from hand to hand, and then drop it on the hot girdle.

The names scone and bannock are applied rather loosely. In modern usage the bannock is the large round scone, about the circumference of a meat-plate, which is baked on the girdle. When the bannock is cut into sections before being fired, or when the dough is cut into small rounds, you have scones.

Bannock: O.Sc. *bannok*, a name that occurs in 1572, derives from Lat. *panicum* (*panis*) probably through the influence of the Church. It may have referred originally to Communion bread.

The etymology of *scone* (pronounced *skonn*, which is Sir John Sinclair's spelling) is uncertain. Chambers suggest the Gaelic *sgonn*, a shapeless mass; Alexander Carmichael, *sgonn*, a block; *sgonn aran*, a block of bread.

On the other hand, Mr. David Murison, the Editor of the *Scottish National Dictionary*, derives it from the Dutch *schoonbrot*, fine bread. (Dutch *sch* is pronounced *ss-ch* (as in *loch*) and regularly becomes sk, as, e.g. *schipper* becomes *skipper*. The name first appears in the sixteenth century. In Gavin Douglas's translation of the seventh Aeneid, we read that at a feast at the mouth of the Tiber,

> The flour sconnis weir set in by and by
> With other messis.

It is surprising that scones, now so popular in England and throughout the English-speaking world, are not even mentioned in the earlier editions of Mrs. Beeton's work (1860).

Bere Or Barley Bannocks

> Leeze me on thee,[1] John Barleycorn,
> Thou king o' grain!
> On thee auld Scotland chaws her cood
> In souple scones, the wale[2] o' food.
>   – Burns: *Scotch Drink.*

> Fair fa'[3] the gudewife and send her gude sale,
> She gies us gude bannocks to drink her ale.
>   – Old Song: *Todlen But and Todlen Ben.*

> At the sight of Dumbarton once again,
> I'll cock up my bonnet and march amain,
> With a gude claymore hanging down at my heel,
> To whang at the bannocks o' barley-meal.
>   – John, Duke of Argyll.

> Wha in a brulyie[4]
> Will first cry a parley?[5]
> Never the lads wi'
> The bannocks o' barley!
> Bannocks o' bere meal,
> Bannocks o' barley,
> Here's to the Hielandman's
> Bannocks o' barley!
>   – Old Song.

'Did our swank country lads know how appetizingly sustaining a barley scone can be made – especially did our comely country lasses . . . realize the virtues, of beauty to the skin and sweetness to the temper, which reside in bannocks of bear-meal – there would be, I am firmly convinced, such a revival of this well-approved ancient feeding-stuff as would send down the price of wheat and drive tapioca and similar foreign stinking ware that jaups in luggies clean out of caup and market.'
    – Hugh Haliburton: *Furth in Field.*

(Old Method)

Barley-meal, butter, salt, sweet milk

Put half a pint of milk into a pan with a pinch of salt and an ounce or more of butter. Bring to the boil and stir in

---

[1] Dear thou to me (Lief is me).   [2] Choicest.   [3] Good befall.
    [4] Broil.   [5] Truce.

quickly enough barley-meal to make a pliable dough. Turn
out on a floured board, roll out thinly, cut into rounds the
size of a meatplate. Bake on a hot girdle, turning them once,
on a rather sharp fire. They should be eaten hot.

In Sutherland the bannocks are often mixed with whey
(unheated), without butter.

(Modern Method)

Barley-meal, flour, bicarbonate of soda, salt, buttermilk

Put into a bowl a pound of barley-meal, four ounces of
flour, two small teaspoonfuls of cream of tartar and half a
teaspoonful of salt. Mix well. Put three teacupfuls of buttermilk into a jug and into it stir two small teaspoonfuls of
bicarbonate of soda. Stir briskly, and, as it fizzes up, pour
it into the flour mixture. Make into a soft dough, turn out on
a floured board, handle as little as possible, but roll out
lightly to about half an inch in thickness; cut into rounds the
size of a meat-plate, place on a hot girdle, and bake (not
too quickly) until the under side is brown; turn the bannock
and brown the other side.

The proportion of flour may be increased to taste.

A survival of an old Druidical belief, mentioned by Sir James Frazer in *The Golden
Bough*, and still prevalent in some parts of the Highlands, is that in kneading bannocks,
stirring porridge or kail, sending a glass round the company, etc., the movement must
be 'deiseal', sunwise – i.e. the right-hand turn. This is the lucky way. Widdershins –
i.e. the left-hand turn – is unlucky.

Pease Bannocks

> Sae brawly[1] did a pease-scon toast
> Biz i' the queff[2] and flie the frost,
> There we got fu' wi' little cost,
> And muckle[3] speed.
> – Alan Ramsay.

Make as barley bannocks, substituting pease-meal for
barley-meal.

[1] Finely.   [2] Quaigh, drinking-cup.   [3] Much.

Mashlum Bannocks

'Twa mashlum bannocks.' – Burns: *Cry and Prayer*.

Bannocks made of any mixture of flours are known as mashlum or meslin bannocks, and in some parts as brash-bread. They are prepared like barley bannocks.

Struan Micheil (St. Michael's Cake). In the Hebrides there is a traditional harvest-cake made of a mixture of oats, barley, and rye (representing the fruits of the field) baked on September 29th in honour of St. Michael. As the bannock gains consistency in the firing, it is covered on both sides with three successive layers of a batter of cream, eggs, and butter, in the manner of the Beltane bannock. Various ingredients are introduced into the small struans, as cranberries, blaeberries, brambles, caraways, and wild honey. The elaborate ritual used in the preparation of this cake is described by Alexander Carmichael in the introduction to his collection, *Carmina Gadelica*, and in my own work, *The Silver Bough*, Vol. II, in the chapter on Michaelmas.

Aran Isenach (Indian Bread) is a bannock made in the Outer Isles of a mixture of flour and fine Indian meal, shortened with butter.

Oatcakes

O whar did ye get the hauvermeal[1] bannock?
O silly blind body, O dinna ye see?
I got it frae a brisk young sodger laddie
Between St. Johnston[2] and bonnie Dundee.
– Old Song.

The carline[3] brought her kebbuck[4] ben
Wi' girdle-cakes well toasted broon.
Weel does the canny kimmer[5] ken[6]
They gar[7] the scuds[8] gae glither[9] doon
– *Andro and his Cutty Gun*.

O gie me the time when auld ploys were in vogue,
An' the cake an' the kebbuck gaed doon wi' the cog.[10]
– Hew Ainslie.

Oatmeal, fat or dripping, baking-soda, salt, hot water

Four special implements are used for baking oatcakes – the *spurtle*, or porridge-stick, for stirring the mixture; a notched *bannock-stick*, or rolling-pin, which leaves a criss-cross pattern on the upper side; the *spathe*, a heart-shaped implement with a long handle, made of iron, used for transferring the cakes from board to girdle; and the *banna-rack*, or toaster.

[1] Oatmeal. [2] Perth. [3] Old woman. [4] Cheese. [5] Gossip.
[6] Know. [7] Make. [8] Liquor. [9] Easier.
[10] Wooden vessel to contain liquor.

If a quantity is to be made, the dough should be rather soft, as it stiffens whilst lying about to be made up. The best results are obtained by mixing enough for one bannock, or round, at a time (using the quantities given below), the next bannock being prepared whilst the last is on the girdle.

Put into a bowl four ounces of oatmeal, a pinch of baking-soda, and a pinch of salt. Melt a teaspoonful of fat (bacon or poultry fat or butter or dripping; goose fat is excellent). Make a well in the centre of the oatmeal and add the melted fat with just enough hot water to make a stiff dough. Rub plenty of meal on to the baking-board; turn out the mixture and form into a smooth ball; knead with gradually spreading knuckles, working as quickly as possible, and roll out as thinly as possible – say an eighth of an inch. The process is not quite easy to one unfamiliar with the work, owing to the stickiness of the dough and the tendency of the edges to break. The dough must be kept from sticking by constant rubbing over on both sides with dry meal, and the edges must be kept as even as possible by pinching with the thumb and forefinger. Invert a plate of from five to seven inches in diameter on the dough and cut neatly into a round. Give a final rub with meal to make the cakes white. They may be left whole (bannocks) or cut into quarters (farls).[1] Place on a moderately hot girdle over a clear fire, smooth side uppermost, and bake steadily till the cakes curl up at the edge. Remove them carefully, rub a little oatmeal over them, and toast the smooth side slightly before a bright smokeless fire. (Toasting-stones with an incised pattern to permit the sweating of the cakes were formerly used on the open hearth. An attachable iron toaster was used on the ordinary coal-range.) Place for a few minutes in a warm place, e.g. a moderate oven. Keep buried in oatmeal in the girnel or meal-chest; or, failing these, in a tin. They are improved by

A.S. *feorth-dael*. Also called *corter* (quarter), Aberdeenshire.
> Wi' sweet-milk cheese i' mony a whang,
> An' farlies baked wi' butter.
> – Burns: *The Holy Fair*.

Some bakers nowadays misuse the term *farl* for the thin quarters and *bannock* for the thick ones of the same dimension.

being heated shortly before they are served, unless they are freshly baked.

'The proper making of these cakes requires both skill and care. Have for the best kind, finely ground, double-sifted oatmeal, such as is only seen to the north of the Spey.' – Meg Dods.

An excellent oatcake is baked with whey, in place of fat and water. Buttermilk and cream, fresh or sour, may be used, but milk renders them flinty.

Oatcakes were at one time the gala-bread of the cottager; barley-bread was the ordinary fare.

'Oatcakes are a delicate relish when eaten warm with ale.' – Burns.

'Oatcakes should always be sent to table with fresh herrings garnished with raw onions and cold butter.' – Mrs. McEwen: *Elements of Cookery*, 1835.

Oatcakes are especially good with herrings, sardines, cheese, curds, buttermilk, broth, and kail; or spread with butter and marmalade to complete the breakfast.

The original oatcake was made of oatmeal and cold water. In the Hebrides, this is called a *potag* or *ollag*. Until quite recent times, the Skye fishermen used to dip a handful of oatmeal over the side of the boat into the sea and, when it was thoroughly moistened, knead into a bannock. On this frugal fare they could subsist, if need were, for days.

According to Froissart, the accoutrements of the Scottish soldier in the fourteenth century included a flat plate at his saddle and a wallet of meal at his back, 'the purpose whereof is this: Whereas a Scottish soldier hath eaten of flesh so long that he beginneth to loathe the same, he casteth this plate into the fire, he moisteneth a little of his meal in water, and when the plate is heated, he layeth his paste thereon and maketh a little cake, the which he eateth to comfort his stomach. Hence it is no marvel that the Scots should be able to make longer marches than other men.'

While staying some time ago in the Mackintosh country, the writer was told of an old woman who lived in a cottage between Culloden and Moy during the Forty-five. On the day of the battle, word having reached her of the Prince's defeat, the old soul carried her table, her girdle, and a quantity of oatmeal down to the roadside, lit a gipsy fire, and baked for all she was worth; and when presently Charlie's men came by, speeding to the hills for safety, each seized an oatcake from the pile.

Some Varieties Of Oatcakes

Branderbannock. A thick bannock cooked on a brander.

Een-cake or *Oon-cake.* Thick cake made of yeast and oatmeal and baked in the oven.

Clauti-scone. A coarse scone of oatmeal and yeast made in Kinross.

Mill-bannock. 'A circular cake of oatmeal, with a hole in the centre, generally a foot in diameter and an inch in thickness. It is baked at milnes and *haurned* or toasted on the burning seeds of shelled oats, which makes it as brittle as if it had been baked with butter.' – *Gallovidian Encyclopedia.*

Soor Poos. Oatcakes moistened with swats (the liquid poured off sowans).

Caper. A piece of oatcake and butter with a slice of cheese on it. Gael. *ceapaire.*

Beltane Bannocks. Oatcakes, prepared in a special way, were used from time immemorial, in the rites of Beltane (May 1st, O.S.). Pennant (1769) writes: 'Everyone takes a cake of oatmeal, upon which are raised nine square knobs, each dedicated to some particular being the supposed preserver of their flocks and herds, or to some particular animal, the real destroyer of them. Each person turns his face to the fire, breaks off a knob, and, flinging it over his shoulder, says: "This I give to thee, preserve thou my horses; this to thee, preserve thou my sheep," and so on. After that, they use the same ceremony to the noxious animals: "This I give to thee, O Fox, spare thou my lambs; this to thee, O Hooded Crow, this to thee, O Eagle!"

'The Beltane cakes with the nine knobs on them,' writes the Rev. Walter Gregor in *Folklore*, 'remind us of the cakes with twelve knobs which the Athenians offered to Cronus and other deities.'

In Badenoch, until recently, oatcakes marked on one side with a cross and on the other with a circle were rolled down the hillside on Beltane morning. (See *The Silver Bough*, Vol. II.)

According to Sir James Frazer, Beltane bannocks were oatcakes baked in the usual way, but washed over with a thin batter composed of whipped egg, milk, and cream, and a little oatmeal. (See *The Golden Bough*.) This batter is called the Beltane caudle. Pennant (1774) describes how in every village the herdsmen light the Beltane fire and on it 'dress a large caudle of eggs, butter, oatmeal, and milk', some of which they spill on the ground 'by way of libation.'

John Ramsay, the Laird of Ochiltree and a contemporary of Burns, mentions 'a large cake baked with eggs and scalloped round the edge, *an bonnach beal-tine*, the Beltane bannock'.

'It is no longer made in Uist,' writes Miss Goodrich-Freer in *More Folk'ore from the Hebrides* (1902), 'but Father Allan[1] remembers seeing his grandmother make one about twenty-five years ago.'

The Beltane bannock appears to be the last survivor of the old Highland Quarter Cakes; the *bonnach Bride*, St. Bride's bannock, baked for the first day of spring; the *bonnach Bealltain*, Beltane bannock, baked for the first day of summer; the *bonnach Lunastair*, Lammas bannock, baked for the first day of autumn; and the *bonnach Samhthain*, Hallowmas bannock, baked for the first day of winter.

Bonnach Salainn (salt bannock). An oatcake, baked in the ordinary way save for the addition of a great deal of salt, which used to be eaten in the Highlands at Hallowe'en to induce dreams that would foretell the future. No water might be drunk, nor any word spoken, after it was eaten, or the charm would not work.

St. Columba's Cake. A bere, rye, or oaten cake, baked on the eve of St. Columba's Day (June 9th). A small silver coin was put into the dough, and the cake was toasted before a fire of rowan, yew, oak, or other sacred wood. The child who got the coin got the crop of lambs for the year.

Yule Bread. The Yule bread proper was a thin bannock of oatmeal. Just as the neighbour wives at a lying-in prepared their 'merrymeat' to celebrate the birth of the child, so the housewife baked the Yule-bannocks in honour of the Virgin's delivery, the usual round bannock having the sign of the Cross made upon it with a sharp knife, which thus divided it into 'farls' (fardels or quarters) before it was placed on the girdle. The cakes were baked before daybreak on Christmas morning. Each member of the family received one, which he endeavoured to keep intact until the time of the evening feast. If it remained whole, the owner might expect unbroken prosperity in the coming year; if it were broken, shattered likewise were his hopes of good fortune.

There is, however, ample evidence that the 'Christianized' bannocks derive from an early pagan source. In Shetland, where traces of the ancient Scandinavian Yule are more marked than anywhere else in these islands, the Yule-brunies, as they are called, are still round in shape, with a hole in the centre (to keep the trows (trolls) away), and the edge pinched in points to symbolize the sun's rays – although the symbolism is doubtless entirely forgotten. In brief, the Yule-bannock, like the Yule-log, is a relic of sun-worship. An oatcake was kneaded for each child, and differed in size as the children differed in age.

[1] The late Father Allan Macdonald of Eriskay, a distinguished folklorist and much-loved priest.

Oat farls, together with a slice of the Yule kebbuck (cheese), were commonly given to the children who went guising (mumming) on Hogmanay.

Cryin'-bannock. When a child was born, in some districts a bannock, called a cryin'-bannock, made of oatmeal, cream, and sugar, and cooked in a frying-pan, was served up to the 'kimmers' (gossips) present.

Teethin'-bannock. When a child first showed symptoms of cutting teeth, a bannock of oatmeal and butter or cream, sometimes with a ring in it, was made and given to the child to play with till broken. The child got a small bit and so did each one present. See *Notes on the Folklore of the North-east of Scotland*, by the Rev. W. Gregor.

The Infar-cake or *Dreaming-bread.* In early times the bride's cake of rural Scotland was a richly shortened oatcake, which was used as infar-cake. The breaking of the infar-cake over the head of the bride on the threshold of her new home is a very ancient custom, having its origin in the Roman rite of *conferratio*, in which the eating of a consecrated cake by the contracting parties constituted marriage. (Scots law, although its roots are native, has been, unlike English law, strongly influenced by the old Roman law.) Portions were distributed to the young unmarried men and maidens 'to dream on'.

A song frequently sung by the wedding-guests at the breaking of the infar cake runs:

> Welcome to your ain fireside!
> Health and wealth attend the bride!
> Wanters[1] noo your true weird[2] make:
> Joes[3] are spaed[4] by th' infar-cake.

The Orkney custom in the late nineteenth century is described by a parish minister, the late Rev. John Firth. After the arrival of the wedding-guests the hansel wife distributed bread and cheese. 'When this had been disposed of, there was a hush of expectancy for a minute as the mester-hoosal came up quietly behind the bride's back, and over her head held the bride's cake on his open palm. With a swing of his arm he came down with his fist on the centre of the cake, which broke into crumbs and fell down in a shower over and around the bride. A most exciting scramble ensued, it being regarded as very lucky to catch a piece of the cake before it reached the ground.

'The cake, then so much prized, was nothing more than an oat bannock made crisp by being baked with butter; but despite its plainness, the smallest particle was supposed to carry a charm. It was placed under their pillows by young girls and never failed to reveal the name or appearance of the future spouse.'

Sour-Skons (*Orkney*)

Oatmeal, flour, baking-soda, sugar, caraway seeds, buttermilk

Soak some oatmeal in buttermilk for a few days, then take it and beat it up with flour into which you have stirred a little baking-soda (allow roughly a teaspoonful to each pound of oatmeal and flour), sugar to taste (don't over-sweeten), and a few caraway seeds. Make into a soft dough, roll out, and bake on the girdle.

---

[1] A bachelor or widower, anyone seeking a wife.
[2] Destiny.　　[3] Sweethearts.　　[4] Foretold.

Rutherglen Sour Cakes

(A Special Cake at St. Luke's Fair)

(Traditional Recipe, abbreviated from the 'New Statistical Account of Scotland', 1845)

Oatmeal, water, sugar, aniseed or cinnamon

Eight or ten days before St. Luke's Fair, a certain quantity of oatmeal was made into a dough with warm water and laid up in a vessel to ferment. Being brought to a proper degree of fermentation and consistency, it was rolled up into balls proportionable to the intended size of the cakes. With the dough there was commonly mixed a small quantity of sugar and a little aniseed or cinnamon. The cakes were beaten out until as thin as a piece of paper, and were toasted on a girdle.

The elaborate ritual with which these cakes were prepared, and which clearly derives from a pagan source, is fully described in the *New Statistical Account* (under *Rutherglen*), and in Vol. III of my own work, *The Silver Bough*.

Sowan Scones *(Orkney)*

Flour, sugar, salt, bicarbonate of soda, the liquid poured off sowans,[1] caraways (optional).

Mix together a pound of flour, a pinch of salt, a teaspoonful of sugar, another of bicarbonate of soda, and a few caraways, if liked. Make this into a thinnish batter with the liquid poured off sowans, adding a little of the sediment. (The amount is a matter of taste: some like it strongly, some mildly flavoured.) Rub a hot girdle with a piece of suet and drop on the batter in spoonfuls, as for Scots crumpets. When ready on one side, turn quickly with a knife and brown the other. Serve hot with butter.

Sowan scones, properly made, resemble golden-brown lace doyleys and are extremely palatable.

[1] For sowans, see p. 268.

Highland Slim Cakes

(Meg Dods's Recipe)

Flour, butter, eggs, hot milk

Are often used in the Highlands, and in country situations,
for breakfast or tea. To a pound of flour allow from two to
four ounces of butter, as much hot milk as will make a dough
of the flour, and two beat eggs, if the cakes are wished to rise.
Handle quickly, and lightly roll out, and stamp of any size
wanted with a basin, a saucer, or tumbler. Bake on the
girdle or in a thick-bottomed frying-pan. They must be
served hot, kept in a heap, and used newly baked, as on
keeping they become tough.

Clap Scones: Make as above, substituting boiling water
for the scalded milk.

Scadded Scones *(Galloway)*

Flour, salt, milk

These are made with 'scadded' (scalded) milk.

Put a pint of milk into a saucepan, bring to the boil, stir
in an approximately equal measure of salted flour, and
continue stirring till the mass comes away from the sides of
the pan, like choux paste, and you have a nice pliable dough.
Form into rounds and pat them out lightly with the palm of
the hand, sprinkling when necessary with flour. They should
be as thin as possible. Bake on a pretty hot girdle, turning
once. Pile one over another as they come off the girdle, and
when nearly cold roll them up tightly in a clean towel. They
do not keep but are excellent when eaten fresh. Spread with
butter and syrup or honey and roll up each separately.

Baps

(Traditional Recipe)

Flour, salt, lard, yeast, sugar, milk, water

Sift a pound of flour into a warm bowl and mix with it a small teaspoonful of salt. Rub in, with the finger-tips, two ounces of lard. In another bowl, cream an ounce of yeast and a teaspoonful of sugar (that is, work them together with a wooden spoon till liquid); add half a pint of tepid milk-and-water (half and half), and strain into the flour. Make into a soft dough, cover, and set to rise for an hour in a warm place. Knead lightly and divide into pieces of equal size to form oval shapes about three inches long and two wide. Brush with milk or water (to give a glaze), and, if 'floury baps' are desired, dust them with flour just after brushing them, and again just before they go into the oven. Place the baps on a greased and floured tin and set again in a warm place, to prove, for fifteen minutes. To prevent blisters, press a finger into the centre of each before they are placed in the oven. Bake in a hot oven for from fifteen to twenty minutes. Baps appear exclusively on the breakfast-table, and should be eaten warm from the oven.

The bap is the traditional morning roll of Scotland. The etymology of the word is unknown, but Dr. Maclagan, the Highland folklorist, suggests an analogy with *pap*, the mammary gland, on account of its shape and size.

We learn from a sixteenth-century document that baps were sold at nine for twelve pence, but later they were popularly known as 'bawbee baps'. (A bawbee is a ha'penny.)

In Allan Ramsay's *Miscellany* one line unites 'sowans, farls and baps'.

The Shearer's or Harvester's Bap is about the size of a large meat-plate. Highland harvesters working in the Lowlands were formerly regaled at midday with buttered baps and ale. – F. M. McN.

'The grandfather of a late Prime Minister of Great Britain[1] kept a shop in Leith Walk, Edinburgh, where he sold "baps", flour, oatmeal, peas, etc., and where he was popularly known to the boys of the neighbourhood as "Sma' Baps", because his baps were reputed to be smaller than those of his brother tradesmen.'
– C. Mackay: *Dictionary of Lowland Scots.*

Unfortunately the post-war baker's bap, which is baked on an iron plate, lacks the delectable flavour of the pre-war bap, which was baked on an honest stone sole, and is now hard to come by. – F. M. McN.

[1] W. E. Gladstone.

Buttery Rowies (*Aberdeen Butter Rolls*)

'Bawbee Baps and Buttery Rowies!'
– Old Aberdeen Street Cry.

Flour, yeast, salt, castor sugar, butter, lard, water

Sift a pound of flour into a warm bowl. Mix an ounce of baker's yeast with a level tablespoonful of castor sugar and a small teaspoonful of salt. Add to the flour along with three-quarters of a pint of tepid water. Mix well and set in a warm place to rise to twice its bulk, keeping it covered with a warm, damp towel until it proves. Beat six ounces of butter and six of lard together until thoroughly blended; then divide into three equal portions. Roll out the dough (which is the better of being chilled after it has risen) on a floured board, in a strip three times as long as it is wide. Place small pats of the butter mixture all over it until the first portion is used up. Fold in three and roll out as for flaky pastry. Repeat this process twice, at intervals of thirty minutes, keeping the dough in a cool place in the intervening periods. Divide into oval shapes. Place a little apart on a greased and floured tray, and prove in a warm place for another thirty minutes. Bake in a fairly hot oven (*c.* 400°F.) for twenty or twenty-five minutes.

'The buttery is really one of the "mysteries" of medieval days. It is a by-product of the old, overnight sponge method.' – A Forres baker in a letter to the author.

'Roast dripping is sometimes used. It makes a most flavoursome roll.' – Id.

Buttermilk Bread (*Or Soda Loaf*)

(*Traditional Recipe*)

Flour, bicarbonate of soda, cream of tartar, salt, sugar, butter (optional), buttermilk or thick sour milk

Mix thoroughly in a basin four teacupfuls of flour, a teaspoonful of bicarbonate of soda (the lumps rubbed out), another of cream of tartar, a pinch of salt and a small tablespoonful of sugar. An ounce of butter is an improvement, but is not necessary. It should be lightly rubbed into the dry ingredients. Make into a soft dough with about half a pint of buttermilk or thick sour milk. Put into a floured tin and bake in a moderate oven for three-quarters of an hour.

White Girdle Scones (*Or Soda Scones*)

Flour, bicarbonate of soda, cream of tartar, salt, buttermilk or thick sour milk

Sieve into a basin a pound of flour, a teaspoonful of bicarbonate of soda, a teaspoonful of cream of tartar, and half a teaspoonful of salt. Add enough buttermilk or thick sour milk to make a very soft dough. Turn out on a floured board and divide into four. Flatten each piece into a round scone, about half an inch in thickness. Cut each in quarters, flour them, and place them on a hot girdle. Let them cook steadily till well risen and of a light brown underneath (about five minutes), then turn with a knife and cook on the other side about the same length of time. When the edges are dry they are ready. Serve fresh-baked with butter. They are especially popular on the breakfast-table.

These scones are often baked as bannocks, i.e. in one large round, the size of a meatplate, and are cut up on the table. They may be made richer by having an ounce or two of butter rubbed into the flour.

Fife Bannocks

Flour, oatmeal, bicarbonate of soda, cream of tartar, salt, sugar, lard, buttermilk

Sieve into a bowl six ounces of flour, four ounces of oatmeal, half a teaspoonful of bicarbonate of soda, three-quarters teaspoonful of cream of tartar, half a teaspoonful of sugar, and a pinch of salt. Rub in a piece of lard the size of a walnut, and add enough buttermilk to make a soft dough. Turn on to a floured board and knead lightly, then roll out into a round. Cut in four and bake on a hot girdle or in a thick-bottomed frying-pan.

Mrs. Macnab's Scones[1] (*Aberdeenshire*)

Flour, butter, salt, bicarbonate of soda, cream of tartar, egg, buttermilk

Mix thoroughly a pound of flour, a teaspoonful of salt, a small teaspoonful of bicarbonate of soda and two small teaspoonfuls of cream of tartar. Rub in two ounces of butter. Stir in gradually a beaten egg and half a pint of buttermilk. Turn out the dough on a floured board, flour the top, and knead with the hand as little as possible. Cut off pieces of dough and flatten them with the knuckles, but do not roll out at all. Prick with a fork and cut into quarters. Bake in a pretty quick oven for from ten to fifteen minutes.

The secret of success lies in not working the dough with the hands except just once kneading it.

Silverweed Bannock (*Hebrides*)

> *Bhrisgein beannachte earraich*
> *Seachdamh aran a' Ghàidheil.*
> The blest silverweed of spring,
> One of the seven breads of the Gael.

The silverweed bannock (*bonnach bhrisgein*) is essentially a spring cake for the months of March and April, when the roots can be obtained.

Silverweed roots, oatmeal or barley-meal, salt, butter, milk or water

Go over a newly ploughed field and collect as many silverweed roots as you require. They are easily recognized, being long, thin, and white or cream-coloured. Wash and rinse the roots thoroughly in cold water. Scrape gently with a blunt knife when required. Spread out on a clean cloth and dry in the sun, turning over and over again. When quite dry and brittle, break into very small bits. Put these back into the cloth, tie tightly and pound with a pestle or smooth

---

[1] Mrs. Macnab was the wife of a farmer who lived near Ballater. Such was her reputation as a baker that King Frederick of Prussia and other distinguished guests at Balmoral used frequently to go over and have tea with her. It is not possible to impart Mrs. Macnab's lightness of touch, or the wine-like air of these regions, which doubtless contributed to her visitors' enjoyment; but here, at least, is the recipe for her celebrated scones.

stone until reduced to powder. Put into a bowl with some oatmeal or barley-meal and a pinch of salt. Mix well and rub in a good pat of butter. Make a well in the centre and pour in, little by little, just enough warm milk or water to make a stiff paste. Roll out into a round from half to three-quarters of an inch thick. Have the bannock slab (*leac nam bonnach*) heating in front of a bright peat fire, and stand the bannock against the slab to toast in front of the fire. When well toasted on one side, turn and toast the other.

A chunk of silverweed cake and a *cuach* (cup) of milk used to make a satisfying meal for the labourer in the field.

(The above is the method used by the mother of Calum Macleod, The Glen, Barra, a hundred years ago.)

'The root was much used in the Highlands and Islands before the potato was introduced. It was cultivated and grew to a considerable size. . . . It was sometimes boiled in pots, sometimes roasted on stoves, and sometimes ground into meal for bread and porridge. It was considered palatable and nutritious.'
– Alexander Carmichael: *Carmina Gadelica:* Vol. IV.

Selkirk Bannock

(*Traditional Recipe*)

'Never was such making of car-cakes and sweet scones and Selkirk bannocks.'
– Scott: *The Bride of Lammermoor.*

Baker's dough, butter, lard, sugar, sultanas

Make or procure from the baker two pounds of dough. Into this rub eight ounces of butter and four of lard until melted but not oiled; then work in eight ounces of castor sugar and two pounds of sultanas. Mould in the form of a large round bun, place in a buttered tin, let it stand in a warm place for thirty minutes to rise, and bake in a moderate oven until lightly browned (about an hour and a quarter).

'Selkirk bannocks were known to discerning folk in Scotland a long time ago, but it was Robbie Douglas who spread their fame throughout the whole world. Robbie opened his little bakery in the corner of Selkirk Market Place in 1859. He was a wonderful baker and he made bannocks of such superb quality and flavour that orders poured in from all parts of the country. Soon his modest business developed out of all recognition.

'Robbie's first bannock was much more than a mere mixture of flour, butter and fruit. He found that the flavour was influenced by different butters, and finally he chose a butter made from milk produced on certain neighbouring pastures. If for any reason this butter could not be procured, well, no bannocks were made. That was one reason why there were no bannocks during war-time. Similarly with the sultanas. They had to be of a certain kind, specially imported from Turkey.

'Besides butter, lard and sultanas, the original Selkirk bannock requires sugar, salt, flour and yeast. And nothing else! No spices, no flavouring, no syrup or colouring. The distinctive, delicious eating quality of the Selkirk bannock has always been the result of the purity and quality of the ingredients and of the exclusive methods of mixing and baking which were perfected by Robbie Douglas.

... The Selkirk bannock is a weighty, rounded loaf, flat on the bottom and curved on top, and about half of its weight is fruit. It is cut into slices and eaten with or without butter. It is rich but not over-rich, and the butter that it contains is very noticeable. It is very economical since little is required and it keeps well. Wrapped in a cloth and placed in a tin, it will keep moist and palatable for a month or longer.' – From a brochure issued by The Border Bakeries, Ltd., successors to Robert Douglas, Selkirk.

Cookies[1]

'Muckle obliged to ye for your cookies, Mrs. Shortcake.
– Scott: *The Antiquary*.

(Traditional Recipe)

Flour, sugar, butter, yeast, salt, eggs, milk

Sieve one and a half pounds of flour into a warm basin and make a hole in the centre. Melt three ounces of butter in a saucepan, add three gills of milk and make lukewarm. Cream an ounce of yeast with a teaspoonful of salt, pour over this the warm milk and butter, and strain into the middle of the flour. Add two well-beaten eggs and beat the mixture till smooth and light. Cover the basin and set it in a warm place till the dough has risen to about twice its original size. Then mix in six ounces of fine sugar. Stiffen the dough with flour so that it will not adhere to the baking-board. Divide into two-ounce pieces, and form into rounds. Place the cookies on greased and floured tins. Set them in a warm place till they begin to swell and puff out, then bake in a good oven. When almost ready, glaze them with a little sugar dissolved in hot milk. Split and spread with butter, jam, or whipped cream.

A richer cookie may be made as follows: Rub six ounces of butter into a pound and a half of flour; put it into a basin and break in four eggs; add one pint of lukewarm water

[1] The 'cukie' is mentioned in *Foulis of Ravelstone's Account Book*, 1671–1707. Teut. *koeck*; Belg. *koekie*.

with an ounce of yeast, mixing them together; cover it up, and let it sponge all night. Proceed as above, adding six ounces of sugar.

A *cooky-shine* is the Scottish equivalent of the English *bun-fight* (tea-party).

Potato Scones

Mashed potatoes, butter, flour, salt

To half a pound of mashed potatoes (preferably warm from the pot) add a good pinch of salt and half an ounce of melted butter. Work in as much flour as the potatoes will take up (about two ounces). Roll out very thin on a floured board, cut into rounds, prick well with a fork, place on a hot girdle and cook for about three minutes on each side. Keep wrapped in a towel till required. The fresher the better.

The butter may be omitted and the scones well buttered.

Aberdeen Softies

(*Soft Biscuits*)

Baker's dough, butter, sugar

Into every pound of baker's dough work three ounces of melted butter and a tablespoonful of sugar. Form into flattened bun shapes, about three or four inches in diameter. Bake in a good oven.

Aberdeen Crulla[1]

(*Mrs. Dalgairns's Recipe*)

Flour, butter, sugar, eggs, lard or suet

Beat to a cream a quarter-pound of fresh butter and mix with it the same quantity of pounded and sifted loaf sugar and four well-beaten eggs; add flour till thick enough to roll out; cut the paste into oblong pieces about four to five

---

[1] A crule is a small cake or bannock, N. of S. Isl. *kril*, anything very small.

– Jamieson.

inches in length; with a paste cutter divide the centre into three or four strips; wet the edges and plait one bar over the other so as to meet in the centre; throw them into boiling lard or clarified suet; when fried of a light brown, drain them before the fire and serve them in a napkin, with or without grated loaf sugar served over them.

Deer Horns

(*Mrs. Dalgairns's Recipe*)

Flour, sugar, almonds, lemon, eggs, cream

Beat one white and six yolks of eggs; mix them with five tablespoonfuls of pounded and sifted loaf sugar, the same quantity of sweet (fresh) cream, ten sweet almonds, blanched and pounded, the grated peel of one lemon, and as much flour as will make the whole into a paste sufficiently thick to roll out. Then cut it with tins for this purpose into the forms of horns, branches, or any other shape, and throw them into boiling lard.

Drop-Scones or Dropped Scones

Flour, castor sugar, bicarbonate of soda, cream of tartar, egg, buttermilk

Mix in a basin a pound of flour, two tablespoonfuls of sugar, a small teaspoonful of bicarbonate of soda, another of cream of tartar, and a good pinch of salt. Make a well in the centre and drop in an egg. Add a little buttermilk and beat well with the back of a wooden spoon for a few minutes; then thin with more buttermilk till of the consistency of thick cream. You will require about three-quarters of a pint in all. Have ready a hot girdle, grease it slightly with a piece of suet wrapped in a clean white rag, and drop on the batter in rounds about three inches across, placing them a little apart, until the girdle is full. Take care that they are a neat round shape. (The batter may be poured through a greased tin ring, which is removed in a moment or two.) When the scones are covered with air bubbles, slip a broad knife under them, and if they are of a golden brown colour, turn and brown the other side. Place in a folded towel as removed and keep thus till all are ready.

Serve warm (or cold but fresh) with butter and honey or jam. Children like them buttered hot, then topped with fine brown sugar.

The scones can be made with fresh milk, provided the quantity of cream of tartar is doubled; but the quality is not quite the same.

Another method is to beat the egg with the sugar till frothy before adding, with the milk, to the dry ingredients.

Scots Crumpets[1]

(*Traditional Recipe*)

Flour, sugar, eggs, milk

Make the batter some hours before it is required.

Beat separately the yolks and whites of four eggs. Pour into a basin and add half a pint of milk and three table-spoonfuls of sugar. Mix well, and gradually add flour till you have a thickish batter. Beat till quite smooth and set aside. Put a girdle or frying-pan on a bright clear fire and rub with suet. To have light, pretty crumpets the fire must be brisk and the girdle hot, so that they will rise quickly. Drop with a spoon as many as the girdle will hold, and before they have time to form a skin and get dry on the top they should be ready to turn. Do this quickly, and a lovely golden-brown skin as smooth as velvet will be formed, and a delightfully light crumpet produced.

[1] These resemble English crumpets only in name, and are much more closely akin to Shrove-Tuesday pancakes. It is extremely probable that they are identical with the old Scottish *car-cakes* (mentioned by Scott in *The Bride of Lammermoor*), which Jamieson defines as 'a kind of thin cake, made of milk, meal or flour, eggs beaten up, and sugar, baked and eaten on Fastern's E'en'.

Scots Pancakes

(Mrs. Dalgairns's Recipe)

Flour, cream, eggs, lemon, sugar, ratafia, butter or lard

Mix with three tablespoonfuls of flour a little cream, add the beaten yolks of three eggs, then mix in half a pint of cream, the grated peel of half a small lemon, a dessert-spoonful of pounded sugar, and a little ratafia. When the batter is very well beaten, and just before using, mix in the whites of the eggs beaten with a knife into a stiff froth. Put a little butter or lard into a frying-pan and when hot pour in a teacupful of the batter; shake it, and when firm prick it a little with a fork, but do not turn it; hold it before the fire for a minute to brown. Serve them with pounded loaf sugar strewed over them.

'In the Cleikum, and probably in some other old-fashioned inns and Scottish families, pancakes were wont to be served with a layer of currant jelly between the folds – a practice for which much might be said by those familiar with it. Is not this the *omelette à la Celestine*, or *aux confitures*, of our old allies, still lingering in remote places of the country? Pancakes are still better with apricot marmalade.'
                                             – P. Touchwood in the *Annals of the Cleikum Club*.

Oatmeal Pancakes

(Mrs. Cleland's Recipe)

Oatmeal, sugar, nutmeg, salt, lemon, eggs, milk

Boil a chopin (quart) of milk and blend it in a mutchkin (pint) of the flour of oatmeal thus: keep a little milk and mix the meal by degrees in it, then stir in the boiling milk; when it is pretty thick put it to cool, then beat up six eggs with sugar, nutmeg, the grate of a lemon, and a little salt. Stir all together and fry them in butter, putting in a spoonful of the batter at a time. Serve them up hot, with beat butter, orange, and sugar.

Sauty Bannocks. These were a variety of oatmeal pancake formerly made on Fastern's E'en (Shrove Tuesday). A thick batter was prepared, consisting of oatmeal, beaten eggs, beef bree or milk, and salt, and was poured, a ladleful at a time, on a hot greased girdle. The making of the bannocks had its own ritual (see the author's *Silver Bough*, Vol. II, chapter on Fastern's E'en).

CAKES AND SHORTBREADS

'In the beginning, the professional baker in the towns may possibly have borrowed his methods from the French. At any rate, being patronized chiefly by the nobles and the wealthier burghers, he was accustomed to use the very best materials, and he rejoiced in every encouragement to devote himself to the perfection of his methods. To beat the Edinburgh baker, you must go – not to London, but – to Paris or Vienna.'
– T. F. Henderson: *Old-World Scotland.*

In the old Edinburgh records we find various references to the 'Caik-baxteris'. In 1503, for instance, they were ordered to make cakes weighing eight ounces for a penny, and in the same year they were convicted of making cakes that were underweight and were threatened with penalties. It is almost certainly to them that we owe such good things as shortbread, almond flory and black bun. Sukkermen (sugarmen or confectioners) are also mentioned, but in Scotland the functions were never completely separated, as were those of the *bäcker* and *konditor* of Germany, or the *boulanger* and *pâtissier* of France.

Our leading bakers have always been noted for their sugarwork, and have specialized in cakes for festive occasions – weddings, christenings and, notably, the seasonal festivals. As in England, there are rich, elaborately iced Christmas cakes, many cleverly decorated with robins, logs, snowmen and so forth; but peculiar to Edinburgh, I think, are those delicious frosted snowball cakes, each with a sprig of berried holly. Hogmanay has its black bun, its spiced currant loaf and its decorated cakes of shortbread. St. Valentine's cake is, of course, heart-shaped, with blush-pink icing, rose-buds, silver arrows and the rest. The variety of Easter cakes is much more limited now than in pre-war days. An old catalogue (MacVitties Guest's) shows nest cakes (containing confectionery eggs), hamper cakes (square, containing chicks), daffodil cakes, primrose cakes, Easter-egg cakes (with floral decorations) and others; as well as Simnel cakes (borrowed from England) and the ubiquitous hot cross bun. Then the confectioner's fancy runs free on our Hallowe'en cakes, which are decorated mainly with witch emblems.[1] – F. M. McN.

Dundee Cake

(*Old Family Recipe*)

Flour, butter, sugar, salt, currants, sultanas, raisins, mixed candied peel, ground almonds, whole Jordan almonds, orange or lemon rind, sherry or brandy or rum (optional)

Prepare the fruit – four ounces each of currants, sultanas and seeded raisins. Shred two ounces of candied peel. Sift eight ounces of flour with a pinch of salt. Beat eight ounces of butter and eight of sugar to a cream. Into this beat six eggs, one at a time, alternately with a spoonful of flour. Add the fruit, three ounces of ground almonds and the zest

[1] See p. 250.

of an orange or lemon. Add, if desired, a tablespoonful of sherry, brandy or rum. The mixture should be fairly stiff. Turn into a cake tin that has been greased and lined with greased paper. Flatten the surface with a palette knife, and over it strew the Jordan almonds, blanched and split. Bake in a very moderate oven (*c.* 300°F.) for about three hours.

For a less rich cake, reduce the quantity of butter to six ounces, the sugar to five, and the number of eggs to four, and add a teaspoonful of baking-powder with sufficient milk to make a rather stiff dough. Bake in a hot oven (400°F.) for an hour and three-quarters.

Montrose Cakes

(*Mrs. Dalgairns's Recipe*)

Flour, sugar, butter, currants (optional), brandy, rose-water, nutmeg, eggs

Of dried and sifted flour, pounded and sifted loaf sugar and of fresh butter, one pound each will be required; also twelve well-beaten eggs, three-quarters of a pound of cleaned and dried currants. Beat the butter to a cream with the sugar; add the eggs by degrees and then the flour and currants with two tablespoonfuls of brandy and one of rose-water and half a grated nutmeg; beat all well together for twenty to thirty minutes, when it is to be put into small buttered tins, half filling them and baking in a quick oven. The currants may be omitted.

Scots Seed Cake

(*Mrs. Dalgairns's Recipe*)

Flour, butter, sugar, almonds, orange and citron peel, nutmeg, ground caraways, eggs, rose-water, brandy, caraway comfits

Take a pound of dried and sifted flour, the same quantity of fresh butter washed in rose-water and of finely pounded loaf sugar, four ounces of blanched sweet almonds, half a pound of candied orange peel, five ounces of citron, all cut into thin narrow strips; a small nutmeg grated, a small teaspoonful of grated caraway seeds, ten eggs, the yolks and whites beaten separately; then with the hand beat the butter to a cream, add the sugar and then the eggs gradually; mix in the flour a little at a time, and then the sweetmeats, almonds, and spice, and, lastly, stir in a glass of brandy; butter the hoop or tin pan, and pour in the cake so as nearly to fill it; smooth it over the top, and strew over it caraway comfits. Bake it in a moderate oven; it must not be moved or turned till nearly done, as shaking it will occasion the sweetmeats sinking to the bottom.

Scots Snow Cake[1]

(*Old Family Recipe*)

Arrowroot, butter, sugar, eggs, lemon, almond or vanilla flavouring

Beat half a pound of butter to a cream. Mix a pound of arrowroot with half a pound of pounded white sugar, and roll them out till perfectly smooth and free from lumps. Stir them gradually into the butter, beating well. Whisk the whites of six eggs to a stiff froth, add, and beat for twenty minutes. Add a few drops of essence of lemon, almonds, or vanilla. Pour into a buttered tin and bake in a moderate oven for an hour or an hour and a half.

Scots Diet Loaf[2]

(*Meg Dods's Recipe*)

Flour, sugar, eggs, lemon, cinnamon

Take a pound of fine sugar sifted, the same weight of eggs very well whisked, and mix and beat these together for

[1] This is practically identical with Mrs. Beeton's 'genuine Scotch recipe'.
[2] Mentioned by Scott in *St. Ronan's Well*.

twenty minutes. Season with lemon grate and cinnamon. Stir in very smoothly three-quarters of a pound of sifted flour. This is a very light cake and will bake quickly. It may either be iced or have sifted sugar strewed over it before baking. (Bake at 400°F.)

Hallowe'en Cake

Prepare a plain white or birthday cake, but just before you put the batter into the cake tin, stir in a few silver or nickel charms,[1] each wrapped in a morsel of greaseproof paper. The cake should be iced appropriately.

Orange and black are the Hallowe'en colours, and in the principal bakers' windows one may see cakes coated with tangerine icing, on which are silhouetted, in chocolate icing, witches on broom-sticks, black cats with arched backs, owls, bats and such-like emblems of witchery. Other cakes are shaped like apples or pumpkins and covered with marzipan icing appropriately moulded and tinted.

Honey Cakes

(*Mrs. Dalgairns's Recipe*)

Flour, honey, sugar, citron and orange peel, ginger, cinnamon

One pound and a half of dried and sifted flour, three-quarters of a pound of honey, half a pound of finely pounded loaf sugar, a quarter of a pound of citron, and half an ounce of orange peel cut small, of pounded ginger and cinnamon three-quarters of an ounce. Melt the sugar with the honey and mix in the other ingredients; roll out the paste and cut it into small cakes of any form. (Bake at 300°F. for fifteen or twenty minutes.)

The Fair Maid of Perth served at breakfast 'thin soft cakes, made of flour and honey according to the family receipt', which were 'not only commended, but done liberal justice to'. Unfortunately her receipt has not survived six centuries! – F. M. McN.

'Scots honey is the best in the world, not because Scottish bees know how to make it

[1] The charms most commonly used are the ring (foretelling marriage to the recipient), the button (bachelordom), the thimble (spinsterhood), the coin (wealth), the wish-bone (the heart's desire), the horse-shoe (good luck), and the swastika (happiness).

250

any better than other bees, but because of the excellence of the clover and heather, which is fuller in nectar.' – Le Vicomte de Mauduit: *The Vicomte in the Kitchen*.

'I have often heard, when I was young, that in the Lewis (whose poetical name in Gaelic is *Eilean nan Fhraoich*, Heather Island) bees were so plentiful in the olden times that the boys were able to collect large quantities of wild honey, which, by applying heat to it, was run into glass bottles and sold at the Stornoway markets. Hunting for wild-bee nests was one of the great ploys for the boys in the autumn. . . . Cameron tells me that, as a young boy, before he left his home, there was an island in Loch Bhacha Chreamha where there was no necessity for hunting for bees' nests, as the whole island seemed under bees, the nests almost touching each other in the moss at the roots of tall heather. . . . My stalker, too, informs me that his home at Kernsary used to be quite famous for its wild bees, but they finally disappeared.

'So much for our degenerate climate.'
– Osgood Mackenzie: *A Hundred Years in the Highlands*.

It is customary to transport the hives to the hills when the heather is in bloom, and set them down where the bees have only short flights to and from the heather. Thus their working-day yields larger returns. When the flow of nectar has ceased, the hives are brought back to the lower levels.

An excellent description of the 'flitting' of the bees is to be found in the novel, *Crossriggs*, by Jane and Mary Findlater.

Heather honey is an ingredient in such classic drinks as Drambuie and Atholl Brose, as well as in cakes. With orange marmalade, it should appear on every Scottish breakfast-table where the old traditions are cherished.

Scots Shortbread

(*A Festive Cake at Hogmanay*)

'The triumph of Scottish baking on the old national lines.
– T. F. Henderson.

Flour, rice flour, butter, castor sugar

Only the best materials should be used. The flour should be dried and sieved. The butter, which is the only moistening and shortening agent, should be squeezed free of all water. The sugar should be fine castor. Two other things are essential for success – the careful blending of the ingredients and careful firing.

The butter and sugar must first be blended. Put eight ounces of butter and four ounces of castor sugar on to a board, and work with the hand until thoroughly incorporated. Mix fourteen ounces of flour with two ounces of rice flour and work gradually into the butter and sugar, until the dough is of the consistency of short crust. Be careful that it does not become oily (a danger in hot weather) or toughened with over-mixing. The less kneading, the more short and crisp the shortbread. Do not roll it out, as rolling,

251

too, has a tendency to toughen it, but press with the hand into two round cakes either in wooden shortbread moulds, oiled and floured, which are then reversed on to a sheet of baking-paper, or direct on the paper, or in ungreased sandwich tins of the same size as the cakes.

The most satisfactory thickness is three-quarters of an inch for a cake eight inches in diameter, or in such proportion. If you make a large thick cake, it is advisable to protect the edges with a paper band or hoop, and to have several layers of paper underneath and possibly one on the top. Pinch the edges neatly all round with the finger and thumb, and prick all over with a fork.

For a festive occasion, decorate with white 'sweetie almonds' (almond comfits) or, in the case of small cakes, with 'sweetie carvies' (caraway comfits), and strips of candied orange or citron peel. Bake in a moderate oven (325°F.) for forty-five to sixty minutes, until it is browned to taste. The shortbread will still be soft when removed from the oven, but should be left to cool a little and then turned out very carefully on to a sieve or wire tray. When quite cold and crisp, it should be wrapped in greaseproof paper and stored in an airtight tin. If left for any length of time, it is the better of being crisped again in the oven, like biscuits.

Only good farm butter gives the true flavour. Many domestic bakers aver that shortbread baked in the old coal-heated oven tastes better than when baked in a gas or electric oven.

The proportion of rice to ordinary flour may be doubled, or it may be omitted altogether; but a small proportion is recommended.

Although it is eaten all the year round, shortbread is associated particularly with the Yule season, which embraces Christmas and Hogmanay (New Year's Eve), and is invariably provided for the 'first-footers' – those who go visiting from house to house in the 'wee sma' 'oors' of New Year morning. The large, round cake of rich, crisp shortbread is, in fact, the lineal descendant of the ancient Yule-bannock, which is notched round the edge to symbolize the sun's ray. (See p. 233, note on the Yule-bannock.) As white flour increased in popularity, our bakers began to experiment and eventually evolved the shortbread we know today. At first a luxury, it gradually superseded the shortened oatcake at Yule, at weddings and on other festive occasions. (But there are still those who prefer a crisp, well-shortened, nutty-flavoured oatcake to the finest shortbread.)

On the approach of Yule, enormous quantities of shortbread are dispatched from the homeland to exiled Scots in every quarter of the globe. Many cakes are decorated with elaborate sugarwork. Especially popular are nostalgic devices – homeland scenes, sprigs of heather, hands-across-the-sea. and so forth, with such legends as 'Frae Bonnie Scotland', 'A gude New Year to Ane an' A' ', 'For Auld Lang Syne', and '*Tir nam Beann, nam Gleann s'nam Gaisgeach*' (The Land of the Bens, the Glens and the Heroes). Many home and professional bakers, however, prefer their shortbread cakes unadorned, save with the traditional notched edge.

The Bride's Bonn (Shetland)

This is simply a large round cake of shortbread to which caraways are usually added, in the proportion of two teaspoonfuls to a pound of flour. Where there is no oven, it is moistened with milk and fired lightly on both sides of the girdle.

'(At the wedding feast) a round cake had been prepared with notches in it, and a sweet, the size of a sixpence, sat in the middle. Each unmarried guest must break off and eat a tiny bit of the cake. Whoever touched the sweet when doing this was to remain unmarried. . . . There was much laughter and jeering when at last some nervous hand came into contact with the ill-omened sweet.'

– Jessie M. B. Saxby: *Shetland Traditional Lore·*

Ayrshire Shortbread

(*Traditional Recipe*)

Flour, rice flour, castor sugar, butter, egg, cream

Sieve four ounces of flour and four ounces of rice flour into a basin and rub in four ounces of butter with the finger-tips. Add four ounces of castor sugar and bind the mixture to a stiff consistency with the beaten yolk of an egg and two tablespoonfuls of cream. Roll out thinly, prick with a fork, and cut into rounds or fingers. Place the cakes on a greased paper and bake in a steady oven for about fifteen minutes or until of a golden brown colour. Cool on a wire sieve.

Pitcaithly Bannock

(*Traditional Recipe*)

Flour, rice flour, butter, sugar, sweet almonds, citron peel

Blanch an ounce of sweet almonds and chop them very finely along with an ounce of candied citron peel. Mix them with six ounces of flour and an ounce of rice flour. With the hand, work three ounces of sugar into four ounces of butter, and work in the dry ingredients, as for shortbread. Ornament, if desired, with large caraways and orange peel. Make into a round flat cake, pinch the edges with the finger and thumb, lay on a sheet of paper on a tin, and bake in a moderate oven for thirty or thirty-five minutes.

Petticoat Tails[1]

(Meg Dods's Recipe)

Flour, butter, sugar, caraway seeds (optional), milk

Mix half an ounce, or fewer or none, caraway seeds[2] with a pound and three-quarters of flour. Make a hole in the middle of the flour and pour in eight ounces of butter melted in a quarter-pint of milk, and three ounces of beat sugar. Knead, but not too much, or it will not be short. Divide it in two and roll it out rather thin. Cut out the cake by running a paste-cutter round a dinner-plate or any large round dish inverted on the paste. Cut a cake from the centre of this one with a small saucer or large tumbler. Keep this inner circle whole, and cut the outer one into eight *petticoat tails*. Bake all these on paper laid on tins, serve the round cake in the middle of the plate, and the petticoat tails as *radii* round it.

The Queen's Tea Cakes

(Mrs. Dalgairns's Recipe)

Flour, sugar, salt, butter, lemon, rose-water, eggs

Mix together half a pound of dried and sifted flour, the same quantity of pounded and sifted loaf sugar, the weight of two eggs in fresh butter, the grated peel of a lemon, and a little salt; beat the two eggs with a little rose-water, and

---

[1] 'An English traveller in Scotland and one very well acquainted with France states in his very pleasant book that our club have fallen into a mistake in the name of these cakes, and that petticoat tails is a corruption of the French *Petites Gatelles*. It may be so: in Scottish culinary terms there are many corruptions, though we rather think the name petticoat tails has its origin in the shape of the cakes, which is exactly that of the bell-hoop petticoats of our ancient Court ladies.' – *Annals of the Cleikum Club*.

[2] These cakes are usually made without caraways.

with them make the ingredients into a paste; roll it out, cut into round cakes, and bake upon floured tins.

Tantallon Cakes

(*Old Edinburgh Recipe*)

Flour, rice flour, butter, sugar, bicarbonate of soda, lemon, eggs

Mix together four ounces of flour, four ounces of rice flour, and a pinch of bicarbonate of soda. Cream four ounces of butter with four ounces of sugar. Beat two eggs and add these alternately with the flour to the butter and cream. Flavour with lemon. Make into a stiff dough, roll out thinly, and cut with a small scalloped round into biscuits. Bake for half an hour in a fairly hot oven. When cool, dust them with fine white sugar.

Black Bun

(*A Festive Cake at Hogmanay*)

> Thou tuck-shop king! Joy of our gourmand youth!
>   What days thou marks't and what blood-curdling nights
> Nights full of shapeless things, hideous, uncouth;
>   Imp follows ghoul, ghoul follows jinn, pell-mell;
> Fierce raisin-devils and gay currant sprites
>   Hold lightsome leap-frog in a pastry hell.
>   – Augustus Bejant: 'Invocation to Black Bun.

> 'A black substance inimical to life.'
>   – Robert Louis Stevenson.

(*Old Family Recipe*)

Muscatel raisins, currants, sweet almonds; orange, lemon, and citron peel; flour, Demerara sugar, ground cloves or cinnamon, ground ginger, Jamaica pepper, black pepper, baking-soda, buttermilk or eggs, brandy; crust: flour, butter, water

Wash and dry two pounds of currants. Stone two pounds of Muscatel raisins. Blanch and chop half a pound of almonds.

Chop half a pound of mixed candied peel. Sift a pound of flour and mix with it four ounces of sugar, half an ounce of ground cloves or cinnamon, half an ounce of ground ginger, a teaspoonful of Jamaica pepper, half a teaspoonful of black pepper, a small teaspoonful of baking-soda. Add to these the prepared fruits. Add just enough buttermilk or beaten egg, with a tablespoonful of brandy, to moisten the mixture.

Make a paste by lightly rubbing half a pound of butter into a pound of flour and mixing in quickly enough water to make a stiff dough. Roll out thinly. Grease a large cake tin and line it evenly with the paste, retaining enough to cover the top. Trim the edges, put the mixture in, and make the surface flat and smooth. Moisten the edges of the pastry with cold water and flatten on the round top. Make all secure and neat. With a skewer make four holes right down to the bottom of the cake. Prick all over with a fork, brush with beaten egg, and bake in a moderate oven (350°F.) for three hours or longer. (Test with skewer.)

Huff paste may be substituted for short paste.[1]

An eighteenth-century recipe: 'Take half a peck of flour, keeping out a little to work it up with; make a hole in the middle of the flour, and break in sixteen ounces of butter; pour in a mutchkin (pint) of warm water, and three gills of yeast, and work it up into a smooth dough. If it is not wet enough, put in a little more warm water; then cut off one-third of the dough, and lay it aside for the cover. Take three pounds of stoned raisins, three pounds of cleaned currants, half a pound of blanched almonds cut long-wise, candied orange and citron peel cut, of each eight ounces; half an ounce of cloves, an ounce of cinnamon, and two ounces of ginger, all beat and sifted. Mix the spices by themselves, then spread out the dough; lay the fruit upon it; strew the spices over the fruit, and mix all together. When it is well kneaded, roll out the cover, and lay the bun upon it; then cover it neatly, cut it round the sides, prickle it, and bind it with paper to keep it in shape; set it in a pretty quick oven, and, just before you take it out, glaze the top with a beat egg.' – Mrs. Frazer: *Practice of Cookery* (Edinburgh, 1791).

'These buns, weighing from four to eight, ten, twelve and sixteen or more pounds, are still (1826) sent from Edinburgh, from the depots of Littlejohn, Mackie and others, to many parts of the three kingdoms.' – Meg Dods.

Black Bun is the old Scottish Twelfth Cake, which was transferred to Hogmanay after the banning of Christmas and its subsidiary festival, Uphalieday, or Twelfth Night, by the Reformers. – F. M. McN.

'Bun: An old word for plumcake or twelfthcake.'
    – Sir John Sinclair: *Observations on the Scottish Dialect* (1782).

[1] *Huff Paste:* This is the name given to the close unleavened paste formerly (and still occasionally) used to wrap round food before baking. It contains less butter and more water than short crust, its object being simply to keep in the juices and the aroma. Though not intended to be eaten, it often absorbed enough fat and flavour to make it appetizing, and bits were cracked off and served to those who liked it.

Scots Currant Loaf[1]

(*Old Family Recipe*)

Flour, sugar, currants, raisins, orange peel, mixed spice, black pepper, ginger, cream of tartar, bicarbonate of soda, buttermilk (or fresh milk); crust: flour, baking-powder, butter, water

Rub half a pound of butter into a pound and a half of flour. Add half a teaspoonful of baking-powder and mix to a paste with water. Roll out rather thin, and line a large cake tin with the paste, reserving enough to cover the top.

Now put into a basin a pound of flour, half a pound of sugar, a pound of currants, washed and dried, half a pound of raisins, cleaned and stoned, a quarter-pound of orange peel, a teaspoonful of mixed spice, half a teaspoonful of ginger and the same of black pepper, one teaspoonful of bicarbonate of soda and one of cream of tartar. Just moisten with buttermilk. About a breakfastcupful will be required. Complete as for Black Bun.

Hawick Banna: 'A rich currant cake in a paste cover.' – *Roxburgh Word-Book.*

Edinburgh Gingerbread

(*Traditional Recipe*)

Flour, butter, sugar, salt, bicarbonate of soda, ground ginger, powdered cinnamon, ground cloves, mixed spice, dates, walnuts, black treacle, eggs, milk

Sift a pound of flour with a quarter teaspoonful of salt, a good teaspoonful apiece of ground ginger, cinnamon, and mixed spice, and half a teaspoonful of ground cloves. Chop eight ounces of dates and four of shelled walnuts, and add. Melt eight ounces of butter, eight of black treacle and six to eight of sugar over a low heat, and pour gradually over the flour mixture. Add four beaten eggs, and a teaspoonful of soda dissolved in a spoonful of warm milk. Beat well, adding a little more warm milk if necessary. The mixture should

[1] This is a poor relation of Black Bun, which it replaces at Hogmanay in all households where the richness or expense of Black Bun is an objection.

be of a dropping consistency, but not too soft. Have ready a well-greased shallow baking-tin smoothly lined with greased paper. Bake in a very moderate oven (335°F. for about twenty minutes, then lowered to 310°) for about three hours.

There are many varieties of gingerbread in Scotland, as in most countries. We give only a small selection.

Fochabers Gingerbread (*Moray*)

(Miss Bella Mitchell's Recipe)

Flour, butter, castor sugar, treacle, sultanas, currants, ground almonds, mixed peel, mixed spices, ground ginger, ground cinnamon, ground cloves, bicarbonate of soda, eggs, beer

Beat a pound of butter and half a pound of sugar to a cream. Warm a pound of treacle slightly and add. Then break in four eggs, one at a time, beating well. Mix together two pounds of flour, half a pound of sultanas, half a pound of currants, six ounces of ground almonds, six ounces of finely chopped candied peel, an ounce of mixed spices, an ounce of ground ginger, half an ounce of ground cinnamon, a quarter-ounce of ground cloves, and add these to the butter, etc. Dissolve two teaspoonfuls of bicarbonate of soda in a pint of beer and add. Mix thoroughly. Put into buttered cake tins and bake in a slow oven for two hours. These quantities make six pounds of cake.

Broonie[1] (*Orkney Oatmeal Gingerbread*)

Oatmeal, flour, brown sugar, butter, ground ginger, baking-soda, treacle, egg, buttermilk

Mix in a basin six ounces of oatmeal and six of flour. Rub in two ounces of butter. Add four ounces of sugar, a teaspoonful of ground ginger and barely three-quarters of a teaspoonful of baking-soda, free from lumps. Melt two

[1] Correctly, *Brüni*, a thick bannock (Orkney and Shetland).

258

tablespoonfuls of treacle, and add, together with a beaten egg and enough buttermilk to make the mixture sufficiently soft to drop from the spoon. Mix thoroughly. Turn into a buttered tin and bake for from one to one and a half hours in a moderate oven till well risen and firm in the centre.

This was the first recipe I ever collected – at the age of five or six. One of my small companions at the island school I first attended gave me a slice of the 'broonie' which she sometimes brought as her midday 'piece'. I begged to know what was 'intill't', and the little lass replied, 'A peerie (little) grain o' flo'or, a peerie grain o' mayle (oatmeal), a peerie grain o' butter, a peerie grain o' shuggar, a peerie grain o' trekkle,' and so forth. Years later, I managed to work out the proportions.

'Broonie' I always assumed to mean a brown cake until I discovered that it was one of the many Norn words that have survived in our Orkney dialect. – F. M. McN.

Parlies (*Parliament Cakes*)

'A species of gingerbread supposed to have its name from being used by the members of the Scottish Parliament.' – Jamieson.

(*Mrs. Fletcher's*[1] *Recipe adapted from Meg Dods's 'Manual'*)

Flour, sugar, ginger, butter, treacle

With two pounds of the best dried flour mix thoroughly one pound of the best brown sugar and a quarter-pound of ground ginger. Melt a pound of fresh butter, add to it one of treacle, boil this, and pour it on the flour. Work up the paste as hot as your hands will bear it and roll out in a rectangular shape, a sixth of an inch or less in thickness, on a sheet of greased paper to fit a baking sheet. Mark into four-inch squares. Grease the baking-sheet lightly and draw the paper carefully on to it. Bake in a slow oven for about forty minutes, when the cakes should be well risen and lightly browned. Separate the squares when soft. They will soon harden.

[1] I am of the opinion that this Mrs. Fletcher, whom I have been unable to identify, is one and the same with the celebrated Mrs. Flockhart (see p. 81) who, Chambers tells us in his *Traditions of Edinburgh*, supplied her customers with gingerbread 'either in thin, crisp cakes called *Parliament* – in round pieces, denominated *Snaps* – or in thick, soft cakes, chequered on the surface and, according to the colour, called *White* or *Brown Quality Cakes*.' – F. M. McN.
'This worthy lady was the universal favourite of the schoolboys of Edinburgh, the contemporaries of Sir Walter Scott. We regret not being able to recover her recipe for White Quality Cakes.' – Note to Mistress Dods's *Manual*.

Parlies used to be sold at stalls in the streets of Edinburgh.

'Gundy, sugar bouls and parliament, a cake compounded of flour and treacle with coloured sweeties known at the time as "Glasgow Jam"[1] sprinkled on top.'
– J. B. S.: *Random Recollections.*

Sweetie-foals: A similar type of gingerbread, baked in flat rounds of about three inches in diameter and sprinkled with 'sweetie carvies' (coloured caraway comfits), that used to be a popular fairing at the Lammas Market in Kirkwall, and is still made by some of the Orkney bakers.

Abernethy Biscuits[2]

Flour, butter, sugar, caraways (optional), baking-powder, egg, milk

Rub three ounces of butter into eight ounces of flour; add three ounces of sugar, half a teaspoonful of baking-powder, and (if liked) a small teaspoonful of caraway seeds. Beat an egg well, and pour it amongst the dry ingredients with a tablespoonful of milk. Mix thoroughly, and turn the paste on to a floured board. Roll out thinly, cut into rounds, place on a greased baking-tin, and bake for ten minutes in a moderate oven.

Manse Biscuits

(Elizabeth Craig's Recipe)

Flour, butter, castor sugar, baking-powder, lemon rind, egg

Rub four ounces of butter into eight ounces of flour. Stir in four ounces of sugar, the grated rind of half a lemon and half a teaspoonful of baking-powder. Moisten with a beaten egg. Roll out to a quarter-inch in thickness. Cut into fancy shapes with biscuit cutters. Bake a little part on a greased baking sheet in a moderate oven for about twenty minutes until pale gold. Dredge with castor sugar.

[1] Nonpareils, 'hundreds and thousands'.
[2] Abernethy biscuits got their name not from the Perthshire burgh, but from a family name that derives from the place-name. The Abernethys removed from Scotland via Ireland to London, where one of the family, Dr. John Abernethy (1764–1831), became chief surgeon to St. Bartholomew's Hospital and the real founder of the medical school attached to 'Bart's'. He used to take lunch at a baker's shop kept by John Caldwell (another Scottish name), where he ate ordinary 'captain's biscuits'. He suggested the addition of sugar and caraways, and the baker gave the new biscuit his patron's name. – F. M. McN.

MISCELLANEOUS

Preparations of Oatmeal, of Blood, of Milk, of Seaweeds, etc.

Oatmeal

Oats are the flower of our Scottish soil, and through that magic cauldron, the porridge pot, Scottish oatmeal has been transmuted through the centuries into Scottish brains and brawn. (Alas for the deterioration wrought in our cities by the Industrial Revolution with its train of slums and the abandonment of the 'halesome farin' ' of rural Scotland for cheap imported food-stuffs!)

Oatmeal, like coffee, must be closely packed and kept airtight. In many old farm-houses there still stands the solid oak chest, or girnal, which after every harvest is packed anew with sweet-smelling, nutty-flavoured oatmeal.[1] In the small croft-houses, a seasoned oak-barrel serves the same purpose. Other woods can be used, provided they are odourless and tasteless, or nearly so. Resinous woods are, naturally, avoided. The receptacle has to stand in a dry place, as dampness ruins the flavour of the meal. Well packed, it may be kept for a year or longer and, indeed, is considered to improve in sweetness and digestibility as it matures. (New oatmeal is heating.) A good miller knows just what samples of grain to select, just how long the process of drying in the kiln requires, just how to set the stones for the correct shelling and grinding of the cleaned and dried oats. The method of kiln-drying is somewhat more arduous than the modern method of mechanical drying, but it is to the kiln that we owe the delectable flavour of the best oatmeal.[2]

In meal from the local mills, as in château wines, there are constant minor differences in taste, due in part to the quality and age of the grain, and in part to the temperature and time taken in the kiln. Country folk with a natural palate always appreciated the fact that the age-old primitive structure of the local mills provided an agreeable variation in the flavour of the meal. Far too much of the meal in the market today is mass-milled by a process which affects adversely both its flavour and its nutritive qualities. That is why so many children do not enjoy their porridge as their parents did. Home-milled meal is, however, still available.

The true flavour is often lacking in meal bought in small stores where the turnover is small and the meal not fresh from the kiln. Meal obtained from a corn dealer is by far the freshest.

The use of fine, medium or coarse oatmeal is mainly a matter of taste.

'A herring fried in nutty oatmeal and accompanied by a mustard sauce,' writes a gourmet, 'makes a noble supper dish, and never better than when coarse oatmeal is

---

[1] In my childhood, when the sacks of meal came back from the mill to the Manse (for we grew our own oats), we smaller children used to have our feet washed and thoroughly dried, and were lifted on to the top of the meal to tramp it down, which we did with great gusto. – F. M. McN.

[2] 'The best oatmeal is well-ripened on the stalk, dried by sunshine and, if necessary, in the gentle warmth of a small kiln, and ground between two honest mill-stones. Some sort of virtue disappears with rapid drying, while high-speed milling between opposed surfaces of steel may possibly add a trace of iron to our diet, but cannot achieve the effect of a little fine sandstone dust.' – Gastrologue in *The Scotsman*.

used and the fish is fried in bacon fat. For brown trout, however, I prefer a dusting of the finest oatmeal; and it should, of course, be cooked in butter.'

As regards porridge, oatcakes, scones and other simple dishes, all their virtue lies in the hands of the cook. Time, temperature and, not least, transmitted skill all count. From perfection, deterioration is rapid.

(On board the vessel that was carrying Dr. Johnson and Boswell to Mull.) 'Col sat at the fire in the forecastle with the captain and Joseph and the rest. I ate some dry oatmeal, of which I found a barrel in the cabin. I had not done this since I was a boy. Dr. Johnson owned that he, too, was fond of it as a boy; a circumstance which I was highly pleased to hear from him, as it gave me an opportunity of observing that notwithstanding his joke in the article on OATS, he was himself a proof that this kind of food was not peculiar to the people of Scotland.'
— James Boswell: *Journal of a Tour to the Hebrides*.

Oatmeal tied in muslin sachets was commonly placed by country maidens in the ewer of rain-water as a beautifier for the complexion. – F. M. McN.

1. PREPARATIONS OF OATMEAL

Porridge

'The halesome parritch, chief o' Scotia's food.' – Burns.

(The One and Only Method)

Oatmeal, salt, water

It is advisable to keep a goblet[1] exclusively for porridge.

Allow for each person one breakfastcupful of water, a handful of oatmeal (about an ounce and a quarter), and a small saltspoonful of salt. Use fresh spring water and be particular about the quality of the oatmeal. Midlothian oats are reputed to be unsurpassed, but the small Highland oats are very sweet.

Bring the water to the boil and as soon as it reaches boiling-point add the oatmeal, letting it fall in a steady rain from the left hand and stirring it briskly the while with the right, sunwise, or the right-hand turn for luck – and convenience. A porridge-stick, called a spurtle,[2] and in some parts a theevil,[3] or, as in Shetland, a gruel-tree, is used for this purpose. Be careful to avoid lumps, unless the children clamour for them. When the porridge is boiling steadily,

---

[1] 'The Carron goblets of Scotland and the saucepans of England and Wales.'
— Meg Dods.
The goblets made at the great Carron foundry, in Falkirk, were of cast iron.
[2] A.S. *sprytle.*   [3] A.S. *thyfel.*

draw the mixture to the side and put on the lid. Let it cook for from twenty to thirty minutes according to the quality of the oatmeal, and do not add the salt, which has a tendency to harden the meal and prevent its swelling, until it has cooked for at least ten minutes. On the other hand, never cook porridge without salt. Ladle straight into *cold* porringers or soup-plates and serve with individual bowls of cream, or milk, or buttermilk. Each spoonful of porridge, which should be very hot, is dipped in the cream or milk, which should be quite cold, before it is conveyed to the mouth.

'The whole principle of porridge-making is to continue to add pinches of fresh meal as the porridge boils, so that when the dish is ready you will have a complete gamut of texture from fully boiled to almost raw meal. The moment when the salt goes in is also important, for the first and bulkiest quantity of oatmeal should have swelled and burst before this happens.' – Gastrologue in *The Scotsman*, 26 May, 1962.

'What meal does Johnnie want for his porridge? I will send it up from Abbotsford. I think it will agree with him better than the southern food of horses.'
– Sir Walter Scott in a letter to his son-in-law, J. G. Lockhart.

The traditional porridge bowl was made of hardwood – preferably birch, because of its sweetness and also because it was easily kept clean. Horn spoons were commonly used with both porridge and broth, and were preferred to metal ones, which are apt to become unpleasantly hot.

Porter, skeachan, and brisk small beer used to be popular accompaniments to porridge. In his poem 'Scotch Drink' (which in his day was ale) Burns writes:

> The poorman's wine,
> His wee drap parritch, or his breid,
> Thou ki†chens[1] fine.

When milk was scarce, drinking-sowans was sometimes substituted.
Children often like a layer of sugar, honey, syrup, or treacle, or of raw oatmeal on top. A morsel of butter in the centre of the plate agrees with some digestions better than milk.

'On Sundays as children, if we had been good during the week we had our initials in treacle put on our porridge, and then cream. Our old Caithness nurse approved of brown sugar on porridge.' – 'Scot' in *Scotsman*, Jan. 1939.

To encourage her reluctan† young porridge-eaters, another nurse used to draw a golden dromedary with syrup on the surface. By the time the dromedary was eaten, the porridge too, had vanished. – F. M. McN.

In Scots, porridge, like broth, is spoken of as 'they'. 'Why do ye no sup yer parritch?' 'I dinna like them; they're unco wersh,[2] gi'e me a wee pickle sau†.'[3] – Jamieson.

The old custom is to stand whilst supping porridge. A friend of the writer's recollects being slapped by her Highland nurse for not standing up to 'them'. As to whether the custom has any mystical significance or is merely an application of the proverb that 'a staunin' (standing) sack fills the fu'est', I profess no opinion. – F. M. McN.

'In spite of the abundance and variety of food with which we were surrounded, porridge easily maintained its pride of place. In our minds it became associated with

[1] Give a relish to.　　　[2] Very insipid.　　　[3] Salt.

263

good manners and even with religion. At Hafton it was laid down that if a child (even an English or Irish child on a visit) was late for morning prayers, that wicked one got no cream with his porridge! The small nursery critics formed their private opinions of guests a great deal on the porridge ceremonial. The worst and most deplorable give-away was when the lady or gentleman took sugar. The next was to sit down at table with the porridge instead of walking about the room with the bowl in one hand and the spoon in the other, as if you were ready to start off for the wars, or shooting, or fishing, next moment.' – General Sir Ian Hamilton: *When I Was a Boy*.

Brochan: the name commonly used for porridge or gruel in the Highlands (Gael. *brochan*).

Bleirie (Lanarkshire) and *Lewands* (Clydesdale): 'oatmeal and buttermilk boiled to a consistency somewhat thicker than gruel with a piece of butter put into the mess.'
– Jamieson.

Bluthrie: the name given in Ettrick and Forfarshire to thin porridge or gruel.

Gogar (Roxburghshire) and *Whillins* (Fife): whey boiled with a little oatmeal.

Whey-whullions: 'Formerly a common dish among the peasantry of Scotland, con-sisting of the porridge left at breakfast, which was beaten down among fresh whey, with an additional quantity of oatmeal.' – Jamieson.

Meal-and-milk or *Milk-meat* or *Milgruel* (Shetland) is porridge made with milk in the ordinary way.

Tartan-purry is thin porridge made with stock in which kail has been boiled.

Brose

> O gi'e my luv brose, brose,
> Gi'e my luv brose and butter.
> – Burns: *Gi'e My Luv Brose*.

Oatmeal, salt, butter, water

Pour into a bowl two handfuls of oatmeal. Add salt and a piece of butter. Pour in boiling water to cover the oatmeal and stir it up roughly with the shank of a horn spoon, allowing it to form knots.[1] Sup with soor dook or sweet milk, and you have a dish that has been the backbone of many a sturdy Scotsman. *Brose and Butter* is as favourite an old tune as this is a nourishing dish.

'I say that oatmeal does not require to be boiled at all. When oatmeal is boiled the starch grains are burst and the starch becomes gluey and semi-transparent; in technical language the starch has become hydrolysed. . . . For many years I have recommended patients to take oatmeal brose made with hot milk instead of hot water. . . . Many people who find that oatmeal porridge does not suit them find that when they take oatmeal not as porridge but as brose made with milk, it suits them splendidly.

'Two dessertspoonfuls of medium ground oatmeal, a small piece of butter and a small quantity of salt, and as much hot milk as will make the brose neither too thin nor too thick. Later, the quantity of oatmeal may be doubled.' – M.B., ChB.

Aigar Brose is brose made of either oatmeal or mashlum meal – equal portions of oatmeal, bere meal and pease meal. (Beggars used to mix the different kinds they received in the same bag.)

[1] The cant designation is *Knotty Tams*. The oatmeal should be raw inside the knots.

Blind Brose or *Water Brose* is brose without butter; 'said to be so denominated from there being none of those small orifices in it called eyes, which appear when butter is used.' – Jamieson.

Cadger's Brose is like aigar brose, only the meal is placed among boiling water in a little pan, and stirred till all the lumps are broken.

Knotty Tam (Caithness) is a brose made of beist milk and oatmeal.

Milk Brose, *Madlocks*, or *Milk-Madlocks* (Renfrewshire), is brose made with milk instead of water.

Pot-brose is a dish consisting of milk and oatmeal made by dashing compressed handfuls of meal into boiling milk and boiling the mixture for a few minutes (Banff-shire).

Wirtiglugs (Shetland) is a brose made of oatmeal and hot wirt (a sweet infusion of malt).

Gruel

In the Best Manner, as made in Scotland.

(*Meg Dods's Recipe*)

Fine oatmeal, water, salt, sugar, wine or honey, etc., to taste

Take very finely ground oatmeal of the best quality. Infuse as much as you wish in cold water for an hour or two. Stir it up, let it settle, and pour the liquid from the grits (or strain it), and boil slowly for a long time, stirring it up.[1] Add a little salt and sugar, with any addition of wine, rum, fruit, jelly, honey, butter, etc., you choose. This gruel will be quite smooth; and when cold will form a jelly. With a toast it makes an excellent luncheon or supper dish for an invalid. It may be thinned at pleasure.

(Allow two ounces of oatmeal, good measure, to a pint of water.)

'For coughs and colds, Water-gruel with a little Butter is the ordinary cure. . . . Water-gruel is also found by experience to be good for Consumptions; it purifies the Blood and procures Appetite when drunk without Salt. The Natives (of St. Kilda) make a pudding of the Fat (of the Solan Goose) in the Stomack of it, and boyl it in their Water-gruel, which they call Brochan; they drink it likewise for removing the Cough: it is by daily experience found to be an excellent Vulnerary.'
– Martin: *Description of the Western Islands*, 1703.

[1] 'The English language is very deficient in terms descriptive of culinary processes. The Scotch retain the word "to skink" in defining the process of continually lifting high a sauce or gruel by spoonfuls, and rapidly letting it fall back into the pan. The French language, which is peculiarly rich in culinary terms, calls what is signified above by stirring, to *vanner* a sauce or soup; and to see a French cook thus engaged at the stove with the *velouté*, or sauce *à la Lucullus*, an Englishman might well suppose that life and death were depending on a process for which *his* language has no name.'
– P. Touchwood, in the *Annals of the Cleikum Club*.

A bowl of gruel, 'laced with usquebaugh', is given to a sick soldier in John Buchan's *Witchwood*.

In Dumfriesshire gruel is called water-berry (Fr. *purée*).

Crowdie or Fuarag

> O that I had ne'er been married,
> I wad never had nae care.
> Now I've gotten wife and weans,
> And they cry crowdie evermair.
>   Ance crowdie, twice crowdie,
>   Three times crowdie in a day;
>   Gin ye crowdie ony mair,
>   Ye'll crowdie a' my meal away.
>   – Old Song, used by Burns.

> My sister Kate cam up the gate
>   Wi' crowdie unto me, man,
> She swore she saw the rebels run
>   Frae Perth unto Dundee, man.
>   – The Battle of Sheriffmuir.

(Traditional Method)

Pour cold spring water or good fresh buttermilk into finely ground oatmeal till as thin as pancake batter. Stir the mixture.

Crowdie was at one time a universal breakfast dish in Scotland. The name was applied generally to all food of the porridge kind. Crowdie-time is an old name for breakfast-time, used by Burns ('Then I gaed hame at crowdie-time.'
                               – The Holy Fair) and by Scott.

Sour milk and meal stirred together in a raw state is known as *Cauld Steer*. *Meal-and-ale* and the original *Athole Brose* (meal and whisky) are also forms of crowdie.

In the Highlands the name *crowdie* (Gael. *gruth*, curd) is given to a species of milk-cheese, and the name *drammach* (Gael. *dramaig*), or *fuarag* (Gael. *fuar*, cold), or *stapag*, is applied to what in Lowland Scotland is called *crowdie* (origin uncertain – S. N. D.).

A mixture of thick kirnmilk and meal was sometimes served as a pudding in cottage homes.

Cranachan or Cream-Crowdie

(A special dish at the Kirn, or Harvest Home)

Oatmeal, cream, sugar and flavouring to taste

Toast some coarse oatmeal lightly before the fire or in the oven. Beat some cream to a stiff froth and stir in the oatmeal. Do not make it too substantial. It may be sweetened and flavoured to taste. The toasted oatmeal gives an agreeable, somewhat nutty, flavour to the dish.

266

This is a very old dish, commonly served in farmhouses on festive occasions. In the Scottish National Museum of Antiquities, there is to be seen, in the section of domestic articles, one of the old fro'ing sticks, having a wooden cross surrounded with a ring of cow's hair at one end, formerly used for beating cream and whey.

Raspberries in Cream-Crowdie: A few handfuls of raspberries buried in a bowl of cream-crowdie make an excellent sweet.

Butter-Crowdie

Oatmeal, butter fresh from the churn, salt or sugar to taste

Make as above, mixing the toasted oatmeal with soft butter fresh from the churn.

Ale-Crowdie or Meal-And-Ale

(A special dish at the Kirn, or Harvest Home)

> A cogie[1] o' yill,[2]
> An' a pickle oatmeal,
> An' a dainty wee drappie o' whisky
> An' hey for the cogie,
> An' hey for the yill –
> Gin ye steer a' thegither, they'll do unco weel.
> – Andrew Shirrefs: *A Cogie o' Yill* (1787).

Ale, treacle, oatmeal, whisky

This is a variety of crowdie.

A large earthenware pot or milk-bowl is filled with ale, and treacle is added to sweeten it. Then oatmeal is stirred in until the whole is of a sufficient consistency, and finally whisky in such quantity as is desired. The dish is prepared on the morning of the festival to allow the meal time to be completely absorbed. It is served up at the end of the feast. A ring is always put into the mixture, and whoever gets it will be the first to be married.

Crowdie-Mowdie

(A Cottage Recipe)

Oatmeal, salt, milk

The night before it is wanted put into a jar oatmeal, salt, and milk, allowing a handful of oatmeal, a small teaspoonful

[1] A wooden vessel.　　[2] Ale.

of salt, and a breakfastcupful of milk for each person. Stir, cover, and let it stand all night. In the morning set the jar in a goblet of water and let it steam for two hours or longer.[1]

Sowans[2]

> Till buttered so'ns wi' fragrant lunt[3]
> Set a' their gabs a-steerin',[4]
> Syne wi' a social glass o' strunt[5]
> They parted aff careerin'
> Fu' blythe that night.
>   – Burns: *Hallowe'en.*

In the days of local mills, when the oats that had been winnowed and threshed were returned as meal, the miller always sent with it a bag of 'sids' – the inner husks of the oat grain – to which adheres some of the finest and most nutritive substance of the meal. This was made into a kind of smooth pudding or gruel called sowans (Gael. *sughan*, pronounced soo-an), an ancient dish of Celtic origin. It has a slightly sour taste which some find unpalatable at first, but which usually 'grows on' one. It is a very wholesome and sustaining food, and is said to be an ideal diet for invalids, especially dyspeptics.

(*Traditional Method*)

Oatmeal sids, water, salt

Put a quantity of sids into the sowan-bowie (a narrow-mouthed wooden tub resembling a small barrel with an open end) or an earthenware jar, and pour over them twice their bulk of lukewarm water. The sids rise to the surface and must be pressed down with a spatula or the back of a wooden spoon until all are wet. Leave them in a warm place until they are quite sour. (The preparation, before the acetous fermentation begins, is called the serf.[6]) They will require anything from four to five days in hot weather to a fortnight in very cold weather. A week is a fair average. Then comes the process known as 'the syein' o' the so'ons', when the contents of the bowie are poured through a fine *sye* (sieve) into a wide-mouthed vessel, the sids being squeezed between the hands to get all the goodness out of them. A little cold water should be added to wash out any remaining

---

[1] This dish goes well with stewed figs.
[2] Spelt also sowens.   [3] Steam.   [4] Mouths watering.   [5] Any spirituous liquor.
[6] Gael. *searbh.*

sediment. The sids are now thrown away (they are usually put into the hens' mash, as they make good roughage) and the liquid is allowed to stand for two days longer, until all the starchy matter has sunk to the bottom. This contains practically all the nutritious properties of the oatmeal in its most easily digested form.

When required for use, pour off all the clear liquid (swats) and put some of the sediment (sowans) into a saucepan, allowing a gill for each person, with two gills of water and salt to taste. Bring to the boil, stirring continuously, and cook gently for ten minutes or longer, until thick and creamy. Serve like porridge, in wooden bowls or deep plates, with cream or rich milk.

I have been told – I do not vouch for the truth of the tale – that a certain wealthy Scottish peer who was for years a martyr to dyspepsia and had been treated with no effect by several London specialists, was cured by an obscure Highland doctor, who prescribed a diet of sowans. – F. M. McN.

Sowans appears on the dietary list (1798) of the Dundee Royal Infirmary.

Sowans can be preserved for months by pouring off the clear swats and adding fresh water.

Sowans may be eaten raw, either with sugar or with the addition of a handful of oatmeal.

In Skye, a mixture of *pronn* (chaff) from the mill and coarse oatmeal in the proportion of three to one is sometimes substituted for the sids.

'It will be remembered with what surprise and doubt the public in general received the news during the Boer War that a hardy Scot kept the starving garrison (at Mafeking) alive on a dish made from the contents of the horses' feed-box. After everything eatable had been consumed, he taught his despondent companions how, from bruised oats, an appetising and sustaining dish could be prepared.' –
　　　　　　　　　　　　– Rev. James Firth: *Reminiscences of an Orkney Parish.*

'An uncle of ours who went to America in the days of sailing-ships, when the voyage took three months or more, took with him a large supply of sowans. They made a big batch of it in a tub, and when it had settled the water was poured off and the sediment allowed to dry until it could be cut like cheese. It was then cut into cubes, which were stored in his travelling-trunk for use on the voyage, with what water was supplied on the ship.' – Hugh Mackay (the Gaelic singer), a native of Sutherland, in a letter to the author.

'It could be cooked like porridge, and this was *brownplate sowans.* Or the sowans was simply heated: this was *gaun-'e-gither* sowans. If something lighter was desired, *duochrea* was produced by pouring a quantity of the raw stuff into boiling water and adding a touch of fresh butter. . . . From the creamy deposit pancakes were made, and these were sowan scones.' – J. Horne: *The County of Caithness.*

Buttered Sowans: Sowans cooked in the usual way with the addition of a little butter. A traditional Hallowe'en dish, in which the 'matrimonial ring' was concealed. (See Burns.)

Drinking-sowans: The sediment mixed with water to the consistency of thin cream or milk.

'As a boy in Golspie,' writes Hugh Mackay, 'we often had sowans in diluted form, of the consistency of milk, with our porridge, in winter, when milk was not to be had. We did not care a great deal for it, but with no alternative we had to thole it. Sowans was used a great deal as a drink in the hay-field, and a very good thirst-quencher it was.'

Sowans-Nicht: The name given in Aberdeenshire and the North-East to Christmas Eve (Old Style), when friends forgathered round a big bowl of sowans, usually laced with whisky.

Bere-Meal Porridge (*Caithness, Orkney and Shetland*)

Bere-meal, salt, water

Pour a pint and a half of cold water into a saucepan. Stir in five ounces of bere-meal. When smooth and free from lumps, bring to the boil. Simmer over boiling water in the upper part of a double boiler, keeping it covered except to stir occasionally, for about twenty-five minutes. Add a scant teaspoonful of salt and serve. (Enough for three.)

White or Mealie Puddings

(*Traditional Method*)

Oatmeal, suet, salt, Jamaica pepper, onions, tripe skins

Toast two pounds of oatmeal in the oven, mix with it from a pound to a pound and a half of good beef suet and three or four fair-sized onions, all finely chopped. Add about a tablespoonful of salt and half that quantity of Jamaica pepper. Prepare your tripe skins as for Black Puddings (p. 274) and fill, not too full, with the oatmeal mixture in the manner there indicated. Boil for an hour, pricking them occasionally with a fork to prevent them from bursting. These puddings will keep good for months if hung up and kept dry, or better, if kept buried in oatmeal in the girnel, or meal-chest. When required, warm them through in hot water and brown them in the frying-pan. They make a savoury addition to a stew.

The same mixture makes an excellent stuffing for a fowl, boiled or roasted, and for a stag's heart.

Mrs. McENEN (1835) recommends plenty of onions, which should be first stewed in a little suet. Don't put in too much salt, she adds, and don't *boil* the puddings, but *stew* them.

Meg Dods recommends one-third of highly toasted oatmeal to two-thirds of beef suet.

In Aberdeenshire, minced cracklings are sometimes substituted for beef suet.

'*Liver Puddings* are made (in the same way), using parboiled liver grated in the proportion of one-fourth; the rest suet and meal, with the above seasonings, and onions shred.' – Meg Dods.

Black and white puddings were sold at the Mercat Cross of Edinburgh as early as the fifteenth century. In his poem, *To the Merchantis of Edinburgh*, William Dunbar (b. *c*. 1461) writes:

> At your hie Croce, quhar gold and silk
> Sould be, thair is bot crudis and milk;
> And at your Trone bot cokill and wilk,
> Pansches, pudingis of Jok and Jame.

Puddings of Jock and James were, I knew, black and white puddings; but which was which? I remained uncertain for years, until, when holidaying in Moray, I chanced to hear a schoolgirl exclaim, 'I adore a mealie jamie!' – in other words, white pudding. But I have never heard the equivalent expression for black puddings. – F. M. McN.

Hie, high; *quhar*, where; *crudis*, curds; *Trone*, Tron, a heavy weighing-machine set up in the market-place; *cokill*, cockle; *wilk*, whelk; *pansches*, tripe.

One of the well-known 'luckies' of the eighteenth-century Edinburgh was Pudden Lizzie, whose tavern was situated at Jock's Lodge, then a little way out of the city. She got her soubriquet from her excellent mealie puddings, which she carried ben to the company seated round her ingle (in the words of a young poet who was a frequent guest):

> A' pipin' like a roastit hen,
> Braw healthy eatin'!
> Wi' timmer pins at ilka en',
> To haud the meat in.
> – Richard Gall.

Timmer, wooden; *ilka*, each; *haud*, hold.

Deer's Puddings

(Recipe from the Kitchen of a Highland Chief)

Deer tripe skins, venison suet, coarse oatmeal, onion, salt, pepper

Take some deer tripe skins, wash in water and a very little salt, turning the skins out to be thoroughly cleansed, but leaving the fat that adheres to the inside of the skins. Take a large cupful of finely chopped venison or beef suet, a handful of coarse oatmeal, some finely chopped onion, and salt and pepper to season. Fill the skins loosely and prick with a needle to prevent their bursting. Boil for forty-five minutes. When required, brown them in a sauté pan with some hot fat, or grill them for fifteen minutes and serve very hot.

271

A Fitless Cock[1]

(Meg Dods's Recipe)

Oatmeal, suet, pepper, salt, onion, egg

This antique Scotch dish, which is now seldom seen at any
table, is made of suet and oatmeal, with a seasoning of
pepper, salt, and onions, as for white puddings, the mixture
bound together with an egg and moulded somewhat in the
form of a fowl. It must be boiled in a cloth like a dumpling.

Skirlie *(Skirl-in-the-Pan)*[2]

(Aberdeenshire and the North-East)

Oatmeal, suet, onion, salt, pepper

Chop two ounces of suet finely. Have a pan very hot and put
in the suet. When it is melted, add one or two finely chopped
onions and brown them well. Now add enough oatmeal to
absorb the fat – a fairly thick mixture. Season to taste.
Stir well till thoroughly cooked (a few minutes). Serve with
potatoes.

'Skirl-in-the-Pan. 1. The noise made by a frying-pan when the butter is put in which
prepares it for receiving the meat. 2. The dish prepared in this manner. 3. A sort of
drink, also called Blythe-meat or Merry-meat, made of oatmeal, whisky, and ale,
mixed and heated in a pan, and given to the gossips at *inlyings*, Mearns.' – Jamieson.

In the south of Scotland, at the Lammas feast the shepherds are provided with a dish
called *Butter Brughtins*, which consists of oatcakes toasted before the fire, crumbled
down and put into a pot with butter and made into a sort of pottage. *Brughtin* is allied
to Gael. *brochan*, gruel or porridge. See Jamieson.

Hodgils *(Borders)*

Oatmeal, pepper, salt, fat, chives (optional)

Put some oatmeal into a bowl, season it with pepper and
salt and a few chopped chives (if liked). Mix with fat from

---

[1] The *Fitless* or *Festy* (Fastyn) *Cock* was formerly eaten on Fastern's E'en, the
evening which precedes the first day of the Fast of Lent. In the eighteenth century,
cock-fights were commonly held in the parish schools to celebrate the festival.

The original *Festy Cock* (called *Dry Goose* in the south of Scotland) was composed
of a handful of the finest meal pressed very close together, dipped in water, and then
roasted among the ashes of a kiln. (See Jamieson.) – F. M. McN.

[2] Mentioned by Scott in *Old Mortality*.

the top of the beef broth. Form into balls and pop into the boiling broth. Cook for twenty minutes. Serve with the meat.

Burstin (*Caithness, Orkney and Shetland*)

Burstin or Burston is a preparation of the hardy type of northern oats combined with bere, a coarse type of barley (*hordeum hexastichon*).

'To make burstin, a good fire of red peat embers and hot ashes was needed. A big three-toed pot was set on the hearth at the foot of the peat fire and packed down on the red hot ashes, the top of the pot sloping slightly towards you. A few handfuls of bere and oats, in roughly equal quantities, were put into the pot to be burst in the drying. It was constantly stirred with a wooden spoon and kept from burning. The mettins cracked away in the pot and were stirred about till they had burst with the heat – hence the original name, burstin. The lot was then whummled (emptied) into a tub, and more put into the pot until enough was burst. It was then chappit in a tub with a spade, winnowed in a sieve called a wecht, ground on a quern or a knocking-stone, and finally rubbed in a coarse cloth or sifted.'

– James Omond: *Orkney Eighty Years Ago* (1911).

'Burstin was always made in the spring for summer use, and when well stirred into louts[1] formed a cooling sequel to the dinner when it did not form the principal meal of the day.' – Rev. John Firth: *Reminiscences of an Orkney Parish.*

Burstin Brunies: 'The meal is of a rich brown colour, highly flavoured and fine as dust. It is made into round cakes, often enriched with butter. It is slowly baked over the fire. . . . When a hungry boy had come in clamouring for his lunch, the burstin was hastily kneaded into a thick cake and well spread with butter. It was then termed a *klind krul.*' – Jessie M. B. Saxby: *Shetland Traditional Lore.*

'Burston brunies, run-milk[2] and blawn cod may assert themselves whereever high game and moving cheese are permitted to appear.'
– Edmonston and Saxby: *The Home of a Naturalist.*

Pramm: Put some burstin into a bowl and pour over it sufficient hot milk to make a drink of the consistency of cream. Add a pinch of salt. Serve hot.

Other preparations of oatmeal will be found under Bannocks, Beverages, etc.

[1] Sour milk or cream ready for churning.   [2] Curdled milk.

2. PREPARATIONS OF BLOOD

Black Puddings

> Puddins a' hot, a' hot,
> Pipin' hot, pipin' hot!
> Hot or cold, they must be sold,
> Puddins a' hot, a' hot!
>   – *Old Edinburgh Street Cry.*[1]

> It fell about the Martinmas time
> And a gay time it was then, O;
> That our gudewife had puddins to mak'
> And she boiled them in the pan, O.
>   – *The Barrin' o' the Door.*

(*East of Scotland Recipe*)

Pig's or ox blood, milk, suet or lard, oatmeal, onions, pepper, salt

Let the blood run into a deep pan; stir it all the time, and when it is nearly cold, throw in a little salt, allowing a large teaspoonful to every quart. Rub it through a hair sieve. To each quart of blood allow half a pint of milk; stir them together and add, again to each quart, a pound of shred suet or of the inward fat of the pig, a large handful of oatmeal, and plenty of minced onions, pepper, and salt.

To clean the pudding-skins, wash them thoroughly, and let them lie a night in salt and water. When they are to be filled, tie one end and turn inside out. Half fill them and tie them in rings or in equal lengths. When the water boils throw in a little cold to put it off the boil and put in the puddings. In five minutes prick them over with a large needle, removing them if necessary for the purpose. Return them to the pot and boil them for half an hour. Hang them up in a dry cool place to keep them. When they are to be used, put them in hot water for ten or fifteen minutes and then broil them.

Pinches of cayenne, grated nutmeg or ground mace, and crushed herbs may be added.

[1] In 1851, the Town Council of Edinburgh ordained 'the pudden mercat to be removit of the calsay and placeit in the flesche mercat'.

(West of Scotland Recipe)

Bullock's or sheep's blood, oatmeal, suet, salt, black pepper,
white pepper, mint, milk, tripe skins

With a quart of blood mix eight ounces of oatmeal, eight
ounces of finely minced suet, a large teaspoonful of salt,
two teaspoonfuls of white pepper, a teaspoonful of black
pepper, and a teaspoonful of powdered mint. Warm half a
pint of skim milk, add and mix thoroughly. Turn the tripe
skins inside out, wash well in warm, salted water, and rinse
well in cold water. Fill three parts full with the mixture, and
tie the two ends together. Put into hot water and boil
slowly for twenty minutes, pricking occasionally with a
darning-needle to let the air escape. Lay them on a cloth to
dry, then hang up for use. When required, place them in
boiling water in a deep saucepan, then toast before a fire
or on a gridiron or under the grill.

At 'the Duck of Montrose's super' in 1715, one of the dishes was 'Scots collips wᵗ
marow and black pudins about them' (see *The Household Book of Lady Grisell Baillie*);
Faujas de St. Fond describes among the dishes served to him in the Highlands in 1784,
a 'pudding of bullock's blood and barley-meal, seasoned with plenty of pepper and
ginger'; and Hogg (the Ettrick Shepherd) mentioned a 'blood ker-cake' of blood and
oatmeal prepared in a frying pan and eaten on Fastern's E'en.

'The wife of one of the most famous judges of the Court of Session, who flourished
sixty years since, was of so exceedingly penurious a nature that she would provide
nothing deemed respectable for the famous Saturday-night suppers at which his Lordship had been accustomed to entertain parties of a dozen or more of his friends of the
bench and bar. His Lordship was driven to invent something which might atone for its
cheapness by its novelty, and introduced a dish to his Saturday-night visitors which
made a great hit. He gave them black puddings! ... They were supplied by an old man
who sold them *al fresco* in the High Street, near John Knox's corner, and his Lordship's cook knew how to send them up to table. With these puddings, a good deal of
anchovy toast, and plenty of good claret, his Lordship happily managed to overcome
his domestic difficulties, and without any check to "the feast of reason and the flow
of soul".' – James Bertram: *Books, Authors and Events* (1893).

In *My Schools and Schoolmasters*, Hugh Miller, describing the 'genuine Highland
breakfasts' he enjoyed on his visits to an aunt in Sutherland, writes: 'On more than one
occasion I shared in a not unpalatable sort of blood-pudding, enriched with butter, and
well seasoned with pepper and salt, the main ingredient of which was derived, through
a judicious use of the lancet, from the *yeld* cattle of the farm. The practice was an
ancient, and a by no means unphilosophic one. In summer and early autumn there is
plenty of grass in the Highlands; but of old, at least, there used to be very little grain
in it before the beginning of October; and as the cattle could, in consequence, provide
themselves with a competent supply of blood from the grass when their masters, who
could not eat grass, and had very little else that they could eat, were able to acquire
very little, it was opportunely discovered that, by making a division in this way of the
all-essential fluid, accumulated as a common stock, the circumstances of the cattle and
their owners could be in some degree equalized.'

275

Neil Munro, too, in his short story, *War*, describes a woman making a *marag* (pudding) with blood drawn from a living cow.

'Some of the stronger cattle were bled in the spring by an expert. The blood was carefully prepared, salted in a tub, and set aside for use. We called it black pudding.

'An Englishman called at the door one day and asked mother if she would supply him with some food. . . . Mother had no bread ready. She brought a sheaf of oats from the barn, passed it rapidly over the red embers of the peat fire that glowed on the hearth, and at the right moment shook off the grain on a clean cloth, which she spread on the floor. After husking it in a stone quern, she cleared away the husks, returned the grain into the quern and ground it with a stone pestle. The meal she baked into an oatcake, and while it was toasting before the fire, she hung the three-legged iron pot over the fire, with a bit of butter in it. When hot, some slices of the above-mentioned black pudding were laid on it to fry, along with a chopped onion.

'The Englishman was delighted with the meal which had thus been prepared before his eyes, and which took only one hour to get ready. He was full of curiosity regarding the nature of the toothsome food given with the no less delicious bread.

'. . . But mother feared he might be shocked should he be made aware of the nature of the ingredient of which it was chiefly composed, so she evaded his questions rather than risk spoiling his appetite.'

– Katherine W. Grant: *Myth, Tradition and Legend from Western Argyll.*

Lamb's Blood Pudding

(Mrs. McIver's Recipe)

Blood, cream, salt, spice, mint, chives or young onions, fat

Take as much blood as with half a mutchkin (half-pint) of cream will fill an ashet; mix the blood and cream together and run through a search. Season with salt and spices, a sprig of mint and chives or young onions, minced small; mince the fat of the near or kidney small; mix all together and fire in the oven or in a frying-pan.

Lamb's blood is the sweetest of all blood.

Goose-Blood Pudding

(Mrs. Glasse's Recipe)

Goose blood, grits, spice, salt, sweet herbs, suet

In Scotland they make a pudding with the blood of a goose. Chop off the head and save the blood, stir it till it is cold, then mix it with grits, spice, salt, and sweet herbs, according to fancy, and some beef suet chopped. Take the skin off the neck, then pull out the wind-pipe and fat, fill the skin, tie it at both ends, so make a pie of the giblets and lay the pudding in the middle.

This pudding is still made in rural districts. It is usually thickened with barley-meal and cooked in the broth.

3. MILKMEATS

'A dinner in the Western Isles differs very little from a dinner in England, except that in the place of tarts there are always set different preparations of milk.'
– Dr. Johnson: *Journey to the Western Isles of Scotland*, 1775.

Milk has always played an important part in the Scottish rural economy. The rich quality of the milk is commented on by many travellers, including Dr. Johnson and Southey. That of the hardy Highland cattle, which lived almost entirely in the clean, sweet air and fed on the clean, sweet pasturage of the hills and glens, enjoyed a reputation for purity and goodness long before the dairy herds of Ayrshire and Galloway achieved fame.[1] Milk, buttermilk and whey were drunk in quantity by all classes, and in the better-to-do households cream was a common accompaniment to porridge, jellies and cold sweets.

Besides cheese and crowdie, our milkmeats included Corstorphine Cream and its *alter ego*, Ru'glen (Rutherglen) Ream, Hattit Kit, O'on (frothed whey), Blaand (sparkling whey) and much beside.

Here are two milking-pictures – one from the Hebrides and one from Aberdeenshire.

'The milking-songs of the people are numerous and varied. They are sung to pretty airs, to please the cows and induce them to give their milk. The cows become accustomed to these lilts and will not give their milk without them. This fondness of Highland cows for music induces owners of large herds to secure milkmaids possessed of good voices and some "go". It is interesting and animating to see three or four comely girls among a fold of sixty, eighty or a hundred picturesque Highland cows on meadow or mountain slope. The moaning and heaving of the sea afar, the swish of the wave on the shore, the carolling of the lark in the sky, the unbroken song of the mavis on the rock, the broken melody of the merle in the break, the lowing of the kine without, the response of the calves within the fold, the singing of the milkmaids in unison with the movement of their hands, and of the soft sound of the snowy milk falling into the pail, the gilding of hill and dale, the glowing of the distant ocean beyond, as the sun sinks into the sea of golden glory, constitute a scene which the observer would not, if he could, forget.' – Alexander Carmichael: *Carmina Gadelica*.

Some of these milking-songs are to be found in the *Songs of the Hebrides*, edited by Marjorie Kennedy-Fraser and Kenneth Macleod.

The other depicts a little sheil, or dairy, set in a howe (valley or glen) in Aberdeenshire.

> On skelfs a' roun' the wa's the cogs were set,
> Ready to ream, and for the cheese be het.
> A hake was frae the riggin' hangin' fu'
> O' quarter kebbucks, tightly made and new.
> Behind the door a calour heather bed
> Flat o' the floor o' stanes and feal was made;
> And Lucky shortly followed owre the gait

[1] 'Speaking of those forgotten pastoral days when the country people drove their cattle to those uplands for the summer months, "There is such a profusion of herbs," he (Munro) remembered, "that the air, water and milk are all impregnated with their virtue." ' – March Cost: *The Bespoken Mi'e*.

Wi' twa fu' leglins foamin' owre and het;
Syne reamed her milk, and set it on the fire,
And bade them eek the blaze, and nae to tyre,
That curds in wamefu' they should get in haste,
As fresh and gueed as ever they did taste.
           – Alexander Ross: *The Fortunate Shepherdess* (1768).

Skelf, shelf; *wa's*, walls; *cog*, wooden milk-vessel; *ream*, cream; *hake*, a frame for drying cheeses; *riggin'*, rafters; *kebbucks*, cheeses; *calour*, fresh; *stanes*, stones; *feal*, turf; *Lucky*, goodwife; *gait*, path; *leglins*, milk-pails; *eek*, increase.

Until comparatively recent times, wild goats, including some ancient and famous herds, were plentiful in Scotland, but their numbers are now sadly depleted.[1] They are to be found chiefly in the high and rocky places in the remoter regions of Skye, Mull, Islay, Jura, Ben Lomond, Ben Venue, and the wilds of Rothiemurchus and Galloway. In the eighteenth century, the drinking of goat's milk and whey was fashionable, and there were resorts in the Ochil hillfoots, at Corrie, in Arran, and elsewhere, that attracted people who sought to benefit their health in this way.[2] Goat's milk or whey, together with moorland air, was especially recommended in cases of consumption.

Corstorphine Cream or Ru'glen Cream

(*Meg Dods's Recipe*)

Milk, moist sugar

Pour a quart of new milk into a jar. On this, next morning, pour another, and mix well; at night do the same; and next day beat up the thickened milk with moist sugar.

'This cooling preparation was patronized by Sir John Sinclair. It may be made like hatted kit, of mixed buttermilk and sweet milk. Indeed, there is a learned controversy on the genuine preparation; and another as to whether its invention really belongs to Corstorphine near Edinburgh, or to the village of Rutherglen in the neighbourhood of the western metropolis.' – *Annals of the Cleikum Club.*

'Rutherglen is famous for making sour cream of an excellent quality. It is made in the following manner. A certain quantity of sweet (i.e. new) milk is put into a wooden vessel or vat, which is placed in a proper degree of heat, and covered with a linen cloth. In due time, the serous or watery part of the milk begins to separate from the rest, and is called *whig*. When the separation is complete, which, according to circumstances, requires more or less time, the whig is drawn off from near the bottom of the vessel. The substance that remains is then beat with a large wooden spoon or ladle, till the particles of which it is composed are properly mixed. A small quantity of sweet milk is sometimes added to correct the acidity if it is in excess. The cream thus prepared is agreeable to the taste and nourishing to the constitution.'
           – *New Statistical Account of Scotland*, 1845.

[1] Some of the goats strayed; some were left behind by the forced emigrants during the Clearances, some were driven off their original habitat by foresters and agricultural improvers; and, more recently, the Holy Isle herd on the Clyde, which numbered about fifty, was reduced by Commandos in training at Lamlash Bay, who found stalking them a useful exercise.

[2] 'Donald McPherson, who I hear is on the way to recoverie of his health, being gone to the Highlands to drink goat's milk.'
           – From the diary of Bailie John Stewart of Inverness, May 20, 1736.

'Both of these are, of course, the Scottish versions of the German *Dickmilch* and of the sour mare's milk of the Cossacks, now so widely known as *Yogurt*, which gave the clue to Metchnikoff. They are quite as conducive to health and long life as the German or the Russian varieties.' – Donald and Catherine Carswell: *The Scots Week-end.*

Hatted Kit

'Their efter I suld meet your lo: in Leith or quietlie in Restal, quhair we sould have preparit ane fyne haitit kit, with suckar and confeittie and wyne, and therefter confer on materis.' – Logan of Restalrig: *Letters*, 1609.

'He has spilled the hatted kit that was for the master's dinner.'
– Scott: *Bride of Lammermoor.*

(*Meg Dods's Recipe*)

Buttermilk, new milk, sugar, nutmeg or cinnamon

Where this cooling and healthy article of diet is in constant use for children or delicate persons, a kit with a double bottom, the upper one perforated with holes and furnished with a fosset and a cover, should be got. Into this vessel put in the proportion of two quarts fresh good buttermilk and a pint of milk hot from the cow. Mix well by jumbling; and next milking add another pint of milk, mixing all well. It will now firm and gather a *hat*. Drain off the whey whenever it runs clear, by the spigot; remove what of the top or hat is necessary to take up the quantity wanted. This dish if to present at table may be moulded for an hour in a perforated mould, and strewed over with a little pounded sugar and then nutmeg or cinnamon. The kit must be well sweetened with lime-water or charcoal every time it is used; and too much should not be made at once, it gets so quickly very acid. A slight degree of coagulation assists digestion, but milk highly acidulated is not wished for in this dish.

(*An Old Highland Recipe*)

Buttermilk, new milk, sugar, nutmeg, double cream

Warm two quarts of buttermilk slightly at milking-time. Carry the vessel to the side of a cow and milk into it a pint of milk. Stir well. At the next milking, add another pint and stir again. Let it stand till it firms and gathers a *hat*. Remove

279

the curd, place it on a hair sieve, and press the whey
through till the curd is stiff.[1] Put into a mould and leave for
half an hour. Turn out and strew with sugar and nutmeg,
and serve with thick cream.

Mrs. Dalgairns's recipe: Make two quarts of new milk scalding hot and pour it
quickly upon four quarts of fresh made buttermilk, after which it must not be stirred.
Let it remain till cold and firm; then take off the top part, drain it in a hair sieve, and
put it into a shape for half and hour. It is eaten with cream, served in a separate dish.

Lady Colebrooke (1877) writes: 'Serve the curds in a glass dish at luncheon, as you
would clotted cream. To eat with stewed fruit or with brown bread and salt, adding
plain cream. Do not butter the brown bread. This kit is instead.'

Cheese

Domestic cheese-making has been carried out in Scotland from time immemorial,
but in this sphere we have sadly lacked the inventiveness and skill of English and
Continental cheese-makers. Against the English Stilton, Cheshire, Cheddar, Double
Gloucester, Wensleydale (described by Morton Shand as 'the premier cheese of England
and one of the world's classic cheeses') and about a dozen more, we can show only one
national cheese – Dunlop. Other types of cheese have been made in Scotland, but with
the exception of the Island of Coll cheese, which has now disappeared from ken, and
Orkney cheese, a traditional product which has only recently emerged from obscurity,
they were never marketed other than locally.

At one time the village of Liberton, now a suburb of Edinburgh, produced cheeses of
repute, and the hilly pastures of Buckholmside were famous for the best ewe-milk
cheese in the South of Scotland.[2]

In his *Reminiscences of a Highland Parish*, Dr. Norman Macleod mentions 'Blue
Highland cheese, finer than Stilton'.

A home-made cheese known as the Crying-kebbuck used to be part of the kimmers'
feast at a lying-in. It was eaten after the new-born babe had uttered its first cry.

Crowdie or Cruddy Butter (*Highlands*)

(*Recipe supplied to the Cleikum Club by P. Touchwood, Esq.*)

Sweet milk curd, fresh butter

In Inverness and the Ross shires there is a rural breakfast
article called crowdie, not the common composition, oatmeal and water or milk, but made thus: Take two parts
fresh sweet-milk curd and one of fresh butter. Work them

---

[1] Failing a cow, the milk may be warmed to blood heat and poured from shoulder
height.
[2] 'The old ewe-milk cheese of the Scottish Border we have found an admirable
substitute for Gruyère.' – Meg Dods.

well together and press them in a basin or small shape and turn it out, when it will slice nicely. When whey is much used for drink in hot weather the curd may be usefully thus disposed of. It is eaten with bread and butter and keeps a long time, if *goût* is liked. This preparation, when the curd is well broken and blended with the butter, is sometimes made up in deep narrow cogs, or wooden moulds, and kept for months, when it becomes very high flavoured though mellow. The celebrated Arabian cheese is made in the same way in vats, and both are uncommonly fine. These preparations deserve trial. In the Lowlands this is sometimes seen but is not kept, and is, for this reason, called a one-day's cheese.

(*Another Recipe*)

Put some thick, sour milk into a pan and heat over a slow fire until a curd is formed. Put the curd into a colander and strain for two hours till quite dry; then mix with a little double cream and salt to taste. Goat-milk crowdie is excellent.

Dunlop Cheese

(*Meg Dods's Recipe*)

As soon as the milk is taken from the cows it is poured into a large pail, or pails, and before it is quite cold the substance called the steep, i.e. rennet, is mixed with it. When it is sufficiently coagulated it is cut transversely with a broad knife made for the purpose, or a broad three-toed instrument, in order to let the curd subside and to procure the separation of the whey from it. When this separation is observed to have taken place the curd is lifted with a ladle, or something similar, into the chessel (for it is to be observed, that where a proper attention is paid to the making of these cheeses, no woman's hand ought ever to touch the curd, from the milking of the cow to the finishing of the whole), where it remains a few hours, till it has acquired something of a hardness or consistency. It is then taken out of the cheese press and cut into small pieces with the instrument above mentioned, of the size of one or two cubic inches, after which it receives the due proportion of salt, and is again replaced in the chessel and put into the press, where it remains a few hours again. Then it is taken out a second time, cut as before, and mixed thoroughly, so as every part may receive the benefit of the salt; and for the last time it is put into the cheese press where it remains until replaced by its successor. After this is done it must be laid in a clean and cool place till sufficiently dried and fit to be carried to market; great care is to be used in frequent turning and rubbing, both to keep the cheese dry and clean and to preserve it from swelling and bursting with the heat, vulgarly 'fire-fanging'. When these cheeses are properly made and dried as they ought to be, they have a rich and delicious flavour.

'This and all sorts of cheese may be pricked, with a bodkin, to allow the escape of air, which, if left, forms what are called *eyes* in the cheese.' – M. D.

'The cheese made here, as well as in other parts of the country, was made of skimmed milk, till about the end of the seventeenth century, when one Barbara Gilmour introduced the practice of using the whole milk.' – *New Statistical Account of Scotland.*

Dunlop is the name of a parish in Ayrshire. During the seventeenth and eighteenth centuries the 'Dunlop' cow, which has since achieved fame as the 'Ayrshire', was being bred with great success, and the farmers were producing more milk than they knew what to do with. During the Covenanting persecutions, a young woman of the district, named Barbara Gilmour, fled to Ireland, and there learned the art of making sweet (unskimmed) milk cheese. On her return to Ayrshire she produced the cheese that was to become widely known as Dunlop cheese. (It differs from any known Irish cheese.) Dunlop, incidentally, was also the name of the young local farmer whom Barbara married.

A new and profitable industry sprang up in the countryside, and with it a new and prosperous body of men, the cheese-merchants, who acted as middlemen, taking the cheese by road to Glasgow. The coming of the railway, however, changed the fortunes of the farmers, for it was now possible to send supplies of fresh milk to the city, and cheese-making became a subsidiary. The creamery closed down in 1932, and the cheese though made elsewhere, is no longer made in its native parish.[1]

Dunlop has always been regarded as the national cheese of Scotland. It is, or used to be, manufactured principally in Ayrshire, Lanarkshire and Renfrewshire. The cheddars of Somerset and the West of Scotland are said to be unrivalled. The standard in Ayrshire used to be very unequal, and in 1855 the Ayrshire Agricultural Association brought in a Somerset farmer and his wife to teach the cheddar method. Since then the average quality in Ayrshire has been higher than in Somerset, though Somerset at its best cannot be surpassed. – See Enc. Brit.: *Ayrshire.*

[1] I am indebted to Mrs. Easton, Manse of Dunlop, for the above information.
– F. M. McN.

Dunlop cheese was popular with the miners of Lanarkshire and the industrial workers of Clydeside because it was moister than other varieties and made an excellent sandwich. Now it follows the lines of the cheddar cheese and is made firmer and drier, in order to retain its flavour in the merchants' stores.

Orkney Cheese

(Recipe from Miss Jessie Tait, Holm)

Take two pailfuls (eight Scots pints) of whole milk and heat to 85°F. Add a teaspoonful of rennet mixed with a little cold water and stir with a wooden spoon for five minutes. Let it stand for half an hour, when it will be a smooth firm curd. With a bread-knife, or any knife with a long blade, cut the curd across in several directions. Let it stand again for a short time. Stir up and strain through a cheese cloth. Break up the curd gently with the hand, add a little salt, and mix well. Place the cheese in a cheese cog or chessit with the cloth underneath. Cover the top smoothly with the cloth, then put on the lid and place on it a seven-pound weight. Take out the cheese every day, put on a clean cloth, replace in the chessit, always turning it the other way. After a day or two add more weight to press out the whey. After eight days remove from the chessit and dry at an open window or shelf.

This cheese is a staple article of diet in Orkney. On the smaller crofts it is usually made with skim milk. Keep buried in oatmeal until required.

Fresh curd, fried in butter, is a popular farmhouse tit-bit.

Sack or Wine Whey

(Mrs. McEwen's Recipe)

Milk, white wine

Put a pint of new milk in a saucepan on the fire; when it boils take it from the fire, put a breakfastcupful of wine to it – sherry, Madeira, or mountain; stir it, cover it up; in a little the curd will fall to the bottom; strain it off; it is now ready.

Green Whey

(In the Highlands) 'Mrs. Macfarlane told me she should send the servant up with a basin of whey, saying, "We make very good whey in this country"; indeed, I thought it the best I had ever tasted.'
– Dorothy Wordsworth: *Recollections of a Tour Made in Scotland* (1803).

(Mrs. McEwen's Recipe)

Have a stew-pan on the fire half full of boiling water; have a quart of new milk in a jug that has a stroup, set it in the stew-pan on the fire, put a tablespoonful of rennet or yearning to it, take it from the fire and let it stand in hot water; if the yearning is good it will be curds in a few minutes; this you will know by leaving a spoon in the jug. If you find that it does not fasten in five minutes put a little more to it; take care that you do not make it too salt; when it is fastened draw the spoon through it two or three times; let it stand; the whey will rise to the top, the curd fall to the bottom. It is now fit for use.

Whey was formerly a common summer drink in Scotland. 'Curds and green whey!' is an old Edinburgh street-cry. – F. M. McN.

Whig (O. Scots *quhig*) is the acetous liquor that subsides from sour cream. This is the origin of the political term, which was first applied by Scottish Episcopalians (who were almost invariably Tories) to Presbyterians, and by Presbyterians of the Established Church to those of the dissenting bodies.

'Whey in which Violets have been boyl'd is used as a cooling and refreshing Drink for such as are ill of Fevers.' – Martin: *Description of the Western Islands* (1703).

Oon[1] or Frothed Whey

(Recipe from Martin's 'Description of the Western Islands' (1703))

'Oon, which in English signifies Froath, is a Dish used by several of the Islanders, and some of the opposite mainland, in the time of scarcity, when they want bread. It is made in the following manner. A quantity of Milk or Whey is boiled in a Pot, and then it is wrought up to the mouth of the Pot with a long Stick of Wood, having a Cross at the lower-end. It is turned about like the Stick for making Chocolat, and being thus made it is supped with Spoons;

[1] Gael. *omhan*, froth of milk or whey, especially the richer whey pressed out of the curds. Called also *onaich*, from *omhanach*, frothy.

284

it is made up five or six times, in the same manner, and the last is always reckoned best, and the first two or three froathings the worst; the Milk or Whey that is in the bottom of the Pot is reckoned much better in all respects than simple Milk.'

'It may be thought that such as feed after this rate are not fit for action of any kind, but I have seen several that lived upon this sort of Food, made of Whey only, for some Months together, and yet they were able to undergo the ordinary Fatigue of their Imployments, whether by Sea or Land, and I have seen them travel to the tops of high Mountains, as briskly as any I ever saw.' – M. Martin.

'Some who live plentifully, make this dish as above said of Goat's Milk, which is said to be nourishing; the Milk is thickened and tastes much better after so much working; some add a little Butter and Nutmeg to it.

'I was treated with this Dish in several Places, and being asked whether this said Dish or Chocolat was best, I told them that if one judge by the Effects, this Dish was preferable to Chocolat, for such as drink often of the former, enjoy a better state of Health than those who use the latter.' – Id.

'At Auchnasheal, we sat down on a green turf-seat at the end of a house; they brought us out two wooden dishes of milk, which we tasted. One of them was frothed like a syllabub. I saw a woman preparing it with such a stick as is used for chocolate, and in the same manner. We had a considerable circle about us, men, women and children, all McCraas, Lord Seaforth's people. Not one of them could speak English.'
– James Boswell: *Journal of a Tour to the Hebrides.*

Blaand or Sparkling Whey

This popular Shetland beverage is simply the whey of butter-milk left to ferment in an oak cask, and used at the proper stage. To make the whey, pour enough hot water on the buttermilk to make it separate, and drain the whey off the curd. (This may be pressed and eaten with cream.) Pour the whey into the cask, and leave it undisturbed until it reaches the fermenting, sparkling stage.

It is a delicious and most quenching drink, and sparkles in the glass like champagne. After the sparkle goes off, it becomes flat and vinegary, but may be kept at the perfection stage by the regular addition of fresh whey.

Blaand used to be in common use in every Shetland cottage, and was at one time given by fashionable doctors to consumptives under the name of the Sour Whey Cure.

285

Frosted Milk

'When I was a very little girl we sometimes had this dish. It was made in a three-legged pot, and Dad in his whimsical way used to say that the pot had to be set out on a frosty night for the fairies to prepare it. In half an hour it was brought indoors and the top of a basin of sweet (fresh) milk was poured in. By rotating a fro'-stick between the palms of the hands the milk quickly frothed up like the white of an egg. It was served in a bowl with very fresh oatmeal, or with burstin.

'Honestly, I did not much care for it. For me, the preparation was the exciting part.'

– Elizabeth Reid, Tongue, the wife of a Sutherland crofter, in a letter to the author.

Buttermilk

The milk that remains in the churn after the butter has been removed was formerly an extremely popular beverage with all classes in Scotland. As a hot-weather drink it was in great demand in the harvest-field. It was valued as both food and drink, and was held to cool the stomach in fever and to aid the cure of dysentery and other ailments.

In old Edinburgh, throughout the summer months, one might witness daily the picturesque sight of milkmaids on horseback riding into town with soor-dook barrels strapped across the saddle behind them. About the middle of the last century, the soor-dook stances extended from the Tron Church to St. Mary's Wynd. It has been estimated that at the end of the eighteenth century a thousand pounds a year was paid in Edinburgh during the months of June, July, August, and September for this very inexpensive beverage, which was sold at a penny the Scots pint (i.e. two Imperial quarts). See 'Street Cries of Edinburgh' by J. Jamieson, in the *Book of the Old Edinburgh Club*.

Other names for buttermilk are *kirn milk*, *sour milk*, *soor dook*, *bladoch* or *blada* (Gael. *blathach*), N. of Scotland, and *bleddoch*, Roxburghshire; and *fochtin milk* (Buchan), possibly from its being produced by fighting at the churn. In Aberdeenshire a cant name is *soutar's brandy*. In Shetland, thin, ill-curdled milk is called *giola*, and in Ettrick Forest, buttermilk very much soured is called *pell*.

Louts (Orkney). Milk or cream poured into a jar previous to churning.
Butter-bells. The froth of the churn after the butter has been removed. It was skimmed off into a bowl as a drink.

Slightly turned milk is called *bleezed* or *blaized* (Angus), *blinked* or *winkit* (Lothians). In Aberdeenshire, skim milk that is slightly turned is called *blenched* (analogous to *blinket*). In Tweeddale the name *whittens* is given to the last part of what is called a

286

'male of milk', which is considered the richest, and is usually milked by the thrifty housewife into a vessel by itself, and put among the cream reserved for the churn.

— See Jamieson's *Dictionary of the Scottish Language*.

Gudeman's Milk is the name given to the milk first skimmed from a sour cog, after the cream has been taken off the churn. The first milk usually contained a little cream and was apportioned to the gudeman, or head of the family.

Bradwardine's Drink. 'A silver jug, which held an equal mixture of cream and butter-milk, was placed for the Baron's share of this repast (breakfast).' — Scott: *Waverley*.

Kirn Milk an' Sourocks. Buttermilk boiled with sorrel.

'Drink off this wersh (insipid) brew, sir. It was my mither's way to caller (cool) the blood — just kirn milk boiled wi' sourocks.' — John Buchan: *Witchwood*.

4. DISHES OF SEAWEED

Seaweeds are rich in potassium iodide.

The edible seaweeds found on our coasts include Carrageen or Sea-moss; Tangle or Redware (Eng. Sea-girdle); Henware or Honeyware (Eng. Bladderlock); Sloke (Eng. Laver); Green Laver; and Dulse (*Fucus palmatus*, Linn.).

'That there is great virtue in seaweed,' writes a native of Caithness, 'is evident from the numbers who went to the "ebb" at least once a year, usually about May — early morning was the proper time — and after a surfeit of dulse, etc., washed down with copious draughts of salt water, they returned set up for the year. It was cheaper and better than Strathpeffer (spa).'

Sea Tangle

In Orkney, children eat the stems of the sea-tangle raw, as they would stalks of rhubarb. In the Hebrides, says Martin Martin, 'the Blade is eat by the Vulgar Natives. . . . I had an Account of a young Man who had lost his Appetite, and taken Pills to no Purpose, and being advised to boil the Blade of the Alga, and drink the Infusion boil'd with a little Butter, was restored to his former State of Health.' He adds that in the islands 'burnt Ashes of Sea-ware preserves Cheese instead of Salt'.

Children in the island of Barra cut the blade away from the fronds and stalk and roast it on both sides over the embers. Placed on a buttered barley bannock, it is eaten with avidity.

A Dulse Dish (*Isle of Barra*)

Dulse, which is said to be in perfection when it has been 'three times bathed in the May flood', played a part in Columban monastic life:

> At times plucking *duileasg* from the rocks.
> – *Hymn of Columba*.

Dulse, water, butter, pepper, salt

Wash the dulse carefully and let it simmer in water till very tender. Strain, cut small, and put into a pan with a little butter, and make thoroughly hot. Add salt and pepper to taste.

Dulse is also eaten raw, or boiled, or cooked over the peat embers on a brander, or rolled about on a stone with a red-hot poker till it turns green. It is often dried and eaten as a savoury or as a relish with potatoes. Pepper dulse is an aromatic variety which is used as a spice. A jelly may be made by letting the dulse simmer in milk until dissolved and set aside to cool, as for Carrageen Mould (q.v.).

'It is eat raw, and then reckoned to be loosning, and very good for the sight: but if boiled it proves more loosning, if the juice be drank with it. The Natives eat it boil'd with butter, and reckon it very wholesome.'
– Martin: *Description of the Western Islands* (1703).

'Caller dulse!' 'Caller dulse and tangles!'

'This once familiar street cry,' writes a citizen of Aberdeen, 'appears to have ceased in recent years, and the clean, tidy fishergirls who carried the succulent seaweed through the streets in round baskets, skilfully balanced against their side with their left arm, must have passed into other lines of life.'

The red form of dulse (f. *Edulis*) is the most popular.

Sloke Jelly

Sloke, slake, or laver is a silky plant of a purplish-brown colour which grows abundantly on our coasts. The leaves are almost transparent, and of so delicate a texture that they dissolve easily into a clear jelly.

The weed is brought home from the rocky pools and carefully washed to remove all sand and dirt. It is then steeped for a few hours in cold water, sometimes with a little salt, sometimes with a little bicarbonate of soda, which is said to remove some of the bitterness.

Put the prepared sloke into a thick-bottomed pot with water to cover and boil gently to a jelly, stirring constantly with a wooden spoon. When thoroughly cooked, it becomes a dark green. Let it cool, then store in earthenware jars. It will keep good for two or three weeks.

The jelly was often spread on bread. The Caithness fishermen used to take a supply of it with them when they went to sea, and ate it with oatcake.

'The Natives eat it (sloke) boil'd and it dissolves into Oil; they say that if a little Butter be added to it, one might live many Years on this alone, without Bread, or any other Food, and at the same Time, undergo any laborious Exercise.' – Martin Martin.

Sloke Sauce:[1] Prepare the sloke as for jelly, and add pepper and lemon juice to taste. The juice of a bitter orange goes excellently with sloke, as with carrageen. Serve very hot. It is especially good with roast mutton.

In Wales, sloke is mixed with oatmeal, made into flat cakes (laverbread) and fried for breakfast.
'Mix with vinegar or lemon juice, a few drops of olive oil, pepper and salt, and serve cold on toast. A delicious hors d'oeuvre or savoury, suggesting a mixture of olives and oysters.' – Jason Hill: *Wild Foods of Britain.*

Slokan (*Isle of Barra*)[2]

Sloke, water, butter, pepper, salt

Prepare the sloke as above. Put it in a pan with a very little sea-water. Make it hot, withdraw it, and beat well; heat it up, withdraw it, and beat again; and continue this process until it is reduced to a pulp. Do not let it cook. Add salt, pepper, and a little butter. Serve hot, with mashed potatoes round it.

Seaweed Soup

Sloke, or dulse, milk, butter, pepper, vinegar or lemon juice

Steep a quantity of sloke as described above; then stew it in sufficient milk to make soup of the right consistency, rub-

[1] In fashionable circles, this used to be known as Marine Sauce.
[2] The *cailleach* from whom this recipe was obtained used to make it for the Big House on the island, and prided herself on being the last of her generation to make the dish properly. – F. M. McN.

bing it hard now and then with a wooden spoon or potato-beetle, until it becomes tender and mucilaginous. Strain if desired, or serve the weed in the soup. Season with pepper, and add butter and vinegar or lemon juice to taste.

To Dry Carrageen

Gather the carrageen or sea-moss in the rock-pools at low tide. (April and May are the best months.) Wash the weed thoroughly in several waters, using sea-water, until free of salt and sand. Clip off the roots and the dark stems with scissors, and spread the carrageen on the grass so that it may get the night dew. It is best to bleach it in showery weather. If there is no rain, sprinkle the weed frequently with fresh water. It will gradually change colour from brown, through beetroot and pink, to a creamy white with pink edges. (This will require several days.) Directly the colour has gone from it, it should be spread either on the rocks or on a tray placed on a wide window-sill so that it may be quickly sun-dried. When perfectly dry, pack into paper bags or aluminium foil and suspend from a hook in a dry place; or store in jars.

Carrageen Mould (*Hebrides*)

Carrageen, salt, castor sugar, milk, egg (optional), fresh lemon rind or other desired flavouring or none

Wash half an ounce of carrageen and steep it for at least half an hour. Pour it into a saucepan with a pint and a half, or rather more, of milk, and a pinch of salt. Add one or two chips of lemon rind if desired. (Most Islanders add no flavouring, preferring the sea-tang of the carrageen.) Bring slowly to the boil and let it barely simmer for about twenty minutes till thick and smooth. Add a tablespoon of sugar and stir until dissolved. Strain over a well-beaten egg, return to the pan and cook, stirring for a second or two without letting it actually boil. Pour through a colander or steamer into a wetted mould. Turn out when set and serve with cream. It is delicious with slightly sour cream.

Another method is to pour the boiling milk over the carrageen, and let it stand for two hours where it will keep hot without coming to the boil. An egg beaten to a froth is often added, but must not be allowed to reach boiling-point. Carrageen thus made, and served with cream, makes a delicate and wholesome sweet.

The strained juice of two Seville oranges may be used to flavour the jelly. An old Manse recipe gives a stick of cinnamon, a bit of lemon peel and lump sugar to taste.

Carrageen is used without bleaching by those who prefer the full flavour of iodine and the sea, which it possesses when it comes direct from the rock. The weed contains sulphur as well as iodine. It is specially recommended for invalids and convalescents, in particular for cases of enteric, internal ulceration and chest troubles. It has been found that when the stomach has rejected even milk, it will sometimes accept carrageen in either jelly or liquid form.

Carrageen Drink: Proceed as for the mould, using double the quantity of milk or water. Simmer for four or five hours. Flavour and sweeten to taste.

PRESERVES

(*Marmalades, Jams and Jellies*)

Although, generally speaking, the Scottish climate is unfavourable to fruit, an exception must be made in favour of berries. It is to the native sweetness of the strawberries and raspberries, which ripen slowly in mild sunshine, that the excellence of Scottish jams is mainly due; whilst 'the Highlands,' remarks Mrs. C. W. Earle in *Pot-pourri from a Surrey Garden*, 'seem to be the home of the gooseberry – such old and hoary bushes, more or less covered by grey lichens, but laden none the less with little hairy gooseberries, both red and green, and full of flavour.'

In Galt's *Annals of the Parish*, the Rev. Micah Balquidder comments on the increase in jam- and jelly-making in Ayrshire in the year 1787:

'I shall not . . . forget to mark a new luxury that got in among the commonality at this time. By the opening of new roads, and the traffic thereon with carts and carriers, and by young men that were sailors going to the Clyde, and sailing to Jamaica and the West Indies, heaps of sugar and coffee-beans were brought home, while many, among the kail-stocks and cabbages in their yards, had planted grozet and berry bushes; which two things happening together, the fashion to make jam and jelly, which hitherto had been known only in the kitchens and confectioneries of the gentry, came to be introduced into the clachan. . . . This occasioned a great fasherie to Mrs. Balquidder; for, in the berry time, there was no end to the borrowings of her brass pan, to make jelly and jam, till Mrs. Toddy, of the Cross Keys, bought one, which, in its turn, came into request, and saved ours.'

> *Grozet*, gooseberry; *clachan*, village; *fasherie*, trouble, annoyance.

Pride of place goes to orange marmalade, which is a Scottish invention.[1] There are many ways of making marmalade, and recipes can be obtained in almost any cookery-book. I give here only one – that of Meg Dods. For the same reason I give only a few of the less-known jams and jellies. – F. M. McN.

Scots Orange-Chip Marmalade

'[At breakfast] there is always, besides butter and toasted bread, honey and jelly of currants and preserved orange peel.' – Bishop Pococke: *Travels in Scotland* (1760).

'My wife is sending you some marmalade of her own making.'
– Boswell to Dr. Johnson on his return from Scotland to London in 1771.

(*Meg Dods's Recipe*)

Seville oranges, lemons, loaf sugar, water, white of egg (to clarify sugar)

Take equal weight of fine loaf sugar and Seville oranges. Wipe and grate the oranges, but not too much. (The outer

---

[1] Marmalade of oranges is mentioned in one or two fairly old cookery-books, but this is in the nature of a *confiture*, usually mixed with apples or other ingredients, and differing in kind from our breakfast marmalade.

grate boiled up with sugar will make an excellent conserve for rice, custard, or batter puddings.) Cut the oranges the cross way and squeeze out the juice through a small sieve. Scrape off the pulp from the inner skins and remove the seeds. Boil the skins till perfectly tender, changing the water to take off part of the bitter. When cool, scrape the coarse, white, thready part from the skins, and, trussing three or four skins together for dispatch, cut them into narrow chips. Clarify the sugar,[1] and put the chips, pulp, and juice to it. Add, when boiled for ten minutes, the juice and grate of two lemons to every dozen of oranges. Skim and boil for twenty minutes; pot and cover when cold.

Marmalade may be served with roast pork, duck, or goose, and with hot boiled ham. Eaten with buttered oatcake, brown bread, or a wheaten meal scone, it is an excellent last mouthful at breakfast.

The name marmalade (from the Portuguese *marmelo*, a quince) was originally applied to a conserve of quinces, as porridge (from the Latin *porrum*, a leek), was originally applied to pottage, or broth. These two dishes are Scotland's chief gifts to the breakfast-table of the English-speaking world.

The original home of orange marmalade is Dundee. Its invention is accredited by long tradition to Janet Keiller, née Pierson, a young woman of 'humble' birth whose marriage to James Keiller on April 1, 1700, is recorded in the Dundee Register. They opened a small business in the city.

One morning a ship from Spain, long buffeted by easterly gales, reached Tayside and deposited a cargo of oranges. Among those who gathered at the quayside was James Keiller. The oranges were going cheap, and James was tempted to buy a considerable quantity – rashly, as it seemed, for owing to their bitter taste he was unable to sell them. What was to be done? His thrifty and resourceful young wife supplied the answer. We may assume that she was already skilled in the making of jams and jellies; but little could she have dreamed, as she stood over her kitchen fire, boiling and testing, that the result of her experiment would achieve world-wide renown.

The new conserve speedily caught on in Dundee, and its fame soon spread to Edinburgh. Recipes began to appear in the eighteenth-century cookery-books published in that city – among them *The Ladies' School of Arts*, by Mrs. Hannah Robertson (who, incidentally, was a 'natural' granddaughter of Charles II), and those written by Mrs. Cleland and Mrs. MacIver (the latter was the daughter of a Highland laird who had been impoverished in the Forty-five), 'chiefly for the benefit of the Young Ladies attending their Schools.'

By a curious coincidence, a descendant of the original Keillers having married one Janet Matthewson, a second Mrs. Janet Keiller came to play an important part in the history of marmalade. The first Janet was born at the dawn of the Industrial Era – that

[1] To clarify sugar: To every pound of broken sugar of the best quality take a quarter-pint of water, and the half of the white of an egg beat up, or less egg will do. Stir this up till the sugar dissolves, and when it boils, and the scum rises strong and thick, pour in another quarter-pint of cold water to each pound. Let it boil, edging the pan forward from the stove till all the scum is thrown up. Set it on the hearth and when it has settled take off the scum with a sugar-skimmer, and lay this on a reversed hair-sieve over a dish, that what syrup is in it may run clear from it. Return the drained syrup into the pan, and boil and skim the whole once more.

is, before the making of jams and 'preserves' of every description was transferred from the home to the factory, but the second Janet, coming considerably later on the scene, had the opportunity and the initiative to establish in 1797, along with her son James, the factory that bears the family name.

In 1859, a Paisley grocer and his wife, by name Robertson, decided to improve the flavour, which was still somewhat sharp and bitter, owing, they conjectured, to the pith and cellulose of the fruit. Together they carried out experiments until they succeeded in blending the juice and sugar into a clear jelly. Then came the crowning touch – the addition of finely shredded peel. Thus Paisley produced her famous 'Golden Shred' marmalade.

At this period marmalade was still reckoned, in Galt's words, 'a curiosity among the English,' and it was not until the 'seventies that its conquest of our southern neighbours began. Oxford was the first centre to capitulate. About the year 1870 (so the present writer was informed by an Oxford lady, the daughter of an historian of the city, who had known the Cooper family) a recipe was brought from a Perthshire manse by an Oxford don and presented to Mrs. Cooper, the wife of a well-known grocer in the city. She placed a few pots of the novelty on her husband's counter, and so popular did it prove among the undergraduates, at whose breakfasts it figured as 'squish,' that the kitchen had soon to be abandoned for the factory. In the course of time, Oxford marmalade acquired a character of its own.

Other firms arose, each with its own type of marmalade. Chivers's Olde English Marmalade 'was born, as one might expect,' says a member of the firm, humorously, 'in England in 1901.'

More recently, Baxter's of Fochabers have shown originality in producing, in addition to their well-known Castle Marmalade, a Vintage Marmalade that has been mellowed and matured for several years in whisky casks.

Whether pale gold and clear, or bronze gold and chunky, or anything in between; whether made by your favourite factory or at home from your favourite recipe, all varieties stem from the invention of young Janet Keiller of Dundee.

Today, marmalade appears on the breakfast-table of all the great cosmopolitan hotels, and the present writer has enjoyed it in private homes in Germany, France, Italy and even Greece (whither the recipe had arrived via Boston, Mass.). 'Voulez-vous du Dundi?' A French hostess will ask, presenting the delicacy with as much pride as we should have in offering a guest *pâté de foie gras*. In jars or cans it accompanies expeditions to the South Pole and the summit of Mount Everest; it dives to the depths of the sea in submarines, it soars far above the clouds in aeroplanes; and, who knows, it may one day be rocketed to the moon! – F. M. McN.

Blaeberry Jam[1]

(A Highland Recipe)

Blaeberries, rhubarb, sugar, water

Allow a pound of sugar to every pound of blaeberries and a pound of thin red rhubarb to every seven pounds of fruit. Wipe the rhubarb and cut it into inch lengths. Put it into the preserving-pan with the sugar and boil rapidly for ten minutes. Add the blaeberries and simmer gently, skimming

[1] Mentioned by Faujas de St. Fond in his account of his travels in the Hebrides in 1784.

well, till it reaches setting point. Test in the usual way. Pour
into pots and seal.

'Fluxes are Cured by taking now and then a Spoonful of the Syrup of blew Berries
that grow on the Mertillus.' – Martin Martin: *Description of the Western Islands* (1703).

Gean[1] Jam

(*A Highland Recipe*)

Geans (*wild cherries*), *gooseberry or currant juice, sugar,*
water

Weigh your wild cherries, stone them, and put them into a
preserving-pan. Cover them with water and boil until nearly
all the juice is dried up (about three-quarters of an hour).
Add sugar, allowing a pound to every six pounds of fruit,
and gooseberry or currant juice, allowing a pint to every six
pounds. Boil all together until it jellies (twenty to thirty
minutes), skimming it well and keeping it well stirred. Pour
into pots and seal.

Rhubarb And Ginger Jam

(*A Family Recipe*)

Rhubarb, sugar, lemon, ginger

Choose a good quality of rhubarb (which varies considerably): Victoria rhubarb, when tender and full grown, is
excellent. Cut off both ends; do not peel the stalks but wipe
them with a cloth and cut them into pieces about an inch
long. To six pounds of rhubarb allow five pounds of sugar,
and put them in a deep dish in alternate layers. Let this
stand for twenty-four hours, by which time the sugar should
be in a liquid state. Pour the liquid into a preserving-pan, add
the grated rind of a lemon and three-quarters of a pound of
preserved ginger cut small, and boil briskly for half an hour.
Then add the rhubarb and boil half an hour longer. Take it
off and let it stand near the fire for half an hour before you
pot it.

[1] The G is hard. From Fr. *guigne.*

Sloe And Apple Jelly

(A Highland Recipe)

Sloes, apples, sugar, water

Wash four apples and cut them up roughly. Put them in a jelly-pan with two pounds of sloes, cleared of stalks. Cover with water and boil to a pulp. Strain through a cheese-cloth, but do not squeeze. Measure the liquid and return to the pan, adding a pound of sugar for every pint of juice. Boil for fifteen minutes and fill your jars.

Rowan Jelly

(Old Family Recipe)

Rowan berries, apples, water, sugar

Gather your rowan berries when almost ripe. Remove the stalks and wash and drain the berries. Put them in a preserving-pan with enough cold water to float them well. Let them simmer for about forty minutes or until the water is red and the berries are quite soft. Strain off the juice, being careful not to press the fruit in the least. Measure the juice and return it to the pan. Add sugar in the proportion of a pound to each pint of juice. Boil rapidly for half an hour or until some of it sets quickly on a plate when cold. Skim it well, pour it into small pots, and tie down quickly.

If you allow pound for pound of apple juice to rowan juice you will get a delightful jelly. Allow a pound of sugar to each pint of apple juice.

Rowan jelly is an excellent accompaniment to grouse, venison, and saddle of mutton.

Bramble And Rose-Hip Jam

Brambles, rose-hips, sugar, butter (unsalted)

Allow a good breakfastcupful of hips to each three pounds of brambles. Chop the hips finely, after denuding them of their seeds, and leave them to steep for two days in just enough water to cover them. Now wash and pick over your freshly gathered brambles (which should not be over-ripe), and put them into a crock along with the drained hips. Leave in a warmish oven for a day to extract the juice. Butter the jelly-pan, empty the crock into it, add sugar pound for pint and stir over a low heat until dissolved. Bring to the boil and boil rapidly until setting-point is reached. Skim. Pour into hot dry jars and cover.

This is a delicious bramble jam with a rose-hip flavour.

Avern Or Wild Strawberry Jelly

Wild strawberries, lemons, sugar, water

Place five pints of berries in the preserving-pan. Add the juice of two lemons and a quart of cold water. Bring slowly to the boil and simmer until all the juice is extracted. Strain and measure juice. Add a pound of sugar to each pint and boil to setting-point. Skim, pot, and seal.

SWEETIES

The Scots, it has been computed, eat more sweets than any other people in the world, the Swiss coming a not too close second. The simple explanation of this not altogether enviable reputation is that since 1680, when sugar began to be shipped in bulk from the West Indies, sugar-refining has been an important West of Scotland industry. Greenock is Scotland's town of sugar, or 'Sugarapolis', as Neil Munro has called it, 'whose numerous factories spread sweetness everywhere.'

It is generally conceded that one of the special skills in the Scots kitchen is sweet-making and sugar-work. Originally most of the sweeties popularly enjoyed were made by simple processes over an open fire.

'In rural districts in Scotland [I quote from an old booklet on cottage cookery] candy-making is a regular adjunct to courting. It draws together all the lads and lasses round for miles, and the fun and the daffing that go on during the boiling, pulling, clipping, cooling, are, both lads and lasses declare, worth the money. . . A few of the lasses club their sixpences together, a night is set, a house is named, and, of course, the young men who are specially wanted are invited to lend a hand and a foot too, for dancing is not an uncommon adjunct to such gatherings.'

At country fairs, the candyman was always in evidence, his wares arranged on a tray that was supported by a cord round his neck, or on a wheel-barrow. At other times his voice would ring from the crown of the causey:

'Here's yer fine cinnamon-rock, for auld rags, banes, copper, iron, brass or broken c-c-r-r-ystal! Gether, gether up! Gether, bairns, gether!'

All over the country, in the vicinity of the burgh and the larger village schools, there was always a sweetie-shop, to whose counter the bairns were lured by the delectable odour of boiling toffee that emanated from the kitchen behind. The sweetie-wives were usually known by some such nickname as Candy Kate, Sweetie Annie, or Taffie (Toffee) Knott. Besides such homely sweets as gundy, glessie, cheugh jeans and black man, there were bottles of 'boilings' (Scotch Mixtures) that glittered like rubies, emeralds, topazes and all the jewels of the Orient, and tasted of all the fruits of the orchard and spices of the Indies. Striped rock in variegated colours and yellow spiral sticks of barley sugar were always prime favourites, and so was 'taiblet' of various flavours. In addition, many localities had their own speciality, some of which achieved national fame.

As with preserve-making, sweet-making is now mainly carried out in the factory, but many children and young folk still derive great enjoyment in concocting the auld-farrant toffees and tablets over the kitchen range. – F. M. McN.

Scots Barley Sugar

(Mrs. McIver's Recipe)

Barley, liquorice, sugar, water, egg (to clarify), butter

Wash a little barley and put it on with boiling water; let it boil a little, then turn out that water and pour more boiling water on it. Put in a pennyworth of liquorice stick, let it boil till all the strength is out of it; then pour off the liquor and let it stand to settle and pour all the clear from the grounds;

then take half a mutchkin (half-pint) of it to the pound of sugar; clarify it with white of egg. It must be on a soft equal fire; you must not stir it much on the fire; it must be boiled until it crackles. Have a stone ready, rubbed with fresh butter or fine oil. Pour the sugar on it. You must double it together and cut it as fast as you can with big scissors. Give it a little twist as you cut it.

If you think the sugar boils too furiously, add a very little bit of fresh butter amongst it.

Both barley water and barley sugar are included in Mrs. McIver's list of Scottish national dishes. See her *Cookery and Pastry* (Edinburgh, 1773).

Butterscotch

(An Edinburgh Recipe)

Brown sugar, butter, ground ginger or lemon

Put a pound of brown sugar into an enamelled saucepan and let it dissolve on the range. Beat four ounces of butter to a cream, add it to the sugar when dissolved, and stir over the fire until it has boiled sufficiently to harden when dropped into cold water. Add a quarter-ounce of powdered ginger dissolved in a little water, or a little essence of lemon. Beat with a fork quickly for a few minutes. Pour on to a buttered slab or dish and when sufficiently cool mark into squares. When cold, a slight tap will break them off.

Grandmamma's Bon-Bons

(Meg Dods's Recipe)

Sugar, lemon grate, citron or orange-peel

Cut candied citron or orange peel into strips an inch long, and then as small dice. String them apart on a fine wire skewer or knitting-needle, and dip them in boiling barley-sugar made as follows: Clarify and boil sugar to the fourth degree or crackling height, and when nearly boiled enough add lemon grate, a drop of citron oil, or a little beat spermaceti.

Have a baking-slab or large flat dish rubbed with oil that they may not stick, and lay them on it to dry. When crisp, pack them in paper bags.

Black Man Or Treacle Candy (*An Old-fashioned Sweetmeat*)

(A Cottage Recipe)

Treacle, vinegar, bicarbonate of soda

Put into a saucepan four pounds of treacle and a dessertspoonful of vinegar. Bring it to the boil and let it boil very slowly, stirring it to prevent burning. When it has boiled for twenty minutes try it by dropping into cold water. If it snaps it is done. Add flavouring to taste – peppermint, almond, or lemon. Then put in half a teaspoonful of bicarbonate of soda and stir hard. Take it off the fire immediately and pour on to buttered dishes. As soon as it is possible to handle it, butter the hands, take it from the dish, and pull it rapidly with both hands as long as it is possible to do so. This makes it light coloured and tender. (Confectioners used to use an iron hook driven into the wall to assist them in pulling it. Two pairs of hands, their owners *vis-à-vis*, can do it even better.) When too hard to work longer, cut the sticks to the desired length (one inch or six or eight inches) with scissors.

(Another Recipe)

Put into a saucepan one pound of brown sugar, one teacupful of treacle, half a cup of water, a teaspoonful of cream of tartar. Prepare exactly as above.

'In the pan, in the little shop where we bought it, it looked like gingerbread, but when it was broken up, it was a crispy crunch, like a petrified sponge, but once it was in the mouth, it melted into the most soul-satisfying, delectable sweet. (It was about an inch thick.) Even after sixty years, I can still taste it in my memory.'
– A native of Kilmarnock.

Black Man: 'A concoction of brown sugar and baking-soda, blown to frothy, swollen nothingness, was splendid value at a big daud (lump) for a faurdin (farthing).'
– E. MacGirr: Art. *The Sweetie Shop* in *The Scots Magazine*, December, 1923.

Yellow Man: Use three parts golden syrup to one of treacle and make as above, adding a little lemon juice.

Gundy (*An Old-fashioned Sweetmeat*)

Brown sugar, syrup or treacle, butter, aniseed or cinnamon

Put into a saucepan a pound of brown sugar, a teaspoonful of syrup or treacle, and two ounces of butter. Boil it to the crack, that is, till it becomes quite hard when a little is put into cold water. Flavour with aniseed or cinnamon. Pour out very thinly on a buttered tin or slab, and when it is cold and hard break up roughly with a small hammer; or when cool enough to handle form into thin round sticks.

In Scott's boyhood 'gundy was sold by Mrs. Flockhart in the Potter-row.'
      – R. Chambers: *Traditions of Edinburgh.*

Glessie (*An Old-fashioned Sweetmeat*)

Moist brown sugar, golden syrup, butter, cream of tartar, water

Put into an enamelled pan two tablespoonfuls of water, a teaspoonful of cream of tartar, half a pound of soft sugar, and a small piece of butter. Boil for five minutes. Add a pound and a half of syrup and boil briskly, without stirring, for half an hour. Try in cold water to see if it is crisp. Pour in thin sheets on buttered tins. When cold, chop it up, or pull out as for Black Man and cut into sticks.

'But the glessie! Who that ever tasted it can forget the stick of sheeny golden rock which stretched while you were eating it to gossamer threads of silver glistening like cobwebs in the sun?'
      – E. MacGirr: Art. *The Glessie Shop* in *The Scots Magazine*, December, 1925.

Claggum Or Clack

Treacle, water

Put two teacupfuls of treacle into a pan with one of cold water. Set on a low heat to dissolve, then boil briskly until, when tested, it forms a soft ball. Pour into a well-buttered shallow dish, and when cool enough to handle, with buttered hands gather it into a lump. 'Tease' or pull it out until it turns a pale cream colour; then twist into long sticks.

'This is the old-fashioned "teasing-candy". We used to make a large pot at Hogmanay time and found long sticks of it tremendously popular with the village children.'
– An Aberdeenshire Housewife.

Mealie Candy

(Old Cottage Recipe)

Sugar, treacle, oatmeal, ginger, water

Put three and a half pounds of loaf sugar and a pound of treacle into a saucepan with one and a quarter pints of water, bring it to the boiling-point and let it boil for ten minutes. Remove it from the fire and, with the back of a wooden spoon, rub the syrup against the sides of the pan until it looks creamy. Then stir in gently half a pound of toasted oatmeal and two ounces of ground ginger. Pour into shallow tins lined with well-oiled paper. When it has cooled a little cut it into cubes, and when cold remove it from the tins and take off the paper. This is a very wholesome sweetmeat, as the oatmeal is soothing and the ginger stimulating.

Almond Cake

Castor sugar, syrup, butter, almonds, lemon, water

Put into a saucepan four teacupfuls of sugar, three tablespoonfuls of syrup, and one and a quarter teacupfuls of water. Boil for twenty minutes. Add a piece of butter the size of an egg, and boil till the mixture hardens. Flavour with lemon. Blanch four ounces of almonds by throwing them into boiling water for two minutes and removing the skins. Halve them and strew them thickly on the bottom of a flat buttered tin. Pour the toffee over them. When fairly cool cut into bars, or break up with a small hammer when cold.

Fig Cake: Make as above and pour over split dried figs.

302

Edinburgh Rock

'Friable, fluted sticks of pastel shades and pastel flavours.'
– Lady Violet Bonham-Carter.

Quelle est cette odeur agréable
  That's wafted on the air?
The perfume of Arabia
  Cannot with it compare.
What makes the crowds to Melbourne Place[1]
  With wide-stretched nostrils flock?
It's Ferguson who's boiling up
  His Edinburgh rock.

– John W. Oliver.

Crushed loaf sugar, cream of tartar, water, colour and flavouring as follows: white, lemon or vanilla; pink, raspberry or rose; fawn, ginger; yellow, orange or tangerine

Put into a pan a pound of crushed loaf sugar and half a pint of cold water. Stir gently over the fire until the sugar is dissolved. When nearly boiling, add a good pinch of cream of tartar and boil without stirring until it reaches 250°F. in cold weather or 260°F. in hot – that is, until it forms a hard lump in cold water. Remove from the fire, add colouring and flavouring, and pour on a buttered marble slab, preferably through buttered candy bars. As it begins to cool, turn the ends and edges inwards with a buttered knife. When cool enough to handle, dust it with powdered sugar, take it up and pull gently (being careful not to twist it) until it is dull. Cut in pieces with a pair of scissors. Place the rock in a warm room and let it remain there for at least twenty-four hours, until the process of granulation is complete, and the rock is powdery and soft.

The original Edinburgh Rock is made by the famous Edinburgh firm of Ferguson. Confectionery is an important industry in the capital, and the world-famous rock is one of the triumphs of the Scottish confectioner's art.

The founder of the firm was Alexander Ferguson, popularly known as 'Sweetie Sandy,' who was born in 1798 in the bien little burgh of Doune, in Perthshire. As a boy, Sandy used to concoct sweet-smelling, bubbling liquids in old tins and disused pans in the parental outhouses. So singular a hobby aroused the wrath and scorn of his father, a joiner and skeely craftsman; but Sandy refused to desist, and eventually left home to learn the business side of his chosen craft with a confectioner in Glasgow. Thence he removed to Edinburgh, set up on his own and prospered exceedingly – thanks mainly to one speciality.

Edinburgh Rock is said to have been 'discovered' more or less accidentally. A batch

---

[1] Until 1959, the site of the factory.

303

of confectionery had been set aside and somehow overlooked. Months later someone came across it, and it became apparent that some mysterious alchemy had been a work. From this batch the delicious mellowness of the new confection was evolved.

Sandy retired to his native Doune with a considerable fortune, enlarged his old home handsomely, formed a considerable library, created a beautiful garden, and entertained both literary and fashionable society. He was long remembered as a kindly old gentleman with a white beard, who went about in a black velvet jacket and white trousers, from the capacious pockets of which he habitually produced handfuls of sweets for the children he chanced to meet – a well-beloved 'Sweetie Sandy.'

Packed in tartan boxes – mainly Ferguson and Royal Stewart – Edinburgh rock now finds its way to every corner of the Commonwealth. – F. M. McN.

Scots Tablets

> 'Taiblet's awfu' guid.'
> – *Wee Macgreegor.*

(Traditional Recipe)

Granulated sugar, thin cream or milk, flavouring

Put into an enamelled saucepan two pounds of granulated sugar and three teacupfuls of thin cream or milk. Bring it gradually to the boiling-point, stirring all the time. Let it boil a few minutes. Test as for toffee, but do not boil it so high. When it has reached the consistency of soft putty when dropped in cold water (about 245°F.), remove the pan from the fire. Add flavouring as below. Now put the pan into a basin of cold water and stir rapidly with a spoon. It soon begins to solidify round the edge, and this must be scraped off repeatedly. Keep stirring until the mass is sufficiently grained, and then pour it immediately on to a buttered slab. If too highly grained, it will not pour out flat; if too thin, it will be sticky. Only practice makes perfection. When sufficiently firm, mark into bars with a knife, or cut into rounds with the lid of a circular tin.

FLAVOURINGS

Cinnamon. Add a few drops of oil of cinnamon.

Coconut. Add four ounces of coconut and boil for two minutes, then add a pinch of cream of tartar and remove from the fire. It should be vigorously stirred till quite creamy.

Fig. Add a pinch of cream of tartar just before removing from the fire. Then stir in four ounces of finely chopped figs, previously washed and dried.

304

Ginger. Add two teaspoonfuls of ground ginger, dissolved in a little cold water, and (if liked) some chopped preserved ginger.

Lemon. Add a small teaspoonful of essence of lemon.

Orange. Add the grated rind and juice of an orange.

Peppermint. Add a few drops of oil of peppermint.

Vanilla. Add a small teaspoonful of essence of vanilla.

Walnut. Add half a teaspoonful of essence of vanilla, and four ounces of shelled and chopped walnuts.

In *The Household Book of Lady Grisell Baillie* (1692–1733), among the purchases recorded we occasionally find 'taiblet for the bairns.'

Helensburgh Toffee

Helensburgh lies just across the water from Greenock, the town of sugar refineries and has given its name to one of the most popular of our Scottish sweets.

Loaf sugar, condensed milk, salt butter, water, vanilla

Put into an iron or enamelled pan two pounds of loaf sugar, the contents of a tin of condensed milk (ordinary size), four ounces of salt butter, and a small teacupful of water. Stir continuously over the fire for forty-five minutes. Add a teaspoonful of vanilla essence and stir off the fire for one minute. Pour into a buttered tin and, when cool, cut into squares.

If desired the toffee may be dotted with halved walnuts immediately after it has been poured out.

Other Popular Sweeties

Berwick Cockles: These have been made at Berwick-on-Tweed for nearly two hundred years. Pale fawn with red stripes, they are mildly flavoured with peppermint. Their resemblance to cockles is hardly striking.

Black-strippit Ba's: Black and white striped balls of hard toffee, strongly flavoured with peppermint. Country folk used to take them to church, where they not only sweetened, but timed the sermon – three balls to a good old forty-minute sermon.

Cheugh Jeans: 'Luscious lumps of sweetness that yield themselves into a liquid satisfaction in the warmth of the mouth.' Made by sweetie-wives practically all over the country. A speciality of 'Ball Allan', the Candy King of Glasgow, in the latter half of the nineteenth century. There was a choice of clove, cinnamon, peppermint, ginger and many other flavours. Eager customers included city magnates as well as schoolboys. Boxes and tins were dispatched to all quarters of the globe where Glesca folk had settled.

Cheugh means tough. The origin of *jean* is uncertain.

Coltart's Candy: Coltart made his celebrated candy in Melrose and sold it mainly there and in Galashiels. It was flavoured with aniseed. He composed a song in its honour.

The sound of his 'signature tune' and merry whistle caused every cottage door to open and the children to troop after him like the followers of the Pied Piper, lured no less by his gay garments, his songs, his jokes and antics, than by his wares.

> Mither, gie's ma thrifty doon,
> Coltart's comin' to the toun,
> Wi' a feather in his croon,
> To sell Coltart's candy!

The chorus is still sung as a lullaby:

> Allabally, Allabally bee,
> Sittin' on your mammie's knee,
> Greetin' for anither bawbee
> To buy Coltart's Candy.

Coltart died in 1890, greatly lamented.

Curly-andra: A white, coral-like sweet with a coriander seed in the centre. The name is a corruption of *curryander*, a Scots form of *coriander*.

'Pink sugar hearts, "curly-andras" and gilt gingerbread were some of the old-world dainties on sale at the Lammas Market (St. Andrews).'
                                                      – *Dundee Courier*, August 10, 1938.

Curly-doddies, curly murlies: Mixed sweets formed on a seed or other foundation such as carvie (caraway), clove or almond, and having a gnarled exterior.

Jeddart Snails: Dark brown toffees which 'taste of the sweetness of brown sugar blended with the richness of real butter and flavoured with mild peppermint.' They are rounded into a curve, with one end formed into a blob for the head and the other flattened for the tail. The recipe is said to have been given to a Jedburgh baker by a French prisoner-of-war of Napoleonic times whom he had taken into his employment.

Oddfellows: A lozenge speciality made for a hundred years by a Wishaw firm. The flavours remain constant – cinnamon, clove and rose. The cinnamon oil still comes from Sri Lanka, the cloves from Malagasy Republic, and the rose (geranium) from the French island of Réunion.

Soor Plooms: A speciality of Galashiels. Ball-shaped, and of a pale clear green colour, they have a refreshing, slightly acid flavour. The 'plooms' commemorate an incident in local history, in 1377, when a band of English marauders, whilst eating the unripe plums in which the district abounded, was surprised and routed by the braw lads of Gala Water.

Starrie Rock: A traditional Angus sweet, still made in Brechin, of various colours and flavours – peppermint, clove, lemon, cinnamon and ginger – in short, thin sticks. Unlike most rock, it does not become brittle in the mouth, but resolves itself into a stubborn ball of hard caramel. The rolling of the rock causes the sections to assume a star-like appearance.

Other favourites include Sugar-ally (liquorice), Sugar-bools (small round sugar-plums like marbles), Lettered Rock, Pan Drops (mint imperials) and such local specialities as Carluke Balls, Hawick Balls and Moffat Whirlies (dark brown glistening toffee twisted with pale amber).

BEVERAGES

In olden times, the common beverage of Lowland Scotland was ale. There is evidence that it was in general use in the thirteenth century; in *The Friars of Berwick* (*c.* 1500) the 'silly friars', Robert and Allen, are regaled on 'stoups of ale with bread and cheese'; and even in the eighteenth century we find that the subject of Burns's poem, *Scotch Drink*, is not whisky, but ale.[1]

In the days of the Auld Alliance, French wines were freely imported. They were drunk at the court of Alexander III (1241–86), and successive travellers comment on their excellence, abundance, and cheapness.

The origin of whisky is wrapped in mystery. The Highlander was content in the ordinary way with water from the spring and milk from the byre and the churn. *Usquebaugh* was reserved for festive occasions, and even then it was used sparingly, for, unlike the Saxon, the Celt was temperate in both eating and drinking. There is good reason to believe that the distillation of whisky received its chief impetus from the acts of the Scottish Privy Council, which in the early seventeenth century forbade the importation of wines into the Isles. The heavy taxation subsequently imposed had the ultimate effect of banishing claret[2] from the Scottish

---

[1] 'To birl the brown bowl' is the old expression for 'to drink ale'.

[2] The Tappit Hen, a measure containing three quarts of claret, was formerly a feature at Scottish country inns.

> Blythe, blythe, and merry was she
> Blythe was she but and ben;
> Weel she loo'ed a Hawick gill,*
> And leugh to see a tappit-hen.
> – *Andro and his Cuttie Gun.*
> * Half an Imperial pint.

'I have seen one of these formidable stoups at Provost Haswell's at Jedburgh in the days of yore. It was a pewter measure. the claret being in ancient days served from the tap, and had a figure of a crested hen upon the lid. In later times, the name was given to a glass bottle of the same dimensions. These are rare apparitions among the degenerate topers of modern days.' – Scott: *Guy Mannering*, Note.

dining-table and substituting the over-alcoholized beverage the misuse of which was to become an evil and a reproach to the Scottish nation.[1]

The women of Lowland Scotland were great brewers in their day.[2] Tibbie Shiel's green grozet (gooseberry) wine,[3] Mrs. Gentle's primrose wine,[4] the elder-flower wine that Mistress Jean, the 'penniless lass wi' a lang pedigree', was making when the Laird o' Cockpen came a-wooing[5] – there are many references in reminiscence and fiction.

The following epigram was written by John Home, author of the tragedy of *Douglas* when the Government at Westminster laid a tax upon claret:

> Firm and erect the Caledonian stood,
> Old was his mutton, and his claret good;
> 'Let him drink port,' an English statesman cried –
> He drank the poison and his spirit died.

The lines, Dean Ramsay tells us, were great favourites with Sir Walter Scott who delighted in repeating them.

[1] See *Leaves from a Physician's Portfolio*, by James Crichton-Browne, M.D., LL.D.

[2] In Kinross, the browst which the guid-wife of Lochrin produced from a peck of malt is thus commemorated:

> Twenty pints o' strong ale,
> Twenty pints o' sma',
> Twenty pints o' hinky-pinky,
> Twenty pints o' plooman's drinkie,
> Twenty pints o' splitter-splatter,
> An' twenty pints was waur nor water.

[3] 'North: Now, sir, you have tasted Tibbie's Green Grozet. St. Mary, what are the vine-covered hills and gay regions of France to the small yellow, hairy gooseberry-gardens of your own forest!' – Christopher North: *Noctes Ambrosianae*.

[4] 'Mrs. Gentle: Mr. Hogg, Mr. North requested me to take charge of the making of his primrose wine this season, and I used the freedom of setting aside a dozen bottles for your good lady at Altrive.' – *Ibid*.

[5] Mistress Jean, she was makin' the elder-flo'er wine:
> 'And what brings the Laird at sic a like time?'
> She put off her apron and on her silk goon,
> Her mutch wi' red ribbons, and gaed awa' doon.
> – Lady Nairne: *The Laird o' Cockpen*.

AN OLD HIGHLAND TOAST*

'Suas e, suas e!	'Up with it, up with it, up with it!
Sios e, sios e, sios e!	Down with it, down with it, down with it!
A null e, a null e, a null e!	Away from me, away from me, away from me!
A nall e, a nall e, a nall e!	Towards me, towards me, towards me!
Sguab as e!	Drink it off!
. . . .	. . . .
Agus cha n'òl neach eile as a ghloine so gu bràth!'	An no other shall ever drink from this glass again!'

* The proposer stands on his chair with one foot on the table, holding the glass in his right hand. He accompanies the toast with appropriate gestures, and at the last words, flings the glass over his left shoulder on to the floor, where it is shattered to atoms. I have seen it drunk thus in the Isle of Skye. – F. M. McN.

Highland Bitters

(Very Old)

Gentian root, coriander seed, bitter-orange peel, camomile flowers, cinnamon stick, whole cloves, whisky

Cut one ounce and three-quarters of gentian root and half an ounce of orange peel into small pieces. Put them into a mortar with one ounce of coriander seed, quarter of an ounce of camomile flowers, quarter of an ounce of cinnamon stick, and half an ounce of cloves. Bruise all together. Put into an earthenware jar, empty two bottles of whisky over it, cover so that the jar is air-tight, and let it stand for about ten days. Strain and bottle. More whisky may be added to the flavouring materials, which remain good for a long time.

'On the sideboard there always stood before breakfast a bottle of whisky, smuggled, of course, with plenty of camomile flowers, bitter orange-peel, and juniper berries in it – "bitters" we called it – and of this he (Sir Hector Mackenzie) had a wee glass always before we sat down to breakfast, as a fine stomachic.'
– Osgood Mackenzie: *A Hundred Years in the Highlands.*

Highland Cordial

(Traditional Recipe)

White currants, lemon, ginger, sugar, whisky

Take a pint of white currants stripped of their stalks, the thin peel of a lemon, a teaspoonful of essence of ginger, and a bottle of whisky. Mix and stand for forty-eight hours. Strain, add a pound of loaf sugar, and stand for a day to dissolve. Bottle and cork. It will be ready in three months, but will keep longer.

Caledonian Liquor

(Mrs. Dalgairns's Recipe)

Whisky, sugar, cinnamon

One ounce of oil of cinnamon is to be dropped on two and a

half pounds of bruised loaf sugar; one gallon of whisky, the best, is to be added, and the sugar being dissolved, it is to be filtered and bottled.

Auld Man's Milk

(*Meg Dods's Recipe*)

Milk or cream, rum, whisky or brandy, eggs, nutmeg or lemon zest

Beat the yolks and whites of six eggs separately. Put to the beat yolks sugar and a quart of new milk or thin sweet cream. Add to this rum, whisky, or brandy to taste (about a half-pint). Slip in the whipt whites, and give the whole a gentle stir up in the china punch-bowl, in which it should be mixed. It may be flavoured with nutmeg or lemon zest. This morning dram is the same as the egg-nogg of America.

Atholl Brose

> Aye since he wore the tartan trews
> He dearly lo'ed the Atholl Brose.
> – Neil Gow.

Oatmeal, water, heather honey, whisky, cream (optional)

(*The Duke of Atholl's Recipe*)[1]

To make a quart, take four dessertspoonfuls of run honey and four sherry glassfuls of prepared oatmeal; stir these well together and put into a quart bottle; fill up with whisky; shake well before serving.

To prepare the oatmeal, put it into a basin and mix with cold water to the consistency of a thick paste. Leave for about half an hour, pass through a fine strainer, pressing with the back of a wooden spoon so as to leave the oatmeal as dry as possible. Discard the meal, and use the creamy liquor for the brose.

[1] Made known by the eighth Duke.

(Williamina Macrae's Recipe)[1]

Beat one and a half teacupfuls of double cream to a froth; stir in one teacupful of very lightly toasted oatmeal; add half a cup of dripped heather honey and, just before serving, two wine-glasses of whisky. Mix thoroughly and serve in shallow glasses.

Atholl Brose emerges from the Highland mists in the year 1475, but may well be much older. It is mentioned by Scott in *The Heart of Midlothian* and by Robert Louis Stevenson in *Kidnapped*. The legends connected with it are given in my book, *The Scots Cellar* – F. M. McN.

It is recorded that when entertaining Sheridan at Blair Castle, the Duke of Atholl of that day 'ordered some Atholl Brose, which the dramatist relishing, partook of rather freely.' Queen Victoria and Prince Albert, too, partook of this 'giant's drink,' let us hope rather less freely, when they visited Blair Atholl in September, 1844. (See the Queen's *Leaves from a Journal of Our Life in the Highlands*.)

A favourite regale for first-footers in the Highlands, and for toasting the New Year in the Highland regiments.

Stapag. Atholl Brose, made strong and very hot. It is said in the Outer Isles to be a soothing and relaxing drink after a long day on the sea or the hill.

Het Pint

(Meg Dods's Recipe)

Ale, sugar, eggs, whisky, nutmeg

Grate a nutmeg into two quarts of mild ale, and bring it to the point of boiling. Mix a little cold ale with sugar necessary to sweeten this, and three eggs well beaten. Gradually mix the hot ale with the eggs, taking care that they do not curdle. Put in a half-pint of whisky, and bring it once more nearly to boil and then briskly pour it from one vessel into another till it becomes smooth and bright.[2]

Het Pint was used also on the night preceding a marriage and at a lying-in. The writer recollects the *Bride's Cog* (Gael. *coggan*), a large wooden vessel with three lugs, or ears,

---

[1] As made at her angling-inn at Lochailort.

[2] 'This beverage carried about in a bright copper kettle is the celebrated New Year's morning Het Pint of Edinburgh and Glasgow. In Honest Aberdeen, half-boiled sowens is used on the same festive occasion. In Edinburgh, in her bright and palmy state – her days of "spice and wine", while she yet had a court and parliament, while France sent her wines and Spain, Italy, and Turkey, fruits and spices – a far more refined composition than the above was made by substituting light wine for ale, and brandy for whisky.' – W. Winterblossom, in the *Annals of the Cleikum Club.*

often of beautiful design and workmanship, which used to circulate like a loving-cup at the Orkney rural weddings. It contained copious libations of new ale, laced with whisky, seasoned with pepper, ginger, and nutmeg, and thickened with beaten eggs and pieces of toasted biscuit.

Toddy

> Sit roun' the table well content
> An' steer aboot the toddy.

(Traditional Recipe)

Whisky, sugar, hot water

Pour boiling water slowly into a tumbler till about half full. Let the water remain until the crystal is thoroughly heated, then pour it out. Put in three or four pieces of loaf sugar, and pour over them a wineglassful of boiling water. When the sugar is dissolved, add a wineglassful of whisky and stir with a silver spoon; add more boiling water, and finally a second glass of whisky. Stir again, and sip the toddy 'with slow and loving care.'

Toddy is excellent as a stimulant and as a cure for a cold (drunk in bed).

In his poem, 'The Morning Interview', published in 1721, Allan Ramsay speaks of 'some kettles full of Todian spring', and appends the note:

'The Todian spring, i.e. Tod's well, which supplies Edinburgh with water. Tod's well and St. Anthony's well, on the side of Arthur's Seat, were two of the wells which very scantily supplied the wants of Edinburgh, and when it is borne in mind that whisky derives its name from water, it is highly probable that Toddy in like manner was a facetious term for the pure element.'

Glasgow Punch[1]

(From 'Peter's Letters')[2]

A hundred years ago and more, the signal toast at the Glasgow clubs was 'The trade of Glasgow and the outward bound'.

Rum, cold water, sugar, lemons, limes

The sugar[3] being melted with a little cold water, the artist

---

[1] 'Rum punch was the universal beverage of the members of the Pig Club at their dinners, as it was at those of all the jovial fraternities in the city.'
  – Strang: *Glasgow Clubs.*

[2] *Peter's Letters to His Kinsfolk*, by J. G. Lockhart and others, 1819.

[3] Allow a tablespoonful to each lemon. – F. M. McN.

squeezed about a dozen lemons through a wooden strainer, and then poured in water enough almost to fill the bowl. In this state the liquor goes by the name of sherbet, and a few of the connoisseurs in his immediate neighbourhood were requested to give their opinion of it – for in the mixing of the sherbet lies, according to the Glasgow creed, at least one half of the whole battle. This being approved by an audible smack of the lips of the umpires, the rum was added to the beverage, I suppose, in something about the proportion from one to seven. Last of all, the maker cut a few limes, and running each section rapidly round the rim of his bowl, squeezed in enough of this more delicate acid to flavour the whole composition. In this consists the true *tour-de-maître* of the punchmaker.

Glasgow punch should be made of the coldest spring water newly taken from the spring. The acid ingredients above mentioned will suffice for a very large bowl.

(*Another way*)

Icing sugar, lemon, rum, ice

Put into a tumbler a tablespoonful of icing sugar, the juice of a lemon, and a wineglassful of Jamaica rum. Fill the glass with chipped ice and stir well.

Scots Noyau (*A Very Pleasant Compound*)

(*Meg Dods's Recipe*)

Proof-spirit, water, syrup, almonds (sweet and bitter)

Two quarts of proof-spirit, a pint and a half of water, a pound and a half of syrup, six ounces of sweet and four bitter almonds blanched and chopped. Infuse for a fortnight, shaking the compound occasionally, and filter. Lemon juice or grate may be added, but the nutty or almond flavour does not harmonize well with acid or citron flavours.

Birk Wine

(Mrs. Dalgairns's Recipe)

Juice from the birch tree,[1] sugar, raisins, almonds, crude tartar

To every gallon of juice from the birch tree, three pounds of sugar, one pound of raisins, half an ounce of crude tartar, and one ounce of almonds are allowed; the juice, sugar, and raisins are to be boiled twenty minutes, and then put into a tub, together with the tartar; and when it has fermented some days, it is to be strained, and put into the cask, and also the almonds, which must be tied in a muslin bag. The fermentation having ceased, the almonds are to be withdrawn, and the cask bunged up, to stand about five months, when it may be fined and bottled. Keep in a cool cellar. Set the bottles upright or they will fly.

Heather Ale

> From the bonny bells of heather,
> They brewed a drink longsyne,
> Was sweeter far than honey,
> Was stronger far than wine,
> – Robert Louis Stevenson
> (*Heather Ale*: a Galloway Legend).[2]

(From an old coverless book of cottage cookery)

Heather, hops, barm, syrup, ginger, water

Crop the heather when it is in full bloom, enough to fill a large pot. Fill the pot, cover the croppings with water, set to

---

[1] About the end of March, or later if the spring is backward, bore a hole in a tree and put in a faucet, and it will run for two or three days together without hurting the tree; then put in a pin to stop it, and the next year you may draw as much from the same hole.

Pennant, writing in 1769, tells us that, in the Aberdeenshire Highlands, the birch, which grows plentifully in this district, was applicable to a great variety of purposes: for all implements of husbandry, for the roofing of houses, and fuel; whilst with its bark leather was tanned, and 'quantities of excellent wine are extracted from the live tree by tapping'.

[2] The poem tells how the Scottish king who slaughtered the Picts tried to wrest the secret of heather ale from the last survivor by offering to spare his life, and how the old man chose death. The legend of the extirpation of the whole race of Picts, who with the Scots, Britons, and a small colony of Angles constituted sixth-century Scotland, has no historical evidence, though there may have been a local massacre.

boil, and boil for one hour. Strain into a clean tub. Measure the liquid, and for every dozen bottles add one ounce of ground ginger, half an ounce of hops, and one pound of golden syrup. Set to boil again and boil for twenty minutes. Strain into a clean cask. Let it stand until milk-warm, then add a teacupful of good barm. Cover with a coarse cloth and let it stand till next day. Skim carefully and pour the liquor gently into a tub so that the barm may be left at the bottom of the cask. Bottle and cork tightly. The ale will be ready for use in two or three days.

This makes a very refreshing and wholesome drink, as there is a good deal of spirit in heather.

In Islay, in the eighteenth century, Pennant tells us, ale was frequently made of the young tops of heath, mixed with about a third part of malt and a few hops. 'This liquor, it appears from Boethius, was first used among the Picts, but when they were extirpated by the Scots, the secret of preparing it perished with them.'

Skeachan or Treacle Ale

(*Meg Dods's Recipe*)

Molasses, hops or ginger or extract of gentian, yeast, water

Boil for twenty minutes four pounds of molasses in from six to eight gallons of soft water, with a handful of hops tied in a muslin rag, or a little extract of gentian. When cooled in the tub, add a pint of good beer-yeast, or from four to six quarts of fresh worts from the brewer's vat. Cover the beer with blankets or coarse cloths.[1] Pour it from the lees and bottle it. A little ginger may be added to the boiling liquid if the flavour is liked, instead of hops. This is a cheap and very wholesome beverage.

Yule Ale, sweetened with honey, was usually made in this manner. – F. M. McN.

[1] Let it stand for one day. – F. M. McN.

White Caudle

(Meg Dods's Recipe)

Oatmeal, water, sugar, nutmeg or lemon juice

Mix two large spoonfuls of finely ground oatmeal in water, two hours previous to using it; strain it from the grits and boil it. Sweeten and add wine and seasonings to taste. Nutmeg or a little lemon juice answers best for seasoning.

Brown Caudle or The Scots Aleberry[1]

(Meg Dods's Recipe)

Is made as White Caudle, using mild sweet small beer instead of water.

'Caudle may be made of rice flour or wheat flour, with milk and water, sweetening it to taste.' – M. D.

Oatmeal Posset

(Mrs. Cleland's Recipe)

Flour of oatmeal, nutmeg, cinnamon, sugar, milk, sack, ale

Take a mutchkin (pint) of milk, boil it with nutmeg and cinnamon, and put in two spoonfuls of flour of oatmeal, and boil it till the rawness is off the oatmeal; then take three spoonfuls of sack and three spoonfuls of ale and two spoonfuls of sugar; set it over the fire till it is scalding hot, then put them to the milk, give it one stir, and let it stand on the fire for a minute or two, and pour it in your bowl; cover it and let it stand a little, then send it up.

A Harvest Drink

Oatmeal, sugar, lemon, water

Put a quarter-pound of oatmeal and six ounces of sugar into a pan. Mix with a little warm water and the juice of a lemon,

[1] Berry is a corruption of Fr. *purée*.

and pour over it, stirring all the time, a gallon of boiling water. Boil (still stirring) for three minutes. Strain and use when cold.

This is said to be very strengthening. Half an ounce of ground ginger may be mixed with the dry ingredients.

Stoorum[1]

Oatmeal, salt, water, milk

Put a heaped teaspoonful of oatmeal into a tumbler; pour a little cold water over it and stir well. Fill up half-way with boiling water, then to the top with boiling milk. Season with salt and serve.

This is said to be splendid for nursing mothers.

Stooradrink (*Shetland*)

Heat some swats (the liquid poured off sowans) in a pan and stir in some oatmeal, making it not too thick. Mix well.

Blenshaw[2]

(*A Cottage Recipe*)

Oatmeal, sugar, milk, water, nutmeg

Put a teaspoonful of oatmeal into a tumbler with the same quantity or less of sugar. Pour in half a gill of good milk, stir to the thickness of cream, and then pour in boiling water, stirring till the tumbler is full. Lastly grate a very little nutmeg over it. Do not drink it too hot. It should be the temperature of milk from the cow. This is a wholesome and nutritious beverage.

The names blenshaw and stoorum seem to be used arbitrarily for any of the many varieties of oatmeal drink. – F. M. McN.

[1] In Aberdeen, *Stouram* is a kind of gruel. In the Hebrides, a similar drink is made with barley-meal; if made with water, a morsel of butter is added.
[2] Fr. *Blanche eau*, whitish water; Strathmore.

Drammach

Oatmeal, salt, pepper, water

This is the hiker's 'special'. Carry some oatmeal, seasoned with salt and pepper, and mix it with cold water until thin enough to drink. This quenches thirst and, in the words of Robert Louis Stevenson, 'provides a good enough dish for a hungry man, and where there are no means of making fire, or good reasons for not making one, it is the chief stand-by of those who have taken to the heather.'

For further beverages, see Milkmeats and Seaweeds.

In my book, *The Scots Cellar: its Traditions and Lore,* which deals with hospitality and convivial life, many more recipes may be found. – F. M. McN.

APPENDICES

I. Franco-Scottish Domestic Terms

'Mrs. Diggity-Dalgetty's forebears must have been exposed to foreign influences, for she interlards her culinary conversation with French terms, and we have discovered that this is quite common. A "jigget" of mutton is, of course, a "gigot", and we have identified an ashet as an "assiette". The petticoat tails she requested me to buy at the confectioner's were somewhat more puzzling, but when they were finally purchased by Susanna Crum they appeared to be ordinary little cakes; perhaps, therefore, petits gastels, since gastels is an old form of gâteau, as bel was for beau. Susanna, for her part, speaks of the wardrobe in my room as an "awmry". It certainly contains no weapons, and we conjecture that her word must be a corruption of armoire.'
   – Kate Douglas Wiggan: *Penelope's Experiences in Scotland* (1890).

Scots	English	French
Accornie.	Horn. 'Half a dozen accornie spoons, 2s.' Lauder of Fountainhall's *Journals*, 1673.	Acorne.
Acorne.	A drinking-vessel with ears.	Acorne.
Ananas.	Pineapple. (Burns.)	Ananas.
Ashet.	A dish on which meat is served. 'To keep me in braws and you in ashets to break, is more than the poor creatures would face, I'm thinkin'.' – Neil Munro: *John Splendid*.	Assiette.
Assol, aisle.	To sun; to dry, mellow, or season in the sun.	Assoler.
Aumrie.	A cupboard. Her cozie box-bed and weel-polished aumrie Wi' massy brass handles a' shinin' sae braw, Her shelf fu' o' pewter a' glancin' like glamrie, An' braw bawbee pictures nailed round on the wa'. – *Janet's Auld Aumrie* (Gaberlunzie's Wallet).	Aumoire.
Backet, back backie.	A small shallow tub for holding ashes (aiss-backet), salt (saut-backet), etc. – *Rob Roy;* Burns.	Bacquet.
Bassie.	A large wooden dish for holding meal.	Bassin.
Battry.	Kitchen utensils.	Batterie.
Beam, bein	To beam the tea-pot: to warm the tea-pot with hot water before putting in the tea.	Baigner.
Berry.	Bread soaked in boiling milk and sweetened is called breadberry. Sim. aleberry, water-berry.	Purée.
Blenshaw.	A drink composed of meal, milk, water, etc.; Strathmore.	Blanche eau.

319

SCOTS	ENGLISH	FRENCH
Bonally.	A *deoch-an-doruis*, or stirrup-cup: a drink to speed the parting guest. 'I will drink it for you, that good customs be not broken. Here's your bonally, my lad.' – Scott: *The Pirate*.	Bon aller.
Boss.	A small cask, a bottle.	Boisson.
Bouvrage.	A drink, a beverage.	Beuvrage.
Bowet.	A hand-lantern. – *Waverley*.	Boete, boîte.
Bowie, milk bowie.	A tub or milk-pail. – *Old Mortality*.	Buie.
Brick.	A small loaf of bread sold in Edinburgh and elsewhere for a penny.	Brique de pain (patois).
Broach.	A flagon or tankard.	Broc.
Broch, brotch.	A spit. – *Bride of Lammermoor*.	Broche.
Brule, brulyie.	To broil.	Brûler.
Bufe.	Beef.	Bœuf.
Buist, meal-buist.	A box or chest. – *Acts James II; The Monastery*.	Boist.
Calander.	A mangle. 'Calandering done here' was once commonly seen on sign-boards.	Calandre.
Cannel.	Cinnamon.	Cannelle.
Caraff.	A decanter for holding water.	Carafe.
Carvi.	Caraway. Carvies: confections in which caraway seeds are enclosed.	Carvi.
Chaffer.	Old Scots type of oven.	Chaufoire.
Chandler.	A candle-stick. 'Hae ye ony pots or pans, Or ony broken chandlers?' – *Clout the Cauldron*.	Chandelier.
Chauffen.	To warm.	Chauffer.
Cheston.	A chestnut.	Chastaigne.
Chopin, choppin.	A measure.	Chopine.
Creish.	Grease. 'Even the slang of the Courts passed from France to Scotland, and to *graisser la patte* became to "creish the hand" of the advocate.' – J. G. Mackay, K.C., LL.D.: *Relations between the Court of Session, the Supreme Civil Court of Scotland, and the Parliament of Paris*.	Graisse.
Crusie, Cruisie.	A small iron lamp.	Creuset.
Cummerfealls.	Entertainment after an in-lying.	Commère and veille.
Debosh.	Festivity, riot – *Mansie Waugh*.	Débauche.
Deis, dess, deas.	A sort of uncushioned sofa.	Dais.
Dine.	Dinner-time. 'We twa ha'e paidl't in the burn Frae morning sun till dine.' – Burns.	Dîné.
Disjeune, disjune.	Breakfast. – *Old Mortality*. 'A kiss and a drink o' water are but a wersh (insipid) disjeune.' – Allan Ramsay.	Desjeune.
Dortor.	A dormitory, bedroom; also a posset or night-cap taken at night-time.	Dortoir.

320

SCOTS	ENGLISH	FRENCH
Dresser.	A kitchen sideboard.	Dressoir.
Dublar.	A large wooden platter. – *Wowing of Jok and Jynny.*	Doublier.
Eel-dolly.	An oil lamp (originally oil for a lamp). – Rev. W. Macgregor: *Folklore.*	Huile d'olive.
Fadge, fage.	A large flat loaf or bannock.	Fouace.
Fenester.	Window.	Fenêtre.
Flam.	A custard.	Flan.
Flamb, to.	To baste (roasted meat).	Flamber.
Fraise.	The pluck of a calf.	Fraise (id).
Furmage.	Cheese. – *Henryson.*	Fromage.
Gallimafray.	A hash, a hotch-potch.	Galimafrée.
Gardevyance, gardeviant.	A cabinet.	Gardeviandes.
Gardyloo.	'Before the days of sanitation, slops were thrown from the upper windows of old Edinburgh houses, with the warning cry of "Gardyloo!" ' – Scott: *Waverley.*	Gare de l'eau.
Gardyveen.	A case for holding wine, a cellaret.	Garde-vin.
Gean.	Wild cherry. 'Brought from Guignes in France to Scotland.' – Sir John Sinclair.	Guigne, guine.
Geil, jeel.	Jelly.	Geler.
Gigot, jiggot.	A leg of mutton.	Gigot.
Girnal.	A meal-chest.	Grenier.
Gout (pr. goo).	Taste. 'They do not know how to cook yonder. They have no gout.' – Galt.	Goût.
Governante.	Housekeeper. – Scott: *Old Mortality.*	Gouvernante.
Grange.	Granary.	Grange.
Grosset, grosert.	Gooseberry. 'A randy-like woman with a basket selling grossets.' – Galt. 'They will jump at them in Edinburgh like a cock at a grosset.' – Scott: *Fortunes of Nigel.*	Groseille.
Hainberries.	Wild berries.	Haie.
Harigals.	Liver and kidneys. 'He that never eats meat Thinks harigals a treat.' – Scots Proverb.	Haricot (a dish of boiled livers).
Havil-crook.	Lowering-crook (for pots over a fire).	Avaler.
Herse.	A frame for lights, a chandelier.	Herse.
Hogue.	Tainted.	Haut goût.
Hotch Potch.	Vegetable soup.	Hochepot.
Howtowdie.	A pullet.	Hutaudeau.
Kickshaw.	Trifle, dainty.	Quelque chose.
Lamoo.	Wassail bowl.	Le moût (new or sweet wine).

SCOTS	ENGLISH	FRENCH
Laundiers.	Andirons.	Landier.
Lavatour.	A vessel to wash in.	Lavatoire.
Lavendar.	A laundress.	Laver.
Lent-fire.	A slow fire. – Baillie.	Lent.
Lepron, leproun.	A young rabbit or hare.	Lapereau.
Longavil.	A species of pear.	Longueville.
Mange.	A meal.	Manger.
Mangerie.	A feast. – Barbour.	Mangerie.
Maniory.	A feast. – Douglas.	Maniairia.
Man-miln.	Hand-mill.	Moulin-main.
Mele.	Honey.	Miel.
Menage.	Housekeeping, establishment. – Scott: *Old Mortality.*	Ménage.
Mobylls.	Furniture.	Meubles.
Mouter.	Miller's perquisite.	Mouture.
Moy.	A measure.	Moyau.
Mutton.	A sheep.	Mouton.
Napery.	House-linen.	Nappe, naperon.
Napron, Naprie.	Apron.	Naperon.
Orlege, orlager.	A clock.	Horloge.
Paip.	A cherry-stone.	Pépin.
Palliase.	Straw mattress.	Paillasse.
Pands.	Valances of bed.	Pands.
Parsell.	Parsley.	Persil.
Pece.	A piece of plate. *Treas. Acts. I.* A vessel for holding liquids. – Douglas.	Pièce.
Pecher.	A pitcher.	Pichier. (Languedoc.)
Petté quarter.	A measure: a small quarter. Aberd. Reg.	Petit.
Petticoat tails.	Thin shortbread cakes.	Petites gatelles.
Pettie-pan.	Small moulds for pies or cakes.	Pâté or petit.
Piertryks, partrik, patrick.	A partridge.	Perdrix.
Plat.	A plate, a dish.	Plat.
Plumedame.	A prune. *Acts James VI.*	Plumebedamas.
Pork.	A pig.	Porc.
Pottisear.	A pastry-cook. – Balfour.	Pâtissier.
Proochey.	'Proochey, leddy, proochey-moo (moi)!' Milk-maids' call to the cows in many parts of Scotland.	Approchez.
Pultie.	A short-bladed knife.	Poêle+te.
Purry.	A kind of porridge, Aberd.	Purée.
Ravelled (bread).	A species of wheaten bread.	Ravailler.
Reefort, ryfart.	Radish.	Raifort.
Regale.	Entertainment. – Scott: *Old Mortality.*	Régale.
Repater.	To feed, to take refreshments – Douglas.	Repaître.
Revay.	Festivity. – *Gawan and Gol.*	Reviaus.

Scots	English	French
Rizards, rizzer-berries.	Currants.	Ressoré.
Rizzared.	Dried in the sun.	Ressoré.
Rooser.	A watering-can.	Arrouser.
Saim.	Lard.	Sain.
Sauty or sooty bannock.	A pancake.	Sauter.
Sawcer, sawster.	A maker or vendor of sauces.	Saucier.
Say.	A bucket.	Seau.
Scaud.	Scald.	Eschauder.
Schoufer.	A chaffern. – *Inventories*.	Eschauffer.
Scrutoire.	A desk, generally forming the upper part of a chest of drawers.	Escritoire.
Serge.	A taper, a torch. – *Wyntoun*.	Cierge.
Servite, Servet.	A napkin.	Serviette.
Soss.	A savoury chop-steak stew.	Sausse.
Spairge.	Sprinkle.	Asperger.

'Auld Hornie, Satan, Nick, or Clootie,
Spairges about the brimstane cootie
      To scaud poor wretches.'
    – Burns: *Address to the Dell.*

Scots	English	French
Spence, spens.	The place where provisions are kept; the room where the family sit at meat.	Despence.

'Our Bardie lanely keeps the spence
    Sin' Mailie's deid.'
    – Burns.

Scots	English	French
Squiss.	To beat up (an egg). – Z. Boyd.	Escousser.
Stoved.	A method of cooking potatoes, howtowdie, etc.	Étuvé.
Sucker.	Sugar. 'Neeps like sucker!' An old Edinburgh street cry.	Sucre.
Sybo.	A young onion, with its green tail.	Cibo.

'A lee dykeside, a sybo tail
An barley-scone shall cheer me.'
    – Burns.

Scots	English	French
Syes.	Chives.	Cives.
Tantonie bell.	A small bell.	Tintoner.
Tappit Hen.	A measure holding a quart.	Topynett.
Tartan purry.	A dish of chopped kail and oatmeal.	Tarte-en-purée.
Tash.	To soil.	Tacher.

'An' cauld and blae her genty hands,
Her feet a' tashed and torn.'
    – W. B. Crawford: *The Wandered Bairn.*

Scots	English	French
Tasse, tassie.	A cup.	Tasse.

'Gae bring to me a pint o' wine
And fetch it in a silver tassie,
That I may drink, before I go,
A service to my bonnie lassie.'
    – Burns.

Scots	English	French
Trayt.	A superior kind of wheaten bread.	Panis de Treyt.
Trest.	The frame of a table. *Acts James V.*	Tresteau.

SCOTS	ENGLISH	FRENCH
Tron, trone.	A public beam for weighing merchandise.	Trone.
	'The beam known as the salt-trone, to distinguish it from the butter-trone in Lawnmarket . . . gave its name to the Tron Church.'	
	– Reid: *New Lights on Old Edinburgh*.	
Vantose.	A cupping-glass.	Ventouse.
Veal, veil.	A calf. – *Acts James VI*.	Veau.
Verry.	Glass or tumbler.	Verre.
Vittall.	To supply with provisions.	Vitaille.
Vivers.	Victuals.	Vivres.
	'The dainty vivers that were set before them.'	
	– Scott: *The Fortunes of Nigel*.	
Vodure.	A tray for removing fragments after a meal. (Lit. a voider or emptier.)	Vodeur.
Wyandour.	'A gud wyandour', one who lives or feeds well.	Viander.
	– Wyntoun.	

II. Old Scottish Measures

4 gills	= 1 mutchkin
2 mutchkins	= 1 choppin
2 choppins	= 1 pint
2 pints	= 1 quart
4 quarts	= 1 gallon
8 gallons	= 1 barrel

SCOTTISH	IMPERIAL
1 mutchkin	= 1 pint
1 choppin	= 1 quart
1 pint	= 2 quarts[1]
1 quart	= 1 gallon
1 lippie	= 1 peck

[1] 'The Scottish pint of liquid measure comprehends four English measures of the same denomination. The jest is well known of my poor countryman who, driven to extremity by the raillery of the Southern on the small denomination of the Scottish coin, at length answered, "Ay, ay! but the deil tak them that has the least pint-stoup!" '
– Scott: *Redgauntlet*, Note.

III. Old Scottish Cuts

The names of the various pieces, according to the Scottish method of dividing the carcass, says Mrs. Dalgairns (1829), are as follows:

BEEF

The Middle Sirloin – Top of the Rump and Hook-Bone – Middle Hook-Bone and Round – the Hough – the Spare Rib – the Flank and part of the Hough – the Fore Saye – the Breast and Nine-Holes – the Lair – Neck and Sticking-piece – the Knap – Cheek and Head.

Besides these are the Tongue and Palate. The Entrails consist of the Heart – Sweetbreads – Kidneys – Skirts – and three kinds of Tripe, the Double, the Roll, and the Red Tripe.

MUTTON

The Leg – the Loin – the Fore Quarter. The two loins joined together are called a Chine. A Saddle of Mutton is the two Necks joined together.

The finest mutton is that of the mountain or black-faced sheep of Scotland, and that of the South Downs and Welsh Sheep.

PORK

Spare Rib – Breast and Shoulder – Sirloin – the Ham or Gigot. The Entrails are named the liver, crow, kidney, skirts, sometimes called the harslet, also the chitterlings and guts.

IV. Old Scottish Festival Cakes and Dishes

'Some of the cakes which have a prominent place in folk usage at certain periods of the year, e.g. Christian festivals and holy days, as well as on other occasions, are probably lineally descended from cakes used sacrificially or sacramentally in pagan times. This is suggested by the customs observed in the making of these cakes, or the eating of them; by their division among the members of the family, or by their being marked with sacred symbols.' – L. A. MacCulloch: *Encyclopædia of Religion and Ethics*, article on 'Cakes and Loaves'.

Jan. 1.	New Year's Day.	See *Hogmanay* (Dec. 31).
Jan. 5.	Twelfth Night.	Twelfth Cake.[1]
Jan. —	Auld Handsel Monday. (First Monday of New Year, O.S.)	Gudebread (various).[2]
Jan. 25.	Burns Night.	Haggis.
Feb. 1.	St. Bride's day (Candlemas Eve).	St. Bride's Bannock (Highland Quarter Cake: Spring).
Mar. or Ap.	Fastern's E'en (Shrove Tuesday).	Fastyn, Festy, or Fitless Cock; Skairskons, Car-cakes, or Sauty Bannocks; Crowdie or Matrimonial Brose or Matrimonial Bannock (with ring).
Mar. or Ap.	Car Sunday (a week before Palm Sunday).	Carlings (peas, birsled or boiled).
Mar. or Ap.	Pasch or Easter.	Pays or Pasch Eggs; Pesse (Pasch) Pie: a chicken pie; Hot Cross Buns.
May 1.	Beltane.	Beltane Bannock (Highland Quarter Cake: Summer); Beltane Caudle.

[1] A rich plum- or pound-cake, ornamented, and containing a lucky bean, the recipient of which became King or Queen of Bane. In one of his Latin epigrams, Buchanan commemorates the choice of Mary Beaton as Queen of the Twelfth Tide Revels at Holyrood. Black Bun was probably the original Twelfth Cake. See p. 256, note to recipe for Black Bun. – F. M. McN.

[2] *Gudebread* is the Scots term for all bread and cakes specially prepared for festive occasion. – F. M. McN.

June 9.	St. Columba's Day.	St. Columba's Cake (with coin) (Hebrides).
Aug. 1.	Lammas.	Lammas Bannock (Highland Quarter Cake: Autumn).
Sept. 29.	Michaelmas.	St. Michael's Cake (Hebrides).
Oct. 18.	St. Luke's Day.	Sour Cakes (Rutherglen).
Oct.	Harvest Home.	Cream Crowdie; Meal-and-Ale (with ring).
Oct. 31.	Hallowe'en.	Buttered Sowans; Crowdie or Champit Tatties (mashed potatoes) or (modern) cake, with charms; *Bonnach Salainn* (Highlands); Apples and Nuts.
Nov. 1.	Hallowmas.	Hallowmas Bannock (Highland Quarter Cake: Winter); Hallowfair Gingerbread.
Nov. 11.	Martinmas.	(Killing of Mart.) Haggis, Black and White Puddings.
Nov. 30.	Anermas (St. Andrew's Day).	Sheep's Head, Haggis, and other national dishes.
Dec. 24 to Auld Handsel Monday (q.v.).	} The Daft Days.	Gude-bread (various).
Dec. 25.	Yule or Christenmas.	Yule Brose; Yule Bread; Sowans; Goose, Goose-pie, or (modern) Turkey; Plum Porridge or (modern) Plum Pudding.
Dec. 31.	Hogmanay.	Cakes and Kebbuck (oat-farls and cheese); Sugared Bread and Sweet Cakes (Shortbread, Black Bun, Currant Loaf, Ankerstock Gingerbread, etc.); Oranges; Het Pint (Edinburgh and Glasgow); Sowans (Aberdeen), Atholl Brose.

When merry Yule-day comes, I trow,
You'll scantlins[1] fin' a hungry mou;[2]
Sma' are our cares, our stamacks fou
    O' gusty gear,[3]
An' kickshaws,[4] strangers to our view,
    Sin' fairn year.[5]
           – R. Fergusson: *The Daft Days.*

Births.	*In-lying:* Blythe Meat, Merry Meat or Wanton Meat; Cheesing Meat[6] (Orkney); Crying Bannock; Crying Kebbuck.
	Christening: Bonnach Baiste or Christening Bannock, or (modern) Christening cake (ornamented).
	Teething: Teething Bannock.
Marriages.	Infar Cake or Wedding-cake (originally a rich oat-cake; later shortbread, ornamented with favours; now more commonly a rich fruit-cake, elaborately iced);[7] The Bride's Pie; The Bride's Cog.
Funerals.	Gude-bread, various (seed-cake perhaps a speciality).

[1] Scarcely.   [2] Mouth.   [3] Savoury fare.   [4] Dainties.   [5] Since yester-year.
[6] This consists of a stoupful of eggalourie (a caudle of eggs and milk) and a cubbie (a special kind of basket) full of bannocks.
[7] Some of the wedding-cakes of the Royal Family are supplied by a well-known Edinburgh firm.

V. Meg Dods's Suggested Bill of Fare for St. Andrew's Day, Burns Clubs, or other Scottish National Dinners.

First Course

Friar's Chicken, or Scots Brown Soup.
(*Remove* – Braised Turkey.)

Brown Fricassee of Duck.   Potted Game.   Minced Collops.

Haggis.

Salt Cod, with Egg Sauce.   (*Remove* – Chicken Pie.)   Crimped Skate.

Smoked Tongue.   Tripe in White Fricassee.

Salt Caithness Goose, or Solan Goose.

Sheep's Head Broth.
(1. *Remove* – Two Tups'[1] Heads and Trotters.)
(2. *Remove* – Haunch of Venison or Mutton,
with Wine Sauce and Currant Jelly.)

———

Second Course

Roast Fowls, with Drappit Egg, or Lamb's Head Dressed.

Buttered Partans.[2]   Small Pastry.   Stewed Onions.

Calves-foot Jelly.   Rich Eating Posset.   Blancmange.
in a China Punch Bowl.

Apple-puddings in skins.   Small Pastry.   Plum-damas[3] Pie.
A Black Cock, or three Ptarmigan.

A MODERN BURNS SUPPER

BILL OF FARE

Het Kail
Cock-a-Leekie.   Bawd Bree.

Caller Fish
Cabbie-Claw.   Herring Fillets Fried in Oatmeal.

Rarebit
THE HAGGIS

Clapshot or Tatties and Neeps.

Het Joints
Roastit Bubblyjock wi'   Roastit Sirloin o' Aberdeen-
Cheston Crappin[4]   Angus Beef
Ayrshire Tatties.   Musselburgh Sprouts.

Ither-Orra Eattocks
Hattit Kit.   Drambuie Cream.
Aipple Frushie wi' Whuppit Cream.

Gusty Kickshaws
Finnan-toasties.
Dunlop Kebbuck or Highland Crowdie
wi' wee Ait Bannocks.

———

A Tassie o' Coffee.

---

[1] Sheeps'.   [2] Crabs.   [3] Prune.
[4] *Bubblyjock,* turkey; *cheston crappin,* chestnut stuffing.

BIBLIOGRAPHY

(1) General

ADAMNAN, SAINT: *Life of St. Columba* (521–597)
ANGUS, J. S.: *Glossary of the Shetland Dialect*, 1914
ANONYMOUS: Old Songs and Ballads
AULD MAKARS: Poems

BAILLIE, LADY GRISELL: *Household Books* (1692–1733)
BARBÉ, LOUIS A.: *In Byways of Scottish History*, 1924
BARRON, EVAN: *The Scottish War of Independence*, 1914
BERTRAM, JAMES G.: *Memories of Books, Authors and Events*, 1893
BLACKIE, JOHN STUART: *Altavona*, 1882
BOECE, HECTOR: *Scotorum Historiae*, 1526
BOSWELL, JAMES: *Journal of a Tour to the Hebrides*, 1786
BROWN, P. HUME: *Early Travellers in Scotland*, 1891
BURNS, ROBERT: Poems
BURT, CAPTAIN: *Letters from the North of Scotland* (1730)

CARMICHAEL, ALEXANDER: *Carmina Gadelica*, 1900
CARRUTHERS, ROBERT: *The Highland Note-Book*, 1843
CARSWELL, DONALD AND CATHERINE: *The Scots Week-end*, 1936
CHAMBERLAYNE, JOHN: *The Present State of Great Britain*, 1708
CHAMBERS, ROBERT: *Traditions of Edinburgh*, 1825
CRICHTON-BROWNE, SIR JAMES: *Stray Leaves from a Physician's Portfolio*, 1927
CROCKETT, W. S.: *The Scott Originals*, 1912

DE AYALA, PEDRO: Letter dated July 25, 1498
DE SAINT-FOND, FAUJAS: *Voyage en Angleterre et en Ecosse* (1784), 1797
DODS, MRS. MARGARET (MRS. ISOBEL CHRISTIAN JOHNSTON): *The Cook and Housewife's Manual*, 1826
DUNBAR, WILLIAM: Poems

FERGUSSON, ROBERT: Poems
FERRIER, SUSAN: Novels
FINDLATER, JANE AND MARY: Novels
FINLAY, IAN: *Scotland*, 1957
FIRTH, REV. JOHN: *Reminiscences of an Orkney Parish*, 1920
FORDUN: *Chronicle* (1384–1387)
FROISSART: Chronicles (Fourteenth Century)

GALT, JOHN: *Annals of the Parish*, 1821
GRAHAM, HENRY GRAY: *Social Life in Scotland in the Eighteenth Century*, 1899
GRANT, MRS. ANNE, OF LAGGAN: *Letters from the Mountains* (1773–1807)
— ELIZABETH, OF ROTHIEMURCHUS: *Memoirs of a Highland Lady* (1797–1827)
— MRS. KATHERINE W.: *Myth, Tradition and Legend from Western Argyll*, 1925
GREGOR, REV. WALTER: *Notes on the Folklore of the North-East of Scotland*, 1881
GULLIVER, L. S.: *So This is Glasgow*, 1938

HALDANE, ELIZABETH S.: *The Scotland of Our Fathers*, 1933
HALIBURTON, HUGH (J. LOGIE ROBERTSON): *Furth in Field*, 1894
HALYBURTON, ANDREW, Merchant in Leith: *Ledger* (1492–1503)

328

HAMILTON, GENERAL SIR IAN: *When I Was a Boy*, 1939
HENDERSON, T. F.: *Old-World Scotland*, 1893
HISLOP, ALEXANDER: *A Book of Scottish Anecdote*, 1875
HORNE, JOHN: *The County of Caithness*, 1907

JAMIESON, DR. JOHN: *Dictionary of the Scottish Language*, 1818
JOHNSON, DR. SAMUEL: *Journey to the Western Isles of Scotland* (1775)

KENNEDY-FRASER, MARJORY, AND KENNETH MACLEOD: *Songs of the Hebrides*, 1909

LOCKHART, J. G.: *Peter's Letters to His Kinsfolk*, 1819

MACDONALD, GEORGE: Novels
MACKAY, JOHN: *A Journey through Scotland* (1722–1723)
MACKENZIE, HENRY: *Anecdotes and Egotisms* (1745–1831), 1927
— OSGOOD: *A Hundred Years in the Highlands* (1800–1900), 1921
MACLAGAN, DR. R. C.: *Occasional Papers*
MACLEOD, DR. NORMAN: *Reminiscences of a Highland Parish*, 1891
MACLURE, VICTOR: *Scotland's Inner Man*, 1935
MACTAGGART, JOHN: *Gallovidian Encyclopaedia*, 1824
MARTIN, MARTIN: *Description of the Western Islands of Scotland* (c. 1695), 1703
MILLER, HUGH: *My Schools and Schoolmasters*, 1852
MORYSON, FYNES: *Itinerary* (1598), 1617
MUNRO, NEIL: Novels; Articles in the Glasgow Press

NAIRNE, BARONESS CAROLINE: Songs
NORTH, CHRISTOPHER: *Noctes Ambrosianae*, 1825–1835

OMOND, JAMES: *Orkney Eighty Years Ago* (1911)

PENNANT, THOMAS: *A Tour in Scotland* (1769); *A Tour in Scotland and Voyage to the Hebrides* (1772)
POCOCKE, BISHOP RICHARD: *Travels in Scotland* (1747, 1750, 1760), 1760
POWER, WILLIAM: Articles in the Glasgow Press

RAMSAY, ALLAN: *A Tea-Table Miscellany*, 1724–1727
— DEAN: *Reminiscences of Scottish Life and Character*, 1858
ROBERTSON, HANNAH: *The Ladies' School of Arts*, 2nd edn., 1767
ROGERS, CHARLES: *Scotland, Social and Domestic*, 1869

SAINTSBURY, GEORGE: Cookery of the Grouse: Chapter in *The Grouse: Natural History* by the Rev. H. A. Macpherson, 1894
— Scrap Books, 1922, 1923
SAXBY, JESSIE M. B.: *Shetland Traditional Lore*, 1932
SCOTT, SIR WALTER: Novels; Poems; *Journal*
SHAND, P. MORTON: *A Book of Food*, 1929
SMOLLETT, TOBIAS: Novels
STEVENSON, R. L.: Novels; Poems
STEUART, JOHN, Bailie of Inverness: *Letters* (1715–1752)
STEWART, REV. ALEXANDER: *Nether Lochaber*, 1883
STUART, PROFESSOR JAMES: *Reminiscences* (privately printed), 1911

TAYLOR, JOHN, the Thames Water-Poet: *A Pennyles Pilgrimage* (1618)
TROTTER, R. DE B.: *Galloway Gossip*, 1901

VICTORIA, QUEEN: *Leaves from a Journal of Our Life in the Highlands* (1846–1861)

WALFORD, MRS. L. B.: *Recollections of a Scottish Novelist*, 1910
WARRACK, JOHN: *Domestic Life in Scotland*, (1488–1688), 1920
WORDSWORTH, DOROTHY: *Recollections of a Tour Made in Scotland* (1803)

Annals of the Cleikum Club (Incorporated in Meg Dods's *Manual*), 1826
Blackwood's Magazine
Book of the Old Edinburgh Club
Caledonian Horticultural Society, Memoirs of
Caledonian Medical Journal
Gaelic Society of Glasgow: Transactions
Scotland: A Description of Scotland and Scottish Life, Ed. H. W. Meikle, 1947
Scots Magazine
Scottish National Dictionary
Statistical Accounts of Scotland, Old and New, 1797 and 1843

(2) *Cookery-Books*

CLARK OF TILLYPRONIE, LADY: *The Cookery-Book of Lady Clark of Tillypronie*, 1909
CLELAND, MRS. ELIZABETH: *A New and Easy Method of Cookery*, 1759
CRAIG, ELIZABETH: *The Scottish Cookery-Book*, 1956

DALGAIRNS, MRS.: *The Practice of Cookery*, 1829
DODS, MRS. MARGARET (MRS. ISOBEL CHRISTIAN JOHNSTON): *The Cook and Housewife's Manual*, 1826

FRAZER, MRS. *The Practice of Cookery*, 1791

GLASSE, MRS.: *The Art of Cookery Made Plain and Easy*, 1747

MCEWEN, MRS.: *Elements of Cookery*, 1835
MCIVER, MRS. SUSANNA[1]: *Cookery and Pastry, as Taught and Practised at her Pastry School in Peebles Wynd*, 1773
MACLEOD, MRS. LILY: *A Cook's Note-Book*, 1958

ROBERTSON, MRS. HANNAH: *The Young Ladies' School of Arts*, 2nd edn., 1767

ST. CLAIR, LADY HARRIET: *Dainty Dishes*, 1886
STOUT, MARGARET: *Cookery for Northern Wives* (including many Shetland Folk-Dishes), 1925

WILLIAMSON, D., AND SON: *The Practice of Cookery and Pastry*, 1862
WREN, JENNY (JAMES BERTRAM): *Modern Domestic Cookery*, 1880
— — *The Highland Feill Cookery-Book*, 1907

OTHER SOURCES: Old Family MSS. Oral Tradition.

[1] 'A celebrated Caledonian professor of the culinary art.'
                    – Dr. Kitchener in *The Cook's Oracle*.

GENERAL INDEX

333

335

INDEX TO RECIPES

(Dishes, etc., mentioned in the notes are printed in italics)

338

341

344

NOTES

NOTES

NOTES

NOTES

NOTES